British Railways

LOCOMOTIVES &

COACHING STOCK

1996

The Complete Guide to all
Locomotives & Coaching Stock
Vehicles Which May Run on Britain's
Main-Line Railways (excluding Service Stock)

Peter Fox

PLATFORM
5

ISBN 1 872524 83 4

© 1996. Platform 5 Publishing Ltd., Wyvern House, Sark Road, Sheffield S2 4HG, England.

Printed in England by B.R. Hubbard Printers Ltd., Callywhite Lane, Dronfield, Sheffield, S18 6XP.

CONTENTS

MANX ELECTRIC

by Mike Goodwyn

Manx Electric is the story of the Manx Electric Railway and the Snaefell Mountain Railway. It traces the history of the island's electric railway systems in detail and charts the development of the lines and their rolling stock to the present day. As well as a comprehensive history of the two lines, there are detailed chapters on the Rolling Stock, Ticketing, Overhead Equipment, Traffic, Buildings and the Training of Motormen. Author Mike Goodwyn is Chairman of the Manx Electric Railway Society and his knowledge of the subject is unsurpassed. He has been connected with the railways for many years, and his achievements include leading the succesful campaign to re-open the section from Laxey to Ramsey in 1977.

A4. Thread Sewn. 112 pages including 8 in colour. £8.95.

ORGANISATION OF BRITAIN'S RAILWAY SYSTEM

The Government's privatisation programme has meant that the whole basis of ownership and operation of railway vehicles and infrastructure has changed. This section gives an overview of the current situation. It should be noted, however, that matters are at present in a state of flux and can change overnight.

INFRASTRUCTURE

Britains state-owned railway infrastructure, i.e. the track, signalling, stations and overhead line equipment is now owned by a new nationalised body known as "Railtrack". It is the Government's intention to sell this body in 1996, but this is not certain to happen. Many stations are leased to train operating companies.

OPERATIONS

Passenger trains are operated by train operating companies (TOCs). As we went to press, two of these had been franchised to private companies (South West Trains and Great Western), but a third one which should have been franchised (LTS Rail) was still in the hands of BR pending the outcome of a fraud investigation. The rest of the TOCs were being operated by BR, but a number of them should be privatised during the currency of this book.

The exception to the above is European Passenger Services (EPS). This company which operates Eurostar services to Paris and Brussels jointly with French Railways (SNCF) and Belgian Railways (NMBS/SNCB) is a Government department. EPS will also operate the Night Service trains jointly with SNCF, Netherlands Railways (NS) and German Railways (DB).

Parcels, mail and the majority of charter trains are operated by Rail Express Systems (RES), a company which has just been bought by the North & South Railway Company, a subsidiary of Wisconsin Central Transportation Corporation in the USA.

The majority of freight train operations are run by five different companies. Three of these are Trainload freight companies known as LoadHaul, Mainline and TransRail. These three companies are at present subsidiaries of BR, but are believed to be being sold to Wisconsin Central. Container trains are operated by Freightliner and general freight, particularly Channel Tunnel traffic is handled by Railfreight Distribution (RfD). Freightliner and RfD are still subsidiaries of BR. Certain other companies e.g. National Power operste freight trains with their own locomotives.

LOCOMOTIVES AND ROLLING STOCK

The locomotives of the freight companies and the locomotives and rolling stock of Rail Express Systems are owned by those companies, as are the vehicles of EPS. Most locomotives, hauled coaching stock and multiple unit vehicles used by the passenger train operating companies are owned by three leasing companies which were originally set up by British Railways as subsidiaries and then privatised. These are:

Eversholt Holdings (formerly Eversholt Leasing)
Great Rolling Stock Company (formerly Angel Trains)
Porterbrook Leasing Company Ltd.

Other vehicles are owned by various private companies such as The Carriage and Traction Co. Ltd., a subsidiary of Flying Scotsman Railways, Carnforth Railway Restoration & Engineering Services Ltd. and the Venice Simplon-Orient Express Ltd.

Further details of these companies will be found in the section on abbreviations and codes. Thus for each vehicle it is generally necessary to specify both the owner and the TOC which currently operates the vehicle.

Finally, a number of 'service' type vehicles are owned by Railtrack (e.g. Sandite vehicles) and others are owned by former BR Headquarters organisations such as Railtest. Royal Train vehicles are also owned by Railtrack at present, but it remains to be seen what will happen to these if and when the threatened privatisation of Railtrack takes place.

BASIS OF INCLUSION OF VEHICLES

One result of privatisation is that the old distinction between 'live' and 'condemned' vehicles has become blurred, particularly with regard to locomotive-hauled stock. Two vehicles, one 'condemned' and one 'off-loan' may be standing next to one another in an Army camp out-of-use, but either could come into use at any time if a TOC wanted to hire one. In addition, as all passenger coaches are now privately-owned, the former 99XXX private-owner series is being discontinued and coaches are generally to receive their former BR number. Thus this book now includes all coaches which might conceivably be used on main lines in future and has meant the re-appearance of classes which formerly had been deleted. Non-leasing company coaches which are not at present registered to run on Railtrack lines show the suffix 'Z' in the owner code.

ACQUISITION OF INFORMATION

This book has been published with great difficulty. Privatisation of the railways and the splitting up of BR into different companies has been used as an excuse to deny the railway press access to official rolling stock library information, breaking a tradition of freely-supplied information which was even available during the Second World War. We hope that readers will find the information accurate, but cannot be responsible for any inaccuracies.

We would like to thank the companies and individuals which have been co-operative in supplying information and would ask other companies which find this book useful to help us in future to make the book as accurate as possible.

The vehicles contained in the book are those which were in service on 1st January 1996.

1. LOCOMOTIVES

The following notes are applicable to locomotives:

DETAILS & DIMENSIONS

Principal details and dimensions are given for each class in metric units. Imperial equivalents are also given for power. Maximum speeds are still quoted in miles per hour since the British railway operating departments still uses imperial units. Since the present maximum permissible speed of certain classes of locomotives is different from the design speed, these are now shown separately in class details. In some cases certain low speed limits are arbitrary and may occasionally be raised raised when necessary if a locomotive has to be pressed into passenger service.

LOCOMOTIVE DETAIL DIFFERENCES

Detail differences which affect the areas and types of train which locos work are shown. Where detail differences occur within a class or part class of locos., these are shown against the individual loco number. Except where shown, diesel locomotives have no train heating equipment. Electric or electro-diesel locomotives are assumed to have train heating unless shown otherwise. Standard abbreviations used are:

a	Train air brakes only.
c	Fitted with Scharfenberg couplers for Eurostar working.
e	Fitted with electric heating apparatus (ETH).
r	Fitted with radio electronic token block equipment.
s	Slow speed control fitted (and operable).
t	Fitted with automatic vehicle identification transponders.
v	Train vacuum brakes only.
x	Dual train brakes (air & vacuum).
y	ETH equipped but equipment isolated.
+	Extended range locos with Additional fuel tank capacity compared with others in class.

After the locomotive number are shown any notes regarding braking, heating etc., the livery code (in bold type), the pool code, the depot code and name if any. Locomotives which have been renumbered in recent years show the last number in parentheses after the current number.

NAMES

All official names are shown as they appear on the locomotive i.e. all upper case or upper & lower case lettering. Where only a few locomotives in a class are named, these are shown in a separate table at the end of the class or sub-class.

DEPOT ALLOCATIONS & POOL CODES

The depot at which a locomotive is allocated is the one at which it receives its main examinations. This depot may be a long way away from where it normally performs its duties, e.g. Class 60s operating from Peak Forest are allocated to Cardiff Canton! The pool code is a better means of ascertaining where a locomotive may operate, but it should be borne in mind that often locomotives of the same company may be used in pools other than their official pool. (S) denotes stored serviceable and (U) stored unserviceable. Locos may not be stored at their home depots. Thus the layout is as follows:

No.	Old No.	Notes	Liv.	Pool	Depot	Name
47777	(47636)	+	RX	PXLB	CD	Restored

GENERAL INFORMATION ON BRITISH RAILWAYS' LOCOMOTIVES

CLASSIFICATION & NUMBERING

Initially BR diesel locomotives were allocated numbers in the 1xxxx series, with electrics allotted numbers in the 2xxxx series. Around 1957 diesel locomotives were allocated new four digit numbers with 'D' prefixes. Diesel electric shunters in the 13xxx series had the '1' replaced by a 'D', but diesel mechanical shunters were completely renumbered. Electric locomotives retained their previous numbers but with an 'E' prefix.

When all standard gauge steam locomotives had been withdrawn, the prefix letter was removed. In 1972, the present TOPS numbering system was introduced whereby the loco number consisted of a two-digit class number followed by a serial number. In some cases the last two digits of the former number were generally retained (classes 20, 37, 50), but in other classes this is not the case. In this book former TOPS numbers carried by converted locos are shown in parentheses. Full renumbering information is to be found in the 'Diesel & Electric loco Register', the new third edition of which is now available.

Diesel locomotives are classified as "types" depending on their engine horsepower as follows:

Type	Engine hp.	Old Number Range	Current Classes
1	800-1000	D 8000-D 8999	20.
2	1001-1499	D 5000-D 6499/D 7500-D 7999	31.
3	1500-1999	D 6500-D 7499	33, 37.
4	2000-2999	D 1-D 1999	47.
5	3000+	D 9000-D 9499	56, 58, 59, 60.
Shunter	Under 300	D 2000-D 2999	03.
Shunter	300-799	D 3000-D 4999	08, 09.

Class 14 (650 hp diesel hydraulics) were numbered in the D95xx series.

Electric and electro-diesel locomotives are classified according to their supply system. Locomotives operating on a d.c. system are allocated classes 71-80, whilst a.c. or dual voltage locomotives start at Class starting at 81. Departmental locomotives which remain self propelled or which are likely to move around on a day to day basis are classified Class 97.

WHEEL ARRANGEMENT

For main line diesel and electric locomotives the system whereby the number of driven axles on a bogie or frame is denoted by a letter (A = 1, B = 2, C = 3 etc.) and the number of undriven axles is noted by a number is used. The letter 'o' after a letter indicates that each axle is individually powered and a + sign indicates that the bogies are intercoupled. For shunters the Whyte notation is used. In this notation, generally used in Britain for steam locomotives, the number of leading wheels are given, followed by the number of driving wheels and then the trailing wheels.

HAULING CAPABILITY OF DIESEL LOCOS

The hauling capability of a diesel locomotive depends basically upon three factors:

1. Its adhesive weight. The greater the weight on its driving wheels, the greater the adhesion and thus more tractive power can be applied before wheel slip occurs.

2. The characteristics of its transmission. In order to start a train the locomotive has to exert a pull at standstill. A direct drive diesel engine cannot do this, hence the need for transmission. This may be mechanical, hydraulic or electric. The current BR standard for locomotives is electric transmission. Here the diesel engine drives a generator or alternator and the current produced is fed to the traction motors. The force produced by each driven wheel depends on the current in its traction motor. In other words the larger the current, the harder it pulls.

As the locomotive speed increases, the current in the traction motors falls hence the *Maximum Tractive Effort* is the maximum force at its wheels that the locomotive can exert at a standstill. The electrical equipment cannot take such high currents for long without overheating. Hence the *Continuous Tractive Effort* is quoted which represents the current which the equipment can take continuously.

3. The power of its engine. Not all of this power reaches the rail as electrical machines are approximately 90% efficient. As the electrical energy passes through two such machines (the generator/alternator and the traction motors), the *Power At Rail* is about 81% (90% of 90%) of the engine power, less a further amount used for auxiliary equipment such as radiator fans, traction motor cooling fans, air compressors, battery charging, cab heating, ETH, etc. The power of the locomotive is proportional to the tractive effort times the speed. Hence when on full power there is a speed corresponding to the continuous tractive effort.

HAULING CAPABILITY OF ELECTRIC LOCOS

Unlike a diesel locomotive, an electric locomotive does not develop its power on board and its performance is determined only by two factors, namely its weight and the characteristics of its electrical equipment. Whereas a diesel locomotive tends to be a constant power machine, the power of an electric locomotive varies considerably. Up to a certain speed it can produce virtually a constant tractive effort. Hence power rises with speed according to the formula given in section 3 above, until a maximum speed is reached at which tractive effort falls, such that the power also falls. Hence the power at the speed corresponding to the maximum tractive effort is lower than the maximum.

BRAKE FORCE

The brake force is a measure of the braking power of a locomotive. This is shown on the locomotive data panels so that railway staff can ensure that sufficient brake power is available on freight trains.

TRAIN HEATING AND POWER EQUIPMENT

The standard system in use on BR for heating loco hauled trains is by means of electricity and is now known as ETS (Electric train supply). Locomotives which were equipped to provide steam heating have had this equipment removed or rendered inoperable (isolated). Electric heat is provided from the locomotive by means of a separate alternator on the loco, except in the case of Class 33 which have a d.c. generator. The *ETH Index* is a measure of the electrical power available for train heating. All electrically heated coaches have an ETH index and the total of these in a train must not exceed the ETH power of a locomotive.

ROUTE AVAILABILITY

This is a measure of a railway vehicle's axle load. The higher the axle load of a vehicle, the higher the RA number on a scale 1 to 10. Each route on BR has an RA number and in theory no vehicle with a higher RA number may travel on that route without special clearance. Exceptions are made, however.

MULTIPLE AND PUSH-PULL WORKING

Multiple working between diesel locomotives on BR has usually been provided by means of an electro-pneumatic system, with special jumper cables connecting the locos. A coloured symbol is painted on the end of the locomotive to denote which system is in use. Class 47s nos. 47701-17 used a time-division multiplex (t.d.m.) system which utilised the existing RCH (an abbreviation for the former railway clearing house, a pre-nationalisation standards organisation) jumper cables for push-pull working. These had in the past only been used for train lighting control, and more recently for public address (pa) and driver-guard communication. A new standard t.d.m. system is now fitted to all a.c. electric locomotives and other vehicles, enabling them to work in both push-pull and multiple working modes. RfD Class 47 locomotives are now being fitted with a 'green circle' multiple working system, as are the privately-owned locomotives of Class 20/3. Full details of the mechanism of these new multiple-working systems are not to hand.

1.1. BR DIESEL LOCOMOTIVES

CLASS 03   BR SHUNTER   0 – 6 – 0

Built: 1960 at BR Doncaster Works.
Engine: Gardner 8L3 of 152 kW (204 hp) at 1200 rpm.
Transmission: Mechanical. Fluidrive type 23 hydraulic coupling to Wilson-Drewry CA5R7 gearbox with SCG type RF11 final drive.
Max. Tractive Effort: 68 kN (15300 lbf).
Brake Force: 13 t.
Weight: 31 t.
Max. Speed: 28 mph.

Length over Buffers: 7.92 m.
Wheel Diameter: 1092 mm.
RA: 1.

Formerly numbered 2079.

| 03079 | v | HZSH | RY | |

CLASS 08   BR SHUNTER   0 – 6 – 0

Built: 1953 – 62 by BR at Crewe, Darlington, Derby, Doncaster or Horwich Works.
Engine: English Electric 6KT of 298 kW (400 hp) at 680 rpm.
Main Generator: English Electric 801.
Traction Motors: Two English Electric 506.
Max. Tractive Effort: 156 kN (35000 lbf).
Cont. Tractive Effort: 49 kN (11100 lbf) at 8.8 mph.
Power At Rail: 194 kW (260 hp).
Brake Force: 19 t.
Design Speed: 20 mph.
Max. Speed: 15 or 20* mph.

Length over Buffers: 8.92 m.
Wheel Diameter: 1372 mm.
Weight: 50 t.
RA: 5.

Non-standard liveries:

08414 is 'D' with RfD brandings and also carries its former number D 3529.
08460 is light grey with a black roof.
08500 is red lined out in black & white.
08519/730/867 are BR black.
08527 is light grey with a black roof and a blue bodyside stripe and 'Ilford Level 5' branding.
08593 is Great Eastern blue lined out in red and also carries its former number D 3760.
08601 is London Midland & Scottish Railway black.
08629 is Royal purple.
08642 is London & South Western Railway black and also carries its former number D 3809.
08689 is 'D' with Railfreight general markings.
08715 is in experimental dayglo orange livery.
08721 is blue with a red & yellow stripe ('Red Star' livery).
08805 is LMS maroon and also carries its former number 3973.
08883 is Caledonian blue.
08907 is London & North Western Railway black.

08933 is 'D' but with two orange cabside stripes.
08938 is grey and red.

n – Waterproofed for working at Oxley Carriage Depot.
z – Fitted with buckeye adaptor at nose end for HST depot shunting.
§ – Fitted with yellow flashing light and siren for working between Ipswich Yard and Cliff Quay.

Formerly numbered in series 3000 – 4192. 08600 was numbered 97800 whilst in departmental use between 1979 and 1989. 08616 carries its former number D 3783.

CLASS 08/0. Standard Design.

08388	a	**FP**	FDSI	IM	08510	a		FDSD	DR
08389	a		DAWE	AN	08511	a		ENSN	TO
08393	a	**D**	DAWE	AN	08512	a	**F**	FDSD	DR
08397	a	**F**	LWSP	SP	08514	a		FDSD	DR
08401	a	**D**	FDSI	IM	08516	a	**D**	FDSK	KY
08402	a	**D**	PXLT	CD	08517	a		EWSX	SF (S)
08405	a	**D**	FDSI	IM	08519	a	**0**	LBBS	BS
08410	a	**D**	HJXX	PM	08523	x	**ML**	EWOC	OC
08411	a		LGML	ML	08525	x	**F**	HISL	NL
08413	a	**D**	DASY	TI	08526	x		EWSF	SF
08414	a* § **0**		EWSF	SF	08527	x	**0**	KCSI	ZI
08415	x		PXXA	SP	08528	x	**D**	ENSN	TO
08417	a		CD.ID	DY	08529	x		ENSN	TO
08418	a	**F**	FDSD	DR	08530	x	**D**	DFLS	AN
08428	a		LBBS	BS	08531	x	**D**	DFLS	AN
08441	a		ENSN	TO	08534	x	**D**	LGML	ML
08442	a	**F**	FDSK	KY	08535	x	**D**	DASY	TI
08445	a		FDSX	IM (U)	08536	x		HISE	DY
08448	a		LNXX	BS (U)	08538	x	**D**	ENSN	TO
08449	a		ENSN	TO	08540	x	**D**	ENSN	TO
08451	x		HFSN	WN	08541	x	**D**	EWSF	SF
08454	x		HFSN	WN	08542	x	**F**	EWSF	SF
08460	a	**0**	EWOC	OC	08543	x	**D**	LBBS	BS
08466	a	**F0**	FDSX	IM (U)	08561	x		LGML	ML
08472	a		HBSH	BN	08567	x		LBBS	BS
08480	az	**G**	EWOC	OC	08568	x		KGSS	ZH
08481	x		LNCF	CF	08569	x		DAAN	AN
08482	a	**D**	DAWE	AN	08571	xz		HBSH	EC
08483	a	**D**	HJXX	PM	08573	x		KCSI	ZI
08484	a	**D**	KWSW	ZN	08575	x		DFLS	TI
08485	a		LWSP	SP	08576	x		LNCF	CF
08489	a	**F**	LWSP	SP	08577	x		FMSY	TE
08492	a		ENSN	TO	08578	x	**R**	PXLS	HT
08493	a		LNCF	CF	08580	x		ENSN	TO
08495	x		ENSN	TO	08581	x	**BS**	FDSX	DR (S)
08499	a	**F**	FDSK	KY	08582	a	**D**	FMSY	TE
08500	x	**0**	FDSD	DR	08585	x		DFLS	AN
08506	x		LGML	ML	08586	a	**F**	LNXX	AY
08509	a	**F**	FDSD	DR	08587	x		FDSD	DR

08588	xz	**BS**	HISL	NL	08693	x		LNWX	ML
08593	x	**0**	EWSF	SF	08694	x		DASY	TI
08594	x		PXLT	CA (U)	08695	x		PXLT	CD
08597	x		ENSN	TO	08696	a	**D**	HFSN	WN
08599	x		PXLS	CD	08697	x		HISE	DY
08600	a	**D**	EWEH	EH	08698	a		EWSU	SU
08601	x	**0**	LBBS	BS	08700	a		EWSX	SF (S)
08605	x		FDSK	KY	08701	x	**R**	PXLS	CD
08607	x		ENSN	TO	08702	x		PXLS	WN
08610	x		LNXX	BS (U)	~~08703~~	~~a~~		~~DAAN~~	~~AN~~
08611	x		HFSL	LO	08706	x		FDSK	KY
08616	x	**G**	HGSS	TS	08709	x		EWSF	SF
08617	x		HFSN	WN	08711	x	**RX**	PXLS	CA
08619	x		LNXX	SP (S)	08713	a		FDSX	DR (U)
08622	x		LNWX	ML	08714	x	**RX**	PXLS	CA
08623	x		LBBS	BS	08715	v	**0**	EWSF	SF
08624	x		DFLS	AN	08718	x		LNWX	ML
08625	x		LBBS	BS	08720	a	**D**	LGML	ML
08628	x		LBBS	BS	08721	x	**0**	HFSL	LO
~~08629~~	~~x~~	**0**	~~KWSW~~	~~ZN~~	08723	x		ENSN	TO (U)
08630	x		LNWX	ML	08724	x		HBSH	BN
08632	x		FDSX	IM (U)	08730	x	**0**	KGSS	ZH
08633	x	**RX**	PXLS	CD	08731	x		LNWX	ML
08635	x		PXLS	CA	08734	x		LBBS	BS
08641	xz	**D**	HJSL	LA	08735	x		LGML	ML
08642	x*	**0**	DFLS	AN	08737	x	**F**	DAWE	AN
08643	xz	**D**	HJXX	PM	08738	x	**D**	LGML	ML
08644	xz	**I**	HJSL	LA	08739	x		DAAN	AN
08645	xz	**D**	HJSL	LA	08740	x	**F**	EWSF	SF
08646	x	**F**	EWOC	OC	08742	x		PXLS	CD
08647	x	**G**	PXXA	CD	08745	xz	**FE**	DFLS	TI
08648	x*	**D**	HJSL	LA	08746	x	**D**	LBBS	BS
08649	x	**G**	KESE	ZG	08750	x		EWSF	SF
08651	xz	**D**	EWOC	OC	08751	x	**FE**	DASY	TI
08653	x*	**FE**	DAAN	AN	~~08752~~	~~x~~	**C**	~~EWSF~~	~~SF~~
08655	x*	**F**	DAWE	AN	08754	x		HASS	IS
08661	a	**FE**	DAAN	AN	08756	x	**D**	LNCF	CF
08662	a		FDSK	KY	08757	x	**RX**	PXLS	HT
08663	a	**D**	HJSL	LA	08758	x		EWSF	SF
08664	x		EWOC	OC	08762	x		HASS	IS
08665	x		FDSX	IM (S)	08765	xn	**D**	LBBS	BS
08668	x		PXXA	CD	08768	x		LGML	ML
08670	a		EWSF	SF	08770	a	**D**	LNCF	CF
08675	x	**F**	LGML	ML	08773	x		ENSX	TO (U)
08676	x		LWSP	SP	08775	x		EWSF	SF
08682	x		KDSD	ZF	08776	a	**D**	FDSK	KY
08683	x		LBBS	BS	08780	x		HJSE	LE
08685	x		PXLS	CA	08782	x		FDSK	KY
08689	a	**0**	EWSF	SF	08783	x		FDSK	KY
08690	x		HISE	DY	08784	x		DAAN	AN
08691	x	**G**	DFLS	AN	08786	a	**D**	LNCF	CF

No.			Code	Abbr.
08790	x		HFSL	LO
08792	x		LNCF	CF
08795	x	M	HJSE	LE
08798	x		LNCF	CF
08799	x		DAAN	AN
08801	x		LNCF	CF
08802	x		PXLS	CD
08804	x		PXLS	CD
08805	x	0	DAAN	TS
08806	a	F	FMSY	TE
08807	x	BS	LBBS	BS
08810	a		HSSN	NC
08811	a*		EWSX	SF (S)
08813	a	D	FMSY	TE
08815	x		LWSP	SP
08817	x	BS	LWSP	SP
08818	x		PXXA	CD
08819	x	D	LNCF	CF
08822	x		HJSE	LE
08823	a		KDSD	ZF
08824	a	F	FDSI	IM
08825	a		DAAN	AN
08826	a		LNWX	ML
08827	a		LGML	ML
08828	a		EWSF	SF
08830	x*		HLSV	CF
08834	x	FD	HBSH	BN
08836	x	I	HJXX	OO
08837	x*	D	DAAN	AN
08842	x		DAYX	AN
08844	x		DAWE	AN
08847	x*		KESE	ZG
08853	xr		HBSH	EC
08854	x*		EWOC	OC
08856	x		DAAN	AN
08865	x		PXLT	CA
08866	x		EWSF	SF
08869	x	G	HSSN	NC
08872	x	D	DAAN	AN
08873	x	M	PXLS	CD
08877	x	D	FDSD	DR
08878	x		EWSX	SF (U)
08879	x		DATI	TI
08880	x		DAYX	TI
08881	x	D	LGML	ML
08882	x		LGML	ML
08883	x	0	LGML	ML
08884	x		LWSP	SP
08886	x		PXLS	HT
08887	x		HFSN	WN
08888	xz	R	PXLS	HT
08890	x	D	PXLS	WN
08891	x		DFLS	AN
08892	x*	D	DFLS	AN
08893	x	D	LNXX	BS (U)
08894	x		LWSP	SP
08896	x		PXLS	CD
08897	x	D	PXLS	CD
08899	x		HISE	DY
08900	x	D	LNCF	CF
08901	xn		LNXX	BS (U)
08902	x		DAAN	AN
08903	x		FDSX	DR (U)
08904	x		EWOC	OC
08905	x		DASY	TI
08906	x		LGML	ML
08907	x	0	DAAN	AN
08908	xz		HISL	NL
08909	x		EWSX	SF
08910	x		LGML	ML
08911	x	D	LWSP	SP
08912	x		LGML	ML
08913	x	D	DAWE	AN
08914	x		LBBS	BS
08915	x	F	LWSP	SP
08918	x	D	LWSP	SP
08919	x	RX	PXLS	CD
08920	x	F	LBBS	BS
08921	x		PXLS	CD
08922	x	D	LGML	ML
08924	x	D	EWOC	OC
08925	x		LWSP	SP
08926	x		DAAN	AN
08927	x		LBBS	BS
08928	x	FR	HSSN	NC
08931	x		FDSX	TE (U)
08932	x		LNCF	CF
08933	x*	0	EWEH	EH
08934	x		HFSN	WN
08938	xr	0	LNWX	ML
08939	x		DAAN	AN
08940	x		EWEH	EH
08941	x		LNCF	CF
08942	x		LNCF	CF
08944	x	D	EWOC	OC
08946	x	FE	DASY	TI
08947	x		EWOC	OC
08948	xc	E	GPSS	OC
08950	x	I	HISL	NL
08951	x	D	DAYX	AN
08952	x		LNWX	ML
08953	x	D	LNCF	CF

08954	x	F	LNCF	CF	08957	x	EWSF	SF
08955	x		LNCF	CF	08958	x	EWSX	SF (U)
08956	x		CDJD	DY				

Names:

08578	~~Libert Dickinson~~	08757	EAGLE C.U.R.C.
08647	Crimpsall	08790	M.A. SMITH
08649	G.H. Stratton	08869	The Canary
08661	Europa	08888	~~Postman's Pride~~
08682	Lionheart	08919	~~Steep Holm~~
08701	The Sorter	08950	Neville Hill 1st
08714	Cambridge		

Class 08/9. Fitted with cut-down cab and headlight for Cwmmawr branch.

08993	(08592)	x	FT	LNCF	CF	ASHBURNHAM
08994	(08462)	a	FR	LNCF	CF	
08995	(08687)	a	FT	LNCF	CF	KIDWELLY

CLASS 09   BR SHUNTER   0-6-0

Built: 1959 – 62 by BR at Darlington or Horwich Works.
Engine: English Electric 6KT of 298 kW (400 hp) at 680 rpm.
Main Generator: English Electric 801.
Traction Motors: English Electric 506.
Max. Tractive Effort: 111 kN (25000 lbf).
Cont. Tractive Effort: 39 kN (8800 lbf) at 11.6 mph.
Power At Rail: 201 kW (269 hp).
Brake Force: 19 t.
Weight: 50 t.
Max. Speed: 27 mph.
Train Brakes: Air & Vacuum.

Length over Buffers: 8.92 m.
Wheel Diameter: 1372 mm.
RA: 5.

Class 09/0 were formerly numbered 3665 – 71, 3719 – 21, 4099 – 4114.

CLASS 09/0. Built as Class 09.

09001		LNCF	CF	09014	D	FDSK	KY
09003		EWHG	SL	09015	D	LNCF	CF
09004		HWSU	SU	09016	D	EWOC	OC
09005	D	FMSY	TE	09018	ML	EWOC	OC
09006	ML	EWOC	OC	09019	D	EWHG	SL
09007	ML	EWOC	OC	09020		EWSF	SF
09008	D	LNCF	CF	09021		DAWE	AN
09009	D	EWHG	SL	09022		DAWE	AN
09010	D	EWSF	SF	09023		EWSU	SU
09011	D	DAWE	AN	09024	ML	EWHG	SL
09012	D	EWOC	OC	09025		HWSU	SU
09013	D	LNCF	CF	09026	D	HWSU	SU

Names:

09009	Three Bridges C.E.D.	09026	William Pearson
09012	Dick Hardy		

CLASS 09/1. Converted from Class 08. 110 V electrical equipment.

09101	(08833)	D	EWOC	OC
09102	(08832)	D	EWOC	OC
09103	(08766)	D	LGML	ML
09104	(08749)	D	LBBS	BS
09105	(08835)	D	LNCF	CF
09106	(08759)	D	FMSY	TE
09107	(08845)	D	LNCF	CF

CLASS 09/2. Converted from Class 08. 90 V electrical equipment.

09201	(08421)	D	ENSN	TO
09202	(08732)	D	LGML	ML
09203	(08781)	D	LNCF	CF
09204	(08717)	D	FMSY	TE
09205	(08620)	D	LGML	ML

CLASS 20   ENGLISH ELECTRIC TYPE 1   Bo–Bo

Built: 1957 – 68 by English Electric Company at Vulcan Foundry, Newton le Willows or Robert Stephenson & Hawthorn, Darlington. 20001 – 128 were originally built with disc indicators whilst 20129 – 228 were built with four character headcode panels.
Engine: English Electric 8SVT Mk. II of 746 kW (1000 hp) at 850 rpm.
Main Generator: English Electric 819/3C.
Traction Motors: English Electric 526/5D (20001 – 48) or 526/8D (others).
Max. Tractive Effort: 187 kN (42000 lbf).
Cont. Tractive Effort: 111 kN (25000 lbf) at 11 mph.
Power At Rail: 574 kW (770 hp).   **Length over Buffers:** 14.25 m.
Brake Force: 35 t.   **Wheel Diameter:** 1092 mm.
Design Speed: 75 mph.   **Weight:** 73.5 t.
Max. Speed: 60 mph.   **RA:** 5.
Train Brakes: Air & Vacuum.
Multiple Working: Blue Star Coupling Code.

Formerly numbered in series 8007 – 8190, 8315 – 8325.

CLASS 20/0. BR-owned Locomotives.

20007 st		TAKX	CE (U)	
20016 st		LNXX	BS (U)	
20032 s		TAKX	ZC (U)	
20057 st		LNXX	BS (U)	
20059 st **FR**		LNXX	BS (U)	
20066		LNXX	BS (U)	
20072 st		TAKX	CE (U)	
20075 st **T**		TAKB	BS	Sir William Cooke
20081 st		LNXX	BS (U)	
20087 st **BS**		LNXX	BS (U)	
20092	**CS**	LNXX	BS (U)	

20104	st	**FR**	TAKX	CE (U)	
20117	st		TAKX	CE (U)	
20118		**FR**	LNWX	BS (U)	
20121	st		TAKX	CE (U)	
20128	st	**T**	TAKB	BS	Guglielmo Marconi
20131	st	**T**	TAKB	BS	Almon B. Strowger
20132	st	**FR**	LNWX	BS (U)	
20138		**FR**	LNWX	BS (U)	
20165		**FR**	LNWX	BS (U)	
20168	st		LNWX	BS (U)	
20169	st	**CS**	LNWX	BS (U)	
20187	st	**T**	TAKB	BS	Sir Charles Wheatstone
20190	st		TAKX	CE (U)	
20215	st	**FR**	TAKX	CE (U)	

CLASS 20/3. Privately-owned by Direct Rail Services

Used on radioactive waste trains between Sellafield, Barrow Docks and Drigg and chemical trains to Northwich.
Non-standard Livery: Dark blue with light blue roof and green lettering.
All have train air brakes only and twin fuel tanks.

20301	(20047)	**0**	XHSD	SD
20302	(20084)	**0**	XHSD	SD
20303	(20127)	**0**		
20304	(20120)	**0**		
20305	(20095)	**0**		

CLASS 20/9. Privately-owned by Hunslet – Barclay Ltd.

Used mainly on weedkilling trains.
Non-standard Livery: Hunslet – Barclay two-tone grey with red lettering.

20901	(20041)	t	**0**	XYPD	ZK	NANCY
20902	(20060)		**0**	XYPD	ZK	LORNA
20903	(20083)		**0**	XYPD	ZK	ALISON
20904	(20101)		**0**	XYPD	ZK	JANIS
20905	(20225)	t	**0**	XYPD	ZK	IONA
20906	(20219)		**0**	XYPD	ZK	Kilmarnock 400

CLASS 31   BRUSH TYPE 2   A1A – A1A

Built: 1957 – 62 by Brush Traction at Loughborough.
31102/5 – 7/10/25/34/44/418/44/50/61 retain two headcode lights. Others have roof-mounted headcode boxes.
Engine: English Electric 12SVT of 1100 kW (1470 hp) at 850 rpm.
Main Generator: Brush TG160-48.
Traction Motors: Brush TM73-68.
Max. Tractive Effort: 160 kN (35900 lbf) (190 kN (42800 lbf)*).
Cont. Tractive Effort: 83 kN (18700 lbf) at 23.5 mph. (99 kN (22250 lbf) at 19.7 mph *.)
Power At Rail: 872 kW (1170 hp).   **Length over Buffers:** 17.30 m.

Brake Force: 49 t.
Design Speed: 90 (80*) mph.
Max. Speed: 60 mph (90 mph 31/4)
RA: 5 or 6.
Train Brakes: Air & Vacuum.
Multiple Working: Blue Star Coupling Code.

Driving Wheel Diameter: 1092 mm.
Centre Wheel Diameter: 1003 mm.
Weight: 107 – 111 t.
ETH Index (Class 31/4): 66.

Communication Equipment: This class is in the process of being fitted with cab to shore radio-telephone.

Non-standard liveries:

31116 is red, yellow, red and grey with 'Infrastructure' branding.
31413 is BR blue with yellow cabsides, a light blue stripe along the bottom of the body and a red band around the bottom of the cabs.

Formerly numbered 5520 – 5699, 5800 – 5862 (not in order).

CLASS 31/1. Standard Design. RA5.

31102	C	LBDB	BS	Cricklewood
31105 *	FT	LBDB	BS	Bescot TMD
31106 *	C	LNWX	BS (U)	The Blackcountryman
31107	C	LNWX	BS (U)	
31110	C	LBDB	BS	
31112 *	CT	LBDB	BS	
31113	C	LBDB	BS	
31116	O	ENXX	TO (U)	
31119	C	LNWX	SP (S)	
31125	C	LNXX	BS (U)	
31126	C	LNWX	SP	
31128	FO	LNXX	BS (U)	
31130	FC	LWNC	SP	Calder Hall Power Station
31132	FO	LNWX	BS (U)	
31134	C	LWNC	SP	
31135	C	ENXX	TO (U)	
31142	C	LWNC	SP	
31144	C	LWDC	SP	
31145	C	LNXX	SP	
31146 r	C	LBDB	BS	Brush Veteran
31147 r	C	LBDB	BS	Floreat Salopia
31149	FR	ENXX	TO (S)	
31154	C	LWNC	SP	
31155	FA	LNXX	BS (U)	
31158	C	LNXX	BS (U)	
31159	C	LWDC	SP	
31160	F	LNXX	SP	
31163	C	LWNC	SP	
31164	FO	LNWX	BS (U)	
31165	G	ENTN	TO	
31166	C	LBDB	BS	
31171	FO	LNXX	BS (U)	
31174	C	LNXX	BS (U)	
31178	C	LNWX	BS (U)	

31180	FR	ENXX	TO (U)
31181	C	ENXX	TO (U)
31184	FO	ENXX	TO (U)
31185	C	LBDB	BS
31186	C	ENXX	TO (U)
31187	C	ENXX	TO (U)
31188	C	LWNC	SP
31190	C	LNWX	SP (S)
31191	C	ENXX	TO (S)
31199	FC	LWNC	SP
31200	FC	LWNC	SP
31201	FC	LWNC	SP
31203	C	LWDC	SP
31205	FR	ENXX	TO (U)
31206	C	LNWX	BS (U)
31207	C	LWNC	SP
31209	FA	ENXX	TO (U)
31219	C	ENXX	TO (U)
31224	C	LNWX	SP (S)
31229	C	LWNC	SP
31230 *	FO	ENXX	TO (U)
31232	C	LNWX	BS (U)
31233	C	LWNC	SP Severn Valley Railway
31235	C	LNWX	SP (S)
31237	C	LNWX	BS (U)
31238	C	LWNC	SP
31242	C	LNWX	SP (S)
31247	FR	ENXX	TO (U)
31248	FO	LNXX	BS (U)
31250	C	ENXX	TO (U)
31252	FO	ENXX	TO (U)
31255	C	LWNC	SP
31263	C	LNXX	SP (U)
31268	C	ENXX	TO (U)
31270	FC	LNWX	SP (S)
31271	FA	ENXX	TO (S)
31273	C	LBDB	BS
31275	FC	LWNC	SP
31276	FC	ENXX	TO (U)
31285	C	LNWX	SP (S)
31290	C	ENXX	TO (U)
31294	FA	ENXX	TO (U)
31301	FR	LNXX	SP (U)
31302	FP	LWNC	SP
31304	FC	LNXX	SP
31306	C	LWDC	SP
31308	C	ENTN	TO
31312	FC	LNXX	SP
31317	FO	LNWX	BS (U)
31319	FC	LWNC	SP
31327	FR	LNWX	SP (S)

CLASS 31/4. Equipped with Train Heating. RA6.
CLASS 31/5. Dedicated for Civil Engineer's Department Use. Train Heating Equipment isolated. RA6.

31403		ENXX	TO (U)	
31405	M	LBDB	BS	Mappa Mundi
31407 (31507)	M	ENTN	TO	
31408		LNXX	SP (S)	
31410	RR	LWNC	SP	Granada Telethon
31411 (31511)	D	LNXX	BS (U)	
31512 (31412)	C	LWDC	SP	
31413	O	LNXX	BS (U)	
31514 (31414)	C	LBDB	BS	
31415		LNXX	BS (U)	
31516 (31416)	C	LNXX	BS (U)	
31417	D	LNXX	BS (U)	
31519 (31419)	C	LNXX	SP	
31420 (31172)	M	LBDB	BS	
31421 (31140)	RR	LWNC	SP	Wigan Pier
31422 (31522)	M	LBDB	BS	
31423 (31197)	M	LBDB	BS	Jerome K. Jerome
31524 (31424)	C	LBDB	BS	
31526 (31426)	C	LNXX	BS (U)	
31427 (31194)		LNWX	SP (S)	
31530 (31430)	C	LNWX	BS (U)	Sister Dora
31531 (31431)	C	ENXX	TO (U)	
31432 (31153)		LWDC	SP	
31533 (31433)	C	LNXX	BS (U)	
31434 (31258)		LBDB	BS	
31435 (31179)	C	LNWX	BS (U)	
31537 (31437)	C	LNWX	BS (U)	
31538 (31438)		LNWX	SP (S)	
31439 (31239)	RR	LWDC	SP	North Yorkshire Moors Railway
31541 (31441)	C	ENXX	TO	
31444 (31544)	C	LNXX	SP	Keighley and Worth Valley Railway
31545 (31445)		LBDB	BS	
31546 (31446)	C	LNWX	BS (U)	
31547 (31447)	C	ENXX	TO (U)	
31548 (31448)	C	LNXX	BS (U)	
31549 (31449)	C	ENTN	TO	
31450 (31133)		LWDC	SP	
31551 (31451)	C	ENTN	TO	
31552 (31452)	C	ENXX	TO (S)	
31553 (31453)	C	ENXX	TO (U)	
31554 (31454)	C	LBDB	BS	
31455 (31555)	RR	LWDC	SP	
31556 (31456)	C	LNWX	SP	
31558 (31458)	C	ENTN	TO	Nene Valley Railway
31459 (31256)		ENTN	TO	
31461 (31129)	D	ENXX	TO (U)	

31462 (31315)	D	LBDB	BS	
31563 (31463)	C	ENTN	TO	
31465 (31565)	RR	LWDC	SP	
31466 (31115)	C	ENTN	TO	
31467 (31216)		LBDB	BS	
31468 (31568)	C	LBDB	BS	The Enginemen's Fund
31569 (31469)	C	ENXX	TO (U)	

CLASS 33   BRCW TYPE 3   Bo – Bo

Built: 1960 – 62 by the Birmingham Railway Carriage & Wagon Company, Smethwick.
Engine: Sulzer 8LDA28 of 1160 kW (1550 hp) at 750 rpm.
Main Generator: Crompton Parkinson CG391B1.
Traction Motors: Crompton Parkinson C171C2.
Max. Tractive Effort: 200 kN (45000 lbf).
Cont. Tractive Effort: 116 kN (26000 lbf) at 17.5 mph.
Power At Rail: 906 kW (1215 hp).   **Length over Buffers:** 15.47 m.
Brake Force: 35 t.   **Wheel Diameter:** 1092 mm.
Design Speed: 85 mph.   **Weight:** 77.5 t (78.5 t Class 33/1).
Max. Speed: 60 mph.   **RA:** 6.
Train Heating: Electric (y isolated). **ETH Index:** 48.
Train Brakes: Air & vacuum.
Multiple Working: Blue Star Coupling Code.
Communication Equipment: This class is in the process of being fitted with cab to shore radio-telephone.

Formerly numbered in series 6500 – 97 but not in order. 33116 carries its original number D 6535.

Class 33/0. Standard Design.

33002	y	C	EWRB	SL	Sea King
33008	y	G	EWDB	SL	Eastleigh
33012	e		ENXX	SL (S)	
33019	e	C	EWDB	SL	Griffon
33021	e	FM	ENXX	SL (U)	
33023	e		ENXX	SL (U)	
33025	e	C	EWDB	SL	Sultan
33026	e	C	EWDB	SL	Seafire
33029	e		ENXX	SL (U)	
33030	e	C	EWDB	SL	
33035	y	N	EWDB	SL	Spitfire
33042	e	FA	ENXX	SL (U)	
33046	y	C	EWDB	SL	Merlin
33048	es		ENXX	SL (S)	
33051	e	C	EWDB	SL	Shakespeare Cliff
33052	e		ENXX	SL (S)	Ashford
33053	e	FA	ENXX	SL (U)	
33057	ys	C	EWDB	SL	Seagull
33063	ys	FM	ENXX	SL (S)	
33065	e	C	EWRB	SL	Sealion

Class 33/1. Fitted with Buckeye Couplings & SR Multiple Working Equipment for use with SR EMUs, TC stock & class 73.

Also fitted with flashing light adaptor for use on Weymouth Quay line.

33103	e	**C**	ENXX	SL (S)	
33109	e	**D**	EWDB	SL	Captain Bill Smith RNR
33116	e		EWDB	SL	Hertfordshire Rail Tours
33117	e		ENXX	SL (U)	

Class 33/2. Built to Former Loading Gauge of Tonbridge – Battle Line.

33202	ys	**C**	EWDB	SL	The Burma Star
33204	es	**FM**	EWRB	SL	
33205	es	**FD**	ENZX	SL (U)	
33206	es	**FD**	ENXX	SL (U)	
33207	ys	**FA**	EWDB	SL	Earl Mountbatten of Burma
33208	es	**C**	EWDB	SL	

CLASS 37   ENGLISH ELECTRIC TYPE 3   Co–Co

Built: 1960 – 5 by English Electric Company at Vulcan Foundry, Newton le Willows or Robert Stephenson & Hawthorn, Darlington. 37003 – 116/340/1/3/5/350/1/9 with the exception of 37019*/047/053/065*/072*/073/074/075*/100* (* one end only) retain box-type route indicators, the remainder having central headcode panels/marker lamps.
Engine: English Electric 12CSVT of 1300 kW (1750 hp) at 850 rpm.
Main Generator: English Electric 822/10G.
Traction Motors: English Electric 538/A.
Max. Tractive Effort: 245 kN (55500 lbf).
Cont. Tractive Effort: 156 kN (35000 lbf) at 13.6 mph.
Power At Rail: 932 kW (1250 hp).   **Length over Buffers:** 18.75 m.
Brake Force: 50 t.   **Wheel Diameter:** 1092 mm.
Design Speed: 90 mph.   **Weight:** 103 – 108 t.
Max. Speed: 80 mph.   **RA:** 5 or 7.
Train Heating: Electric (Class 37/4 only). **ETH Index:** 38
Train Brakes: Air & Vacuum.
Multiple Working: Blue Star Coupling Code.
Communication Equipment: Cab to shore radio-telephone.

a Vacuum brake isolated.

Formerly numbered 6600 – 8, 6700 – 6999 (not in order). 37274 is the second loco to carry that number. It was renumbered to avoid confusion with Class 37/3 locos.

Note: 37070 has had its roof and bodyside panels removed for transportation and maintenance of Class 37 power units at Toton depot. It has had the rest of the body painted dark grey.

Class 37/0. Unrefurbished Locos. Technical details as above. RA5.

37003	+	**C**	FDYX	IM (U)
37004		**FS**	LNXX	ML (U)
37010		**C**	ENTN	TO

37012		C	ENTN	TO	
37013	+	F	EWDS	SF	
37019	+	FD	FDYX	IM (U)	
37023		ML	EWDS	SF	Stratford TMD Quality Approved
37025		BR	LBLB	BS	Inverness TMD Quality Assured
37026	(37320) +	FD	LWCC	SP	Shapfell
37035		C	EWRB	SL	
37037	(37321)	FS	EWDB	SL	
37038		C	ENTN	TO	
37040		F	EWRB	SL	
37042	+	FM	EWCN	TO	
37043	(37354)	CT	LGBM	ML	
37045	(37355) +	F	FDYX	TE (U)	
37046		C	ENTN	TO	
37047	+	ML	EWDS	SF	
37048		FM	ENTN	TO	
37051		FM	ENTN	TO	
37054		C	EWDB	SL	
37055	+	ML	EWCN	TO	RAIL Celebrity
37057	+	BR	EWCN	TO	
37058	+	C	FDKI	IM	
37059	+	FD	FDKI	IM	
37063	+	FD	FDYX	TE (U)	
37065	+	ML	EWCN	TO	
37066	+	C	LWCC	SP	
37068	(37356) +	FD	FDYX	IM (U)	
37069	+	C	LGBM	ML	
37070		0	ENXX	TO	
37071	+	C	LBLB	BS	
37072	+	D	EWCN	TO	
37073	+	FT	LGBM	ML	Fort William/An Gearasdan
37074	+	ML	EWDB	SL	
37075	+	F	FDYX	TE (U)	
37077		ML	EWDB	SL	
37078	+	FS	LNXX	ML (U)	
37079	(37357) +	FD	FDYX	IM (U)	
37080		FP	LNXX	CD	
37083	+	C	FDYX	IM (U)	
37087		C	LBLB	BS	
37088	(37323)	C	LGBM	ML	Clydesdale
37092		C	ENTN	TO	
37095	+	C	FDKI	IM	
37097		C	ENTN	TO	
37098	+	C	EWCN	TO	
37099	(37324)	C	LBLB	BS	Clydebridge
37100	+	FS	LGBM	ML	
37104		C	FDYX	IM (U)	
37106	+	C	EWDS	SF	
37107	+	FD	LWCC	SP	
37108	(37325) +	F	LWCC	SP	
37109		FM	EWDB	SL	

37110		+	**F**	FDYX	IM (U)
37111	(37326)		**FT**	LBLB	BS	Glengarnock
37114		+	**C**	EWCN	TO	City of Worcester
37116		+	**BR**	LBLB	BS
37131		+	**F**	FDKI	IM
37133			**C**	LNSK	CF
37137	(37312)		**FM**	ENTN	TO	Clyde Iron
37138			**FS**	ENXX	TO (U)
37139		+	**FC**	FDYX	IM (U)
37140	.		**C**	EWDS	SF
37141			**C**	LNDK	CF
37142			**C**	LBLB	BS
37144		r	**FA**	FDYX	IM (U)
37146			**C**	LNDK	CF
37152	(37310)		**I**	LGBM	ML
37153			**CT**	LGBM	ML
37154		+	**FT**	LBLB	BS
37156	(37311)	r	**FT**	LGBM	ML
37158			**C**	LNDK	CF
37162		+	**D**	EWCN	TO
37165	(37374)	+	**C**	LGBM	ML
37167		+	**ML**	EWDB	SL
37170		r	**C**	LGBM	ML
37174			**C**	EWRB	SL
37175			**C**	LGBM	ML
37178		+	**F**	LNSK	CF
37184			**C**	LBLB	BS
37185		+	**C**	EWCN	TO	Lea & Perrins
37188			**C**	LBLB	BS
37191			**C**	LBLB	BS
37194		+	**FM**	EWRB	SL	British International Freight Association
37196			**C**	LGBM	ML
37197		+	**CT**	LNSK	CF
37198		+	**ML**	EWDB	SL
37201			**CT**	LBLB	BS	Saint Margaret
37203			**ML**	EWDB	SL
37207			**C**	LBLB	BS
37209			**BR**	FDYX	IM (U)
37211			**C**	LBLB	BS
37212		+	**FT**	LGBM	ML
37213		+	**FC**	LNSK	CF
37214		+	**FA**	LNDK	CF
37216		r+	**G**	EWDS	SF	Great Eastern
37217		+		FDYX	IM (U)
37218		+	**F**	FDYX	IM (U)
37219		r	**ML**	EWDB	SL
37220		+	**FM**	EWRB	SL
37221			**FT**	LGBM	ML
37222		+	**FM**	EWCN	TO
37223		+	**FC**	FDYX	IM (U)

37225		+	F	FDKI	IM	
37227		+	FM	EWCN	TO	
37229		+	FC	LNSK	CF	
37230		+	CT	LNSK	CF	
37232	r		C	LGBM	ML	The Institution of Railway Signal Engineers
37235		+	F	FDYX	IM (U)	
37238		+	F	FDYX	IM (U)	
37240		+	C	LBLB	BS	
37241			FS	EWDS	SF	
37242		+	ML	EWDS	SF	
37244		+	F	EWCN	TO	
37245			C	EWRB	SL	
37248		+	ML	EWCN	TO	Midland Railway Centre
37250		+	FT	LGBM	ML	
37251		+	I	LGBM	ML	The Northern Lights
37254		+	C	LNSK	CF	
37255		+	C	LBLB	BS	
37258		+	C	LNSK	CF	
37261		+	FD	LGBM	ML	Caithness
37262		+	D	LGBM	ML	Dounreay
37263			C	LNDK	CF	
37264			C	ENTN	TO	
37274 (37308)		+	ML	EWDB	SL	
37275		+		LBLB	BS	Oor Wullie
37278		+	FC	ENXX	TO (U)	
37293		+	FM	EWRB	SL	
37294		+	C	LGBM	ML	
37298		+	F	FDYX	IM (U)	

Class 37/3. Unrefurbished locos fitted with regeared (CP7) bogies.
Details as Class 37/0 except:
Max. Tractive Effort: 250 kN (56180 lbf).
Cont. Tractive Effort: 184 kN (41250 lbf) at 11.4 mph.

37330 (37128)	+	BR	FDRI	IM	
37331 (37202)		F	FDYX	IM (U)	
37332 (37239)	+	FC	FDRI	IM	
37333 (37271)	+	FD	FDYX	IM (U)	
37334 (37272)	+	F	FDRI	IM	
37335 (37285)	+	F	FDYX	IM (U)	
37340 (37009)	+	FD	FDYX	IM (U)	
37341 (37015)	+	F	FDYX	TE (U)	
37343 (37049)		C	FDYX	IM (U) Imperial	
37344 (37053)	+	FD	FDKI	IM	
37345 (37101)	+	FD	FDYX	IM (U)	
37350 (37119)	+	FP	FDKI	IM	
37351 (37002)	+	C	LGPM	ML	
37358 (37091)		F	FDKI	IM	
37359 (37118)		FP	FDYX	TE (U)	
37370 (37127)		C	EWRB	SL	
37371 (37147)	+	C	EWDB	SL	

```
37372 (37159)   C    EWRB      SL
37375 (37193) +  C    EWDB      SL
37376 (37199) +  FC   EWCN      TO
37377 (37200) +  C    EWDB      SL
37378 (37204) +  FD   FDYX      IM
37379 (37226)   C    EWDS      SF    Ipswich WRD Quality Assured
37380 (37259)   FM   EWRB      SL
37381 (37284) +  FD   FDYX      IM (U)
37382 (37145)   FP   FDYX      IM (U)
```

Class 37/4. Refurbished locos fitted with train heating. Main generator replaced by alternator. Regeared (CP7) bogies. Details as class 37/0 except:

Main Alternator: Brush BA1005A.
Max. Tractive Effort: 256 kN (57440 lbf).
Cont. Tractive Effort: 184 kN (41250 lbf) at 11.4 mph.
Power At Rail: 935 kW (1254 hp).
All have twin fuel tanks.

```
37401 (37268) r  FT   LGHM      ML   Mary Queen of Scots
37402 (37274) r  F    LWMC      CD   Bont Y Bermo
37403 (37307) r  G    LGHM      ML   Ben Cruachan
37404 (37286) r  FT   LGHM      ML   Loch Long
37405 (37282) r  M    LWCC      SP   Strathclyde Region
37406 (37295) r  FD   LGHM      ML   The Saltire Society
37407 (37305) r  FT   LWMC      CD   Blackpool Tower
37408 (37289)    BR   LWMC      CD   Loch Rannoch
37409 (37270) r  FT   LGHM      ML   Loch Awe
37410 (37273) r  FT   LGHM      ML   Aluminium 100
37411 (37290)    FT   LNDK      CF
37412 (37301)    FT   LNDK      CF   Driver John Elliot
37413 (37276) r  FT   LNDK      CF   Loch Eil Outward Bound
37414 (37287) r  RR   LWMC      CD   Cathays C&W Works
                                     1846 – 1993

37415 (37277) r  M    LWCC      SP
37416 (37302) r  M    LWCC      SP
37417 (37269) r  F    LWMC      CD   Highland Region
37418 (37271) r  RR   LWMC      CD   East Lancashire Railway
37419 (37291) r  M    LWCC      SP
37420 (37297) r  M    LWCC      SP   The Scottish Hosteller
37421 (37267) r  RR   LWMC      CD   The Kingsman
37422 (37266) r  RR   LWMC      CD   Robert F. Fairlie Locomotive
                                     Engineer 1831 – 1885
37423 (37296) r  FT   LGHM      ML   Sir Murray Morrison
                 1873 – 1948 Pioneer of British Aluminium Industry
37424 (37279) r  FT   LGHM      ML
37425 (37292) r  RR   LWMC      CD   Sir Robert McAlpine/
                                     Concrete Bob (opp. sides)
37426 (37299) r  M    LWCC      SP
37427 (37288) r  RR   LNDK      CF   Highland Enterprise
37428 (37281) r  FT   LGHM      ML   David Lloyd George
37429 (37300) r  RR   LWMC      CD   Eisteddfod Genedlaethol
```

```
37430 (37265) r  FT LGHM    ML   Cwmbrân
37431 (37272) r  M  LGHM    ML
```

Class 37/5. Refurbished locos. Main generator replaced by alternator. Regeared (CP7) bogies. Details as class 37/4 except:

Max. Tractive Effort: 248 kN (55590 lbf).
All have twin fuel tanks.

```
37503 (37017)    FS FDCI    IM
37504 (37039)    FS FEPS    IM
37505 (37028)    I  LGBM    ML
37508 (37090) s  FS FEPS    IM
37509 (37093)    FT LWCC    SP
37510 (37112)    I  LGBM    ML
37513 (37056)    LH FDDI    IM
37515 (37064) s  LH FDDI    IM
37516 (37086) s  LH FDDI    IM
37517 (37018) as LH FDCI    IM   St. Aidan's CE Memorial School
                                 Hartlepool Railsafe Trophy Winners 1995
37518 (37076)    FS LWCC    SP
37519 (37027)    FS FDRI    IM
37520 (37041)    FS LWCC    SP
37521 (37117)    FP LNLK    CF
```

Class 37/6. Refurbished locos for use on Channel Tunnel Night services. Train air brakes only, UIC brake and coaching stock jumpers, RCH jumpers, ETH through wires.

```
37601 (37501)    E  GPSV    PM
37602 (37502)    E  GPSV    PM
37603 (37504)
37604 (37506)    E  GPSV    PM
37605 (37507)    E  GPSV    PM
37606 (37508)
37607 (37511)    E  GPSV    PM
37608 (37512)    E  GPSV    PM
37609 (37514)    E  GPSV    PM
37610 (37687)    E  GPSV    PM
37611 (37690)    E  GPSV    PM
37612 (37691)    E  GPSV    PM
```

Class 37/5 continued.

```
37667 (37151) as F  EWDS    SF
37668 (37257) s  FP LNLK    CF
37669 (37129)    FT LNLK    CF
37670 (37182)    FT LNLK    CF   St. Blazey T&RS Depot
37671 (37247)    FD LNLK    CF   Tre Pol and Pen
37672 (37189) s  FD LNLK    CF   Freight Transport Association
37673 (37132)    FT LNLK    CF
37674 (37169)    FT LNLK    CF   Saint Blaise Church 1445 – 1995
37675 (37164) s  FT LGPM    ML
37676 (37126)    F  EWDS    SF
```

37677	(37121)		**F** FDRI	IM
37678	(37256)		**FA** EWDS	SF
37679	(37123)		**F** EWDS	SF
37680	(37224)		**FA** FDRI	IM
37682	(37236)		**FA** FDCI	IM
37683	(37187)		**FT** LGBM	ML
37684	(37134)		**F** FDCI	IM	Peak National Park
37685	(37234)		**I** LGBM	ML
37686	(37172)		**FA** FDCI	IM
37688	(37205)		**FA** FDDI	IM	Great Rocks
37689	(37195)	s	**F** FDCI	IM
37692	(37122)	s	**FC** LGPM	ML	The Lass O' Ballochmyle
37693	(37210)	s	**FT** LGPM	ML
37694	(37192)	s	**FC** FDDI	IM
37695	(37157)	s	**FT** LNLK	CF
37696	(37228)	s	**FT** LNLK	CF
37697	(37243)	s	**FC** FDCI	IM
37698	(37246)	s	**LH** FDCI	IM
37699	(37253)	s	**FC** FDCI	IM

Class 37/7. Refurbished locos. Main generator replaced by alternator. Regeared (CP7) bogies. Ballast weights added. Details as class 37/4 except:
Main Alternator: GEC G564AZ (37796 – 803) Brush BA1005A (others).
Max. Tractive Effort: 276 kN (62000 lbf).
Weight: 120 t.   **RA:** 7.
All have twin fuel tanks.

37701	(37030)	s	**FC** LNCK	CF
37702	(37020)	s	**FC** LNCK	CF	Taff Merthyr
37703	(37067)	s	**FM** EWDB	SL
37704	(37034)	s	**FC** LNCK	CF
37705	(37060)	a	**FM** ESBB	SL
37706	(37016)	a	**FP** FDCI	IM	Conidae
37707	(37001)	a	**FP** FDCI	IM
37708	(37089)	a	**FP** FDCI	IM
37709	(37014)	a	**FM** ESBB	SL
37710	(37044)		**FP** FDCI	IM
37711	(37085)		**FS** FDCI	IM
37712	(37102)		**FP** LGPM	ML	Teesside Steelmaster
37713	(37052)		**LH** FDCI	IM
37714	(37024)		**FS** LGPM	ML
37715	(37021)		**FM** ESBB	SL	British Petroleum
37716	(37094)		**FS** FDCI	IM	British Steel Corby
37717	(37050)		**FP** FDCI	IM	Stainless Pioneer
37718	(37084)		**FS** FDCI	IM	Hartlepool Pipe Mill
37719	(37033)	a	**FP** FDCI	IM
37796	(37105)	s	**FC** LNCK	CF
37797	(37081)	s	**FC** LNCK	CF
37798	(37006)	s	**ML** EWDB	SL
37799	(37061)	s	**FT** LNCK	CF	Sir Dyfed/County of Dyfed
37800	(37143)	s	**FM** EWDB	SL
37801	(37173)	s	**FC** LGPM	ML

37802	(37163)	s	**FC**	LNCK	CF	
37803	(37208)	s	**ML**	EWDB	SL	
37883	(37176)		**FP**	FDCI	IM	
37884	(37183)		**FP**	FDCI	IM	Gartcosh
37885	(37177)		**FP**	FDCI	IM	
37886	(37180)		**FS**	FDCI	IM	
37887	(37120)	s	**FC**	LNCK	CF	Caerphilly Castle/Castell Caerffili
37888	(37135)		**F**	FDCI	IM	
37889	(37233)		**FT**	LNCK	CF	
37890	(37168)	a	**FM**	ESBB	SL	The Railway Observer
37891	(37166)		**FM**	EWDB	SL	
37892	(37149)		**FM**	EWDB	SL	Ripple Lane
37893	(37237)		**FT**	LGPM	ML	
37894	(37124)	s	**FC**	LNCK	CF	
37895	(37283)	s	**FC**	LNCK	CF	
37896	(37231)	s	**FT**	LNCK	CF	
37897	(37155)	s	**FT**	LNCK	CF	
37898	(37186)	s	**FC**	LNCK	CF	Cwmbargoed DP
37899	(37161)	s	**FC**	LNCK	CF	County of West Glamorgan/
						Sir Gorllewin Morgannwg

Class 37/9. Refurbished Locos. Fitted with manufacturers prototype power units and ballast weights. Main generator replaced by alternator. Details as Class 37/0 except:

Engine: Mirrlees MB275T of 1340 kW (1800 hp) at 1000 rpm (37901 – 4), Ruston RK270T of 1340 kW (1800 hp) at 900 rpm (37905 – 6).
Main Alternator: Brush BA1005A (GEC G564, 37905/6).
Max. Tractive Effort: 279 kN (62680 lbf).
Cont. Tractive Effort: 184 kN (41250 lbf) at 11.4 mph.
Weight: 120 t.   **RA:** 7.
All have twin fuel tanks.

37901	(37150)		**FT**	LNHK	CF	Mirrlees Pioneer
37902	(37148)		**FS**	LNHK	CF	
37903	(37249)		**FS**	LNHK	CF	
37904	(37125)		**FS**	LNHK	CF	
37905	(37136)	s	**FS**	LNHK	CF	Vulcan Enterprise
37906	(37206)	s	**FT**	LNHK	CF	

CLASS 43   HST POWER CAR   Bo – Bo

Built: 1976 – 82 by BREL Crewe Works. Formerly numbered as coaching stock but now classified as locomotives. Fitted with luggage compartment.
Engine: Paxman Valenta 12RP200L of 1680 kW (2250 hp) at 1500 rpm. (Mirrlees MB190 of 1680 kW (2250 hp) m) (Paxman VP185 of 1680 kW (2250 hp) *).
Main Alternator: Brush BA1001B.
Traction Motors: Brush TMH68 – 46 or GEC G417AZ (43124 – 151/180). Frame mounted.
Max. Tractive Effort: 80 kN (17980 lbf).
Cont. Tractive Effort: 46 kN (10340 lbf) at 64.5 mph.

Power At Rail: 1320 kW (1770 hp).   **ETH:** Non standard 3-phase system.
Brake Force: 35 t.   **Length over Buffers:** 17.79 m.
Weight: 70 t.   **Wheel Diameter:** 1020 mm.
Max. Speed: 125 mph.   **RA:** 5.
Train Brakes: Air.
Multiple Working: With one other similar vehicle.
Communication Equipment: All equipped with driver – guard telephone and cab
to shore radio-telephone.

§ Modified to be able to remotely control a class 91 locomotive and to be remotely controlled by a class 91 locomotive. Fitted with buffers. Tdm and Class 91
control equipment now isolated.

Note: Cross-country and Midland Main Line locos are owned by Porterbrook
Leasing Company (owner codes SBH for ICCS/ICCP and SBI for IMLP). East
Coast and Great Western locos are owned by Angel Train Contracts (owner
codes SCB for IECP and SCJ for IWRP). The above does not apply to Cross Country locos 43006 – 8, 43178/184 which are owned by Angel Train Contracts
(owner codes SCH).

43002	I	IWRP	LA	Top of the Pops
43003	I	IWRP	PM	
43004	I	IWRP	LA	
43005	I	IWRP	LA	
43006	I	ICCP	LA	
43007	I	ICCP	LA	
43008	I	ICCP	LA	
43009	I	IWRP	LA	
43010	I	IWRP	LA	
43011	I	IWRP	LA	Reader 125
43012	I	IWRP	LA	
43013 §	I	ICCS	EC	
43014 §	I	ICCS	EC	
43015	I	IWRP	LA	
43016	I	IWRP	PM	
43017	I	IWRP	LA	
43018	I	IWRP	LA	
43019	I	IWRP	LA	Dinas Abertawe/City of Swansea
43020	I	IWRP	LA	John Grooms
43021	I	IWRP	LA	
43022	I	IWRP	LA	
43023	I	IWRP	LA	County of Cornwall
43024	I	IWRP	LA	
43025	I	IWRP	LA	Exeter
43026	I	IWRP	LA	City of Westminster
43027	I	IWRP	LA	Glorious Devon
43028	I	IWCP	LO	
43029	I	IWCP	LO	
43030	I	IWRP	PM	
43031	I	IWRP	PM	
43032	I	IWRP	PM	The Royal Regiment of Wales
43033	I	IWRP	PM	

43034		I	IWRP	PM	The Black Horse
43035		I	IWRP	PM	
43036		I	IWRP	PM	
43037		I	IWRP	PM	
43038		I	IECP	NL	National Railway Museum
					The First Ten Years 1975 – 1985
43039		I	IECP	NL	
43040		I	IWRP	PM	
43041		I	IWCP	LO	City of Discovery
43042		I	IWCP	LO	
43043		I	IMLP	NL	
43044		I	IMLP	NL	Borough of Kettering
43045		I	IMLP	NL	The Grammar School Doncaster AD 1350
43046		I	IMLP	NL	Royal Philharmonic
43047	*	I	IMLP	NL	Rotherham Enterprise
43048		I	IMLP	NL	
43049		I	IMLP	NL	Neville Hill
43050		I	IMLP	NL	
43051		I	IMLP	NL	The Duke and Duchess of York
43052		I	IMLP	NL	City of Peterborough
43053		I	IMLP	NL	Leeds United
43054		I	IMLP	NL	
43055		I	IMLP	NL	Sheffield Star
43056		I	IMLP	NL	University of Bradford
43057		I	IMLP	NL	Bounds Green
43058		I	IMLP	NL	
43059		I	IMLP	NL	
43060		I	IMLP	NL	County of Leicestershire
43061		I	IMLP	NL	City of Lincoln
43062		I	ICCS	EC	
43063		I	ICCS	EC	
43064		I	IMLP	NL	City of York
43065	§	I	ICCS	EC	
43066		I	IMLP	NL	Nottingham Playhouse
43067	§	I	ICCS	EC	
43068	§	I	ICCS	EC	
43069		I	ICCS	EC	
43070		I	ICCS	EC	
43071		I	ICCS	EC	
43072		I	IMLP	NL	Derby Etches Park
43073		I	IMLP	NL	
43074		I	IMLP	NL	
43075	*	I	IMLP	NL	
43076		I	IMLP	NL	BBC East Midlands Today
43077		I	IMLP	NL	County of Nottingham
43078		I	ICCS	EC	Shildon County Durham
43079		I	ICCS	EC	
43080	§	I	ICCS	EC	
43081		I	IMLP	NL	
43082		I	IMLP	NL	
43083		I	IMLP	NL	

43084 §	I	ICCS	EC	County of Derbyshire
43085	I	IMLP	NL	City of Bradford
43086	I	ICCS	EC	
43087	I	ICCS	EC	
43088	I	ICCS	EC	XIII Commonwealth Games Scotland 1986
43089	I	ICCS	EC	
43090	I	ICCS	EC	
43091	I	ICCS	EC	Edinburgh Military Tattoo
43092	I	ICCS	EC	
43093	I	ICCS	EC	York Festival '88
43094	I	ICCS	EC	
43095	I	IECP	NL	
43096	I	IECP	NL	The Queens Own Hussars
43097	I	ICCS	EC	
43098	I	ICCS	EC	
43099	I	ICCS	EC	
43100	I	ICCS	EC	Craigentinny
43101	I	ICCP	LA	Edinburgh International Festival
43102	I	ICCP	LA	
43103	I	ICCP	LA	John Wesley
43104	I	IECP	NL	County of Cleveland
43105	I	IECP	NL	Hartlepool
43106	I	IECP	NL	Songs of Praise
43107	I	IECP	NL	
43108	I	IECP	NL	
43109	I	IECP	NL	Yorkshire Evening Press
43110	I	IECP	EC	Darlington
43111	I	IECP	EC	
43112	I	IECP	EC	
43113	I	IECP	EC	City of Newcastle-upon-Tyne
43114	I	IECP	EC	National Garden Festival Gateshead 1990
43115	I	IECP	EC	Yorkshire Cricket Academy
43116	I	IECP	EC	City of Kingston Upon Hull
43117	I	IECP	EC	
43118	I	IECP	EC	Charles Wesley
43119	I	IECP	EC	
43120 .	I	IECP	EC	
43121	I	ICCP	LA	West Yorkshire Metropolitan County
43122	I	ICCP	LA	South Yorkshire Metropolitan County
43123 §	I	ICCS	EC	
43124	I	IWRP	PM	
43125	I	IWRP	PM	Merchant Venturer
43126	I	IWRP	PM	City of Bristol
43127	I	IWRP	PM	
43128	I	IWRP	PM	
43129	I	IWRP	PM	
43130	I	IWRP	PM	Sulis Minerva
43131	I	IWRP	PM	Sir Felix Pole
43132	I	IWRP	PM	
43133	I	IWRP	PM	
43134	I	IWRP	PM	County of Somerset

43135	I	IWRP	PM	
43136	I	IWRP	PM	
43137	I	IWRP	PM	
43138	I	IWRP	PM	
43139	I	IWRP	PM	
43140	I	IWRP	PM	
43141	I	IWRP	PM	
43142	I	IWRP	PM	
43143	I	IWRP	PM	
43144	I	IWRP	PM	
43145	I	IWRP	PM	
43146	I	IWRP	PM	
43147	I	IWRP	PM	The Red Cross
43148	I	IWRP	PM	
43149	I	IWRP	PM	BBC Wales Today
43150	I	IWRP	PM	Bristol Evening Post
43151	I	IWRP	PM	
43152	I	IWRP	PM	
43153	I	ICCP	LA	University of Durham
43154	I	ICCP	LA	INTERCITY
43155	I	ICCP	LA	BBC Look North
43156	I	ICCP	LA	
43157	I	ICCP	LA	Yorkshire Evening Post
43158	I	ICCP	LA	Dartmoor The Pony Express
43159	I	ICCP	LA	
43160	I	ICCP	LA	Storm Force
43161	I	ICCP	LA	Reading Evening Post
43162	I	ICCP	LA	Borough of Stevenage
43163	I	IWRP	LA	
43164	I	IWCP	LO	
43165	I	IWCP	LO	
43166	I	IWCP	LO	
43167	* I	IECP	NL	
43168	m I	IWRP	PM	
43169	* I	IWRP	PM	The National Trust
43170	* I	IWRP	LA	Edward Paxman
43171	I	IWRP	LA	
43172	I	IWRP	LA	
43173	I	IWRP	LA	
43174	I	IWRP	LA	
43175	I	IWRP	LA	
43176	I	IWRP	LA	
43177	I	IWRP	LA	University of Exeter
43178	I	ICCP	LA	
43179	I	IWRP	LA	Pride of Laira
43180	I	SBXL	NL	
43181	I	IWRP	LA	Devonport Royal Dockyard 1693-1993
43182	I	IWRP	LA	
43183	I	IWRP	LA	
43184	I	ICCP	LA	
43185	I	IWRP	LA	Great Western

▲ BR blue liveried Class 03 No. 03079 stabled at Sandown, Isle of Wight on 15th July 1995. This loco is now the only remaining member of the class.
Martyn Hilbert

▼ Class 08 No. 08994 'GWENDRAETH', one of three locos from the class which have cut down cabs, is pictured here at Cwmmawr opencast disposal point, Dyfed after arriving with a train of coal empties from Coedbach Washery. The date is 28th September 1995.
Nic Joynson

▲ Class 09 No. 09006 stands by the turntable at Old Oak Common TMD on 2nd October 1995. This loco has been repainted into the house colours of the Mainline freight company. *Brian Morrison*

▼ Hunslet-Barclay owned and liveried Class 20 No. 20901 is pictured stabled with a weed killing train at Clapham on 9th September 1995. Sister loco 20904 is attached to the rear of the train. *Chris Wilson*

▲ A pair of old Railfreight liveried Class 31s Nos. 31128 & 31317 pause next to Evesham signal box whilst working a ballast train on 12th February 1995. Both of these locos are now stored. *Stephen Widdowson*

▼ Class 31s Nos. 31455 'Our Eli' & 31421 'Wigan Pier' at Hargrave, east of Chester with the 15.15 Crewe-Llandudno service on 14th August 1994. Both locos are in Regional Railways livery. *Hugh Ballantyne*

▲ Class 33s Nos. 33025 'Sultan' & 33030, both in Civil-link livery, enter Camden Road on 30th August 1995 with the 09.49 Hoo Junction-Temple Mills engineers train. *Kevin Conkey*

▼ Class 43 No. 43042 leads the 13.38 Holyhead-London Euston out of Penmaenbach tunnel, near Conway on 27th June 1995. Power Car No. 43 165 was at the rear. *G.W. Morrison*

Transrail liveried Class 37 No. 37407 'Blackpool Tower' skirts the North Wales coast at Penmaenmawr whilst working the 12.24 Crewe-Holyhead on 24th June 1995.

Paul D. Shannon

New Railfreight Distribution liveried Class 47 No. 47201 passes Shakespeare Cliff with 10.10 Paddock Wood-Dover 'European' trip. The date is 16th August 1995.

Nic Joynson

▲ Still carrying the obsolete Trainload livery, Class 56 No. 56088 passes Burton Salmon with a south bound m.g.r. on 16th August 1995.

Hugh Ballantyne

▼ Class 56 No. 56106, in Loadhaul colours, approaches Gretna Green on 26th May 1995 with the 12.09 Tyne Yard-Falkland Junction empty coal train.

Kevin Conkey

▲ In two-tone grey livery with Mainline brandings, Class 58 No. 58013 brings up the rear of a Asfordby-Toton coal train at Cossington on 22nd August 1995. *John A. Day*

▼ Class 58 No. 58050 'Toton Traction Depot', in Mainline freight livery, hauls the 10.10 March-Kennett Redland aggregates train at Ely on 17th August 1995. *John A. Day*

National Power Class 59/2 No. 59201 'Vale of York' leaves Peak Forest on 29th June 1995 with a Tunstead-Drax Power Station limestone train.

Les Nixon

Trainload Petroleum liveried Class 60 No. 60025 'Joseph Lister' crosses Ais Gill viaduct on 10th August 1995 with a Gypsum train from Kirby Thore.

Hugh Ballantyne

The 09.30 Roxby-Bredbury waste train passes over the Pennines with Trainload Construction liveried Class 60 No. 60084 'Cross Fell' at the head. The date is 29th March 1994.

Vincent Eastwood

▲ Merseytravel Departmental liveried Class 73/0 No. 73006 is between duties at Hall Road EMUD on 9th October 1994. *Martyn Hilbert*

▼ Few locos now remain in the old Intercity livery. One of the few, a Class 73/1, is 73104 pictured here shunting at Eastleigh TMD on 18th June 1995. *Brian Denton*

Rail Express Systems liveried Class 86 No. 86419 passes through Lune Gorge on 8th July 1995 with the 12.38 Glasgow Central-Brighton service.

Kevin Conkey

▲ Class 87 No. <u>87032 'Kenilworth'</u>, in Intercity livery, passes Grayrigg with a northbound express on 26th July 1995.　　　　*Ian A. Lyall*

▼ Old Railfreight Distribution liveried Class 90 No. <u>90140</u> passes Belstead, near Ipswich with a lightly loaded Felixstowe-Coatbridge freightliner on 10th March 1995.　　　　*John A. Day*

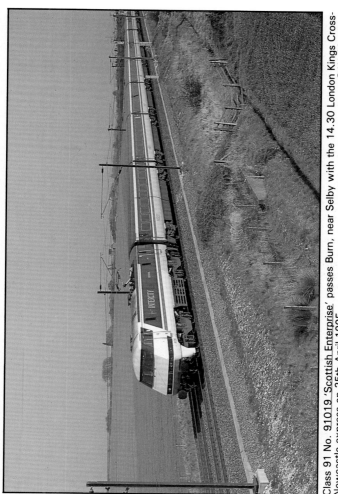

Class 91 No. 91019 'Scottish Enterprise' passes Burn, near Selby with the 14.30 London Kings Cross-Newcastle express on 25th April 1995. *G.W. Morrison*

Class 92 No. 92014 'Emile Zola', in European Passenger Services livery, sweeps through Lune Gorge on 7th June 1995 with a return Carlisle-Crewe test train. Note the Class 47 No. 47555 attached to the rear incase of failure.

Kevin Conkey

43186	I	IWRP	LA	Sir Francis Drake
43187	I	IWRP	LA	
43188	I	IWRP	LA	City of Plymouth
43189	I	IWRP	LA	RAILWAY HERITAGE TRUST
43190	I	IWRP	LA	
43191	I	IWRP	LA	Seahawk
43192	I	IWRP	LA	City of Truro
43193	I	ICCP	LA	Plymouth SPIRIT OF DISCOVERY
43194	I	ICCP	LA	
43195	I	ICCP	LA	British Red Cross 125th Birthday 1995
43196	I	ICCP	LA	The Newspaper Society Founded 1836
43197	I	ICCP	LA	
43198	I	ICCP	LA	

CLASS 47   BRUSH TYPE 4   Co – Co

Built: 1963 – 67 by Brush Traction, Loughborough or BR Crewe Works.
Engine: Sulzer 12LDA28C of 1920 kW (2580 hp) at 750 rpm.
Main Generator: Brush TG160-60 Mk2, TG 160-60 Mk4 or TM172-50 Mk1.
Traction Motors: Brush TM64-68 Mk1 or Mk1A (axle hung).
Max. Tractive Effort: 267 kN (60000 lbf).
Cont. Tractive Effort: 133 kN (30000 lbf) at 26 mph.
Power At Rail: 1550 kW (2080 hp).   **Length over Buffers:** 19.38 m.
Brake Force: 61 t.   **Wheel Diameter:** 1143 mm.
Design Speed: 95 mph.   **Weight:** 120.5 – 125 t.
Max. Speed: various.   **RA:** 6 or 7.
Train Brakes: Air & vacuum.
Multiple Working: Green Circle m (Blue Star*) Coupling Code. Otherwise not equipped.
ETH Index (47/4, 47/6 and 47/7): 66 (75 Class 47/6).
Communication Equipment: Cab to shore radio-telephone.

Non standard liveries:

47145 is dark blue with Railfreight Distribution markings.
47798/9 are Royal train purple.
47803 is grey, red and yellow.
Note: 47520/8, 47972/3 and 47981 are owned by RES.

Formerly numbered 1100 – 11, 1500 – 1999 not in order.

Class 47/0. Built with train heating boiler. RA6. Max. Speed 75 mph.
a Vacuum brake isolated (Class 47/2).

47004		G	ENXX	SF (S)	Old Oak Common
					Traction & Rolling Stock Depot
47016		FO	ENRN	SF	ATLAS
47019		FO	DAYX	TI (U)	
47033	am +	FE	DAET	TI	The Royal Logistics Corps
47049	am +	FD	DAET	TI	
47051	am +	FE	DAET	TI	
47052		F	DFLT	CD	
47053	am +	FE	DAET	TI	Dollands Moor International

47060	a	**FD** DFLT	CD	
47079		**FE** DAST	TI	
47085	am +	**FE** DAET	TI	REPTA 1893 – 1993
47095	am +	**FE** DAET	TI	
47114	am +	**FD** DAET	TI	
47121		**ENXX**	SF (U)	Pochard
47125	am +	**FE** DAET	TI	
47142		**FR** DFLT	CD	
47144	am +	**FD** DAET	TI	
47145	am	**0** DAET	TI	MERDDIN EMRYS
47146	am	**FE** DAET	TI	Loughborough
				Grammar School
47147		**F** DFLT	CD	
47150 (47399)	am +	**FD** DAET	TI	
47152 (47398)	am +	**FD** DAET	TI	
47156	am +	**FD** DAET	TI	
47157		**FF** DFLT	CD	Johnson Stevens Agencies
47186	am +	**FE** DAET	TI	Catcliffe Demon
47187		**F** DFLT	CD	
47188	am +	**FD** DAET	TI	
47193		**FP** LNWX	BS (U)	
47194	am +	**FD** DAET	TI	
47197		**F** DFLT	CD	
47200	am +	**FE** DAYX	TI	Herbert Austin
47201	am +	**FE** DAET	TI	
47204 (47388)	am +	**FD** DAET	TI	
47205 (47395)	am +	**FD** DAET	TI	
47206		**F** DFLT	CD	The Morris Dancer
47207		**FD** DAYX	TI	
47209 (47393)	am +	**FD** DAET	TI	
47210	+	**FD** DAST	TI	
47211 (47394)	am +	**FD** DAET	TI	
47212	+	**F** DFLT	CD	
47213	am +	**FD** DAET	TI	Marchwood Military Port
47217	am +	**FE** DAET	TI	
47218	am +	**FD** DAET	TI	United Transport Europe
47219	am +	**FD** DAET	TI	Arnold Kunzler
47221	+	**FP** FDDI	IM	
47222	am +	**FD** DAET	TI	
47223	+	**F** ENXX	SF (U)	
47224	+	**FP** FDDI	IM	
47225		**FD** DFLT	CD	
47226 (47384)	am +	**FD** DAET	TI	
47228	am +	**FE** DAET	TI	axial
47229	am +	**FD** DAET	TI	
47231		**FD** DFLT	CD	
47234	am +	**FE** DAYX	TI	
47236	am +	**FD** DAET	TI	
47237	am +	**FE** DAET	TI	
47238		**FD** LNXX	BS (U)	Bescot Yard
47241	am +	**FE** DAET	TI	Halewood Silver Jubilee 1988

47245		am +	FE	DAET	TI	The Institute of Export
47249			FR	DAYX	TI (U)	
47256			FD	FDYX	IM	
47258		am +	FD	DAET	TI	
47270			FF	DFLT	CD	
47276		+	FD	DAST	TI	
47277			FD	FDYX	IM (U)	
47278			FP	ENXX	SF (U)	
47279		F		DFLT	CD	
47280		am +	FD	DAET	TI	Pedigree
47281		am +	FD	DAET	TI	
47283			FD	DFLT	CD	
47284		+	FD	DAST	TI	
47285		am +	FE	DAET	TI	
47286		am +	FE	DAET	TI	Port of Liverpool
47287		am +	FE	DAET	TI	
47289		a	FD	DFLT	CD	
47290		am +	FE	DAET	TI	
47291		a +	FD	DAYX	TI	
47292		am +	FD	DAET	TI	
47293		am +	FD	DAET	TI	
47294		+	FD	FDDI	IM	
47295		+	FP	LNWX	BS (U)	
47296		F		DFLT	CD	
47297		am +	FE	DAET	TI	Cobra RAILFREIGHT
47298		+	FD	DAST	TI	Pegasus
47299	(47216)	am +	FE	DAET	TI	

Class 47/3. Built without Train Heat. (except 47300). RA6. Max. Speed 75 mph.
All equipped with slow speed control.

a Vacuum brake isolated (Class 47/2).

47300	(47468)		C	LNWX	BS (U)	
47301			FF	DFLT	CD	Freightliner Birmingham
47302		a	FR	DAYX	TI	
47303	(47397)	am +	FD	DAET	TI	
47304	(47392)	am +	FD	DAET	TI	
47305		F		DFLT	CD	
47306		am +	FE	DAET	TI	The Sapper
47307		am +	FE	DAET	TI	
47308			C	LNWX	BS (U)	
47309	(47389)	am +	FD	DAET	TI	The Halewood Transmission
47310		am +	FD	DAET	TI	Henry Ford
47312		am +	FE	DAET	TI	
47313		am +	FD	DAET	TI	
47314	(47387)	am +	FD	DAET	TI	Transmark
47315			C	ENRN	SF	Templecombe
47316		am +	FE	DAET	TI	
47317		F		DFLT	CD	
47319		+	FP	FDYX	IM (U) Norsk Hydro	
47322			FR	DFLT	CD	

47323		am +	FE	DAET	TI	ROVER GROUP
						QUALITY ASSURED
47325			FO	DAYX	TI (U)	
47326		am +	FE	DAET	TI	Saltley Depot
						Quality Approved
47328	(47396)	am +	FD	DAET	TI	
47329			C	LNWX	BS (U)	
47330	(47390)	am +	FD	DAET	TI	
47331			C	FDYX	IM	
47332			C	LNWX	BS (U)	
47333			C	LNWX	BS (U)	Civil Link
47334			C	LBCB	BS	
47335		am +	FD	DAET	TI	
47337			FO	DFLT	CD	
47338		am +	FE	DAET	TI	
47339			FD	DFLT	CD	
47340			C	DAYX	TI	
47341			C	LBCB	BS	
47344		am +	FE	DAET	TI	
47345			FR	DFLT	CD	
47346			C	FDDI	IM	
47347		a	FD	DFLT	CD	
47348		am	FE	DAET	TI	St. Christopher's
						Railway Home
47349			F	DFLT	CD	
47350			FO	DAST	TI	
47351		am +	FE	DAET	TI	
47352			C	FDYX	IM (U)	
47353			C	LNWX	BS (U)	
47354		a	FD	DFLT	CD	
47355	(47391)	am +	FD	DAET	TI	
47356			FO	DAST	TI	
47357			C	LNXX	BS (U)	
47358			FO	DFLT	CD	
47359			FD	FDDI	IM	
47360		am +	FE	DAET	TI	
47361		am +	FD	DAET	TI	Wilton Endeavour
47362		am +	FD	DAET	TI	
47363	(47385)	am +	F	DAET	TI	
47365		am +	FE	DAET	TI	ICI Diamond Jubilee
47366			C	ENRN	SF	Capital Radio's
						Help a London Child
47367			FR	DAST	TI	
47368			F	ENXX	SF (U)	
47369			FD	FDDI	IM	
47370			FE	DAST	TI	
47371			FO	DFLT	CD	
47372			C	LBCB	BS (U)	
47375		am +	FE	DAET	TI	Tinsley Traction Depot
						Quality Approved
47376			FF	DFLT	CD	Freightliner 1995

47377	a	**FD** DFLT	CD	
47378 (47386)	am +	**FD** DAET	TI	
47379	+	**FD** DAST	TI	

Class 47/4. Equipped with train heating. RA6. Max. Speed 95 mph (§ 75 mph).
47488 is owned by Carriage & Traction Co. Ltd.

47462		**R** ENXX	SF (S)	
47467		**BR** PXLC	CD	
47471	§	**IO** PXLH	CD	Norman Tunna G.C.
47473		**BR** DAYX	TI	
47474		**R** PXLC	CD	Sir Rowland Hill
47475		**RX** PXLC	CD	Restive
47476		**R** PXLC	CD	Night Mail
47478		LNWX	BS (U)	
47481	§	**BR** PXLD	CD (U)	
47484		**G** ENXX	SF (S)	ISAMBARD KINGDOM BRUNEL
47488		**W** PWLO	CF	DAVIES THE OCEAN
47489		**R** PXLC	CD	Crewe Diesel Depot Quality Approved
47492		**RX** PXLC	CD	
47501		**R** PXLC	CD	Craftsman
47513	§	**BR** PXLH	CD	Severn
47519	+	**G** PXLG	CD	
47520		**I** DFLT	CD	
47522	§	**R** PXLH	CD	Doncaster Enterprise
47523		**M** PXLC	CD	
47524		**RX** PXLC	CD	Res Gestae
47525		**FE** DAST	TI	
47526		**BR** ENXX	SF (S)	
47528		**M** DFLT	CD	The Queen's Own Mercian Yeomanry
47530		**RX** PXLC	CD	
47532		**RX** PXLC	CD	
47535		**RX** PXLC	CD	Saint Aidan
47536	§	**RX** PXLH	CD	
47539	§	**RX** PXLH	CD	
47540 (47975)		**C** DAST	TI	The Institution of Civil Engineers
47543		**R** PXLC	CD	
47547	§	**N** PXLH	CD	
47550		**M** FDDI	IM	University of Dundee
47555 (47126)		**FE** DAST	TI	The Commonwealth Spirit
47565 (47039)		**RX** PXLC	CD	Responsive
47566 (47043)		**RX** PXLC	CD	
47572 (47168)		**R** PXLC	CD	Ely Cathedral
47574 (47174)		**R** PXLC	CD	Benjamin Gimbert G.C.
47575 (47175)		**R** PXLC	CD	City of Hereford
47576 (47176)		**RX** PXLC	CD	
47583 (47172)		**RX** PXLC	CD	
47584 (47180)		**RX** PXLC	CD	THE LOCOMOTIVE & CARRIAGE INSTITUTION
47596 (47255)		**RX** PXLC	CD	

47624 (47087)		**RX** PXLC	CD	Saint Andrew
47627 (47273)		**RX** PXLC	CD	
47628 (47078)		**RX** PXLC	CD	
47634 (47158)		**R** PXLC	CD	Holbeck
47635 (47029)		**R** PXLC	CD	
47640 (47244)		**R** PXLC	CD	University of Strathclyde

Class 47/6. Fitted with high phosphorus brake blocks. RA6. Max. Speed 75 mph.

| 47676 (47586) | | **I** FDYX | IM (U) Northamptonshire |
| 47677 (47617) | | **I** FDDI | IM University of Stirling |

Class 47/7. Fitted with an older form of TDM. RA6. Max. Speed 95 mph.
47701/3/5/9/10/12 are owned by Carriage & Traction Co. Ltd.

47701 (47493)	+	**RX** PWLO	CD	
47702 (47504)	+	**F** ENRN	SF	County of Suffolk
47703 (47514)	+	**W** PWLO	CD	LEWIS CARROLL
47704 (47495)	+	**RX** PXLG	CD	
47705 (47554)	+	**W** PWLO	CD	GUY FAWKES
47707 (47506)	+	**RX** PXLG	CD	Holyrood
47709 (47499)	+	**RX** PWLO	CD	
47710 (47496)	+	**W** PWLO	CD	LADY GODIVA
47711 (47498)	+	**N** ENRN	SF	County of Hertfordshire
47712 (47505)	+	**W** PWLO	CD	DICK WHITTINGTON
47714 (47511)	+	**RX** PXLG	CD	
47715 (47502)	+	**N** PXLG	CD	Haymarket
47716 (47507)	+	**RX** PXLG	CD	
47717 (47497)	+	**R** PXLG	CD	

Class 47/7. Parcels dedicated locos. RA6. Max. Speed 95 mph.

a Vacuum brake isolated.

47721 (47557)	+	**RX** PXLB	CD	~~Saint Bede~~
47722 (47558)	+	**RX** PXLB	CD	The Queen Mother
<u>47723</u> (47)				
<u>47724</u> (47)				
47725 (47567)	+	**RX** PXLB	CD	The Railway Mission
<u>47726</u> (47568)	+	**RX** PXLB	CD	~~Progress~~
47727 (47569)	a+	**RX** PXLB	CD	Duke of Edinburgh's Award
<u>47728</u> (47)				
<u>47729</u> (47)				
<u>47730</u> (47)				
<u>47731</u> (47)				
47732 (47580)	+	**RX** PXLB	CD	Restormel
47733 (47582)	+	**RX** PXLB	CD	Eastern Star
<u>47734</u> (47)				
<u>47735</u> (47)				
47736 (47587)	a+	**RX** PXLB	CD	Cambridge Traction & Rolling Stock Depot
<u>47737</u> (47588)	+	**RX** PXLB	CD	Resurgent
47738 (47592)	a+	**RX** PXLB	CD	Bristol Barton Hill
47739 (47594)	a+	**RX** PXLB	CD	Resourceful

47740 (47)				
47741 (47597)	+	**RX** PXLB	CD	Resilient
47742 (47598)	+	**RX** PXLB	CD	The Enterprising Scot
47744 (47600)	a+	**RX** PXLB	CD	Saint Edwin
47745 (47603)	+	**RX** PXLB	CD	Royal London Society for the Blind
47746 (47605)	a+	**RX** PXLB	CD	The Bobby
47747 (47615)	a+	**RX** PXLB	CD	Res Publica
47748 (47)				
47749 (47625)	+	**RX** PXLB	CD	Atlantic College
47750 (47626)	+	**RX** PXLB	CD	
47751 (47)				
47752 (47)				
47753 (47)				
47754 (47)				
47755 (47)				
47756 (47644)	+	**RX** PXLB	CD	Royal Mail Tyneside
47757 (47585)	a+	**RX** PXLB	CD	Restitution
47758 (47517)	+	**RX** PXLB	CD	
47759 (47559)	+	**RX** PXLB	CD	
47760 (47562)	+	**RX** PXLB	CD	Restless
47761 (47564)	+	**RX** PXLB	CD	
47762 (47573)	+	**RX** PXLB	CD	
47763 (47581)	+	**RX** PXLB	CD	
47764 (47630)	+	**RX** PXLB	CD	Resounding
47765 (47631)	+	**RX** PXLB	CD	Ressaldar
47766 (47642)	+	**RX** PXLB	CD	Resolute
47767 (47641)	+	**RX** PXLB	CD	
47768 (47490)	+	**RX** PXLB	CD	Resonant
47769 (47491)	+	**RX** PXLB	CD	Resolve
47770 (47500)	+	**RX** PXLB	CD	Reserved
47771 (47503)	+	**RX** PXLB	CD	Heaton Traincare Depot
47772 (47537)	+	**RX** PXLB	CD	
47773 (47541)	+	**RX** PXLB	CD	Reservist
47774 (47551)	+	**RX** PXLB	CD	Poste Restante
47775 (47531)	+	**RX** PXLB	CD	Respite
47776 (47578)	+	**RX** PXLB	CD	Respected
47777 (47636)	+	**RX** PXLB	CD	Restored
47778 (47606)	+	**RX** PXLB	CD	Irresistible
47779 (47612)	+	**RX** PXLB	CD	
47780 (47618)	+	**RX** PXLB	CD	
47781 (47653)	+	**RX** PXLB	CD	Isle of Iona
47782 (47824)	+	**RX** PXLB	CD	
47783 (47809)	+	**RX** PXLB	CD	Saint Peter
47784 (47819)	+	**RX** PXLB	CD	Condover Hall
47785 (47820)	+	**RX** PXLB	CD	The Statesman
47786 (47821)	a+	**RX** PXLB	CD	Roy Castle OBE
47787 (47823)	+	**RX** PXLB	CD	Victim Support
47788 (47833)	a+	**RX** PXLB	CD	Captain Peter Manisty RN
47789 (47616)	a+	**RX** PXLB	CD	Lindisfarne
47790 (47673)	a+	**RX** PXLB	CD	Saint David/Dewi Sant

47791	(47675)	a+	**RX**	PXLB	CD	VENICE SIMPLON
						ORIENT EXPRESS
47792	(47804)	+	**RX**	PXLB	CD	Saint Cuthbert
47793	(47579)	+	**RX**	PXLB	CD	
47798	(47834)	+	**0**	PXLD	CD	Prince William
47799	(47835)	+	**0**	PXLD	CD	Prince Henry

Class 47/4 continued. RA6. Max. Speed 95 mph (100 mph §).
a Vacuum brake isolated.

Note: Inter City Cross-Country and Great Western Trains locos are owned by
Porterbrook Leasing Company (owner codes SBH for ILRA and SBJ for IWBR).

47802	(47552)	+	I	ENXX	SF (S)	
47803	(47553)	+	0	ENXX	SF (S)	
47805	(47650)	a+	I	ILRA	CD	
47806	(47651)	a+	I	ILRA	CD	
47807	(47652)	a+	I	SBXL	CD (S)	
47810	(47655)	a+	I	ILRA	CD	
47811	(47656)	a+	I	IWBR	PM	
47812	(47657)	a+	I	ILRA	CD	
47813	(47658)	a+	I	SBXL	CD (S)	
47814	(47659)	a+	I	ILRA	CD	
47815	(47660)	a+	I	IWBR	PM	
47816	(47661)	a+	I	IWBR	PM	Bristol Bath Road
						Quality Approved
47817	(47662)	a+	I	SBXL	CD	
47818	(47663)	a+	I	ILRA	CD	
47822	(47571)	a+	I	ILRA	CD	
47825	(47590)	a+	I	ILRA	CD	Thomas Telford
47826	(47637)	a+	I	ILRA	CD	
47827	(47589)	a+	I	ILRA	CD	
47828	(47629)	a+	I	ILRA	CD	
47829	(47619)	a+	I	ILRA	CD	
47830	(47649)	a+	I	SBXL	CD	
47831	(47563)	a+	I	ILRA	CD	Bolton Wanderer
47832	(47560)	a+	I	IWBR	PM	Tamar
47839	(47621)	a+	I	ILRA	CD	
47840	(47613)	a+	I	ILRA	CD	NORTH STAR
47841	(47622)	a+	I	ILRA	CD	The Institution of
						Mechanical Engineers
47843	(47623)	a+	I	ILRA	CD	
47844	(47556)	a+	I	ILRA	CD	Derby & Derbyshire Chamber
						of Commerce & Industry
47845	(47638)	a+	I	SBXL	CD (S)	County of Kent
47846	(47647)	a+	I	SBXL	CD (S)	THOR
47847	(47577)	a+	I	ILRA	CD	
47848	(47632)	a+	I	ILRA	CD	
47849	(47570)	a+	I	ILRA	CD	
47851	(47639)	a+	I	ILRA	CD	
47853	(47614)	a+	I	ILRA	CD	
47854	(47674)	a+	I	ILRA	CD	Women's Royal
						Voluntary Service

47971 (97480)	§*	BR	PXLK	CD	Robin Hood
47972 (97545)	§	CS	DFLT	CD	The Royal Army
					Ordnance Corps
47973 (97561)	§	M	DFLT	CD	Derby Evening Telegraph
47976 (47546)	§*	C	PXLK	CD	Aviemore Centre

Class 47/3 continued. RA6. Max. Speed 100 mph.

| 47981 (47364) | | C | DFLT | CD | |

CLASS 56   BRUSH TYPE 5   Co – Co

Built: 1976 – 84 by Electroputere at Craiova, Romania (as sub contractors for Brush) or BREL at Doncaster or Crewe Works.
Engine: Ruston Paxman 16RK3CT of 2460 kW (3250 hp) at 900 rpm.
Main Alternator: Brush BA1101A.
Traction Motors: Brush TM73-62.
Max. Tractive Effort: 275 kN (61800 lbf).
Cont. Tractive Effort: 240 kN (53950 lbf) at 16.8 mph.
Power At Rail: 1790 kW (2400 hp).   **Length over Buffers:** 19.36 m.
Brake Force: 60 t.   **Wheel Diameter:** 1143 mm.
Design Speed: 80 mph.   **Weight:** 125 t.
Max. Speed: 80 mph.   **RA:** 7.
Train Brakes: Air.
Multiple Working: Red Diamond coupling code.
Communication Equipment: Cab to shore radio-telephone.
All equipped with slow speed control.

§ Derated to 1790 kW (2400 hp).
* Derated to 2060 kW (2800 hp).

56001	FA	LNWX	CF (U)	
56003	LH	FMBY	TE	
56004		LWBK	CF	
56005	FC	FDYX	IM	
56006	LH	FMBY	TE	Ferrybridge 'C' Power Station
56007	FC	LWBK	CF	
56008		FDYX	IM (U)	
56009	FC	LWBK	CF	
56010	FT	LNBK	CF	
56011	F	FDBK	IM	
56012	FC	FDYX	IM (U)	
56014	FC	FDYX	IM (U)	
56016	FC	LNWX	CF (U)	
56018	FT	LWBK	CF	
56019	FR	LWBK	CF	
56020		LNWX	CF (U)	
56021	FC	FDBI	IM	
56022	FT	LWBK	CF	
56024	FO	FDYX	IM (U)	
56025	FT	LWBK	CF	
56026		FDYX	IM (U)	
56027	LH	FDBK	IM	

56029	F	LWBK	CF	
56031	C	FMBY	TE	Merehead
56032	FS	LNBK	CF	Sir De Morgannwg/
				County of South Glamorgan
56033	FT	LWBK	CF	Shotton Paper Mill
56034	LH	FDBK	IM	Castell Ogwr/Ogmore Castle
56035	FA	FMBY	TE	
56036	CT	LWBK	CF	
56037	FA	LWBK	CF	Richard Trevithick
56038	FT	LNBK	CF	Western Mail
56039	LH	FMBY	TE	ABP Port of Hull
56040	FT	LNBK	CF	Oystermouth
56041	FA	FDBI	IM	
56043	FS	FDBK	IM	
56044	FT	LNBK	CF	Cardiff Canton Quality Assured
56045	LH	FMBY	TE	
56046	C	FMBY	TE	
56047	CT	LWBK	CF	
56048	C	FMBY	TE	
56049	CT	LWBK	CF	
56050	LH	FMBY	TE	
56051	FA	FDBK	IM	Isle of Grain
56052	FT	LNBK	CF	
56053	FT	LNBK	CF	Sir Morgannwg Ganol/
				County of Mid Glamorgan
56054	FT	LWBK	CF	British Steel Llanwern
56055	LH	FDBI	IM	
56056	FA	LGAM	ML	
56057	FA	LGAM	ML	
56058	FT	LGAM	ML	
56059	FA	LWBK	CF	
56060	FS	LNBK	CF	The Cardiff Rod Mill
56061	FS	FMBY	TE	
56062	F	FMBY	TE	Mountsorrel
56063	F	FMBY	TE	Bardon Hill
56064	FT	LNBK	CF	
56065	FA	FMBY	TE	
56066	FC	LNBK	CF	
56067	FC	FDBK	IM	
56068	FC	FDBI	IM	
56069 § FS		FMBY	TE	Thornaby TMD
56070	FT	LWBK	CF	
56071	FT	LWBK	CF	
56072	FT	LGAM	ML	
56073	FT	LNBK	CF	Tremorfa Steelworks
56074	LH	FDBK	IM	Kellingley Colliery
56075	F	FDKI	IM	West Yorkshire Enterprise
56076	FS	LNBK	CF	
56077 § LH		FDBK	IM	Thorpe Marsh Power Station
56078	F	FDBK	IM	
56079	FT	LGAM	ML	

56080	F	FDBK	IM	Selby Coalfield
56081	F	FMBY	TE	
56082	F	FDBK	IM	
56083	* LH	FDBK	IM	
56084	* LH	FMBY	TE	
56085	LH	FDBK	IM	
56086	* FT	LWBK	CF	The Magistrates' Association
56087	FS	FDBK	IM	
56088	FC	FDBK	IM	
56089	FC	FDBK	IM	
56090	LH	FDBI	IM	
56091	F	FDBK	IM	Castle Donington Power Station
56092	F	LWBK	CF	
56093	F	LWBK	CF	The Institution of Mining Engineers
56094	FC	FDBK	IM	Eggborough Power Station
56095	F	FDBK	IM	Harworth Colliery
56096	FC	LGAM	ML	
56097	FS	FMBY	TE	
56098	F	FMBY	TE	
56099	FT	LWBK	CF	Fiddlers Ferry Power Station
56100	LH	FDBI	IM	
56101	FT	LGAM	ML	Mutual Improvement
56102	F	FDBI	IM	Scunthorpe Steel Centenary
56103	FA	LGAM	ML	
56104	FC	LGAM	ML	
56105	FA	LWBK	CF	
56106	LH	FDBI	IM	
56107 § LH		FDBI	IM	
56108	F	FMBY	TE	
56109	LH	FDBI	IM	
56110	LH	FMBY	TE	Croft
56111	LH	FDBI	IM	
56112	FC	FMBY	TE	
56113	FT	LNBK	CF	
56114	FT	LNBK	CF	Maltby Colliery
56115	FT	LNBK	CF	
56116	LH	FDBK	IM	
56117	FC	FMBY	TE	Wilton-Coalpower
56118	LH	FDBI	IM	
56119	FT	LNBK	CF	
56120	FC	FMBY	TE	
56121	FC	LGAM	ML	
56123	FC	LGAM	ML	Drax Power Station
56124	FC	LGAM	ML	
56125	FC	LWBK	CF	
56126	FC	FDBK	IM	
56127	FT	LWBK	CF	
56128	FC	LGAM	ML	
56129	FC	LGAM	ML	
56130	LH	FMBY	TE	Wardley Opencast
56131	F	FDBK	IM	Ellington Colliery

56132	FT	LWBK	CF	
56133	FT	LWBK	CF	Crewe Locomotive Works
56134	FC	FMBY	TE	Blyth Power
56135	F	FMBY	TE	Port of Tyne Authority

CLASS 58   BREL TYPE 5   Co – Co

Built: 1983 – 87 by BREL at Doncaster Works.
Engine: Ruston Paxman RK3ACT of 2460 kW (3300 hp) at 1000 rpm.
Main Alternator: Brush BA1101B.
Traction Motors: Brush TM73-62.
Max. Tractive Effort: 275 kN (61800 lbf).
Cont. Tractive Effort: 240 kN (53950 lbf) at 17.4 mph.
Power At Rail: 1780 kW (2387 hp).   **Length over Buffers:** 19.13 m.
Brake Force: 62 t.   **Wheel Diameter:** 1120 mm.
Design Speed: 80 mph.   **Weight:** 130 t.
Max. Speed: 80 mph.   **RA:** 7.
Train Brakes: Air.
Multiple Working: Red Diamond coupling code.
Communication Equipment: Cab to shore radio-telephone.
All equipped with slow speed control.

58001	FM	ENBN	TO	
58002	ML	ENBN	TO	Daw Mill Colliery
58003	F	ENBN	TO	Markham Colliery
58004	FM	ENBN	TO	
58005	F	ENBN	TO	
58006	F	ENBN	TO	
58007	FM	ENBN	TO	Drakelow Power Station
58008	FM	ENBN	TO	
58009	FM	ENBN	TO	
58010	F	ENBN	TO	
58011	FM	ENBN	TO	Worksop Depot
58012	FM	ENBN	TO	
58013	FM	ENBN	TO	
58014	ML	ENBN	TO	Didcot Power Station
58015	FM	ENBN	TO	
58016	FM	ENBN	TO	
58017	FM	ENBN	TO	Eastleigh Depot
58018	FM	ENBN	TO	High Marnham Power Station
58019	FM	ENBN	TO	Shirebrook Colliery
58020	F	ENBN	TO	Doncaster Works
58021	ML	ENBN	TO	Hither Green Depot
58022	FM	ENBN	TO	
58023	ML	ENBN	TO	Peterborough Depot
58024	F	ENBN	TO	
58025	FM	ENBN	TO	
58026	FM	ENBN	TO	
58027	FM	ENBN	TO	
58028	FM	ENBN	TO	
58029	FM	ENBN	TO	

58030	FM	ENBN	TO	
58031	FM	ENBN	TO	
58032	ML	ENBN	TO	Thoresby Colliery
58033	FM	ENBN	TO	
58034	FM	ENBN	TO	Bassetlaw
58035	FM	ENBN	TO	
58036	FM	ENBN	TO	
58037	FM	ENBN	TO	
58038	ML	ENBN	TO	
58039	FM	ENBN	TO	Rugeley Power Station
58040	F	ENBN	TO	Cottam Power Station
58041	FM	ENBN	TO	Ratcliffe Power Station
58042	ML	ENBN	TO	Ironbridge Power Station
58043	FM	ENBN	TO	Knottingley
58044	FM	ENBN	TO	Oxcroft Opencast
58045	FM	ENBN	TO	
58046	ML	ENBN	TO	Asfordby Mine
58047	FM	ENBN	TO	Manton Colliery
58048	FM	ENBN	TO	Coventry Colliery
58049	ML	ENBN	TO	Littleton Colliery
58050	ML	ENBN	TO	Toton Traction Depot

CLASS 59   GENERAL MOTORS TYPE 5   Co – Co

Built: 1985 (59001 – 4), 1989 (59005) by General Motors, La Grange, Illinois, U.S.A. or 1990 (59101 – 4), 1994 (59201) and 1995 (59202 – 6) by General Motors, London, Ontario, Canada.
Engine: General Motors 645E3C two stroke of 2460 kW (3300 hp) at 900 rpm.
Main Alternator: General Motors AR11 MLD-D14A.
Traction Motors: General Motors D77B.
Max. Tractive Effort: 506 kN (113 550 lbf).
Cont. Tractive Effort: 291 kN (65 300 lbf) at 14.3 mph.
Power At Rail: 1889 kW (2533 hp).   **Length over Buffers:** 21.35 m.
Brake Force: 69 t.   **Wheel Diameter:** 1067 mm.
Design Speed: 60 mph.   **Weight:** 121 t.
Max. Speed: 60 mph.   **RA:** 7.

Class 59/0. Owned by Foster-Yeoman Ltd. Blue/silver/blue livery with white lettering and cast numberplates.

59001	0	XYPO	MD	YEOMAN ENDEAVOUR
59002	0	XYPO	MD	YEOMAN ENTERPRISE
59003	0	XYPO	MD	YEOMAN HIGHLANDER
59004	0	XYPO	MD	YEOMAN CHALLENGER
59005	0	XYPO	MD	KENNETH J. PAINTER

Class 59/1. Owned by ARC Limited. Yellow/grey with grey lettering and cast numberplates.

59101	0	XYPA	WH	Village of Whatley
59102	0	XYPA	WH	Village of Chantry
59103	0	XYPA	WH	Village of Mells
59104	0	XYPA	WH	Village of Great Elm

Class 59/2. Owned by National Power. Grey, red, white and blue with white and red lettering and cast numberplates.

59201	0	XYPN	FB	Vale of York
59202	0	XYPN	FB	
59203	0	XYPN	FB	Vale of Pickering
59204	0	XYPN	FB	
59205	0	XYPN	FB	
59206	0	XYPN	FB	

CLASS 60   BRUSH TYPE 5   Co − Co

Built: 1989 − 1993 by Brush Traction at Loughborough.
Engine: Mirrlees MB275T of 2310 kW (3100 hp) at 1000 rpm.
Main Alternator: Brush .
Traction Motors: Brush separately excited.
Max. Tractive Effort: 500 kN (106500 lbf).
Cont. Tractive Effort: 336 kN (71570 lbf) at 17.4 mph.
Power At Rail: 1800 kW (2415 hp). **Length over Buffers:** 21.34 m.
Brake Force: 74 t.   **Wheel Diameter:** 1118 mm.
Design Speed: 62 mph.   **Weight:** 129 t.
Max. Speed: 60 mph.   **RA:** 7.
Multiple Working: Within class.
Communication Equipment: Cab to shore radio-telephone.
All equipped with slow speed control.

60001	FA	ESAB	SL	Steadfast
60002	FP	FDAI	IM	Capability Brown
60003	FP	FDAI	IM	Christopher Wren
60004	FC	FDAI	IM	Lochnagar
60005	FT	LWCK	CF	Skiddaw
60006	FM	ENAN	TO	Great Gable
60007	FP	FMAY	TE	Robert Adam
60008	LH	FDAI	IM	GYPSUM QUEEN II
60009	FM	ENAN	TO	Carnedd Dafydd
60010	FM	ENAN	TO	Pumlumon Plynlimon
60011	ML	ENAN	TO	
60012	FM	ENAN	TO	Glyder Fawr
60013	FP	FDAI	IM	Robert Boyle
60014	FP	FDAI	IM	Alexander Fleming
60015	FT	LNAK	CF	Bow Fell
60016	FA	LWCK	CF	Langdale Pikes
60017	FM	ENAN	TO	Arenig Fawr
60018	FM	ESAB	SL	Moel Siabod
60019	FM	ESAB	SL	Wild Boar Fell
60020	FS	FMAY	TE	Great Whernside
60021	FS	FDAI	IM	Pen-y-Ghent
60022	FS	FMAY	TE	Ingleborough
60023	FS	FMAY	TE	The Cheviot
60024	FP	FDAI	IM	Elizabeth Fry
60025	FP	FDAI	IM	Joseph Lister

60026	FP	FDAI	IM	William Caxton
60027	FP	FDAI	IM	Joseph Banks
60028	FP	FDAI	IM	John Flamsteed
60029	FT	LNAK	CF	Ben Nevis
60030	FS	FMAY	TE	Cir Mhor
60031	FS	FMAY	TE	Ben Lui
60032	FT	LWAK	CF	William Booth
60033	FP	LNAK	CF	Anthony Ashley Cooper
60034	FS	LNAK	CF	Carnedd Llewelyn
60035	FT	LNAK	CF	Florence Nightingale
60036	FS	LNAK	CF	Sgurr Na Ciche
60037	FT	LNAK	CF	Helvellyn
60038	LH	FDAI	IM	
60039	FM	ESAB	SL	Glastonbury Tor
60040	FM	ESAB	SL	Brecon Beacons
60041	FM	ESAB	SL	High Willhays
60042	FM	ESAB	SL	Dunkery Beacon
60043	FA	ESAB	SL	Yes Tor
60044	FM	ENAN	TO	Ailsa Craig
60045	FC	LWAK	CF	Josephine Butler
60046	FT	LWAK	CF	William Wilberforce
60047	FT	LWAK	CF	Robert Owen
60048	FM	ENAN	TO	Saddleback
60049	FS	FMAY	TE	Scafell
60050	FL	FDAI	IM	Roseberry Topping
60051	FP	FDAI	IM	Mary Somerville
60052	FS	FMAY	TE	Goat Fell
60053	FP	FMAY	TE	John Reith
60054	FP	FDAI	IM	Charles Babbage
60055	FT	LWAK	CF	Thomas Barnardo
60056	F	LWAK	CF	William Beveridge
60057	FC	LWAK	CF	Adam Smith
60058	FT	LWAK	CF	John Howard
60059	LH	FDAI	IM	Swinden Dalesman
60060	FC	LWCK	CF	James Watt
60061	FT	LWAK	CF	Alexander Graham Bell
60062	FT	LNAK	CF	Samuel Johnson
60063	FT	LNAK	CF	James Murray
60064	FP	FDAI	IM	Back Tor
60065	FP	LNAK	CF	Kinder Low
60066	FT	LWAK	CF	John Logie Baird
60067	F	FDAI	IM	James Clerk-Maxwell
60068	F	FDAI	IM	Charles Darwin
60069	F	FMAY	TE	Humphry Davy
60070	FC	FDAI	IM	John Loudon McAdam
60071	FM	ENAN	TO	Dorothy Garrod
60072	FM	ENAN	TO	Cairn Toul
60073	FM	ENAN	TO	Cairn Gorm
60074	FM	ENAN	TO	Braeriach
60075	FM	ENAN	TO	Liathach
60076	FM	ENAN	TO	Suilven

60077	FM	ENAN	TO	Canisp
60078	FM	ENAN	TO	Stac Pollaidh
60079	FM	ENAN	TO	Foinaven
60080	FT	LWCK	CF	Kinder Scout
60081	FT	LNAK	CF	Bleaklow Hill
60082	FA	LNAK	CF	Mam Tor
60083	FM	ENAN	TO	Shining Tor
60084	FT	LNAK	CF	Cross Fell
60085	FA	LWCK	CF	Axe Edge
60086	FM	ENAN	TO	Schiehallion
60087	FM	ENAN	TO	Slioch
60088	FM	ENAN	TO	Buachaille Etive Mor
60089	FT	LNAK	CF	Arcuil
60090	FC	FMAY	TE	Quinag
60091	FC	FMAY	TE	An Teallach
60092	FC	LNAK	CF	Reginald Munns
60093	FT	LNAK	CF	Jack Stirk
60094	FM	ENAN	TO	Tryfan
60095	FA	LWCK	CF	Crib Goch
60096	FT	LNAK	CF	Ben Macdui
60097	FT	LWCK	CF	Pillar
60098	FM	ENAN	TO	Charles Francis Brush
60099	FM	ESAB	SL	Ben More Assynt
60100	FM	ESAB	SL	Boar of Badenoch

1.2. BR ELECTRIC LOCOMOTIVES

CLASS 73/0   ELECTRO – DIESEL   Bo – Bo

Built: 1962 by BR at Eastleigh Works.
Supply System: 660 – 850 V d.c. from third rail.
Engine: English Electric 4SRKT of 447 kW (600 hp) at 850 rpm.
Main Generator: English Electric 824/3D.
Traction Motors: English Electric 542A.
Max. Tractive Effort: Electric 187 kN (42000 lbf). Diesel 152 kN (34100 lbf).
Continuous Rating: Electric 1060 kW (1420 hp) giving a tractive effort of 43 kN (9600 lbf) at 55.5 mph.
Cont. Tractive Effort: Diesel 72 kN (16100 lbf) at 10 mph.
Maximum Rail Power: Electric 1830 kW (2450 hp) at 37 mph.
Brake Force: 31 t.   **Length over Buffers:** 16.36 m.
Design Speed: 80 mph.   **Weight:** 76.5 t.
Max. Speed: 60 mph.   **RA:** 6.
Wheel Diameter: 1016 mm.   **ETH Index (Elec. power):** 66
Train Brakes: Air, Vacuum and electro-pneumatic.
Multiple Working: Within sub-class, with Class 33/1 and various 750 V d.c. EMUs.
Communication Equipment: All equipped with driver – guard telephone.
Couplings: Drop-head buckeye.

Non-standard Livery: 73005 is Network SouthEast blue.

Formerly numbered E 6002 – 3/5/6.

73002	**BR**	HEBD	BD (U)
73003	**G**	ENXX	SL (S) Sir Herbert Walker
73005	**O**	HEBD	BD (U)
73006	**MD**	HEBD	BD

CLASS 73/1 & 73/2   ELECTRO – DIESEL   Bo – Bo

Built: 1965 – 67 by English Electric Co. at Vulcan Foundry, Newton le Willows.
Supply System: 660 – 850 V d.c. from third rail.
Engine: English Electric 4SRKT of 447 kW (600 hp) at 850 rpm.
Main Generator: English Electric 824/5D.
Traction Motors: English Electric 546/1B.
Max. Tractive Effort: Electric 179 kN (40000 lbf). Diesel 160 kN (36000 lbf).
Continuous Rating: Electric 1060 kW (1420 hp) giving a tractive effort of 35 kN (7800 lbf) at 68 mph.
Cont. Tractive Effort: Diesel 60 kN (13600 lbf) at 11.5 mph.
Maximum Rail Power: Electric 2350 kW (3150 hp) at 42 mph.
Brake Force: 31 t.   **Length over Buffers:** 16.36 m.
Design Speed: 90 mph.   **Weight:** 77 t.
Max. Speed: 60 (90*) mph.   **RA:** 6.
Wheel Diameter: 1016 mm.   **ETH Index (Elec. power):** 66
Train Brakes: Air, Vacuum and electro-pneumatic.

Multiple Working: Within sub-class, with Class 33/1 and various 750 V d.c. EMUs.

Communication Equipment: All equipped with driver – guard telephone.

Couplings: Drop-head buckeye.

Non-standard Livery: 73101 is Pullman umber & cream.

Class 73/2 are locos dedicated to Gatwick Express services. They are owned by Porterbrook Leasing Company (owner code SBV) and have the vacuum brake isolated.

Formerly numbered E 6001 – 20/22 – 26/28 – 49 (not in order).

73101		**O**	EWHB	SL	The Royal Alex'
73103		**IO**	EWEB	SL	
73104		**IO**	EWEB	SL	
73105		**C**	EWEB	SL	
73106		**D**	EWEB	SL	
73107		**C**	EWHB	SL	Redhill 1844 – 1994
73108		**C**	EWEB	SL	
73109	*	**N**	HYSB	BM	Battle of Britain 50th Anniversary
73110		**C**	EWEB	SL	
73112		**N**	IVGA	SL (U)	University of Kent at Canterbury
73114		**ML**	EWHB	SL	Stewarts Lane
					Traction Maintenance Depot
73117		**IO**	EWEB	SL	University of Surrey
73118	c	**E**	GPSN	SL	
73119		**C**	EWHB	SL	Kentish Mercury
73126		**N**	EWRB	SL	Kent & East Sussex Railway
73128		**C**	EWRB	SL	OVS BULLEID C.B.E.
					1937 1949
					C.M.E. SOUTHERN RAILWAY
73129		**N**	EWHB	SL	City of Winchester
73130	c	**E**	GPSN	SL	
73131		**C**	EWRB	SL	
73132		**IO**	EWRB	SL	
73133		**N**	EWEB	SL	The Bluebell Railway
73134		**IO**	EWEB	SL	Woking Homes 1885 – 1985
73136		**N**	EWEB	SL	Kent Youth Music
73138		**C**	EWEB	SL	
73139		**IO**	EWEB	SL	
73140		**IO**	EWRB	SL	
73141		**IO**	EWRB	SL	
73201 (73142)	a*	**GE**	IVGA	SL	Broadlands
73202 (73137)	a*	**GE**	IVGA	SL	Royal Observer Corps
73203 (73127)	a*	**GE**	IVGA	SL	
73204 (73125)	a*	**GE**	IVGA	SL	Stewarts Lane 1860 – 1985
73205 (73124)	a*	**GE**	IVGA	SL	
73206 (73123)	a*	**GE**	IVGA	SL	Gatwick Express
73207 (73122)	a*	**GE**	IVGA	SL	County of East Sussex
73208 (73121)	a*	**GE**	IVGA	SL	Croydon 1883 – 1983
73209 (73120)	a*	**GE**	IVGA	SL	
73210 (73116)	a*	**GE**	IVGA	SL	Selhurst

73211 (73113) a* **GE** IVGA   SL
73212 (73102) a* **GE** IVGA   SL   Airtour Suisse
73235 (73135) a* **GE** IVGA   SL

CLASS 73/9   ELECTRO – DIESEL   Bo – Bo

For details see Class 73/0. Sandite fitted loco.

Formerly numbered E 6001.

73901 (73001) **MD** HEBD   BD

NOTES FOR CLASSES 86 – 91.

The following common features apply to all locos of Classes 86 – 91.
Supply System: 25 kV a.c. from overhead equipment.
Communication Equipment: Driver – guard telephone and cab to shore radio-
telephone.
Multiple Working: Time division multiplex system.

Note: Class 86 were formerly numbered E 3101 – 3200 (not in order).
a vacuum brakes isolated.

Note: All IANA, ICCA AND IWPA locos are owned by Eversholt Train Leasing
Company (owner codes SAF for IWPA, SAH for ICCA and SAS for IANA).

CLASS 86/1   BR DESIGN   Bo – Bo

Built: 1965 – 66 by English Electric Co. at Vulcan Foundry, Newton le Willows
or BR at Doncaster Works. Rebuilt with Class 87 type bogies and motors. Tap
changer control.
Traction Motors: GEC G412AZ frame mounted.
Max. Tractive Effort: 258 kN (58000 lbf).
Continuous Rating: 3730 kW (5000 hp) giving a tractive effort of 95 kN (21300
lbf) at 87 mph.
Maximum Rail Power: 5860 kW (7860 hp) at 50.8 mph.
Brake Force: 40 t.   **Length over Buffers:** 17.83 m.
Design Speed: 110 mph.   **Weight:** 87 t.
Max. Speed: 110 mph.   **RA:** 6.
ETH Index: 74   **Wheel Diameter:** 1150 mm.
Train Brakes: Air & Vacuum.   **Electric Brake:** Rheostatic.

86101 (86201)   **I**   SAXL   LG   Sir William A Stanier FRS
86102 (86202) a **I**   SAXL   LG   Robert A Riddles
86103 (86203)   **I**   SAXL   LG   André Chapelon

CLASS 86/2   BR DESIGN   Bo – Bo

Built: 1965 – 66 by English Electric Co. at Vulcan Foundry, Newton le Willows
or BR at Doncaster Works. Later rebuilt with resilient wheels and flexicoil suspension. Tap changer control.
Traction Motors: AEI 282BZ.
Max. Tractive Effort: 207 kN (46500 lbf).

Continuous Rating: 3010 kW (4040 hp) giving a tractive effort of 85 kN (19200 lbf) at 77.5 mph.
Maximum Rail Power: 4550 kW (6100 hp) at 49.5 mph.

Brake Force: 40 t.	**Length over Buffers:** 17.83 m.
Design Speed: 125 mph.	**Weight:** 85 t – 86 t.
Max. Speed: 100 (110§) mph.	**RA:** 6.
ETH Index: 74	**Wheel Diameter:** 1156 mm.
Train Brakes: Air & Vacuum.	**Electric Brake:** Rheostatic.

86204			I	IWPA	WN (S)	City of Carlisle
86205	(86503)	a	I	ICCA	LG	City of Lancaster
86206		a	I	ICCA	LG	City of Stoke on Trent
86207		a	I	IWPA	WN	City of Lichfield
86208		a	I	PXLE	CE	City of Chester
86209		a§	I	IWPA	WN	City of Coventry
86210			RX	PXLE	CE	C.I.T. 75th Anniversary
86212			I	ICCA	LG	Preston Guild 1328 – 1992
86213			I	IWPA	WN (S)	Lancashire Witch
86214			I	ICCA	LG	Sans Pareil
86215		a	I	IANA	NC	Joseph Chamberlain
86216		a	I	ICCA	LG	Meteor
86217	(86504)	a	I	IANA	NC	City University
86218			I	IANA	NC	Harold MacMillan
86219		a	I	IWPA	WN (S)	Phoenix
86220		a	I	IANA	NC	The Round Tabler
86221		a	I	IANA	NC	B.B.C. Look East
86222	(86502)		I	ICCA	LG	Clothes Show Live
86223		a	I	IANA	NC	Norwich Union
86224		a§	I	IWPA	WN	Caledonian
86225		a§	I	IWPA	WN	Hardwicke
86226			M	ICCA	LG	Royal Mail Midlands
86227		a	I	ICCA	LG	Sir Henry Johnson
86228			I	IANA	NC	Vulcan Heritage
86229			I	ICCA	LG	Sir John Betjeman
86230		a	I	IANA	NC	The Duke of Wellington
86231		a§	I	IWPA	WN	Starlight Express
86232		a	I	IANA	NC	Norfolk and Norwich Festival
86233	(86506)		I	ICCA	LG	Laurence Olivier
86234			I	ICCA	LG	J B Priestley OM
86235		a	I	IANA	NC	Crown Point
86236		a	I	IWPA	WN	Josiah Wedgwood MASTER POTTER 1736 – 1795
86237		a	I	IANA	NC	University of East Anglia
86238		a	I	IANA	NC	European Community
86239	(86507)		RX	PXLE	CE	
86240		a	I	IWPA	WN	Bishop Eric Treacy
86241	(86508)		RX	PXLE	CE	Glenfiddich
86242			I	IWPA	WN	James Kennedy GC
86243			RX	PXLE	CE	
86244			I	ICCA	LG	The Royal British Legion
86245		a	I	IWPA	WN	Dudley Castle

86246	(86505)	a	I	IANA	NC		Royal Anglian Regiment
86247		a	I	ICCA	LG		Abraham Darby
86248			I	IWPA	WN		Sir Clwyd/County of Clwyd
86249		a	I	IWPA	WN	(S)	County of Merseyside
86250		a	I	IANA	NC		The Glasgow Herald
86251			I	IWPA	WN		The Birmingham Post
86252			I	ICCA	LG		The Liverpool Daily Post
86253	(86044)	a	I	IWPA	WN		The Manchester Guardian
86254	(86047)		RX	PXLE	CE		
86255	(86042)		I	ICCA	LG		Penrith Beacon
86256	(86040)		I	IWPA	WN		Pebble Mill
86257	(86043)	a	I	ICCA	LG		Snowdon
86258	(86501)	a	I	IWPA	WN		Talyllyn – The First Preserved Railway
86259	(86045)	a	I	ICCA	LG		Greater MANCHESTER THE LIFE & SOUL OF BRITAIN
86260	(86048)	a	I	ICCA	LG		Driver Wallace Oakes G.C.
86261	(86041)		RX	PXLE	CE		

CLASS 86/4 & 86/6   BR DESIGN   Bo – Bo

Built: 1965 – 66 by English Electric Co. at Vulcan Foundry, Newton le Willows or BR at Doncaster Works. Later rebuilt with resilient wheels and flexicoil suspension. Tap changer control.
Traction Motors: AEI 282AZ.
Max. Tractive Effort: 258 kN (58000 lbf).
Continuous Rating: 2680 kW (3600 hp) giving a tractive effort of 89 kN (20000 lbf) at 67 mph.
Maximum Rail Power: 4400 kW (5900 hp) at 38 mph.
Brake Force: 40 t.   **Length over Buffers:** 17.83 m.
Design Speed: 100 mph.   **Weight:** 83 t – 84 t.
Max. Speed: 100 (75*) mph.   **RA:** 6.
ETH Index: 74   **Wheel Diameter:** 1156 mm.
Train Brakes: Air & Vacuum.   **Electric Brake:** Rheostatic.

Class 86/6 have the ETH equipment isolated.

86401	(86001)		RX	PXLE	CE	
86602	(86402)	*	FD	DANC	CE	
86603	(86403)	*	FD	DANC	CE	
86604	(86404)	*	FE	DANC	CE	
86605	(86405)	a*	FD	DANC	CE	Intercontainer
86606	(86406)	*	FE	DANC	CE	
86607	(86407)	*	FD	DANC	CE	The Institution of Electrical Engineers
86608	(86408)	*	FE	DANC	CE	St. John Ambulance
86609	(86409)	*	FD	DANC	CE	
86610	(86410)	*	FD	DANC	CE	
86611	(86411)	*	FD	DANC	CE	Airey Neave
86612	(86412)	*	F	DFNC	CE	Elizabeth Garrett Anderson
86613	(86413)	*	FD	DFNC	CE	County of Lancashire
86614	(86414)	*	FD	DFNC	CE	Frank Hornby

86615 (86415)	*	**FD** DFNC	CE	Rotary International
86416 (86316)		**RX** PXLE	CE	
86417 (86317)		**RX** PXLE	CE	
86618 (86418)	*	**FE** DFNC	CE	
86419 (86319)		**RX** PXLE	CE	
86620 (86420)	*	**FD** DFNC	CE	
86621 (86421)	*	**FD** DFNC	CE	London School of Economics
86622 (86422)	*	**FE** DFNC	CE	
86623 (86423)	*	**FD** DFNC	CE	
86424 (86324)		**RX** PXLE	CE	
86425 (86325)		**RX** PXLE	CE	Saint Mungo
86426 (86326)		**RX** PXLE	CE	
86627 (86427)	*	**FD** DFNC	CE	The Industrial Society
86628 (86428)	*	**F** DFNC	CE	Aldaniti
86430 (86030)		**RX** PXLE	CE	
86631 (86431)	*	**FD** DFNC	CE	
86632 (86432)	*	**FD** DFNC	CE	Brookside
86633 (86433)	*	**FD** DFNC	CE	Wulfruna
86634 (86434)	*	**FD** DFNC	CE	University of London
86635 (86435)	*	**FD** DFNC	CE	
86636 (86436)	*	**FD** DFNC	CE	
86637 (86437)	*	**FD** DFNC	CE	
86638 (86438)	*	**FD** DFNC	CE	
86639 (86439)	*	**FD** DFNC	CE	

CLASS 87   BR DESIGN   Bo – Bo

Built: 1973 – 75 by BREL at Crewe Works.
Traction Motors: GEC G412AZ frame mounted (87/0), G412BZ (87/1).
Max. Tractive Effort: 258 kN (58000 lbf).
Continuous Rating: 3730 kW (5000 hp) giving a tractive effort of 95 kN (21300 lbf) at 87 mph (Class 87/0), 3620 kW (4850 hp) giving a tractive effort of 96 kN (21600 lbf) at 84 mph (Class 87/1).
Maximum Rail Power: 5860 kW (7860 hp) at 50.8 mph.
Brake Force: 40 t.
Design Speed: 110 mph
Max. Speed: 110 (75*) mph.
ETH Index: 95
Train Brakes: Air.
Length over Buffers: 17.83 m.
Weight: 83.5 t.
RA: 6.
Wheel Diameter: 1150 mm.
Electric Brake: Rheostatic.

Note: All IWCA locos are owned by Porterbrook Leasing Company (owner code SBF).

Class 87/0. Standard Design. Tap Changer Control.

87001	I	IWCA	WN	Royal Scot
87002	I	IWCA	WN	Royal Sovereign
87003	I	IWCA	WN	Patriot
87004	I	IWCA	WN	Britannia
87005	I	IWCA	WN	City of London
87006	I	IWCA	WN	City of Glasgow
87007	I	IWCA	WN	City of Manchester

87008	I	IWCA	WN	City of Liverpool
87009	I	IWCA	WN	City of Birmingham
87010	I	IWCA	WN	King Arthur
87011	I	IWCA	WN	The Black Prince
87012	I	IWCA	WN	The Royal Bank of Scotland
87013	I	IWCA	WN	John O' Gaunt
87014	I	IWCA	WN	Knight of the Thistle
87015	I	IWCA	WN	Howard of Effingham
87016	I	IWCA	WN	Willesden Intercity Depot
87017	I	IWCA	WN	Iron Duke
87018	I	IWCA	WN	Lord Nelson
87019	I	IWCA	WN	Sir Winston Churchill
87020	I	IWCA	WN	North Briton
87021	I	IWCA	WN	Robert the Bruce
87022	I	IWCA	WN	Cock o' the North
87023	I	IWCA	WN	Velocity
87024	I	IWCA	WN	Lord of the Isles
87025	I	IWCA	WN	County of Cheshire
87026	I	IWCA	WN	Sir Richard Arkwright
87027	I	IWCA	WN	Wolf of Badenoch
87028	I	IWCA	WN	Lord President
87029	I	IWCA	WN	Earl Marischal
87030	I	IWCA	WN	Black Douglas
87031	I	IWCA	WN	Hal o' the Wynd
87032	I	IWCA	WN	Kenilworth
87033	I	IWCA	WN	Thane of Fife
87034	I	IWCA	WN	William Shakespeare
87035	I	IWCA	WN	Robert Burns

Class 87/1. Thyristor Control.

| 87101 | * | DAMC | CE | STEPHENSON |

CLASS 90   GEC DESIGN   Bo – Bo

Built: 1987 – 90 by BREL at Crewe Works. Thyristor control.
Traction Motors: GEC G412CY separately excited frame mounted.
Max. Tractive Effort: 258 kN (58000 lbf).
Continuous Rating: 3730 kW (5000 hp) giving a tractive effort of 95 kN (21300 lbf) at 87 mph.
Maximum Rail Power: 5860 kW (7860 hp) at 68.3 mph.
Brake Force: 40 t.   **Length over Buffers:** 18.80 m.
Design Speed: 110 mph.   **Weight:** 84.5 t.
Max. Speed: 110 (75*) mph.   **RA:** 7.
ETH Index: 95   **Wheel Diameter:** 1156 mm.
Train Brakes: Air.   **Electric Brake:** Rheostatic.
Couplings: Drop-head buckeye (removed on Class 90/1).

Non-standard Liveries:

90128 is in SNCB/NMBS (Belgian Railways) electric loco livery.
90129 is in DB (German Federal Railways) 'neurot' livery.
90130 is in SNCF (French Railways) 'Sybic' livery.

90136 is in livery 'FE', but with full yellow ends and roof and red 'Railfreight Distribution' lettering.

Note: All IWCA locos are owned by Porterbrook Leasing Company (owner code SBF).

Class 90/0. As built.

90001	I IWCA	WN	BBC Midlands Today
90002	I IWCA	WN	The Girls' Brigade
90003	I IWCA	WN	THE HERALD
90004	I IWCA	WN	The D' Oyly Carte Opera Company
90005	I IWCA	WN	Financial Times
90006	I IWCA	WN	High Sheriff
90007	I IWCA	WN	Lord Stamp
90008	I IWCA	WN	The Birmingham Royal Ballet
90009	I IWCA	WN	The Economist
90010	I IWCA	WN	275 Railway Squadron (Volunteers)
90011	I IWCA	WN	The Chartered Institute of Transport
90012	I IWCA	WN	British Transport Police
90013	I IWCA	WN	The Law Society
90014	I IWCA	WN	'The Liverpool Phil'
90015	I IWCA	WN	BBC North West
90016	RX PXLA	CE	
90017	RX PXLA	CE	Rail express systems Quality Assured
90018	RX PXLA	CE	
90019	RX PXLA	CE	Penny Black
90020	RX PXLA	CE	Colonel Bill Cockburn CBE TD
90021	FD DAMC	CE	
90022	FD DAMC	CE	Freightconnection
90023	FD DAMC	CE	
90024	FD DAMC	CE	

Class 90/1. ETH equipment isolated. Renumbered from 90025 – 90050.

90125	* FD DAMC	CE	Crewe International
90126	* FE DAMC	CE	Electric Maintenance Depot
90127	* FD DAMC	CE	Allerton T&RS Depot Quality Approved
90128	* 0 DAMC	CE	Vrachtverbinding
90129	* 0 DAMC	CE	Frachtverbindungen
90130	* 0 DAMC	CE	Fretconnection
90131	* FE DAMC	CE	
90132	* FE DAMC	CE	Cerestar
90133	* FE DAMC	CE	
90134	* FE DAMC	CE	
90135	* FE DAMC	CE	Crewe Basford Hall
90136	* 0 DAMC	CE	
90137	* FD DAMC	CE	
90138	* FD DAMC	CE	
90139	* FD DAMC	CE	
90140	* FD DAMC	CE	
90141	* FD DFLC	CE	

90142	*	FD	DFLC	CE
90143	*	FD	DFLC	CE
90144	*	F	DFLC	CE
90145	*	FD	DFLC	CE
90146	*	FD	DFLC	CE
90147	*	FD	DFLC	CE
90148	*	FD	DFLC	CE
90149	*	FD	DFLC	CE
90150	*	FD	DFLC	CE

CLASS 91   GEC DESIGN   Bo – Bo

Built: 1988 – 91 by BREL at Crewe Works. Thyristor control.
Traction Motors: GEC G426AZ.
Continuous Rating: 4540 kW (6090 hp).
Maximum Rail Power: 4700 kW (6300 hp).
Brake Force: 45 t.   **Length over Buffers:** 19.40 m.
Design Speed: 140 mph.   **Weight:** 84 t.
Max. Speed: 140 mph.   **RA:** 7.
ETH Index: 95   **Wheel Diameter:** 1000 mm.
Train Brakes: Air.   **Electric Brake:** Rheostatic.
Couplings: Drop-head buckeye.

Note: This class is owned by Eversholt Train Leasing Company (owner code SAB).

91001	I	IECA	BN	Swallow
91002	I	IECA	BN	Durham Cathedral
91003	I	IECA	BN	THE SCOTSMAN
91004	I	IECA	BN	The Red Arrows
91005	I	IECA	BN	Royal Air Force Regiment
91006	I	IECA	BN	
91007	I	IECA	BN	Ian Allan
91008	I	IECA	BN	Thomas Cook
91009	I	IECA	BN	Saint Nicholas
91010	I	IECA	BN	Northern Rock
91011	I	IECA	BN	Terence Cuneo
91012	I	IECA	BN	
91013	I	IECA	BN	Michael Faraday
91014	I	IECA	BN	Northern Electric
91015	I	IECA	BN	
91016	I	IECA	BN	
91017	I	IECA	BN	Commonwealth Institute
91018	I	IECA	BN	Robert Louis Stevenson
91019	I	IECA	BN	Scottish Enterprise
91020	I	IECA	BN	
91021	I	IECA	BN	
91022	I	IECA	BN	Robert Adley
91023	I	IECA	BN	
91024	I	IECA	BN	Reverend W Awdry
91025	I	IECA	BN	BBC Radio One FM
91026	I	IECA	BN	Voice of the North

91027	I	IECA	BN	Great North Run
91028	I	IECA	BN	Guide Dog
91029	I	IECA	BN	Queen Elizabeth II
91030	I	IECA	BN	Palace of Holyroodhouse
91031	I	IECA	BN	Sir Henry Royce

CLASS 92   BRUSH DESIGN   Co–Co

Built: 1993–5 by Brush Traction at Loughborough. Thyristor control.
Supply System: 25 kV a.c. from overhead equipment and 750 V d.c. third rail.
Electrical equipment: ABB Transportation, Zürich, Switzerland.
Traction Motors: Brush.
Max. Tractive Effort: 400 kN (90 000 lbf).
Continuous Rating at Motor Shaft: 5040 kW (6760 hp).
Maximum Rail Power (25 kV a.c.): 5000 kW (6700 hp).
Maximum Rail Power (750 V d.c.): 4000 kW (5360 hp).
Brake Force: t.   **Length over Buffers:** 21.34 m.
Design Speed: 140 km/h.   **Weight:** 126 t.
Max. Speed: 140 km/h (87.5 mph).   **RA:** 7.
ETH Index: 108.   **Wheel Diameter:** 1160 mm.
Train Brakes: Air.
Electric Brake: Rheostatic & regenerative.
Multiple Working: Time division multiplex system.
Communication Equipment: Driver – guard telephone and cab to shore radio-telephone.
Cab Signalling: Fitted with TVM430 cab signalling for Channel Tunnel.

Note: Locos are in one common pool. They are owned by Railfreight Distribution (RfD) except where stated as 'f' – SNCF or p – European Passenger Services (EPS). Railfreight Distribution and EPS or SNCF logos are being applied.

92001		E	DAEC	CE	Victor Hugo
92002		E	DAEC	CE	H G Wells
92003		E	DAEC	CE	Beethoven
92004		E	DAEC	CE	Jane Austen
92005		E	DAEC	CE	Mozart
92006	f	E	DAEC	CE	Louis Armand
92007		E	DAEC	CE	Schubert
92008		E	DAEC	CE	Jules Verne
92009		E	DAEC	CE	Elgar
92010	f	E	DAIC	CE	Molière
92011		E	DAIC	CE	Handel
92012		E	DAIC	CE	Thomas Hardy
92013		E	DAIC	CE	Puccini
92014	f	E	DAIC	CE	Emile Zola
92015		E	DAIC	CE	D H Lawrence
92016		E	DAIC	CE	Brahms
92017		E	DAIC	CE	Shakespeare
92018	f	E	DAEC	CE	Stendhal
92019	*	E	DAIC	CE	Wagner
92020	p	E	DAIC	CE	Milton
92021	p	E	DAIC	CE	Purcell

92022	E	DAIC	CE	Charles Dickens
92023 f	E	DAIC	CE	Ravel
92024	E	DAIC	CE	J S Bach
92025	E	DAIC	CE	Oscar Wilde
92026	E	DAIC	CE	Britten
92027	E	DAEC	CE	George Eliot
92028 f	E	DAIC	CE	Saint Saëns
92029	E	DAIC	CE	Dante
92030	E	DAIC	CE	De Falla
92031	E	DAIC	CE	
92032 p	E	DAIC	CE	César Franck
92033 f	E	DAIC	CE	Berlioz
92034	E	DAIC	CE	Kipling
92035	E	DAIC	CE	Mendelssohn
92036	E	DAIC	CE	Bertolt Brecht
92037	E	DAIC	CE	Sullivan
92038 f	E	DAIC	CE	Voltaire
92039	E	DAIC	CE	Johann Strauss
92040 p	E	DAIC	CE	Goethe
92041	E	DAEC	CE	Vaughan Williams
92042	E	DAEC	CE	Honegger
92043 f	E	DAIC	CE	Debussy
92044 p	E	DAEC	CE	Couperin
92045 p	E	DAEC	CE	Chaucer
92046 p	E	DAEC	CE	Sweelinck

1.3. SERVICE LOCOMOTIVES

CLASS 97/6   RUSTON SHUNTER   0-6-0

Built: 1959 by Ruston & Hornsby at Lincoln.
Engine: Ruston 6VPH of 123 kW (165 hp).
Main Generator: British Thomson Houston RTB6034.
Traction Motor: One British Thomson Houston RTA5041.
Max. Tractive Effort: 75 kN (17000 lbf).
Brake Force: 16 t.   **Length over Buffers:** 7.62 m.
Weight: 31 t.   **Wheel Diameter:** 978 mm.
Max. Speed: 20 mph.   **RA:** 1.

Non-Standard Livery: Civil Engineer's Yellow.

| 97651 | (PWM 651) | v | 0 | LNCF | CF |
| 97654 | (PWM 654) | v | 0 | EWOC | OC |

CLASS 97/8   EE SHUNTER   0-6-0

For details see Class 09. Severn Tunnel emergency train locomotive.

Non-Standard Livery: BR blue with grey cab.

| 97806 | (09017) | xo | 0 | LNCF | CF | Normally kept at Sudbrook. |

1.4. BR LOCOMOTIVES AWAITING DISPOSAL

03179	N	Ryde T&RSMD
08222		Bounds Green T&RSMD
08390		ABB Crewe Works
08419		ABB Crewe Works
08473		Leicester LIP
08515		Gateshead WRD
08562		Stratford TMD
08565		Motherwell TMD
08609		Willesden TMD
08618		Gateshead WRD
08634		Stratford TMD
08666		Allerton TMD
08673	IO	Allerton TMD
08677		Willesden TMD
08707		ABB Crewe Works
08733		Motherwell TMD
08755		Millerhill FP
08760		Wessex Traincare
08777		Hull Botanic Gardens FP
08793	0	Aberdeen T&RSMD
08829		Toton TMD
08849		ABB Crewe Works
08855		Aberdeen T&RSMD
08895		Margam WRD
08898		Bescot TMD
20073		Bescot Yard
20119		Toton TMD
20154		Toton TMD
20177		Toton TMD
25083		Crewe Carriage Shed
31168		Bescot Yard
31196	C	Stratford TMD
31217	FC	Toton TMD
31282	FR	Bescot Yard
31283	0	Stratford TMD
31286		Bescot Yard
31289		Bescot Yard
31296	FA	Crewe Carriage Shed
31299	FO	Stratford TMD
31320		Stratford TMD
31402		Bescot Yard
31428		Bescot Yard
31442		Crewe Carriage Shed
31460		Bescot Yard
31970	0	ABB Crewe Works
33009	C	Wessex Traincare
33020		Stewarts Lane T&RSMD

33033	FA	Stewarts Lane T&RSMD
33038		Stratford TMD
33040		Stewarts Lane T&RSMD
33047	C	Eastleigh Yard
33050	FA	Stewarts Lane T&RSMD
33064	FA	Old Oak Common TMD
33101	D	Eastleigh T&RSMD
33108	C	Eastleigh T&RSMD
33113		Stewarts Lane T&RSMD
33114	N	Eastleigh T&RSMD
33118	C	Eastleigh T&RSMD
33201	C	Stewarts Lane T&RSMD
33211	FD	Stewarts Lane T&RSMD
37008	FR	ABB Crewe Works
37031	FD	Cardiff Canton T&RSMD
37252	FD	ABB Doncaster Works
37280	FP	Old Oak Common TMD
37373	FR	Old Oak Common TMD
45015		Toton TMD
47050	FD	Tinsley TMD
47063	FA	ABB Crewe Works
47096		Tinsley TMD
47102		Tinsley TMD
47108		Old Oak Common TMD
47112	FO	Old Oak Common TMD
47190	FP	Tinsley TMD
47214	FD	Tinsley TMD
47288	FD	Tinsley TMD
47318	FO	Bescot Yard
47320	FO	ABB Crewe Works
47321	F	Tinsley TMD
47421		ABB Crewe Works
47423		Old Oak Common TMD
47425		Old Oak Common TMD
47426	BR	Old Oak Common TMD
47430	FA	Old Oak Common TMD
47431	BR	Old Oak Common TMD
47433	BR	ABB Crewe Works
47438	BR	ABB Crewe Works
47439	BR	ABB Crewe Works
47440	BR	Old Oak Common TMD
47441	BR	ABB Crewe Works
47442	BR	ABB Crewe Works
47443	BR	ABB Crewe Works
47446	BR	Old Oak Common TMD
47448	BR	Holbeck FP
47452	BR	Old Oak Common TMD

47453	**BR**	Old Oak Common TMD
47457	**BR**	Old Oak Common TMD
47458	**R**	Holbeck FP
47463		ABB Crewe Works
47465	**BR**	Old Oak Common TMD
47466	**BR**	ABB Crewe Works
47472		Old Oak Common TMD
47483	**M**	ABB Crewe Works
47485	**BR**	ABB Crewe Works
47515	**M**	Crewe Horse Landing

47538	**BR**	Crewe TMD (D)
47850	**I**	ABB Crewe Works
56013	**FC**	Toton TMD
56015	**FC**	ABB Doncaster Works
56023	**FC**	Toton TMD
56028	**FC**	Margam WRD
56030	**FC**	Margam WRD
73004	**0**	Birkenhead N. T&RSMD
73111	**I0**	Stewarts Lane T&RSMD
97653	**0**	Reading T&RSMD

Non-Standard Liveries:

08793 is in London & North Eastern Railway apple green.
31283 is BR blue with large numbers.
31970 is BR Research light grey, dark grey, white and red.
73004 is Network SouthEast blue.
97653 is Departmental yellow.

2. LOCOMOTIVE-HAULED PASSENGER STOCK

Coaches are listed in batches, according to their class, with lot number information for the various batches being shown above the listings. Where a coach has been renumbered, the former number is shown in parentheses. If the coach has been renumbered more than once, both the original number and last number are shown in parenthese,. Where the old number of a coach due to be converted or renumbered is known and the conversion or renumbering has not yet taken place, the coach is listed both under its old number with its depot allocation, and under its new number without an allocation. See page 5 for details of the new scope of this section.

NUMBERING SYSTEMS

Six different numbering systems were in use on BR. These were the BR series, the four pre-nationalisation companies' series' and the Pullman Car Company's series. BR number series coaches are listed first, then former Pullman Car Company series ones. Finally, a list of pre-nationalistaion coaches registered to run on Railtrack metals is given. Please note that the Mark 2 Manchester Pullman vehicles were ordered after the Pullman Car Company had been nationalised and are therefore numbered in the BR series.

DETAILED INFORMATION AND CODES

After the heading, the following details are shown:

● Diagram code. This consists of the first three characters of the TOPS code followed by two numbers which relate to the particular design of vehicle.
● 'Mark' of coach (see below).
● Number of first class seats , standard class seats and lavatory compartments shown as F/S nT respectively.
● Bogie type (see below).
● Brake type. (see below).
● Additional features.
● ETH Index.

TOPS CODES

TOPS (Total operations processing system) codes are allocated to all coaching stock. For passenger stock the code consists of:

(1) Two letters denoting the layout of the vehicle as follows:

AA	Gangwayed Corridor
AB	Gangwayed Corridor Brake
AC	Gangwayed Open (2 + 2 seating)
AD	Gangwayed Open (2 + 1 seating)
AE	Gangwayed Open Brake
AF	Gangwayed Driving Open Brake
AG	Micro-Buffet

AH	Brake Micro-Buffet
AI	As 'AC' but fitted with drop-head buckeye and no gangway at one end.
AJ	Restaurant Buffet with Kitchen
AK	Kitchen Car
AL	As 'AC' but with disabled person's toilet (Mark 4 only)
AN	Miniature Buffet
AP	Pullman First with Kitchen
AQ	Pullman Parlour First
AR	Pullman Brake First
AS	Sleeping Car
AT	Royal Train Coach
AU	Sleeping Car with Pantry
AX	Generator Van
AY	Eurostar Barrier Vehicle
AZ	Special saloon
GF	DMU/EMU/Mark 4 Barrier Vehicle
GX	Generator Van
NM	Sandite Coach

(2) A digit for the class of passenger accommodation:

1	first
2	standard (formerly second)
3	Composite
4	Unclassified
5	None

(3) A suffix relating to the build of coach.

1 Mark 1	A Mark 2A	C Mark 2C	E Mark 2E	G Mark 3 or	H Mark 3B
Z Mark 2	B Mark 2B	D Mark 2D	F Mark 2F	Mark 3A	J Mark 4

OPERATOR CODES

The normal operator codes are given in brackets after the TOPS codes. These are as follows:

B	Brake	C	Composite
F	First	O	Open
S	standard (formerly second)	K	Side corridor with lavatory

Various other letters are in use and the meaning of these can be ascertained by referring to the titles at the head of each class.

BOGIE TYPES

BR Mk 1 (BR1). Standard double bolster leaf spring bogie. Generally 90 m.p.h. but certain vehicles were allowed to run at 100 m.p.h. with special maintenance. Weight: 6.1 t.
BR Mk 2 (BR2). Single bolster leaf-spring bogie used on certain types of non-passenger stock and suburban stock (all now withdrawn). Weight: 5.3 t.
COMMONWEALTH (C). Heavy, cast steel coil spring bogie. 100 m.p.h. Weight: 6.75 t.
B4. Coil spring fabricated bogie for 100 m.p.h. Weight: 5.2 t.

B5. Heavy duty version of B4. 100 m.p.h. Weight: 5.3 t.
BT10. A fabricated bogie designed for 125 m.p.h. Air suspension.
T4. A recent 125 m.p.h. bogie from BREL.
BT41. Fitted to Mark 4 vehicles. Manufactured by the Swiss firm of SIG.

BRAKE TYPE CODES.

a	Air braked.
v	Vacuum braked.
x	Dual braked (air and vacuum).

HEATING

Heating codes have now been discontinued, as all haeting on British main-line trains is now electric. Certain coaches for use on charter trains may, hoewever have steam heating facilities also.

PUBLIC ADDRESS

It is assumed that all coaches are now fitted with public address, although certain stored coaches may not have the feature. In addition, it is assumed that all vehicles with a guard''s compartment have public address transmission facilities, as have catering vehicles.

ADDITIONAL FEATURE CODES.

d	Secondary door locking provided.
f	Facelifted or fluorescent lighting provided.
k	Composition brake blocks (instead of cast iron).
n	Day/night lighting.
p	Fitted with public telephone.
pg	Public address transmission and driver-guard communication.
q	Fitted with catering staff to shore telephone.
w	Fitted with wheelchair space.
z	Fitted with wheelchair space and disabled persons' toilet.

NOTES ON ETH INDICES.

The sum of ETH indices in a train must not be more than that of the locomotive. The normal voltage on BR is 1000. Suffix 'X' denotes 600 amp wiring instead of 400 amp. Trains whose ETH index comes to more than 66 must be formed completely with 600 amp wired stock.

THE DEVELOPMENT OF BR STANDARD COACHES

The standard BR coach built from 1951 to 1963 is the mark 1. This has a separate underframe and body. The underframe is normally 64'6'' long, but certain vehicles were built on short (57') frames. Tungsten lighting is standard and until 1961, BR mark 1 bogies were generally provided. In 1959 TSOs to lot No. 30525 appeared with fluorescent lighting and melamine interior panels and from 1961 onwards Commonwealth bogies were fitted in an attempt to improve the quality of ride which became very poor when the tyre profiles on the wheels of the Mark 1 bogies became worn. The further batches of TSOs and BSOs retained the features of lot 30525, but the BSKs, SKs, BCKs and CKs, whilst utilising melamine panelling in standard class, still retained tungsten lighting. Wooden interior finish was retained in first class compartments. The FOs had fluorescent lighting with wooden panelling except for lot No. 30648 which had tungsten lighting. In later years many mark 1s had their mark 1 bogies replaced by B4s.

In 1964, a new train was introduced. Known as "XP64", it featured new seat designs, pressure ventilation, aluminium compartment doors and corridor partitions, foot pedal operated toilets, and B4 bogies. The vehicles were on standard mark 1 underframes. Folding doors were fitted but these proved troublesome and were later replaced with hinged doors. All XP64 coaches have now been withdrawn, but some have been preserved.

The prototype mark 2 vehicle (W 13252) was produced in 1963. This was an FK of semi-integral construction and was pressure ventilated. Tungsten lighting was provided and B4 bogies. This vehicle has been preserved by the National Railway Museum. The production build was similar, but wider windows were used. The standard class open vehicles used the new seat design similar to that in the XP64 and fluorescent lighting was provided. Interior finish reverted to wood. MK 2s were built from 1964-66.

The mark 2As, built 1967-68, incorporated the rest of the novel features first used in the XP64 set, i.e. foot pedal operated toilets (except BSOs), new first class seat design, aluminium compartment doors and partitions together with fluorescent lighting in first class compartments. Folding gangway doors (lime green coloured) were used instead of the traditional variety. The following list summarises the changes made in the later Mk 2 variants:

Mk 2B: Wide wrap round doors, no centre doors, slightly longer body. In standard class, one toilet at each end instead of two at one end as previously . Red gangway doors.

Mk 2C: Lowered ceiling with twin strips of fluorescent lighting, ducting for air conditioning, but no air conditioning.

Mk 2D: Air conditioning. No opening lights in windows.

Mk 2E: Smaller toilets with luggage racks opposite. Fawn gangway doors.

Mk 2F: Plastic interior panels. Inter-City 70 seats. Modified air conditioning system.

The Mark 3 coach has BT10 bogies, is 75' long and is of fully integral construction with Inter-City 70 seats. Gangway doors are yellow (red in RFB). Loco-hauled coaches are classified Mark 3A, Mark 3 being reserved for HST trailers. A new batch of FOs and BFOs classified Mark 3B was built in 1985 with APT style seating and revised lighting. The last vehicles in the Mark 3 series were the driving brake vehicles (officially called driving van trailers) which have been built for West Coast Main Line services.

The Mark 4 coach built by Metro-Cammell for the East Coast Main Line electrification scheme features a body profile suitable for tilting trains, although tilt is not fitted, and is not intended to be. They are suitable for 140 m.p.h. running, although are restricted to 125 m.p.h. pending the installation of a more advanced signalling system on the East Coast Main Line.

PRESERVED LOCOMOTIVES OF BRITISHRAILWAYS 9th edition

Peter Fox & Peter Hall

The complete guide to all remaining Ex-British Railways and Constituent Companies, steam, diesel & electric locomotives, and diesel & electric multiple units. Technical details are provided for each class of vehicle, including builder, year of manufacture, wheel arrangement and tractive effort. Further details of numbers carried, names and locations are provided for each individual vehicle. For the first time, this popular volume now includes locomotives and multiple units of London Underground Limited and its predecessors, plus expanded coverage of locomotives once owned by the British Military. Also includes a full list of preservation sites and industrial locations. Fully updated to June 1995. A5 size. Thread Sewn. Illustrated in colour and black & white. £7.95.

PRESERVED COACHING STOCK OF BRITISH RAILWAYS 1st edition.
PART 1 - BR DESIGN STOCK

Peter Hall & Peter Fox.

The ideal companion to 'Preserved Locomotives of British Railways' is now available. This book contains full details of all BR Design Coaching Stock and Pullman cars from the same era. Background information and brief design details are included, plus all numbers carried and current locations for every vehicle. A complete BR hauled coaching stock lot number list is also provided. This is the first time such a listing has been published in the clear Platform 5 format which also includes a full index to preservation sites including OS grid references. A5. Thread Sewn. 104 pages including 8 in colour. £7.95.

For a full list of titles available by mail order, see the list at the back of this book.

2.1. BR NUMBER SERIES STOCK

AJ11 (RF)   RESTAURANT FIRST

Dia. AJ106. Mark 1. Gas cooking. 24/ – . B5 bogies. ETH 2. This coach spent most of its life as a Royal train vehicle and was numbered 2907 for a time.

Lot No. 30633 Swindon 1961. a. 41 t.

325		WV	XWR		BN

AP1Z(PK)   PULLMAN FIRST WITH KITCHEN

Dia. AP101. Mark 2. Pressure Ventilated. Electric cooking. 18/ – 2T. B4 bogies. a. ETH 6.

Lot No. 30755 Derby 1966. 40 t.

Non-Standard Livery: Statesman Pullman maroon & beige.

504	0	XMA	CS	THE WHITE ROSE
506	0	XMA	CS	THE RED ROSE

AQ1Z(PC)   PULLMAN PARLOUR FIRST

Dia. AQ101. Mark 2. Pressure Ventilated. 36/ – 2T. B4 bogies. a. ETH 5.

Lot No. 30754 Derby 1966. 35 t.

Non-Standard Livery: Statesman Pullman maroon & beige.

546	0	XMA	CS	CITY OF MANCHESTER
548	0	XMA	CS	ELIZABETHAN
549	0	XMA	CS	PRINCE RUPERT
550	0	XMA	CS	GOLDEN ARROW
551	0	XMA	CS	CALEDONIAN
552	0	XMA	CS	SOUTHERN BELLE
553	0	XMA	CS	KING ARTHUR

AR1Z(PB)   PULLMAN BRAKE FIRST

Dia. AQ101. Mark 2. Pressure Ventilated. 30/ – 2T. B4 bogies. x. ETH 4.

Lot No. 30753 Derby 1966. 35 t.

Non-Standard Livery: Statesman Pullman maroon & beige.

586	0	XMA	CS	TALISMAN

AJ1F(RFB)   BUFFET OPEN FIRST

Dia. AJ104. Mark 2F. Air conditioned. Electric cooking. Converted 1988 – 9/91 at BREL, Derby from Mark 2F FOs. 1200/1/3/6/11/14 – 17/20/21/50/2/5/6/9 have Stones equipment, others have Temperature Ltd. – /26 1T. B4 bogies. a.

payphone. Catering staff – shore telephone. Secondary door locks. ETH 6X.

1200/3/6/11/14/16/20/52/5/6. Lot No. 30845 Derby 1973. 33 t.
1201/4/5/7/8/10/12/13/15/17 – 9/21/50/1/4/7/9. Lot No. 30859 Derby 1973 – 4. 33 t.
1202/9/53/8. Lot No. 30873 Derby 1974 – 5. 33 t.

1200 (3287, 6459)	I	SAH	DY
1201 (3361, 6445)	I	SAH	PC
1202 (3436, 6456)	I	SAH	PC
1203 (3291)	I	SAH	DY
1204 (3401)	I	SAH	PC
1205 (3329, 6438)	I	SAH	DY
1206 (3319)	I	SAH	MA
1207 (3328, 6422)	I	SAH	MA
1208 (3393)	I	SAH	MA
1209 (3437, 6457)	I	SAH	DY
1210 (3405, 6462)	I	SAH	PC
1211 (3305)	I	SAH	MA
1212 (3427, 6453)	I	SAH	DY
1213 (3419)	I	SAH	DY
1214 (3317, 6433)	I	SAH	MA
1215 (3377)	I	SAH	PC
1216 (3302)	I	SAH	PC
1217 (3357, 6444)	I	SAOL	ZH
1218 (3332)	I	SAOL	Long Marston
1219 (3418)	I	SAH	PC
1220 (3315, 6432)	I	SAH	PC
1221 (3371)	I	SAH	MA
1250 (3372)	I	SAH	MA
1251 (3383)	I	SAH	MA
1252 (3280)	I	SAH	PC
1253 (3432)	I	SAH	MA
1254 (3391)	I	SAH	PC
1255 (3284)	I	SAH	MA
1256 (3296)	I	SAH	MA
1258 (3322)	I	SAH	PC
1259 (3439)	I	SAH	MA
1260 (3378)	I	SAH	PC

AK51(RKB)   KITCHEN BUFFET

Dia. AK502. Mark 1. Gas Cooking. No seats. B5 bogies. a. ETH 1.

Lot No. 30624 Cravens 1960 – 1. 41 t.

1566	G	XVSZ	SL	I

AJ41 (RBR)   RESTAURANT BUFFET

Dia. AJ403. Mark 1. Gas cooking. Built with 23 loose chairs (dia. AJ402). All remaining vehicles refurbished with 23 (21 w) fixed polypropylene chairs and fluorescent lighting. ETH 2 (2X*).

r Further refurbished with 21 chairs, payphone, wheelchair space and carpets (Dia. AJ417).

1644 – 1699. Lot No. 30628 Pressed Steel 1960 – 61. Commonwealth bogies. 39 t.
1730. Lot No. 30512 BRCW 1960 – 61. B5 bogies. 37 t.

1644 a	I	MPNW	Ferme Park
1645 a	I	XWRZ	BN
1646 a	I	XWRZ	BQ
1647 a	I	SAOL	Long Marston
1649 aw	I	SAXZ	BN
1650 aw	I	MPNW	Ferme Park
1652 aw	I	MPNW	Ferme Park
1653 aw	I	XWR	BN
1655 a	I	MPNW	Carlisle Yard
1658 a	I	XWR	BN
1659 a	I	XWRZ	BN
1663 x*	I	MPNW	Ferme Park
1666 x*	I	MPNW	Ferme Park
1667 x	I	XWR	BN
1670 x*w	I	MPNW	Ferme Park
1671 x*	I	XWR	BN
1672 x*	I	MPNW	Ferme Park
1673 aw	I	SAXZ	BN
1674 a	I	XWR	BN
1675 x*	I	XWRZ	BN
1678 x*	M	XWR	BN
1679 a	I	XWR	BN
1680 x*w	WV	XWR	BN
1683 x	I	SAS	NC
1684 x*	I	MPNW	Carlisle Yard
1686 ar	I	SAOL	Long Marston
1688 aw	I	MPNW	Ferme Park
1689 ar	I	SAOL	Long Marston
1691 ar	I	SAS	NC
1692 ar	I	SAOL	Long Marston
1693 x*	I	XWR	BN
1696 a	G	XWRZ	Ferme Park
1697 ar	I	SAS	NC
1698 a	I	XWRZ	BN
1699 ar	I	SAS	NC
1730 x	M	XSC	BQ

AN21 (RMB)   MINIATURE BUFFET CAR

Dia. AN203. Mark 1. Gas cooking. – /44 2T. These vehicles are basically an open standard with two full window spaces removed to accommodate a buffet counter, and four seats removed to allow for a stock cupboard. All remaining vehicles now have fluorescent lighting. All vehicles have Commonwealth bogies except 1850 (B5). ETH 3 (3X*).

1813 – 1832. Lot No. 30520 Wolverton 1960. 38 t.
1842 – 1850. Lot No. 30507 Wolverton 1960. 37 t (1850 is 36 t).
1853 – 1863. Lot No. 30670 Wolverton 1961 – 2. 38 t.
1866 – 1882. Lot No. 30702 Wolverton 1962. 38 t.

1842/50/71 have been been refurbished and are fitted with a microwave oven and payphone. Dia. AN208.

1813 x	CC	XWR	BN
1816 x*		XWRZ	BQ
1832 x	I	XWR	HT
1842 x	I	SAS	NC
1850 a	I	SAS	NC
1853 x	I	XWR	BN
1859 x	M	XSC	BO
1860 x	I	XCRZ	CS
1861 x	M	XWR	BN
1863 x	M	XRP	CO
1871 x	I	SAS	NC
1882 x	M	XCR	CS

AJ41 (RBR)   RESTAURANT BUFFET

Dia. AJ414. Mark 1. Gas cooking. These vehicles were built as unclassified restaurant (RU). All remaining vehicles were rebuilt with buffet counter and 21 fixed polypropylene chairs (RBS). They were then further refurbished by fitting fluorescent lighting and reclassified RBR. a. w. ETH 2 (2X*).

1953 – 1954. Lot No. 30575 Ashford/Eastleigh 1960. B4/B5 bogies. 36.5 t.
1966 – 1984. Lot No. 30632 Ashford/Eastleigh 1960 – 61. Commonwealth bogies. 39 t.

1953 *	I	XVSZ	SL	1971	I	SAXZ	Ferme Park
1954	I	SAXZ	Norwich Goods	1972		SAXZ	Ferme Park
1966	I	SAXZ	Ferme Park	1984		SAXZ	Ferme Park

AS41 FIRST CLASS SLEEPING CAR

Dia. AU101. Mark 1. Pressure Ventilated. 11 single-berth compartments plus an attendant's compartment with gas cooking. a. ETH 3 (3X*).

2013. Lot No. 30159 Wolverton 1958. B5 bogies. 39 t.
2127. Lot No. 30687 Wolverton 1961. Commonwealth bogies. 41 t.

Note: 2013 was numbered 2908 for a time when in use with the Royal Train.

2013	**M**	XWRZ	SO	2127 *	**M**	XGS	EN

AU51 CHARTER TRAIN STAFF COACHES

Dia. AU501. Mark 1. Converted from BCKs. ETH 2.

Lot No. 30732 Derby 1964. Commonwealth bogies. a. 37 t.

2833 (21270)	I	XWR	BN	2834 (21267)	**WV**	XWR	BN

AT5 ROYAL SALOONS

Non-standard livery: All Royal vehicles are in Royal purple.

AT5G. The Queen's Saloon.

Dia. AT525. Mark 3. Converted from a mark 3 FO built 1972. Consists of a lounge, bedroom and bathroom for the Queen, and a combined bedroom and bathroom for the Queen's dresser. One entrance vestibule has double doors. Air conditioned. a. BT10 bogies.

Lot No. 30886 Wolverton 1977. ETH 9X. 36 t.

2903 (11001)	**0**	MC	ZN

AT5G. The Duke of Edinburgh's Saloon.

Dia. AT526. Mark 3. Converted from a mark 3 TSO built 1972. Consists of a combined lounge/dining room, a bedroom and a shower room for the Duke, a kitchen and a valet's bedroom and bathroom. Air conditioned. a. BT10 bogies.

Lot No. 30887 Wolverton 1977. ETH 15X. 36 t.

2904 (12001)	**0**	MC	ZN

AT5B. Staff Couchette/Power Brake.

Dia. AT527. Mark 2B. Converted from a Mk. 2B BFK built 1969. Consists of luggage accommodation, guard's compartment, 350 kW diesel generator and Staff sleeping accommodation. Pressure ventilated. a. B5 bogies.

Lot No. 30888 Wolverton 1977. ETH 5X. 46 t.

| 2905 (14105) | **0** | MC | ZN |

AT5B. Staff Couchette.

Dia. AT528. Mark 2B. Converted from a Mk. 2B BFK built 1969. Pressure ventilated. a. B5 bogies.

Lot No. 30889 Wolverton 1977. ETH 4X. 35.5 t.

| 2906 (14112) | **0** | MC | ZN |

AT5G. Royal Train Staff Sleeping Cars.

Dia. AT531. Mark 3A Details as for 10646 – 732 except that controlled emission toilets are not fitted. ETH11X.

Lot No. 31002 Derby/Wolverton 1985. 42.5 t 2915 is 44 t.

| 2914 (2914) | **0** | MC | ZN |
| 2915 (2915) | **0** | MC | ZN |

AT5G Royal Dining Car.

Lot No. 31059 Wolverton 1988. Converted from HST TRUK. Dia. AT537.

| 2916 (40512) | **0** | MC | ZN |

AT5G Royal Vehicles. Converted from HST TRUKs.

Lot Nos. 31084 Wolverton 1990. Dia. AT539. 43 t. ETH13X.

| 2917 (40514) | **0** | MC | ZN |

Lot Nos. 31083 Wolverton 1989. Dia. AT538. 41.05 t. ETH10X.

| 2918 (40515) | **0** | MC | ZN |

Lot Nos. 31085 Wolverton 1989. Dia. AT540.

| 2919 (40518) | **0** | MC | ZN |

AT5B. Royal Train Staff/Generator Vehicle. Dia. AT536. Mark 2B. B5 bogies. 48 t. ETH2X.

Lot Nos. 31044 Wolverton 1986.

| 2920 (14109, 17109) | **0** | MC | ZN |

AT5B. Royal Staff Couchette. Dia. AT541. Mark 2B. Converted from BFK. B4 bogies. Dia. AT541. 41.5 t. ETH7X.

Lot No. 31086 Wolverton 1990.

| 2921 (14107, 17107) | **0** | MC | ZN |

AT5G. Royal Sleeping Car.

Lot No. 31035 Derby/Wolverton 1987. Dia. AT534.

| 2922 (2922) | **0** | MC | ZN |

AT5G. The Prince of Wales's Saloon.

Lot No. 31036 Derby/Wolverton 1987. Dia. AT535.

2923 (2923)   **0**   MC   ZN

AD11 (FO)   OPEN FIRST

Dia. AD103. Mark 1. 42/– 2T. ETH 3. d. Many now fitted with table lights.

3063 – 3069. Lot No. 30169 Doncaster 1955. B4 bogies. 33 t.
3096 – 3100. Lot No. 30576 BRCW 1959. B4 bogies. 33 t.

3063 a		XVSZ	SL		3096 x	**M**	XSC	BO
3064 a		XVSZ	SL		3097 a	**WV**	XWR	BN
3066 a	**G**	XVS	SL		3098 a	**I**	XWRZ	Crewe Coal S
3068 a	**G**	XVS	SL		3100 x	**CC**	XWR	BN
3069 a	**G**	XVS	SL					

Later design with fluorescent lighting, aluminium window frames and Commonwealth bogies.

3105 – 3128. Lot No. 30697 Swindon 1962 – 3. 36 t.
3130 – 3150. Lot No. 30717 Swindon 1963. 36 t.

Note: 3128/35/6/41/3/4/6/7/8 were renumbered 1058/9/60/3/5/6/8/9/70 when reclassified RUO, then 3600/1/5/8/9/2/6/4/10 when declassified, but have now regained their original numbers.

3105 x	**M**	XCR	CS	3127 a	**I**	XWR	BN
3106 x	**M**	XWRZ	Basford Hall	3128 x	**M**	XCR	CS
3107 x	**I**	XWR	BN	3130 v	**M**	XCRZ	CS
3109 x	**I**	XWRZ	Basford Hall	3131 x	**M**	XWR	BN
3110 x	**CC**	XWR	BN	3132 x	**M**	XWR	BN
3111 x	**I**	XWR	BN	3133 x	**M**	XWR	BN
3112 x	**M**	XWRZ	Basford Hall	3134 x	**I**	XWR	BN
3113 x	**M**	XCR	CS	3135 a	**I**	SAXZ	BN
3114 a	**I**	XWR	BN	3136 a	**I**	XWR	BN
3115 x	**I**	XWR	BN	3140 x	**I**	XWR	BN
3117 x	**M**	XCR	CS	3141 a	**I**	XWR	BN
3118 x	**I**	XWR	BN	3143 a	**I**	XWR	BN
3119 x	**I**	XWR	BN	3144 x	**CC**	XWR	BN
3120 a	**I**	XWR	BN	3146 a	**I**	XWR	BN
3121 a	**WV**	XWR	BN	3147 a	**WV**	XWR	BN
3123 a	**I**	XWR	BN	3148 a	**I**	XWR	BN
3124 a	**I**	XWRZ	BN	3149 a	**I**	XWR	BN
3125 v	**M**	XRFZ	CS	3150 a	**I**	XWR	BN

AD1D (FO)   OPEN FIRST

Dia. AD105. Mark 2D. Air conditioned. 3172 – 88 have Stones equipment. 3192/3202 have Temperature Ltd and require at least 800 V train heating supply. 42/– 2T. B4 bogies. a. ETH 5.

Lot No. 30821 Derby 1971 – 2. 32.5 t.

3172	I	XWRZ	DY		3186	I	XWRZ	DY
3174	I	XWRZ	BN		3187	I	MPNW	Carlisle Yard
3178	I	XWRZ	DY		3188	I	XWRZ	DY
3181	I	XWRZ	BN		3192	I	MPNW	Carlisle Yard
3182	I	XWRZ	DY		3202	I	MPNW	Carlisle Yard

AD1E (FO)   OPEN FIRST

Dia. AD106. Mark 2E. Air conditioned. Stones equipment. Require at least 800 V train heating supply. 42/– 2T (41/– 2T w). B4 bogies. a. ETH 5.

* Seats removed to accommodate catering module. 40F 1T.
§ Fitted with power supply for Mk. 1 RBR.

Lot No. 30843 Derby 1972 – 3. 32.5 t.

3221 w	I	SAOL	Long Marston		3248	I	XWRZ	DY
3223	I	XWRZ	Long Marston		3249 *	I	SAOL	BN
3224	I	XWRZ	BN		3250 w	I	XWRZ	Ferme Park
3225	I	MPNW	Kineton		3251 w*	I	XWRZ	Ferme Park
3226	I	MPNW	Kineton		3252 w	I	SAOL	Long Marston
3227	I	XWRZ	BN		3256 w	I	SAOL	Long Marston
3228 d §	I	SAOL	Long Marston		3257 w	I	XWRZ	Ferme Park
3229 d	I	SAOL	Long Marston		3258 n	I	MPNW	Kineton
3230	I	XWRZ	DY		3259 dw*	I	SAOL	BN
3231	I	XWRZ	Ferme Park		3260	I	XCRZ	CS
3232 dw	I	SAOL	Long Marston		3261 dw	I	SAOL	Longtown
3233		MPNW	Kineton		3262	I	XWRZ	BN
3234 w	I	XWRZ	Ferme Park		3263	I	XWRZ	BN
3235 §	I	SAOL	Long Marston		3265	I	XWRZ	BN
3237	I	XWRZ	BN		3266 §	I	XWRZ	DY
3239	I	XWRZ	BN		3267	I	XWRZ	BN
3240	I	XWRZ	BN		3268	I	XWRZ	Kineton
3241	I	SAOL	Long Marston		3269 d	I	SAOL	Long Marston
3242 w §	I	SAOL	Long Marston		3270	I	XWRZ	BN
3244 dw	I	SAOL	Long Marston		3272	I	XWRZ	BN
3245	I	MPNW	Kineton		3273	I	XWRZ	Crewe Coal Sd
3246 w	I	XWRZ	BN		3275	I	XWRZ	BN
3247	I	XWRZ	Ferme Park					

AD1F (FO)   OPEN FIRST

Dia. AD107. Mark 2F. Air conditioned. 3277 – 3318/58 – 81 have Stones equipment, others have Temperature Ltd. 42/– 2T. All now refurbished with power-operated vestibule doors, new panels and new seat trim. B4 bogies. a. Secondary door locks. ETH 5X.

3277 – 3318. Lot No. 30845 Derby 1973. 33 t.
3325 – 3428. Lot No. 30859 Derby 1973 – 4. 33 t.
3429 – 3438. Lot No. 30873 Derby 1974 – 5. 33 t.

§ Fitted with power supply for Mk. 1 RBR.

3277	I	SAS	NC	3362	I	SAF	OY
3278	I	SAF	OY	3363	I	SAF	OY
3279 §	I	SAS	NC	3364	I	SAF	OY
3285	I	SAF	OY	3366	I	SAF	OY
3290	I	SAS	NC	3368	I	SAS	NC
3292	I	SAS	NC	3369	I	SAF	OY
3293	I	SAF	OY	3373	I	SAF	OY
3295	I	SAS	NC	3374	I	SAF	OY
3299	I	SAF	OY	3375	I	SAS	NC
3300	I	SAF	OY	3379 §	I	SAS	NC
3303	I	SAS	NC	3381	I	SAF	OY
3304	I	SAF	OY	3384	I	SAF	OY
3309	I	SAS	NC	3385	I	SAF	OY
3312	I	SAF	OY	3386	I	SAF	OY
3313	I	SAF	OY	3387	I	SAF	OY
3314	I	SAF	OY	3388	I	SAS	NC
3318	I	SAS	NC	3389	I	SAF	OY
3325	I	SAF	OY	3390	I	SAF	OY
3326	I	SAF	OY	3392	I	SAF	OY
3330	I	SAF	OY	3395	I	SAF	OY
3331	I	SAS	NC	3397	I	SAF	OY
3333	I	SAF	OY	3399 §	I	SAS	NC
3334	I	SAS	NC	3400	I	SAS	NC
3336 §	I	SAS	NC	3402	I	SAF	OY
3337	I	SAF	OY	3403	I	SAF	OY
3338 §	I	SAS	NC	3408	I	SAF	OY
3340	I	SAF	OY	3411	I	SAF	OY
3344	I	SAF	OY	3414	I	SAS	NC
3345	I	SAF	OY	3416	I	SAS	NC
3348	I	SAF	OY	3417	I	SAS	NC
3350	I	SAF	OY	3424	I	SAS	NC
3351	I	SAS	NC	3425	I	SAF	OY
3352	I	SAF	OY	3426	I	SAF	OY
3353	I	SAF	OY	3428	I	SAF	OY
3354	I	SAF	OY	3429	I	SAF	OY
3356	I	SAF	OY	3431	I	SAF	OY
3358	I	SAS	NC	3433	I	SAF	OY
3359	I	SAF	OY	3434	I	SAF	OY
3360	I	SAF	OY	3438	I	SAF	OY

AG1E (FOt)   OPEN FIRST (PANTRY)

Dia. AG101. Mark 2E. Air conditioned. Converted from FO. Fitted with pantry, microwave oven and payphone for use on sleeping car services. 36/– 1T. B4 bogies. a. Secondary door locks. ETH 5X.

Lot No. 30843 Derby 1972 – 3. 32.5 t.

3520 (3253)	I	SAJ	LA	3523 (3238)	I	SAA	IS
3521 (3271)	I	SAJ	LA	3524 (3254)	I	SAA	IS
3522 (3236)	I	SAJ	LA	3525 (3255)	I	SAA	IS

AC21 (TSO)   OPEN STANDARD

Dia. AC204. Mark 1. This vehicle has 2 + 2 seating and is classified TSO ('Tourist second open' – a former LNER designation). It has narrower seats than later vehicles. − /64 2T. x. ETH 4.

Lot No. 30079 York 1953. Commonwealth bogies. 36 t.

| 3766 | M | XCR | CS | |

AC21 (TSO)   OPEN STANDARD

Dia. AC201. Mark 1. These vehicles are a development of Dia. AC204 with fluorescent lighting and modified design of seat headrest. − /64 2T. d. ETH 4.

4831 − 4836. Lot No. 30506 Wolverton 1959. Commonwealth (BR1*) bogies. k. 33 t.
4842 − 4891. Lot No. 30525 Wolverton 1959 − 60. B4 bogies. 33 t.

4831 x		M	XSC	BO		4860 x B4	M	XWRZ	Bristol K.Rd.
4832 x*		M	XSC	BO		4866 x	RR	SAD	LL
4836 x		M	XSC	BO		4869 x	I	XWR	BN
4842 x		I	XWRZ	BN		4873 x	RR	SAD	LL
4849 x		RR	SAD	LL		4875 x	RR	SAD	LL
4854 x		RR	SAD	LL		4876 x	RR	SAD	LL
4856 x		M	XSC	BO		4880 x	RR	SAD	LL
4858 x		I	MPNW	Carlisle Yard		4891 v C	N	XWRZ	Basford Hall

Lot No. 30646 Wolverton 1961. Built with Commonwealth bogies, but BR1 bogies substituted by the SR on 4902/5/9/10/12/15/16. All now re-rebogied. 34 t B4, 36 t C.

4902 x B4	I	MPNW	BN		4912 x C	M	XCRK	BK
4905 x	M	XWR	BN		4915 x B4	W	XWR	BN
4909 x B4	I	XWR	BN		4916 x B4	I	XWR	BN
4910 v C	M	XWR	BN		4917 x C	RR	SAD	LL

These two lots have Commonwealth bogies and aluminium window frames. 37 t. Note: 4923/89 have BR2 bogies substituted and weigh 35.5 t.
4923 − 5044. Lot No. 30690 Wolverton 1961 − 2.
5067. Lot No. 30724 York 1963. Converted to 'LMS Club Car'.

4923 v	M	XWRZ	Basford Hall		4951 v	M	XWR	BN
4925 v	I	XWR	HT		4954 v	M	XCR	CS
4927 a	I	XWRZ	Basford Hall		4956 a	I	XWR	HT
4930 a	I	XWRZ	Basford Hall		4958 v		XCRZ	CS
4931 v		XCR	CS		4959 a	I	XWR	BN
4932 v	M	XCRZ	CS		4960 v	M	XWR	BN
4936 v	M	MPNW	Fort William		4961 a	I	XWRZ	Basford Hall
4938 a	M	XWR	BN		4963 x	CH	XTS	CM
4939 a	I	XWR	HT		4966 a	I	XWRZ	Basford Hall
4940 v	M	XWR	BN		4973 v	M	XWR	BN
4946 x	CC	XWR	BN		4977 a	I	XWR	BN
4949 a	I	XWR	HT		4979 a	I	XWRZ	Basford Hall

4980 v	N	XWRZ	Basford Hall
4984 v	M	XWR	BN
4986 a	I	XWR	BN
4989 v	N	XWRZ	Basford Hall
4991 a	W	XWR	HT
4993 a	I	XWR	HT
4994 v	M	XWR	BN
4996 x	CC	XWR	BN
4997 v		XCRZ	CS
4998 a	I	XWR	BN
4999 a	I	XWR	BN
5001 a	I	SAXZ	Long Marston
5002 a	W	XWR	HT
5005 a	W	XWR	BN
5007 a	I	XWR	BN
5008 x	CC	XWR	BN
5009 a	I	XRPZ	CO

5010 a	I	XWRZ	Carlisle Yard
5023 a	I	XWR	BN
5025 x	CH	XTS	CO
5027 a	I	XWR	HT
5028 x	M	XSCZ	BO
5029 x	CH	XTS	CO
5030 x	CH	XTS	CM
5032 x	M	XWRZ	Bristol K.Rd.
5033 x	M	XCRK	BK
5035 x	M	XWRZ	Bristol K.Rd.
5037 a	I	XWR	HT
5038 x	I	MPNW	BN
5040 x	I	XWRZ	Carlisle Yard
5041 a	I	XWRZ	Carlisle Yard
5042 x	I	XWR	BN
5044 x	M	XCRK	BK
5067	M	XRF	CS

AC2Z (TSO)   OPEN STANDARD

Dia. AC205. Mark 2. Pressure ventilated. – /64 2T. B4 bogies. v. ETH 4.

Lot No. 30751 Derby 1965 – 7. 32 t.

5132	H	SAOL	Longtown
5133	RR	SAOL	Longtown
5135	RR	SAOL	Longtown
5138	RR	SAOL	Longtown
5139	H	SAOL	Longtown
5148	RR	SAOL	Longtown
5154	H	SAOL	Longtown
5156	RR	SAOL	Longtown
5157	RR	SAOL	Longtown
5158	RR	SAOL	Longtown
5159	RR	SAOL	Longtown
5161	RR	SAOL	Longtown
5163	RR	SAOL	Longtown
5166	H	SAOL	Longtown
5167	RR	SAOL	Longtown
5173	RR	SAOL	Longtown
5174	RR	SAOL	Longtown
5175	N	XWRZ	CP
5177	RR	SAOL	Longtown
5179	RR	SAOL	Longtown

5180	RR	SAOL	Longtown
5183	RR	SAOL	Longtown
5184	RR	SAOL	Longtown
5186	RR	SAOL	Longtown
5191	H	SAOL	Longtown
5193	H	SAOL	Longtown
5194	RR	SAOL	Longtown
5198	RR	SAOL	Longtown
5199	N	XWRZ	BQ
5207	RR	SAOL	Longtown
5209	RR	SAOL	Longtown
5210	RR	SAOL	Longtown
5212	H	SAOL	Longtown
5213	RR	SAOL	Longtown
5216	N	XWRZ	BQ
5221	RR	SAOL	Longtown
5224	N	XCRZ	CS
5225	RR	SAOL	Longtown
5226	RR	SAOL	Longtown

Named vehicles:

5132 CLAN MUNRO	5191 CLAN DONALD
5139 CLAN ROSS	5193 CLAN MACLEOD
5154 CLAN FRASER	5212 CAPERKAILZIE
5166 CLAN MACKENZIE	

AD2Z (SO)   OPEN STANDARD

Dia. AD203. Mark 2. Pressure ventilated. −/48 2T. B4 bogies. a. ETH 4.

Lot No. 30752 Derby 1966. 32 t.

| 5254 | SAXZ | DY | 5255 | XCRZ | CS |

AC2A (TSO)   OPEN STANDARD

Dia. AC206. Mark 2A. Pressure ventilated. −/64 2T (−/62 2T w). B4 bogies. a. ETH 4.

5259 – 5345. Lot No. 30776 Derby 1967 – 8. 32 t.
5350 – 5433. Lot No. 30787 Derby 1968. 32 t.

5259	RR	SAXZ	LL		5337		SAOL	Long Marston
5264	RR	SAXZ	Long Marston		5341	RR	SAD	LL
5265	RR	SAOL	Westbury		5345	RR	SAD	LL
5266	RR	SAOL	Long Marston		5350	NR	SAOL	Crewe S. Yd.
5267	RR	SAOL	BK		5353	RR	SAOL	Long Marston
5271	RR	SAOL	Long Marston		5354	RR	SAOL	BK
5272	RR	SAOL	Long Marston		5364	RR	SAK	Westbury
5275	RR	SAD	LL		5365	RR	SAD	LL
5276	RR	SAD	LL		5366	RR	SAD	LL
5277		SAOL	Long Marston		5373	RR	SAD	LL
5278	RR	SAD	LL		5376	NR	SAK	BK
5279		SAOL	Long Marston		5378	NR	SAK	Crewe S. Yard
5282	RR	SAOL	Long Marston		5379	RR	SAXZ	Long Marston
5290	NR	SAXZ	Long Marston		5381 w		SAD	LL
5291	RR	SAOL	ZF		5384	N	SAOL	Long Marston
5292	NR	SAOL	Long Marston		5386 w	RR	SAD	LL
5293	NR	SAOL	Long Marston		5389 w	RR	SAD	LL
5299	N	XCR	CS		5392		SAOL	Long Marston
5300		SAOL	Long Marston		5393	RR	SAOL	Long Marston
5304	RR	SAOL	Long Marston		5396	RR	SAK	BK
5307	RR	SAD	LL		5401	RR	SAOL	Long Marston
5309	RR	SAD	LL		5410	N	SAXZ	Long Marston
5314		SAOL	Long Marston		5412 w	RR	SAD	LL
5316	RR	SAD	LL		5414	RR	SAXZ	LL
5322	RR	SAD	LL		5419 w	RR	SAD	LL
5323	RR	SAXZ	Long Marston		5420 w	RR	SAD	LL
5331	RR	SAD	LL		5432	RR	SAXZ	LL
5335	RR	SAD	LL		5433 w	RR	SAD	LL

AC2B (TSO)   OPEN STANDARD

Dia. AC207. Mark 2B. Pressure ventilated. −/62 2T. B4 bogies. a. ETH 4.

Lot No. 30791 Derby 1969. 32 t.

| 5439 | N | SAXZ | Long Marston | | 5446 | N | SAXZ | Long Marston |
| 5443 | N | SAXZ | Long Marston | | 5447 | N | SAXZ | Long Marston |

5449	N	XWRZ	Basford Hall
5450	N	SAXZ	Long Marston
5453	RR	XCRZ	CS
5454	N	SAXZ	Long Marston
5456	N	SAXZ	Longtown
5462	N	XWRZ	Basford Hall
5463	M	XCRK	BK
5464	N	XWRZ	Basford Hall
5468	N	SAXZ	Longtown

5471	N	SAXZ	Long Marston
5472	N	SAXZ	Long Marston
5475	N	SAXZ	Long Marston
5478		XCRZ	CS
5480	N	SAXZ	Long Marston
5487	M	XCRK	BK
5491	RR	XCRZ	CS
5494	N	XWRZ	Basford Hall

AC2B (TSO)   OPEN STANDARD

Dia. AC208. Mark 2C. Pressure ventilated. –/62 2T. B4 bogies. a. ETH 4.

Lot No. 30795 Derby 1969 – 70. 32 t.

5505	RR	XCRZ	CS
5520	RR	SAXZ	Norwich Goods
5554	RR	SAXZ	Long Marston

5569	M	XCRK	BK
5600	M	XCR	CS
5614	RR	SAXZ	Long Marston

AC2D (TSO)   OPEN STANDARD

Dia. AC209. Mark 2D. Air conditioned. Stones (5653 has Temperature Ltd.) equipment. –/62 2T. B4 bogies. a. ETH 5.

Non-Standard Livery: Waterman VIP without lining.

Lot No. 30822 Derby 1971. 33 t.

5616	I	XWRZ	BN
5617	I	MPNW	Long Marston
5618	I	SAOL	Long Marston
5620	I	SAOL	Longtown
5623	I	SAOL	Longtown
5624	I	SAOL	Long Marston
5625	I	SAOL	Long Marston
5626 d	I	SAOL	Long Marston
5628	I	SAOL	Long Marston
5629	I	SAOL	Longtown
5630	0	XWRL	BK
5631 d	I	SAOL	Long Marston
5632 d	I	SAOL	Long Marston
5633	I	MPNW	Long Marston
5634	I	SAOL	Long Marston
5636 d	I	SAOL	Long Marston
5637	I	MPNW	Long Marston
5638	I	SAOL	Longtown
5639	I	SAXZ	ABB Crewe Wks
5640	I	SAXZ	Longtown
5642	I	XCRZ	CS
5645	I	XCRZ	CS
5646 d	I	SAOL	Long Marston
5647	0	XWRL	BK

5648	I	MPNW	Long Marston
5650	I	SAOL	Longtown
5651	I	SAOL	Long Marston
5652 d	I	SAOL	Long Marston
5653 d	I	SAOL	Longtown
5654 d	I	SAOL	Long Marston
5657	I	SAOL	Long Marston
5658	I	SAOL	Longtown
5659	I	SAXZ	PC
5660	I	SAOL	Long Marston
5661	I	SAOL	Kineton
5662	I	SAOL	Long Marston
5663	I	SAOL	Kineton
5665	I	SAOL	Long Marston
5669 d	I	SAOL	Longtown
5670	I	SAXZ	ZN
5671 d	I	SAOL	Longtown
5673 d	I	SAOL	PC
5674	I	SAOL	Kineton
5675	I	MPNW	Long Marston
5676 d	I	SAOL	Long Marston
5679 d	I	SAOL	Long Marston
5682 d	I	SAOL	Long Marston
5685	I	SAOL	Long Marston

5686	I	SAOL	Long Marston	5717	I	SAOL	Kineton
5687	I	SAOL	Kineton	5718	I	SAOL	Kineton
5689	I	XWRZ	BN	5719	I	SAOL	Long Marston
5690	I	SAOL	Longtown	5722	I	MPNW	Carlisle Yard
5692	I	SAOL	Long Marston	5723	I	SAOL	Longtown
5693	I	SAOL	Long Marston	5724	I	SAOL	Longtown
5694	I	SAOL	Kineton	5726	I	SAOL	Long Marston
5695	I	SAOL	Long Marston	5727	M	XCR	CS
5699	I	SAOL	Kineton	5728	I	SAOL	Long Marston
5700 d	I	SAOL	Long Marston	5729	I	XWRZ	Long Marston
5701	I	SAOL	Kineton	5730	I	SAOL	Long Marston
5703 d	I	SAOL	Long Marston	5731	I	SAOL	Kineton
5704	M	XCR	CS	5732	0	XWRL	BK
5705	I	SAOL	Long Marston	5734	I	SAOL	ZN
5709	I	XCRZ	CS	5735	I	SAOL	Long Marston
5710 d	I	SAOL	Long Marston	5737 d	I	SAOL	Long Marston
5711	I	SAOL	Longtown	5738	I	SAOL	Kineton
5712	I	XCRZ	CS	5739	0	XWRL	BK
5714	M	XCR	CS	5740 d	I	SAOL	Long Marston
5715	I	SAOL	Longtown	5743	I	SAOL	Longtown
5716	I	SAOL	Kineton				

AC2E (TSO) OPEN STANDARD

Dia. AC210. Mark 2E. Air conditioned. Stones equipment. −/64 2T (−/62 2T w). B4 bogies. Require at least 800 V train heat supply. a. ETH 5.

5744 – 5803. Lot No. 30837 Derby 1972. 33.5 t.
5810 – 5907. Lot No. 30844 Derby 1972 – 3. 33.5 t.

5744	I	SAH	PC	5773 d	I	SAH	PC
5745 d	I	SAH	PC	5775 d	I	SAH	PC
5746 d	I	SAH	MA	5776 d	I	SAH	PC
5747	I	XWR	DY	5777	I	XWRZ	DY
5748 dw	I	SAH	PC	5778 dw	I	SAH	PC
5750 d	I	SAH	PC	5779	I	SAH	MA
5751 dw	I	SAOL	ZD	5780 dw	I	SAH	PC
5752 dw	I	SAH	PC	5781 dw	I	SAH	PC
5754 dw	I	SAH	MA	5784 d	I	SAH	MA
5755	I	XWR	DY	5785	I	SAOL	Kineton
5756	M	XCR	CS	5786	I	SAXZ	IMI Witton
5759	I	XWRZ	DY	5787 d	I	SAH	PC
5760	I	SAOL	ZN	5788 dw	I	SAH	PC
5761	W	XWR	DY	5789 d	I	SAH	MA
5762	I	XWRZ	DY	5791 dw	I	SAH	MA
5763	I	SAOL	Kineton	5792 d	I	SAH	PC
5764 d	I	SAOL	Longtown	5793 d	I	SAH	PC
5766	I	SAOL	Longtown	5794 dw	I	SAH	MA
5768	I	SAOL	Kineton	5795	I	SAOL	Kineton
5769 d	I	SAH	MA	5796 dw	I	SAH	MA
5770	I	XWR	DY	5797 d	I	SAH	PC
5772 dw	I	SAOL	ZN	5799 d	I	SAOL	ZD

5800	W	XWR	DY
5801 d	I	SAH	MA
5803	I	XWR	DY
5810 d	I	SAH	PC
5811	I	XWRZ	DY
5812 dw	I	SAH	PC
5814 d	I	SAH	PC
5815	I	SAH	PC
5816 d	I	SAH	PC
5818	I	XWR	DY
5820	I	XWR	DY
5821 d	I	SAH	MA
5822 d	I	SAH	MA
5824 dw	I	SAH	MA
5826 d	I	SAOL	ZN
5827 dw	I	SAH	MA
5828 dw	I	SAH	MA
5829	I	XWR	DY
5831	I	XWR	DY
5832	I	SAXZ	ZC
5833 d	I	SAH	PC
5834	I	SAOL	Kineton
5835	I	XWR	DY
5836	I	XWR	DY
5837	I	XWR	DY
5838	I	SAOL	Kineton
5840 d	I	SAOL	ZD
5842 w	I	XWR	DY
5843 dw	I	SAH	DY
5844	I	SAOL	ZN
5845 dw	I	SAH	MA
5847 dw	I	SAH	MA
5849	I	SAOL	Kineton
5851	I	SAOL	ZD
5852	W	XWR	DY
5853 d	I	SAOL	Longtown
5854 d	I	SAH	MA
5859 d	I	SAH	MA
5860 w	W	XWR	DY
5861	I	XWR	DY
5863	I	XWR	DY
5866 d	I	SAH	MA
5868 d	I	SAH	MA
5869 d	I	SAOL	Long Marston
5870	I	SAOL	Kineton
5871 d	I	SAOL	ZN
5873	I	XWR	DY
5874 w	I	SAOL	Long Marston
5875 d	I	SAOL	Longtown
5876 d	I	SAH	PC
5878	I	XWRZ	DY
5879	I	MPNW	Long Marston
5881 d	I	SAH	PC
5883	W	XWR	DY
5884	I	SAOL	ZC
5885	I	SAOL	Crewe Coal S.
5886 d	I	SAH	PC
5887 dw	I	SAH	MA
5888 dw	I	SAH	MA
5889 d	I	SAH	MA
5890 d	I	SAOL	ZD
5891	I	XWR	DY
5892 d	I	SAOL	Long Marston
5893 d	I	SAH	MA
5897 d	I	SAH	MA
5899 d	I	SAH	PC
5900 d	I	SAH	PC
5901 d	I	SAH	PC
5902	I	SAH	PC
5903	I	SAH	MA
5904	I	SAOL	PC
5905 d	I	SAH	PC
5906 d	I	SAH	MA
5907	I	SAOL	Longtown

AC2F (TSO)   OPEN STANDARD

Dia. AC211. Mark 2F. Air conditioned. Temperature Ltd. equipment. – /64 2T.
Inter-City 70 seats. All now refurbished with power-operated vestibule doors,
new panels and new seat trim. B4 bogies. a. Secondary door locks. ETH 5X.

* – Early Mark 2 style seats.

5908 – 5958. Lot No. 30846 Derby 1973. 33 t.
5959 – 6170. Lot No. 30860 Derby 1973 – 4. 33 t.
6171 – 6184. Lot No. 30874 Derby 1974 – 5. 33 t.

w Wheelchair space. – /62 2T.

5908	I	SAF	OY		5963	I	SAF	OY
5910 w	I	SAF	OY		5964	I	SAS	NC
5911	I	SAH	MA		5965 w	I	SAH	DY
5912	I	SAH	DY		5966	I	SAS	NC
5913	I	SAH	DY		5967 w	I	SAH	MA
5914	I	SAF	OY		5968	I	SAS	NC
5915	I	SAF	OY		5969 w	I	SAF	OY
5916 w	I	SAH	DY		5971	I	SAH	MA
5917	I	SAH	DY		5973	I	SAS	NC
5918 w	I	SAH	DY		5975 *	I	SAH	PC
5919	I	SAH	PC		5976 w	I	SAH	MA
5920	I	SAF	OY		5977	I	SAF	OY
5921	I	SAS	NC		5978 *	I	SAF	OY
5922	I	SAS	NC		5980	I	SAF	OY
5924	I	SAS	NC		5981	I	SAH	MA
5925 w	I	SAH	PC		5983	I	SAH	DY
5926	I	SAS	NC		5984 *	I	SAF	OY
5927	I	SAS	NC		5985	I	SAS	NC
5928	I	SAS	NC		5986	I	SAF	OY
5929	I	SAS	NC		5987 *	I	SAF	OY
5930 w	I	SAH	PC		5988 w	I	SAF	OY
5931 w	I	SAF	OY		5989 w	I	SAH	MA
5932	I	SAF	OY		5991	I	SAH	MA
5933	I	SAF	OY		5993 *w	I	SAS	NC
5934	I	SAF	OY		5994 *	I	SAH	MA
5935	I	SAS	NC		5995	I	SAH	DY
5936	I	SAS	NC		5996	I	SAH	MA
5937	I	SAF	OY		5997	I	SAF	OY
5939	I	SAF	OY		5998	I	SAS	NC
5940 w	I	SAF	OY		5999	I	SAH	MA
5941	I	SAF	OY		6000	I	SAH	PC
5943 w	I	SAF	OY		6001 w	I	SAF	OY
5944 w	I	SAS	NC		6002	I	SAF	OY
5945 w	I	SAF	OY		6005 *	I	SAH	MA
5946	I	SAF	OY		6006	I	SAS	NC
5947	I	SAH	MA		6008	I	SAH	MA
5948 w	I	SAF	OY		6009	I	SAF	OY
5949 w	I	SAF	OY		6010 n	I	SAH	MA
5950	I	SAS	NC		6011	I	SAH	PC
5951	I	SAH	MA		6012 *	I	SAF	OY
5952	I	SAF	OY		6013 *	I	SAH	DY
5953	I	SAF	OY		6014	I	SAH	DY
5954	I	SAS	NC		6015 w	I	SAH	PC
5955	I	SAF	OY		6016	I	SAF	OY
5956	I	SAS	NC		6018 *	I	SAH	PC
5957	I	SAF	OY		6021	I	SAF	OY
5958	I	SAH	MA		6022 w	I	SAH	DY
5959 n	I	SAS	NC		6024	I	SAH	MA
5960	I	SAH	PC		6025 *w	I	SAH	MA
5961	I	SAH	PC		6026 *	I	SAH	PC
5962	I	SAH	DY		6027 w	I	SAF	OY

6028	I	SAS	NC	6121	I	SAF	OY
6029	I	SAF	OY	6122	I	SAH	PC
6030 w	I	SAH	MA	6123	I	SAS	NC
6031	I	SAF	OY	6124	I	SAH	DY
6034	I	SAS	NC	6134	I	SAF	OY
6035 w	I	SAH	DY	6135	I	SAH	DY
6036 *	I	SAS	NC	6136	I	SAF	OY
6037	I	SAS	NC	6137	I	SAH	MA
6038	I	SAH	PC	6138	I	SAF	OY
6041	I	SAH	DY	6139 *n	I	SAS	NC
6042	I	SAS	NC	6141 w	I	SAF	OY
6043	I	SAF	OY	6142 *	I	SAF	OY
6045 w	I	SAF	OY	6144 *	I	SAF	OY
6046	I	SAH	PC	6145 *	I	SAH	DY
6047 *n	I	SAF	OY	6146 *	I	SAS	NC
6049	I	SAF	OY	6147 *	I	SAF	OY
6050	I	SAH	DY	6148 *	I	SAH	DY
6051 *	I	SAF	OY	6149 *w	I	SAH	DY
6052 w	I	SAH	MA	6150 *	I	SAH	DY
6053 *	I	SAS	NC	6151 *	I	SAF	OY
6054	I	SAF	OY	6152 *	I	SAS	NC
6055	I	SAF	OY	6153 *	I	SAF	OY
6056	I	SAF	OY	6154 *	I	SAH	DY
6057	I	SAF	OY	6155 *	I	SAS	NC
6059	I	SAH	MA	6157 *	I	SAH	PC
6060 *	I	SAF	OY	6158 *	I	SAF	OY
6061 *	I	SAH	MA	6159 *n	I	SAH	PC
6062 *	I	SAF	OY	6160 *	I	SAS	NC
6063 w	I	SAF	OY	6161 *	I	SAF	OY
6064	I	SAH	PC	6162	I	SAH	MA
6065	I	SAF	OY	6163	I	SAF	OY
6066	I	SAH	DY	6164	I	SAF	OY
6067	I	SAH	PC	6165	I	SAF	OY
6073	I	SAH	PC	6166	I	SAS	NC
6100 *	I	SAF	OY	6167	I	SAS	NC
6101	I	SAF	OY	6168	I	SAH	DY
6102	I	SAF	OY	6170	I	SAH	PC
6103	I	SAS	NC	6171	I	SAF	OY
6104	I	SAF	OY	6172	I	SAH	MA
6105	I	SAH	DY	6173	I	SAH	PC
6106	I	SAF	OY	6174	I	SAS	NC
6107	I	SAF	OY	6175	I	SAF	OY
6110 w	I	SAS	NC	6176 w	I	SAH	PC
6111	I	SAF	OY	6177	I	SAH	PC
6112	I	SAH	MA	6178 w	I	SAH	MA
6113	I	SAF	OY	6179	I	SAF	OY
6115	I	SAH	DY	6180 w	I	SAF	OY
6116	I	SAF	OY	6181 wn	I	SAF	OY
6117 w	I	SAH	PC	6182	I	SAH	DY
6119 w	I	SAH	PC	6183	I	SAH	MA
6120	I	SAH	MA	6184 *	I	SAH	MA

AC2D (TSO)   OPEN STANDARD

Dia. AC217. Mark 2D. Air conditioned. Stones. –/58 2T. (–/58 1T*). B4 bogies. a. ETH 5X. Rebuilt from FO with new style 2+2 seats.

Lot No. 30821 Derby 1971 – 2. 33:5 t.

6200	(3198)	d	I	SAJ	LA
6201	(3210)	d*	I	SAOL	Longtown
6202	(3191)	d*	I	SAOL	Kineton
6203	(3180)	d	I	SAOL	Kineton
6204	(3216)		I	XWRZ	BN
6205	(3193)		I	SAOL	Long Marston
6206	(3183)	d	I	SAJ	LA
6207	(3204)	d	I	SAOL	Kineton
6208	(3205)	d	I	SAOL	Kineton
6209	(3177)		I	XWRZ	BN
6210	(3196)	d*	I	SAOL	Longtown
6211	(3215)	d	I	SAOL	Longtown
6212	(3176)	d	I	SAOL	Kineton
6213	(3208)	d	I	SAJ	LA
6214	(3211)	d	I	SAOL	Long Marston
6215	(3170)	d	I	SAOL	Long Marston
6216	(3179)		I	SAOL	Kineton
6217	(3184)	d	I	SAOL	Kineton
6218	(3209)	d	I	SAOL	Longtown
6219	(3213)	d	I	SAOL	Kineton
6220	(3175)	d	I	SAOL	Longtown
6221	(3173)	d	I	SAOL	Kineton
6222	(3171)	d	I	SAOL	Kineton
6223	(3194)		I	XWRZ	BN
6224	(3195)	d*	I	SAOL	Long Marston
6225	(3200)		I	XWRZ	BN
6226	(3203)	d	I	SAJ	LA
6227	(3197)		I	SAOL	Long Marston
6228	(3201)	d*	I	SAOL	Long Marston
6229	(3212)		I	SAOL	Kineton
6230	(3185)		I	SAOL	Long Marston
6231	(3189)		I	XWRZ	BN
6232	(3199)	d*	I	SAOL	Kineton
6233	(3206)		I	SAOL	Long Marston
6234	(3207)	d	I	SAOL	Kineton
6235	(3190)		I	XWRZ	BN

AD4Z (OC)   OBSERVATION CAR

Dia. AD401. Converted 1987 from DMU DTCL. DMU bogies. –/42 1T. v.

Lot No. 30468 Metro-Cammell 1958. 25.5 t.

6300 (56356, 54356)	H	SAOL	IS		HEBRIDEAN

GX51 GENERATOR VAN

Dia. GX501. Renumbered 1989 from BR departmental series. Three-phase supply generator van for use with HST trailers. Used to be used at times of low availability of HST power cars. Rebuilt from NDA. May be converted to provide conventional e.t.h. a. B5 bogies.

Lot No. 30400 Pressed Steel 1958.   t.

6310	(81448, ADB 975325)	I	XWRZ	Bristol Kingsland Road

AX51 GENERATOR VAN

Dia. AX501. Converted to generator vans for use with pairs of Class 37s on Anglo-Scottish sleeping car services. Now either stored or leased for use by a private operator. B5 bogies.

6311. Lot No. 30162 Pressed Steel 1958.   t.
6312. Lot No. 30224 Cravens 1956.   t.
6313. Lot No. 30484 Pressed Steel 1958.   t.

6311	(80903, 92911)	I	SBOL	Kineton
6312	(81023, 92925)	I	SBOL	Kineton
6313	(81553, 92167)	PC	SBVS	SL

AZ5Z SPECIAL SALOON

Dia. AZ501. Renumbered 1989 from LMR departmental series. Formerly the LMR General Manager's saloon. Rebuilt from LMS period 1 BFK M 5033 M to dia. 1654 and mounted on the underframe of BR suburban BS M 43232. B5 bogies. This vehicle has a maximum speed of 100 mph, but is restricted to 60 mph when carrying passengers with screw coupling operative.

LMS Lot No. 326 Derby 1927. x.   t.

6320	(5033, 395707)	M	XWR	BN

GS5(HSBV) HST BARRIER VEHICLE

Various diagrams. Renumbered from departmental stock, or converted from various types. a. B4 bogies (Commonwealth bogies *).

6330. Lot No. 30786 Derby 1968. 32 t.
6334. Lot No. 30400 Pressed Steel 1957 – 8. 31.5 t.
6335. Lot No. 30775 Derby 1967 – 8. 32 t.
6336/8/44. Lot No. 30715 Gloucester 1962. 31 t.
6340. Lot No. 30669 Swindon 1962. 36 t.
6343. Lot No. 30795 Derby 1969/70. 32 t.
6346. Lot No. 30777 Derby 1967. 31.5 t.
6347. Lot No. 30787 Derby 1968. 31.5 t.
6348. Lot No. 30163 Pressed Steel 1957. 31.5 t.

6330	(14084, 975629)		I	SCM	LA
6334	(81478, 92128)		PL	SBOL	NL
6335	(14065, 975655)		I	SBOL	NL
6336	(81591, 92185)		I	SCM	LA
6338	(8158, 92180)		I	SCM	LA
6340	(21251, 975678)	*	I	SCM	LA
6343	(5522)		I	SBOL	NL
6344	(81263, 92080)		I	SCM	EC
6346	(9422)		I	SCM	EC
6347	(5395)		I	SCM	LA
6348	(81233, 92963)		I	SCM	LA

GF5 (MFBV)   MARK 4 BARRIER VEHICLE

Various diagrams. Renumbered from departmental stock, or converted from FK, BSO or BG. a. B4 bogies.

6351. Lot No. 30091 Doncaster 1954. 33 t.
6352/3. Lot No. 30774 Derby 1968. 33 t.
6354 – 6. Lot No. 30820 Derby 1970. 32 t.
6357. Lot No. 30798 Derby 1970. 32 t.
6358 – 9. Lot No. 30788 Derby 1968. 31.5 t.
6390. Lot No. 30136 Metro-Cammell 1955. 31.5 t.

6351	(3050, 975435)	I	SAB	EC
6352	(13465, 19465)		SAB	BN
6353	(13478, 19478)		SAB	EC
6354	(9459)	I	SAB	BN
6355	(9477)		SAB	BN
6356	(9455)		SAB	BN
6357	(9443)		SAB	BN
6358	(9432)		SAB	BN
6359	(9429)		SAB	BN
6390	(80723, 92900)	I	SAB	BN

GF5 (BV)   DMU/EMU* BARRIER VEHICLE

Various diagrams. Converted from BFK, BSO or BG. a. B4 (BR1*) bogies.

6360. Lot No. 30777 Derby 1967. 31.5 t.
6361 – 2. Lot No. 30820 Derby 1970. 32 t.
6363. Lot No. 30796 Derby 1970. 32 t.
6364. Lot No. 30039 Derby 1954. 32 t.
6365. Lot No. 30323 Pressed Steel 1957. 32 t.

6360	(9420)		RR	SBOL	NL
6361	(9460)		RR	SBOL	NL
6362	(9467)		RR	SCM	LL
6363	(14117, 17117)		RR	SCM	LL
6364	(80565)	*	RR	SBG	TS
6365	(81296, 84296)	*	RR	SBG	TS

AX5G   EURONIGHT GENERATOR VAN

Dia. AX502. Generator vans for European Night Services trains. Operate sandwiched between two Class 37 locomotives. Converted from Mark 3A sleeping cars. Gangways removed. Two Cummins diesel generator groups providing a 1500 V train supply. Hydraulic parking brake. 61-way ENS interface jumpers.

6371	(10545)	E	GPSG	PM
6372	(10564)	E	GPSG	
6373	(10568)	E	GPSG	
6374	(10585)	E	GPSG	
6375	(10587)	E	GPSG	

AY5 (BV)   EUROSTAR BARRIER VEHICLE

Dia. AY501. Converted from GUVs. Bodies removed to allow for nose of Eurostar set. a. B4 bogies.

6380 – 6382/9. Lot No. 30417 Pressed Steel 1958 – 9.
6383. Lot No. 30565 Pressed Steel 1959.
6384/6/7. Lot No. 30616 Pressed Steel 1959 – 60.
6385. Lot No. 30343 York 1957.
6388. Lot No. 30403 York/Glasgow 1958 – 60. 30 t.

6380	(86386, 93386)	B	GPSM	PI
6381	(86187, 93187)	B	GPSM	PI
6382	(86295, 93295)	B	GPSM	PI
6383	(86664, 93664)	B	GPSM	PI
6384	(86955, 93955)	B	GPSM	PI
6385	(86515, 93515)	B	GPSM	PI
6386	(86859, 93859)	B	GPSM	PI
6387	(86973, 93973)	B	GPSM	PI
6388	(86562, 93562)	B	GPSM	PI
6389	(86135, 93135)	B	GPSM	PI

GS5(HSBV)   HST BARRIER VEHICLE

Dia. Converted from BG. a. B4 bogies.

6392. Lot No. 30715 Gloucester 1962. 29.5 t.
6393/6/7. Lot No. 30716 Gloucester 1962. 29.5 t.
6394. Lot No. 30162 Pressed Steel 1956 – 7. 30.5 t.
6395. Lot No. 30484 Pressed Steel 1958. 30.5 t.
6398/9. Lot No. 30400 Pressed Steel 1957 – 8. 30.5 t.

6392	(81588, 92183)	PL	SBOL	NL
6393	(81609, 92196)	PL	SBOL	NL
6394	(80878, 92906)	PL	SBOL	NL
6395	(81506, 92148)	PL	SBOL	NL
6396	(81606, 92195)	PL	SBOL	NL
6397	(81600, 92190)	PL	SBOL	NL
6398	(81471, 92126)	PL	SBOL	NL

6399   (81367, 92994)   **PL** SBOL   NL

AG2C (TSOT)   OPEN STANDARD (TROLLEY)

Dia. AG201. Mark 2C. Converted from TSO by removal of one seating bay and replacing this by a counter with a space for a trolley. Adjacent toilet removed and converted to steward's washing area/store. Pressure ventilated. −/54 1T. B4 bogies. a. ETH 4.

Lot No. 30795 Derby 1969 – 70. 32.5 t.

6510 (5518)		SAXZ	Norwich Goods		
6513 (5538)	N	SAXZ	OM	6523 (5568)	XCRZ CS
6517 (5499)	N	SAXZ	OM	6528 (5592)	XCRZ CS

AG2D (TSOT)   OPEN STANDARD (TROLLEY)

Dia. AG202. Mark 2D. Converted from TSO by removal of one seating bay and replacing this by a counter with a space for a trolley. Adjacent toilet removed and converted to steward's washing area/store. Air conditioned. Stones equipment. −/54 1T. B4 bogies. a. ETH 5.

Lot No. 30822 Derby 1971. 33 t.

6609 (5698)	I	SAOL	Kineton	6619 (5655)	I	SAOL Kineton

AN2D (RMBT)   MINIATURE BUFFET CAR

Dia. AN207. Mark 2D. Converted from TSOT by the removal of another seating bay and fitting a proper buffet counter with boiler and microwave oven. Air conditioned. Stones equipment. −/46 1T. B4 bogies. a. payphone. Catering staff – shore telephone. ETH 5.

Lot No. 30822 Derby 1971. 33 t.

6652 (5622, 6602)	d	I	SAOL	Long Marston
6660 (5627, 6610)		I	SAOL	Long Marston
6661 (5736, 6611)	d	I	SAOL	Long Marston
6662 (5641, 6612)	d	I	SAOL	Long Marston
6665 (5721, 6615)	d	I	SAOL	Long Marston

AN1F (RLO)   SLEEPER RECEPTION CAR

Dia. AN101 (AN102*). Mark 2F. Converted from FO, these vehicles consist of pantry, microwave cooking facilities, seating area for passengers, telephone booth and staff toilet. 6703 – 8 also have a bar. Converted at RTC, Derby (6700), Ilford (6701 – 5) and Derby (6706 – 8). Air conditioned. 26/ – 1T. B4 bogies. a. payphone. Catering staff – shore telephone. Secondary door locks. ETH 5X.

6700 – 2/4/8. Lot No. 30859 Derby 1973 – 4. 33.5 t.
6703/5 – 7. Lot No. 30845 Derby 1973. 33.5 t.

6700 (3347)		I	SAA	IS
6701 (3346)	*	I	SAA	IS

6702 (3421)	* I	SAA	IS
6703 (3308)	I	SAA	IS
6704 (3341)	I	SAA	IS
6705 (3310, 6430)	I	SAA	IS
6706 (3283, 6421)	I	SAA	IS
6707 (3276, 6418)	I	SAA	IS
6708 (3370)	I	SAA	IS

AC2F (TSO)   OPEN STANDARD

Dia. AC224. Mark 2F. Renumbered 1985 – 6 from FO. Converted 1990 to TSO with mainly unidirectional seating and power-operated sliding doors. Air conditioned. B4 bogies. –/74 2T + one tip-up seat. 6800 – 14 were converted by BREL Derby and have Temperature Ltd. air conditioning. 6815 – 29 were converted by RFS Industries Doncaster and have Stones air conditioning. a. Secondary door locks. ETH 5X.

6800 – 07. 6810 – 12. 6813 – 14. 6819/22/28. Lot No. 30859 Derby 1973 – 4. 33 t.
6808 – 6809. Lot No. 30873 Derby 1974 – 5. 33.5 t.
6815 – 18. 6820 – 21. 6823 – 27. 6829. Lot No. 30845 Derby 1973. 33 t.

6800 (3323, 6435)	I	SAS	NC
6801 (3349, 6442)	I	SAS	NC
6802 (3339, 6439)	I	SAS	NC
6803 (3355, 6443)	I	SAS	NC
6804 (3396, 6449)	I	SAS	NC
6805 (3324, 6436)	I	SAS	NC
6806 (3342, 6440)	I	SAS	NC
6807 (3423, 6452)	I	SAS	NC
6808 (3430, 6454)	I	SAS	NC
6809 (3435, 6455)	I	SAS	NC
6810 (3404, 6451)	I	SAS	NC
6811 (3327, 6437)	I	SAS	NC
6812 (3394, 6448)	I	SAS	NC
6813 (3410, 6463)	I	SAS	NC
6814 (3422, 6465)	I	SAS	NC
6815 (3282, 6420)	I	SAS	NC
6816 (3316, 6461)	I	SAS	NC
6817 (3311, 6431)	I	SAS	NC
6818 (3298, 6427)	I	SAS	NC
6819 (3365, 6446)	I	SAS	NC
6820 (3320, 6434)	I	SAS	NC
6821 (3281, 6458)	I	SAS	NC
6822 (3376, 6447)	I	SAS	NC
6823 (3289, 6424)	I	SAS	NC
6824 (3307, 6429)	I	SAS	NC
6825 (3301, 6460)	a. I	SAS	NC
6826 (3294, 6425)	I	SAS	NC
6827 (3306, 6428)	I	SAS	NC
6828 (3380, 6464)	I	SAS	NC
6829 (3288, 6423)	I	SAS	NC

NM5D (BFK)   INTER-CITY SANDITE COACH

Dia. NM503. Mark 2D. Air conditioned (Stones equipment). BFKs converted for use as Sandite coaches. –/24 1T. B4 Bogies. pg. ETH 4.

Lot No. 30823 Derby 1971 – 2. 33.5 t.

6900	(14145, 977837)	I	QAC	CD
6901	(14142, 17142)	I	QAC	EN

NM51   MERSEYRAIL SANDITE COACH

Dia. NM504. Mark 1. Former Class 501 750 V d.c. third rail EMU driving trailers converted for use as Sandite / de-icing coaches. Mark 1 Bogies.

Lot No. 30328 Ashford/Eastleigh 1958. . t.

6910	(75178, 977346)	MD	HE	BD
6911	(75180, 977348)	MD	HE	BD

AH2Z (BSOT)   OPEN BRAKE STANDARD (MICRO-BUFFET)

Dia. AH203. Mark 2. Converted from BSO by removal of one seating bay and replacing this by a counter with a space for a trolley. Adjacent toilet removed and converted to a steward's washing area/store. –/23 0L. vd. ETH 4.

Lot No. 30757 Derby 1966.

9100	(9405)	RR	SAOL	Longtown
9101	(9398)	RR	SAOL	Longtown
9105	(9404)	RR	SAOL	Longtown

AE21 (BSO)   OPEN BRAKE STANDARD

Dia. AE201. Mark 1. –/39 1T. Mark 1 bogies. xk. ETH 3.

Lot No. 30170 Doncaster 1955. 34 t.

9227	M	XSC		BO	I

AE2Z (BSO)   OPEN BRAKE STANDARD

Dia. AE203. Mark 2. These vehicles use the same body shell as the mark 2 BFK and have first class seat spacing and wider tables. Pressure ventilated. –/31 1T. B4 bogies. v. ETH 4.

Lot No. 30757 Derby 1966. 31.5 t.

9382	N	XWRZ		BQ
9385	H	SAOL	BALMACARA	Longtown
9388	H	SAOL	BRAHAN SEER	Longtown
9391	N	XWRZ		BQ
9414	H	SAOL	BAILECHAUL	Longtown

AE2A (BSO)   OPEN BRAKE STANDARD

Dia. AE204. Mark 2A. These vehicles use the same body shell as the mark 2A
BFK and have first class seat spacing and wider tables. Pressure ventilated. –/31
1T. B4 bogies. a. ETH 4.

9417 – 9424. Lot No. 30777 Derby 1967. 31.5 t.
9428 – 9438. Lot No. 30788 Derby 1968. 31.5 t.

9417	**RR**	SAD	LL	9428	**RR**	SAOL	Westbury
9418	**RR**	SAOL	Long Marston	9431	**RR**	SAOL	Long Marston
9419	**RR**	SAOL	Long Marston	9434	**RR**	SAOL	LL
9421	**RR**	SAOL	Long Marston	9435	**RR**	SAOL	Long Marston
9424	**RR**	SAD	LL	9438	**RR**	SAOL	Westbury

AE2C (BSO)   OPEN BRAKE STANDARD

Dia. AE205. Mark 2C. Pressure ventilated. –/31 1T. B4 bogies. a. ETH 4.

Lot No. 30820 Derby 1970. 32 t.

9440	**M**	XCRZ	CS	9448	**M**	XCRK	BK
9444		SAXZ	Norwich Goods	9458	**RR**	SAOL	LL

AE2D (BSO)   OPEN BRAKE STANDARD

Dia. AE206. Mark 2D. Air conditioned (Stones). –/31 1T. B4 bogies. a. pg.
ETH 5.

Lot No. 30824 Derby 1971. 33 t.

9479	d I	SAH	MA	9488	d I	SAOL	Long Marston
9480	d I	SAH	PC	9489	d I	SAH	MA
9481	d I	SAJ	LA	9490	d I	SAOL	Longtown
9482	d I	SAXZ	NL	9492	d I	SAJ	LA
9483	I	SAOL	Long Marston	9493	d I	SAOL	Long Marston
9484	d I	SAOL	Longtown	9494	I	SAOL	Long Marston
9485	I	SAOL	Longtown	9495	I	SAOL	ABB Crewe Wks
9486	I	SAOL	Long Marston				

AE2E (BSO)   OPEN BRAKE STANDARD

Dia. AE207. Mark 2E. Air conditioned (Stones). –/32 1T. B4 bogies. a. pg.
ETH 5.

Lot No. 30838 Derby 1972. 33 t.

9496	d I	SAH	PC	9503	d I	SAH	PC
9497	d I	SAH	MA	9504	d I	SAH	PC
9498	d I	SAH	PC	9505	d I	SAH	MA
9499	I	SAOL	ZH	9506	d I	SAH	MA
9500	d I	SAH	MA	9507	d I	SAH	MA
9501	d I	SAJ	LA	9508	d I	SAH	DY
9502	d I	SAH	PC	9509	d I	SAH	MA

AE2F (BSO)   OPEN BRAKE STANDARD

Dia. AE208. Mark 2F. Air conditioned (Temperature Ltd.). All now refurbished with power-operated vestibule doors, new panels and seat trim. –/32 1T. B4 bogies. Secondary door locks. a. pg. ETH 5X.

Lot No. 30861 Derby 1974. 34 t.

9513	I	SAH	PC	9526 n	I	SAH	DY
9516	I	SAH	MA	9527 d	I	SAH	PC
9520 n	I	SAH	PC	9529	I	SAH	MA
9521	I	SAH	DY	9531	I	SAH	MA
9522	I	SAH	MA	9537 n	I	SAH	DY
9523	I	SAH	MA	9538	I	SAH	PC
9524 n	I	SAH	DY	9539	I	SAH	DY
9525	I	SAH	PC				

AF2F (DBSO)   DRIVING OPEN BRAKE STANDARD

Dia. AF201. Mark 2F. Air conditioned (Temperature Ltd.). Push & pull (t.d.m. system). Converted from BSO, these vehicles originally had half cabs at the brake end. They have since been refurbished and have had their cabs widened and the outer gangways removed. Fitted with cowcatchers. Cab to shore communication. BR Cellnet phone and data transmitter. Secondary door locks. –/32 1T. B4 bogies. a. pg. ETH 5X.

9701 – 9710. Lot No. 30861 Derby 1974. Converted 1979. Disc brakes. 34 t.
9711 – 9713. Lot No. 30861 Derby 1974. Converted Glasgow 1985. 34 t.
9714. Lot No. 30861 Derby 1974. Converted Glasgow 1986. Disc brakes. 34 t.

9701 (9528)	I	SAS	NC	9709 (9515)	I	SAS	NC
9702 (9510)	I	SAS	NC	9710 (9518)	I	SAS	NC
9703 (9517)	I	SAS	NC	9711 (9532)	I	SAS	NC
9704 (9512)	I	SAS	NC	9712 (9534)	I	SAS	NC
9705 (9519)	I	SAS	NC	9713 (9535)	I	SAS	NC
9707 (9511)	I	SAS	NC	9714 (9536)	I	SAS	NC
9708 (9530)	I	SAS	NC				

AJ1G (RFM)   RESTAURANT BUFFET FIRST (MODULAR)

Dia. AJ103 (10200/1 are Dia. AJ101). Mark 3A. Air conditioned. Converted from HST TRFKs, RFBs and FOs. 22/– (24/– *). BT10 bogies. a. q. Fitted with payphone. Secondary door locks. ETH 14X.

10200 – 10211. Lot No. 30884 Derby 1977.
10212 – 10229. Lot No. 30878 Derby 1975–6. 39.80 t.
10230 – 10260. Lot No. 30890 Derby 1979. 39.80 t.

10200 (40519) *	I	SBA	IS	10205 (40503)	I	SBF	OY
10201 (40520) *	I	SBF	OY	10206 (40507)	I	SBF	PC
10202 (40504)	I	SBF	OY	10207 (40516)	I	SBF	MA
10203 (40506)	I	SBS	NC	10208 (40517)	I	SBF	PC
10204 (40502)	I	SBF	MA	10209 (40508)	I	SBF	PC

10210 (40509)	I	SBF	MA	10234 (10004)	I	SBF	PC
10211 (40510)	I	SBF	PC	10235 (10015)	I	SBF	OY
10212 (11049)	I	SBF	PC	10236 (10018)	I	SBF	PC
10213 (11050)	I	SBF	MA	10237 (10022)	I	SBF	PC
10214 (11034)	I	SBS	NC	10238 (10017)	I	SBF	OY
10215 (11032)	I	SBF	PC	10240 (10003)	I	SBF	OY
10216 (11041)	I	SBS	NC	10241 (10009)	I	SBOL	ZD
10217 (11051)	I	SBF	OY	10242 (10002)	I	SBF	PC
10218 (11053)	I	SBF	MA	10245 (10019)	I	SBF	MA
10219 (11047)	I	SBF	OY	10246 (10014)	I	SBF	OY
10220 (11056)	I	SBF	OY	10247 (10011)	I	SBS	NC
10221 (11012)	I	SBF	PC	10248 (10005)	I	SBF	PC
10222 (11063)	I	SBF	MA	10249 (10012)	I	SBF	PC
10223 (11043)	I	SBS	NC	10250 (10020)	I	SBF	OY
10224 (11062)	I	SBF	MA	10251 (10024)	I	SBF	OY
10225 (11014)	I	SBF	OY	10252 (10008)	I	SBF	MA
10226 (11015)	I	SBF	PC	10253 (10026)	I	SBF	MA
10227 (11057)	I	SBF	MA	10254 (10006)	I	SBF	PC
10228 (11035)	I	SBS	NC	10255 (10010)	I	SBF	OY
10229 (11059)	I	SBF	OY	10256 (10028)	I	SBF	PC
10230 (10021)	I	SBF	PC	10257 (10007)	I	SBF	MA
10231 (10016)	I	SBF	PC	10258 (10023)	I	SBF	MA
10232 (10027)	I	SBF	OY	10259 (10025)	I	SBF	OY
10233 (10013)	I	SBF	MA	10260 (10001)	I	SBF	MA

AJ1J (RFM)   RESTAURANT BUFFET FIRST (MODULAR)

Dia. AJ105. Mark 4. Air conditioned. 20/– 1T. SIG bogies (BT41). a. ETH   X.
Lot No. 31045 Metro-Cammell 1989 onwards. 45.5 t.

10300	I	SAB	BN	10317	I	SAB	BN
10301	I	SAB	BN	10318	I	SAB	BN
10302	I	SAB	BN	10319	I	SAB	BN
10303	I	SAB	BN	10320	I	SAB	BN
10304	I	SAB	BN	10321	I	SAB	BN
10305	I	SAB	BN	10322	I	SAB	BN
10306	I	SAB	BN	10323	I	SAB	BN
10307	I	SAB	BN	10324	I	SAB	BN
10308	I	SAB	BN	10325	I	SAB	BN
10309	I	SAB	BN	10326	I	SAB	BN
10310	I	SAB	BN	10327	I	SAB	BN
10311	I	SAB	BN	10328	I	SAB	BN
10312	I	SAB	BN	10329	I	SAB	BN
10313	I	SAB	BN	10330	I	SAB	BN
10314	I	SAB	BN	10331	I	SAB	BN
10315	I	SAB	BN	10332	I	SAB	BN
10316	I	SAB	BN	10333	I	SAB	BN

AU4G (SLEP)   SLEEPING CAR WITH PANTRY

Dia. AU401. Mark 3A. Air conditioned. 12 compartments with a fixed lower berth and a hinged upper berth, plus an attendants compartment with 2T (controlled emission). BT10 bogies. a. ETH 7X.

Lot No. 30960 Derby 1981 – 3.

10500	I	XWRZ	BN
10501 d	I	SBA	IS
10502 d	I	SBA	IS
10503	I	XWR	BN
10504 d	I	SBA	IS
10506 d	I	SBA	IS
10507 d	I	SBA	IS
10508 d	I	SBA	IS
10510 d	I	SBA	IS
10512 d	I	SBOL	Kineton
10513 d	I	SBA	IS
10514	I	XWR	BN
10515 d	I	SBA	IS
10516 d	I	SBA	IS
10519 d	I	SBA	IS
10520 d	I	SBA	IS
10522 d	I	SBA	IS
10523 d	I	SBA	IS
10526 d	I	SBA	IS
10527 d	I	SBA	IS
10529 d	I	SBA	IS
10530 d	I	SBOL	ZD
10531 d	I	SBA	IS
10532 d	I	SBJ	LA
10533	I	SBOL	ZD
10534 d	I	SBJ	LA
10535 d	I	SBOL	ZD
10536 d	I	SBOL	Kineton
10537 d	I	SBOL	ZD
10538 d	I	SBOL	Kineton
10539 d	I	SBOL	Kineton
10540 d	I	SBOL	ZD
10541 d	I	SBOL	Kineton
10542 d	I	SBA	IS
10543 d	I	SBA	IS
10544 d	I	SBA	IS
10546 d	I	SBOL	ZD
10547 d	I	SBA	IS
10548 d	I	SBA	IS
10549 d	I	SBOL	ZD
10550 d	I	SBXZ	IMI Witton
10551 d	I	SBA	IS
10552 d	I	SBXZ	WB
10553 d	I	SBA	IS
10554 d	I	SBOL	ZD
10555 d	I	SBOL	Kineton
10556 d	I	SBOL	Kineton
10557 d	I	SBOL	ZD
10558 d	I	SBOL	ZH
10559 d	I	SBOL	WB
10560 d	I	SBOL	ZD
10561 d	I	SBA	IS
10562 d	I	SBA	IS
10563 d	I	SBJ	LA
10565 d	I	SBA	IS
10566 d	I	SBOL	ZD
10567	I	SBXZ	Kineton
10569 d	I	SBOL	ZD
10570	I	SBXZ	Kineton
10571	I	XWRZ	BN
10572 d	I	SBOL	ZD
10573 d	I	SBOL	ZD
10574	I	XWR	BN
10575	I	XWRZ	BN
10577	I	SBXZ	ZD
10578	I	SBXZ	Kineton
10579	I	SBXZ	Kineton
10580 d	I	SBA	IS
10582 d	I	SBOL	ZD
10583 d	I	SBJ	LA
10584 d	I	SBJ	LA
10586 d	I	SBOL	Kineton
10588 d	I	SBJ	LA
10589 d	I	SBJ	LA
10590 d	I	SBJ	LA
10591	I	SBXZ	Kineton
10592	I	SBXZ	Kineton
10593 d	I	SBOL	Kineton
10594 d	I	SBJ	LA
10595	I	SBXZ	Kineton
10596 d	I	SBOL	Kineton
10597 d	I	SBA	IS
10598 d	I	SBA	IS
10599	I	SBXZ	Kineton
10600 d	I	SBA	IS
10601	I	SBOL	ZD

10602	I	SBOL	ZD
10603	I	SBXZ	Kineton
10604	I	SBOL	Kineton
10605 d	I	SBA	IS
10606	I	SBXZ	Kineton
10607 d	I	SBA	IS
10609		SBXZ	Kineton

10610 d	I	SBA	IS
10612 d	I	SBJ	LA
10613	I	SBA	IS
10614 d	I	SBA	IS
10615	I	SBXZ	WB
10616	I	SBJ	LA
10617 d	I	SBA	IS

AS4G (SLE)   SLEEPING CAR

Dia. AS403. Mark 3A. Air conditioned. 13 compartments with a fixed lower berth and a hinged upper berth. 2T (controlled emission). BT10 bogies. a. ETH 6X.

Lot No. 30961 Derby 1980 – 4.

10646 d	I	XWR	BN
10647 d	I	SBOL	Kineton
10648 d	I	SBA	IS
10649 d	I	SBOL	Kineton
10650 d	I	SBA	IS
10651 d	I	SBOL	ZD
10653 d	I	SBOL	ZD
10654 d	I	SBOL	ZD
10655	I	XWR	BN
10656	I	SBXZ	Kineton
10657	I	XWR	BN
10658 d	I	SBOL	WB
10660 d	I	SBOL	ZD
10662	I	SBXZ	ZD
10663 d	I	SBA	IS
10665	I	SBXZ	Ferme Park
10666 d	I	SBA	IS
10668 d	I	SBA	IS
10670	I	SBXZ	Kineton
10672 d	I	SBOL	Kineton
10674 d	I	SBOL	Kineton
10675 d	I	SBA	IS
10678		SBXZ	Kineton
10679		SBXZ	Kineton
10680 d	I	SBA	IS
10682 d	I	SBOL	ZD
10683 d	I	SBA	IS
10684		SBXZ	Kineton
10685 d	I	SBOL	IS
10686 d	I	SBA	IS
10687 d	I	SBA	IS
10688 d	I	SBA	IS
10689 d	I	SBA	IS
10690 d	I	SBA	IS
10691 d	I	SBA	IS
10692 d	I	SBOL	ZD

10693 d	I	SBA	IS
10696 d	I	SBOL	Kineton
10697 d	I	SBOL	Kineton
10699 d	I	SBA	IS
10700		SBXZ	Kineton
10701 d	I	SBOL	Kineton
10702	I	XWR	BN
10703 d	I	SBA	IS
10704 d	I	SBXZ	ZD
10706 d	I	SBA	IS
10707	I	SBXZ	BN
10708 d	I	SBA	IS
10709 d	I	SBOL	ZD
10710 d	I	SBOL	Kineton
10711 d	I	SBOL	ZD
10712 d	I	SBA	IS
10713 d	I	SBOL	ZD
10714 d	I	SBA	IS
10715 d	I	SBOL	ZD
10716 d	I	SBA	IS
10717 d	I	SBOL	ZD
10718 d	I	SBA	IS
10719 d	I	SBA	IS
10720		SBXZ	Kineton
10722 d	I	SBA	IS
10723 d	I	SBA	IS
10724	I	XWRZ	BN
10725	I	XWRZ	BN
10726	I	XWR	BN
10727	I	XWR	BN
10728	I	SBXZ	ZN
10729	I	XWR	BN
10730 d	I	SBA	IS
10731 d	I	SBOL	Kineton
10732 d	I	SBOL	Kineton

▲ **Mark 1 Stock.** Intercity liveried RMB No. 1832 at Carlisle Upperby on 16th July 1994.
Kevin Conkey

▼ Charter train staff coach No. 2834 in Waterman Railways VIP livery at Blackpool North on 20th July 1995.
C.J. Marsden

▲ FO 3144 is pictured at the Railway Age, Crewe shortly after receiving a repaint in the old BR carmine and cream livery commonly known as 'blood and custard'. The date is 8th June 1995. *C.J. Marsden*

▼ Porterbrook train leasing company owned and liveried barrier vehicle 6396 at ABB Crewe works on 17th July 1995. *C.J. Marsden*

Regional Railways liveried BSK No. 35453 is pictured bringing up the rear of the 09.45 Manchester Piccadilly–Blackpool North at Chorley on 3rd August 1995.

Martyn Hilbert

BSK No. 35469 is fitted with an ETH generator for use on charter trains. The maroon liveried vehicle is pictured at Long Rock on 13 March 1995.

Mark 2A Stock. A train of Regional Railways liveried Mark 2As forming the 07.21 Blackpool North-Manchester Piccadilly service departs from Bolton with Class 31 No. 31 455 'Our Eli' providing the power. The date is 4th May 1995. Note that the first two coaches are in modified Network SouthEast livery.

Nic Joynson

Mark 2E Stock. TSO 5890 is seen descending Acton Bank in the formation of the 09.20 Brighton-Glasgow Central on 23rd June 1995. *Kevin Conkey*

Mark 2F Stock. RFB 1219 in the formation of the 09.20 Brighton-Glasgow Central at Acton Bank on 14th September 1995.

Kevin Conkey

DBSO 9705 leading the 10.30 London Liverpool Street-Norwich at Kelvedon on 21st October 1995.

Les Nixon

Mark 3 Stock. HST TGS No. 44015 at Worcester Shrub Hill on 30th July 1995.

Stephen Widdowson

Mark 3A Stock. European Passenger Services liveried generator coach No. 6371 stands between two EPS Class 37s after being rolled out of ABBs Doncaster Works after conversion from a surplus sleeping car. The date is 25th October 1995.

Peter Fox

Kevin Conkey

FO 11060 at Carlisle on 8th July 1995.

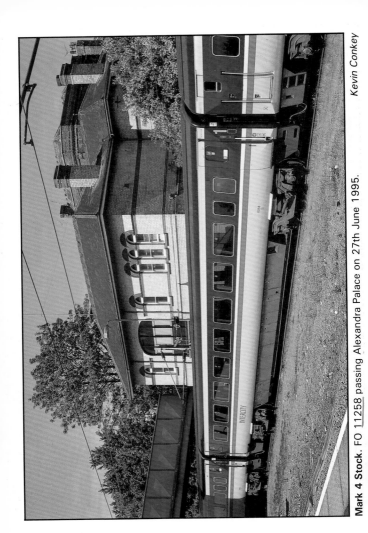

Mark 4 Stock. FO 11258 passing Alexandra Palace on 27th June 1995.

Kevin Conkey

NPCCS. NS (POS) 80316 in Royal Mail livery at Norwich Crown Paint T&RSMD on 16th August 1995.
C.J. Marsden

NZ (DLV) 82116 leads a Manchester Piccadilly-London Euston service at Brinklow on 23rd September 1995. *Michael J. Collins*

NZ (DLV) 82228 passes through Finsbury Park on 27th June 1995 whilst leading the 13.05 Leeds-London Kings Cross.

Kevin Conkey

▲ NF (BG) 92644 in red livery with yellow stripes at Carlisle on 5th August 1995. *Dave McAlone*

▼ NBA Super Brake Van No. 94457 in Rail Express Systems livery is pictured stabled at Newport on 2nd September 1995.

Stephen Widdowson

AD1G (FO)   OPEN FIRST

Dia. AD108. Mark 3A. Air conditioned. All now facelifted with new upholstery, carpets etc. 11005 – 7 have regained their original numbers, having being converted back from open composites 11905 – 7. 48/– 2T. BT10 bogies (BT15 b). Secondary door locks. a. ETH 6X.

Lot No. 30878 Derby 1975 – 6. 34.30 t.

11005	l	SBF	PC	11031	l SBF	PC
11006	l	SBF	PC	11033	l SBF	PC
11007	l	SBF	PC	11036	l SBF	PC
11011 z	l	SBF	PC	11037	l SBF	PC
11013	l	SBF	PC	11038	l SBF	PC
11016	l	SBF	PC	11039	l SBF	PC
11017	l	SBF	PC	11040	l SBF	PC
11018	l	SBF	PC	11042	l SBF	PC
11019	l	SBF	PC	11044	l SBF	PC
11020	l	SBF	PC	11045	l SBF	PC
11021	l	SBF	PC	11046	l SBF	PC
11023	l	SBF	PC	11048	l SBF	PC
11024	l	SBF	PC	11052	l SBF	PC
11026	l	SBF	PC	11054	l SBF	PC
11027	l	SBF	PC	11055	l SBF	PC
11028	l	SBF	PC	11058	l SBF	PC
11029	l	SBF	PC	11060	l SBF	PC
11030	l	SBF	PC			

AD1H (FO)   OPEN FIRST

Dia. AD109. Mark 3B. Air conditioned. Inter-City 80 seats. 48/– 2T. BT10 bogies. a. Secondary door locks. ETH 6X.

Lot No. 30982 Derby 1985. 36.46 t.

11064	l	SBF	MA	11081	l	SBF	MA
11065	l	SBF	MA	11082	l	SBF	MA
11066	l	SBF	MA	11083 p	l	SBF	MA
11067	l	SBF	MA	11084 p	l	SBF	MA
11068	l	SBF	MA	11085 p	l	SBF	MA
11069	l	SBF	MA	11086 p	l	SBF	MA
11070	l	SBF	MA	11087 p	l	SBF	MA
11071	l	SBF	MA	11088 p	l	SBF	MA
11072	l	SBF	MA	11089 p	l	SBF	MA
11073	l	SBF	MA	11090 p	l	SBF	MA
11074	l	SBF	MA	11091 p	l	SBF	MA
11075	l	SBF	MA	11092 p	l	SBF	MA
11076	l	SBF	MA	11093 p	l	SBF	MA
11077	l	SBF	MA	11094 p	l	SBF	MA
11078	l	SBF	MA	11095 p	l	SBF	MA
11079	l	SBF	MA	11096 p	l	SBF	MA
11080	l	SBF	MA	11097 p	l	SBF	MA

| 11098 p | I | SBF | MA | 11100 p | I | SBF | MA |
| 11099 p | I | SBF | MA | 11101 p | I | SBF | MA |

AD1J (FO)   OPEN FIRST

Dia. AD111. Mark 4. Air conditioned. Known as 'Pullman open' by BR. 46/–
1T. SIG bogies (BT41). a. ETH 6.

Note: 11264 – 71 were cancelled.

Lot No. 31046 Metro-Cammell 1989 onwards. 39.70 t.

11200	I	SAB	BN	11235 p	I	SAB	BN
11201 p	I	SAB	BN	11236	I	SAB	BN
11202	I	SAB	BN	11237 p	I	SAB	BN
11203 p	I	SAB	BN	11238	I	SAB	BN
11204 p	I	SAB	BN	11239 p	I	SAB	BN
11205	I	SAB	BN	11240	I	SAB	BN
11206	I	SAB	BN	11241	I	SAB	BN
11207	I	SAB	BN	11242 p	I	SAB	BN
11208	I	SAB	BN	11243 p	I	SAB	BN
11209	I	SAB	BN	11244	I	SAB	BN
11210	I	SAB	BN	11245 p	I	SAB	BN
11211 p	I	SAB	BN	11246 p	I	SAB	BN
11212	I	SAB	BN	11247 p	I	SAB	BN
11213 p	I	SAB	BN	11248	I	SAB	BN
11214 p	I	SAB	BN	11249 p	I	SAB	BN
11215	I	SAB	BN	11250	I	SAB	BN
11216	I	SAB	BN	11251 p	I	SAB	BN
11217 p	I	SAB	BN	11252	I	SAB	BN
11218	I	SAB	BN	11253 p	I	SAB	BN
11219 p	I	SAB	BN	11254	I	SAB	BN
11220	I	SAB	BN	11255 p	I	SAB	BN
11221 p	I	SAB	BN	11256	I	SAB	BN
11222 p	I	SAB	BN	11257 p	I	SAB	BN
11223	I	SAB	BN	11258	I	SAB	BN
11224	I	SAB	BN	11259 p	I	SAB	BN
11225 p	I	SAB	BN	11260	I	SAB	BN
11226	I	SAB	BN	11261 p	I	SAB	BN
11227 p	I	SAB	BN	11262	I	SAB	BN
11228 p	I	SAB	BN	11263 p	I	SAB	BN
11229 p	I	SAB	BN	11272	I	SAB	BN
11230	I	SAB	BN	11273	I	SAB	BN
11231 p	I	SAB	BN	11274	I	SAB	BN
11232	I	SAB	BN	11275	I	SAB	BN
11233 p	I	SAB	BN	11276	I	SAB	BN
11234	I	SAB	BN				

AC2G (TSO)   OPEN STANDARD

Dia. AC213 (AC220 z). Mark 3A. Air conditioned. All now refurbished with
modified seat backs and new layout. 12169 – 72 have been converted from open

composites 11908 – 10/22, formerly FOs 11008 – 10/22. – /76 2T (– /74 2T z). BT10 (BREL T4*, BT15 b) bogies. a. Secondary door locks. ETH 6X.

Lot No. 30877 Derby 1975 – 7. 34.30 t.

12004	I	SBF	PC	12054 z	I SBF	PC
12005	I	SBF	PC	12055	I SBF	MA
12007	I	SBF	PC	12056	I SBF	MA
12008	I	SBF	PC	12057	I SBF	PC
12009	I	SBF	MA	12058	I SBF	PC
12010 b	I	SBF	PC	12059 w	I SBF	MA
12011	I	SBF	PC	12060	I SBF	MA
12012	I	SBF	MA	12061 w	I SBF	MA
12013	I	SBF	PC	12062	I SBF	MA
12014	I	SBF	PC	12063	I SBF	PC
12015	I	SBF	PC	12064	I SBF	PC
12016	I	SBF	PC	12065	I SBF	PC
12017	I	SBF	PC	12066	I SBF	PC
12019	I	SBF	PC	12067	I SBF	PC
12020	I	SBF	MA	12068	I SBF	MA
12021	I	SBF	MA	12069	I SBF	PC
12022	I	SBF	PC	12070	I SBF	MA
12023	I	SBF	PC	12071	I SBF	MA
12024	I	SBF	PC	12072	I SBF	MA
12025	I	SBF	PC	12073	I SBF	PC
12026	I	SBF	PC	12075	I SBF	MA
12027	I	SBF	PC	12076	I SBF	MA
12028	I	SBF	PC	12077	I SBF	MA
12029	I	SBF	PC	12078	I SBF	PC
12030	I	SBF	PC	12079	I SBF	PC
12031	I	SBF	PC	12080	I SBF	MA
12032	I	SBF	PC	12081	I SBF	PC
12033 z	I	SBF	PC	12082	I SBF	PC
12034	I	SBF	MA	12083	I SBF	MA
12035	I	SBF	MA	12084	I SBF	MA
12036	I	SBF	MA	12085 w	I SBF	PC
12037	I	SBF	MA	12086 w	I SBF	MA
12038	I	SBF	MA	12087 w	I SBF	MA
12040	I	SBF	PC	12088 z	I SBF	PC
12041	I	SBF	PC	12089	I SBF	PC
12042 w	I	SBF	MA	12090	I SBF	MA
12043	I	SBF	PC	12091	I SBF	MA
12044	I	SBF	PC	12092	I SBF	PC
12045	I	SBF	PC	12093	I SBF	MA
12046	I	SBF	PC	12094	I SBF	PC
12047 z	I	SBF	PC	12095	I SBF	PC
12048	I	SBF	PC	12096	I SBF	PC
12049	I	SBF	PC	12097	I SBF	PC
12050 w	I	SBF	PC	12098	I SBF	MA
12051	I	SBF	PC	12099	I SBF	PC
12052	I	SBF	PC	12100 z	I SBF	PC
12053	I	SBF	PC	12101 w	I SBF	MA

12102		I	SBF	MA	12137		I	SBF	PC
12103	z	I	SBF	PC	12138		I	SBF	MA
12104		I	SBF	PC	12139		I	SBF	MA
12105		I	SBF	MA	12140	*z	I	SBF	PC
12106		I	SBF	MA	12141		I	SBF	MA
12107		I	SBF	MA	12142	z	I	SBF	PC
12108	w	I	SBF	MA	12143		I	SBF	MA
12109	w	I	SBF	MA	12144	w	I	SBF	MA
12110		I	SBF	MA	12145		I	SBF	PC
12111		I	SBF	PC	12146		I	SBF	MA
12112	z	I	SBF	PC	12147		I	SBF	PC
12113		I	SBF	MA	12148		I	SBF	PC
12114		I	SBF	PC	12149		I	SBF	PC
12115		I	SBF	PC	12150		I	SBF	PC
12116		I	SBF	PC	12151		I	SBF	PC
12117		I	SBF	PC	12152		I	SBF	MA
12118		I	SBF	MA	12153		I	SBF	PC
12119		I	SBF	PC	12154		I	SBF	MA
12120		I	SBF	MA	12155	w	I	SBF	MA
12121		I	SBF	PC	12156		I	SBF	PC
12122	z	I	SBF	PC	12157		I	SBF	MA
12123		I	SBF	PC	12158		I	SBF	MA
12124		I	SBF	MA	12159		I	SBF	MA
12125		I	SBF	MA	12160	w	I	SBF	MA
12126		I	SBF	PC	12161	z	I	SBF	PC
12127		I	SBF	MA	12163		I	SBF	PC
12128	w	I	SBF	MA	12164		I	SBF	MA
12129		I	SBF	MA	12165		I	SBF	PC
12130		I	SBF	PC	12166		I	SBF	PC
12131		I	SBF	MA	12167		I	SBF	MA
12132		I	SBF	MA	12168	w	I	SBF	MA
12133		I	SBF	PC	12169	z	I	SBF	PC
12134		I	SBF	MA	12170	z	I	SBF	PC
12135		I	SBF	PC	12171	z	I	SBF	PC
12136		I	SBF	MA	12172	z	I	SBF	PC

AI2J (TSOE)   OPEN STANDARD (END)

Dia. AI201. Mark 4. Air conditioned. –/74 2T. SIG bogies (BT41). a. ETH 6.

Note: 12232 was converted from the original 12405.

Lot No. 31047 Metro-Cammell 1989 onwards. 39.5 t.

12200	I	SAB	BN	12208	I	SAB	BN
12201	I	SAB	BN	12209	I	SAB	BN
12202	I	SAB	BN	12210	I	SAB	BN
12203	I	SAB	BN	12211	I	SAB	BN
12204	I	SAB	BN	12212	I	SAB	BN
12205	I	SAB	BN	12213	I	SAB	BN
12206	I	SAB	BN	12214	I	SAB	BN
12207	I	SAB	BN	12215	I	SAB	BN

12216	I	SAB	BN	12225	I	SAB	BN
12217	I	SAB	BN	12226	I	SAB	BN
12218	I	SAB	BN	12227	I	SAB	BN
12219	I	SAB	BN	12228	I	SAB	BN
12220	I	SAB	BN	12229	I	SAB	BN
12222	I	SAB	BN	12230	I	SAB	BN
12223	I	SAB	BN	12231	I	SAB	BN
12224	I	SAB	BN	12232	I	SAB	BN

AL2J (TSOD) OPEN STANDARD (DISABLED ACCESS)

Dia. AL201. Mark 4. Air conditioned. –/72 + wheelchair space 1T (suitable for a disabled person). SIG bogies (BT41). a. p. ETH 6.

Lot No. 31048 Metro-Cammell 1989 onwards. 39.4 t.

12300	I	SAB	BN	12316	I	SAB	BN
12301	I	SAB	BN	12317	I	SAB	BN
12302	I	SAB	BN	12318	I	SAB	BN
12303	I	SAB	BN	12319	I	SAB	BN
12304	I	SAB	BN	12320	I	SAB	BN
12305	I	SAB	BN	12321	I	SAB	BN
12306	I	SAB	BN	12322	I	SAB	BN
12307	I	SAB	BN	12323	I	SAB	BN
12308	I	SAB	BN	12324	I	SAB	BN
12309	I	SAB	BN	12325	I	SAB	BN
12310	I	SAB	BN	12326	I	SAB	BN
12311	I	SAB	BN	12327	I	SAB	BN
12312	I	SAB	BN	12328	I	SAB	BN
12313	I	SAB	BN	12329	I	SAB	BN
12314	I	SAB	BN	12330	I	SAB	BN
12315	I	SAB	BN				

AC2J (TSO)   OPEN STANDARD

Dia. AC214. Mark 4. Air conditioned. –/74 2T. SIG bogies (BT41). a. ETH 6X.

Notes: 12405 is the second coach to carry that number. It was built from the bodyshell originally intended for 12221. The original 12405 is now 12232. 12490 – 12512 were cancelled.

Lot No. 31049 Metro-Cammell 1989 onwards. 39.9 t.

12400	I	SAB	BN	12409	I	SAB	BN
12401	I	SAB	BN	12410	I	SAB	BN
12402	I	SAB	BN	12411	I	SAB	BN
12403	I	SAB	BN	12412	I	SAB	BN
12404	I	SAB	BN	12413	I	SAB	BN
12405	I	SAB	BN	12414	I	SAB	BN
12406	I	SAB	BN	12415	I	SAB	BN
12407	I	SAB	BN	12416	I	SAB	BN
12408	I	SAB	BN	12417	I	SAB	BN

12418	I	SAB	BN	12467	I	SAB	BN
12419	I	SAB	BN	12468	I	SAB	BN
12420	I	SAB	BN	12469	I	SAB	BN
12421	I	SAB	BN	12470	I	SAB	BN
12422	I	SAB	BN	12471	I	SAB	BN
12423	I	SAB	BN	12472	I	SAB	BN
12424	I	SAB	BN	12473	I	SAB	BN
12425	I	SAB	BN	12474	I	SAB	BN
12426	I	SAB	BN	12475	I	SAB	BN
12427	I	SAB	BN	12476	I	SAB	BN
12428	I	SAB	BN	12477	I	SAB	BN
12429	I	SAB	BN	12478	I	SAB	BN
12430	I	SAB	BN	12479	I	SAB	BN
12431	I	SAB	BN	12480	I	SAB	BN
12432	I	SAB	BN	12481	I	SAB	BN
12433	I	SAB	BN	12482	I	SAB	BN
12434	I	SAB	BN	12483	I	SAB	BN
12435	I	SAB	BN	12484	I	SAB	BN
12436	I	SAB	BN	12485	I	SAB	BN
12437	I	SAB	BN	12486	I	SAB	BN
12438	I	SAB	BN	12487	I	SAB	BN
12439	I	SAB	BN	12488	I	SAB	BN
12440	I	SAB	BN	12489	I	SAB	BN
12441	I	SAB	BN	12513	I	SAB	BN
12442	I	SAB	BN	12514	I	SAB	BN
12443	I	SAB	BN	12515	I	SAB	BN
12444	I	SAB	BN	12516	I	SAB	BN
12445	I	SAB	BN	12517	I	SAB	BN
12446	I	SAB	BN	12518	I	SAB	BN
12447	I	SAB	BN	12519	I	SAB	BN
12448	I	SAB	BN	12520	I	SAB	BN
12449	I	SAB	BN	12521	I	SAB	BN
12450	I	SAB	BN	12522	I	SAB	BN
12451	I	SAB	BN	12523	I	SAB	BN
12452	I	SAB	BN	12524	I	SAB	BN
12453	I	SAB	BN	12525	I	SAB	BN
12454	I	SAB	BN	12526	I	SAB	BN
12455	I	SAB	BN	12527	I	SAB	BN
12456	I	SAB	BN	12528	I	SAB	BN
12457	I	SAB	BN	12529	I	SAB	BN
12458	I	SAB	BN	12530	I	SAB	BN
12459	I	SAB	BN	12531	I	SAB	BN
12460	I	SAB	BN	12532	I	SAB	BN
12461	I	SAB	BN	12533	I	SAB	BN
12462	I	SAB	BN	12534	I	SAB	BN
12463	I	SAB	BN	12535	I	SAB	BN
12464	I	SAB	BN	12536	I	SAB	BN
12465	I	SAB	BN	12537	I	SAB	BN
12466	I	SAB	BN	12538	I	SAB	BN

AA11 (FK)   CORRIDOR FIRST

Dia. AA101. Mark 1. 42/– 2T. ETH 3. d.

13225 – 13230. Lot No. 30381 Ashford/Eastleigh 1959. B4 bogies. 33 t.
13306 – 13344. Lot No. 30667 Swindon 1962. Commonwealth bogies. 36 t.

f – Fitted with fluorescent lighting.

13225 xk **RR** SAD LL		13318 a **I** XWR BN
13227 xk **RR** SAOL Long Marston		13320 x **M** XCRZ CS
13228 xk **M** XSCZ BO		13321 x **M** XCR CS
13229 xk **M** XSC BO		13323 x **M** XCRZ CS
13230 xk **M** XSC BO		13331 vf **N** XWRZ Basford Hall
13306 v **MPNW** Carlisle Yard		13341 af **I** XWR BN
13317 x **M** XCRZ CS		13344 vf **XWRZ** Carlisle Yard

AA1A (FK)   CORRIDOR FIRST

Dia. AA106. Mark 2A. Pressure ventilated. 42/– 2T. B4 bogies. d. ETH 4.

13440 – 13462. Lot No. 30774 Derby 1968. 33 t.
13467 – 13474. Lot No. 30785 Derby 1968. 33 t.

13462 was renumbered 19462 for a time when declassified.

13440 v **N** XWRZ BO	13467 v **N** XWRZ Basford Hall
13462 a **N** XWRZ Basford Hall	13474 a **N** XWRZ BO

AA1B (FK)   CORRIDOR FIRST

Dia. AA107. Mark 2B. Pressure ventilated. 42/– 2T. B4 bogies. d. ETH 4.

Lot No. 30789 Derby 1969. 33 t.

13479 was renumbered 19479 for a time when declassified.

13479 a **N** XWRZ Basford Hall	13482 a **N** XWRZ Basford Hall

AA1D (FK)   CORRIDOR FIRST

Dia. AA109. Mark 2D. Air conditioned (Stones). 42/– 2T. B4 bogies. a.
ETH 5. 13585 – 13607 require at least 800 V train heat supply.

Lot No. 30825 Derby 1971 – 2. 34.5 t.

13575 **N** SAXZ OM		13585 **I** XWRZ Kineton
13581 **I** SAXZ WB		13593 **I** SAXZ ZN
13582 **I** MPNW Kineton		13604 **I** XWRZ BN
13583 **I** SAXZ WB		13607 **I** XWRZ BN

AA31 (CK)   CORRIDOR COMPOSITE

Dia. AA301. Mark 1. 24/18 1T. v. ETH 2.

Lot No. 30665 Derby 1961. Commonwealth bogies and metal window frames. 37 t. Numbered 7187/91 for a time.

16167	v	**N**	XVSZ	SL			
16168	v	**N**	XCRZ	CO			
16187	x	**CH** XTS		CM			

16190	v	**N** XCRZ		CO
16191	x	**CH** XTS		CM

AB11 (BFK)   CORRIDOR BRAKE FIRST

Dia. AB101. Mark 1. 24/– 1T. v. ETH 2.

Originally numbered 14007/13/15/21/23.

17007. Lot No. 30382 Ashford/Eastleigh 1959. B4 bogies. 33 t.
17013 – 17015. Lot No. 30668 Swindon 1961. Commonwealth bogies. 36 t.
17021 – 17023. Lot No. 30718 Swindon 1963. Commonwealth bogies and metal window frames. 36 t.

17007	x	**PC**	XVS	SO
17013	v	**M**	XWRZ	SO
17015	x	**W**	XWR	BN

17021	vk	**M**	XHLZ	SO
17023	x	**I**	XWR	BN

Note: 17007 is named 'MERCATOR'.

AB1Z (BFK)   CORRIDOR BRAKE FIRST

Dia. AB102. Mark 2. Pressure ventilated. 24/– 1T. B4 bogies. vd. ETH 4.

Lot No. 30756 Derby 1966. 31.5 t.

Originally numbered 14039/41/54.

17039	v	**RX** SAXZ	CD
17041	v	**M** XCI	DI

17054	v		SAXZ	Crewe Brook S

AB1A (BFK)   CORRIDOR BRAKE FIRST

Dia. AB103. Mark 2A. Pressure ventilated. 24/– 1T. B4 bogies. d. ETH 4.

17056 – 17077. Lot No. 30775 Derby 1967 – 8. 32 t.
17086 – 17102. Lot No. 30786 Derby 1968. 32 t.
Non-Standard Livery: Statesman Pullman maroon & beige. Named 'ATTENDANTS CAR' Originally numbered 14056 – 102. 17089/90 were renumbered 35502/3 for a time when declassified.

17056	a	**N**	XWRZ	Basford Hall
17058	a	**N**	SAXZ	Long Marston
17064	v	**RR**	SAOL	Longtown
17068	v	**RR**	SAOL	Longtown
17073	a	**N**	SAXZ	Long Marston
17076	a	**N**	SAXZ	Eastl'h Dn CS
17077	a	**N**	SAOL	Long Marston

17086	a	**N**	SAOL	Long Marston
17089	v	**RR**	SAOL	Longtown
17090	v	**RR**	SAOL	Longtown
17091	v	**RR**	SAOL	Longtown
17096	a	**G**	SAVS	SL
17099	v	**RR**	SAA	Long Marston
17102	a	**0**	XMA	CS

AB1D (BFK)   CORRIDOR BRAKE FIRST

Dia. AB106. Mark 2D. Air conditioned (Stones equipment). 24/– 1T. B4 Bogies.
17163 – 17172 require at least 800 V train heat supply. a. ETH 5.
Non-Standard Livery: Waterman VIP without lining.

Originally numbered 14141 – 72.

Lot No. 30823 Derby 1971 – 2. 33.5 t.

17141	0	XWRL	BK		17163	I	SAOL	Kineton
17144	I	XWR	DY		17164	0	XWRL	BK
17146	I	XWRZ	DY		17165	I	XWR	BN
17148	I	SAOL	Kineton		17166	I	SAOL	Longtown
17151	I	XWRZ	HT		17167	I	XWRZ	HT
17153	W	XWR	DY		17168	M	XCR	CS
17155	I	SAOL	Kineton		17169	I	XWR	DY
17156	I	XWR	DY		17170	I	XWRZ	DY
17158	I	SAOL	ZN		17171	I	MPNW	Carlisle Yard
17159	I	XWRZ	BN		17172	I	XWR	BN
17161	I	MPNW	BN					

AE1G (BFO)   OPEN BRAKE FIRST

Dia. AE101. Mark 3B. Air conditioned. Fitted with hydraulic handbrake. 36/–
1T. BT10 bogies. a. pg. Secondary door locks. ETH 5X.

Lot No. 30990 Derby 1986. 35.81 t.

17173	I	SBF	MA		17175	I	SBF	MA
17174	I	SBF	MA					

AB31 (BCK)   CORRIDOR BRAKE COMPOSITE

Dia. AB301 (AB302*). Mark 1. There are two variants depending upon whether
the standard class compartments have armrests. Each vehicle has two first class
and three standard class compartments. 12/18 2T (12/24 2T*). ETH 2.

21096. Lot No. 30185. Metro-Cammell 1956. BR1 bogies. Steam heat only.
32.5 t.
21236 – 21246. Lot No. 30669 Swindon 1961 – 2. Commonwealth bogies.
36 t.
21256. Lot No. 30731 Derby 1963. Commonwealth bogies. 37 t.
21265 – 21272. Lot No. 30732 Derby 1964. Commonwealth bogies. 37 t.

21096	x	M	XSN	BQ		21265	a*	MPNW	Carlisle Yard
21236	v	M	XRP	ZG		21266	a* I	XWR	BN
21241	x	I	XWR	HT		21268	a* I	XWR	HT
21245	x	CC	XWR	BN		21269	a*	WV	XWR	BN
21246	a	I	XWR	BN		21272	x*	M	XWRZ	Ferme Park
21256	x	M	XCRK	BK					

AA21 (SK)   CORRIDOR STANDARD

Dia. AB201. Mark 1. Each vehicle has eight compartments. All remaining vehicles have metal window frames and melamine interior panelling x. Commonwealth bogies. – /48 1T. ETH 4.
Non-Standard Livery: Pilkington's K (green with white red chevron and light blue block).

25729 – 25893. Lot No. 30685 Derby 1961 – 2. 36 t.
25955. Lot No. 30686 Derby 1962. 36 t.
26013. Lot No. 30719 Derby 1962. 37 t.

f – Facelifted with fluorescent lighting.

Before preservation, these coaches were renumbered 18729 – 19013.

25729	*f	M	XCR	CS		25837		O	XCR	CS
25756		O	XCR	CS		25862		O	XCR	CS
25767		O	XCR	CS		25893		O	XCR	CS
25806		O	XCR	CS		25955	*f	M	XCR	CS
25808		O	XCR	CS		26013		O	XCR	CS

AB21 (BSK)   CORRIDOR BRAKE STANDARD

Dia. AB201. Mark 1. Each vehicle has four compartments. – /24 1T (– /32 1T*).
Non-Standard Liveries: 30290 is black. 35407 is in London & North Western Railway livery.

34525 – 34556. Lot No. 30095 Wolverton 1955. BR1 bogies. 34 t. (34525 C 36 t.).
34952 – 34991. Lot No. 30229 Metro-Cammell 1956 – 7. BR1 bogies. 34 t. (34991 C 36 t.).
35073. Lot No. 30233 Gloucester 1956 – 7. BR1 bogies. 35 t.
35185 – 35207. Lot No. 30427 Wolverton 1959. BR1 bogies. 35 t. (35207 B4 33 t.).
35290. Lot No. 30573 Gloucester 1960. B4 bogies. 33 t.

34525	a	M	XGS	EN		35073		M	XCRZ	CS
34556	v		XVSZ	SL		35185	v		XVSZ	SL
34952	v		XVSZ	SL		35207	x*B4	G	XVS	SL
34991	a*C	PC	XVS	SL						

These lots have metal window frames and melamine interior panelling Commonwealth bogies. ETH 2.

35317 – 35337. Lot No. 30699 Wolverton 1962 – 3. Commonwealth bogies. 37 t.
35449. Lot No. 30728 Wolverton 1963. Commonwealth bogies. 37 t.
35407, 35452 – 35486. Lot No. 30721 Wolverton 1963. 37 t.

f – Facelifted with fluorescent lighting.
g – Converted to ETH generator vehicle.
§ – Converted to charter train support coach.

35290	v	O	XWRZ	Basford Hall		35322	x*f	M	XBL	DI
35317	v	M	XWR	BN		35337	v	CH	XRTZ	CO

35407	xg	0	XSH	CJ	35463	v	M	XCR	CS
35449	v	M	XBC	DI	35465	x §	WV	XWR	BN
35452	x	RR	SAD	LL	35467	v	M	XRP	KR
35453	x	RR	SAOL	Long Marston	35468	v	CH	XNR	YM
35457	v	M	XST	BO	35469	xg	WV	XWR	BN
35459	x	M	XCR	CS	35476	v	CC	XMR	SK
35461	x	CH	XTS	CO	35479	v	M	XWR	BN

AB2A/AB2C (BSK)   CORRIDOR BRAKE STANDARD

Dia. AB204. Mark 2A (2C*). Pressure ventilated. Renumbered from BFK. –/24 1T. B4 bogies. ETH 4.

35500/15 – 18. Lot No. 30786 Derby 1968. 32 t.
35505 – 9/11. Lot No. 30796. Derby 1969 – 70. 32.5 t.
35510/12 – 14. Lot No. 30775 Derby 1967 – 68. 32 t.

§ – Cage removed from brake compartment.

35486	(35486)		v	M	XJBZ	MK
35500	(14094, 17094)		v	M	SAOL	Longtown
35505	(14118, 17118)	a*	RR	SAXZ	LL
35506	(14122, 17122)	a*	RR	XCRZ	CS
35507	(14123, 17123)	a*	RR	SAXZ	Long Marston
35508	(14128, 17128)	a*	RR	XWRZ	Basford Hall
35509	(14138, 17138)	a*	RR	SAXZ	Long Marston
35510	(14075, 17075)	a	RR	SAXZ	Long Marston
35511	(14130, 17130)	a*	RR	SAXZ	Nottingham CS
35512	(14057, 17057)	a§	RR	SAD	LL
35513	(14063, 17063)	a§	RR	SAD	LL
35514	(14069, 17069)	a§	RR	SAD	LL
35515	(14079, 17079)	a§	RR	SAD	LL
35516	(14080, 17080)	a§	RR	SAD	LL
35517	(14088, 17088)	a§	RR	SAD	LL
35518	(14097, 17097)	a§	RR	SAD	LL

2.2. COACHES AWAITING DISPOSAL

This list contains the last known locations of condemned coaches awaiiting disposal. The definition of which coaches are ''awaiting disposal'' is somewhat vague, but generally speaking these are coaches of types not now in normal service, coaches which have been damaged by fire, vandalism or collision. Most stored coaches have now been included in the main lists.

2900	ZN	10608	ZN
4485	SP	13237	Hull Paragon Station
6332	ZK	13325	Margam EY
6339	EC	13342	Margam EY
7183	CP	18416	Crewe Brook Sidings
7213	Long Marston	18750	Crewe Brook Sidings
9533	MA	19500	CP

2.3. HIGH SPEED TRAIN TRAILER CARS

HSTs run in formations of 7 or 8 trailer cars with a driving motor brake (power car) at each end. All trailer cars have BT10 bogies with disc brakes. Heating is by a three-phase supply and vehicles have air conditioning. Max. Speed is 125 mph.

GN4G (TRB)   TRAILER BUFFET FIRST

Dia. GN401. Converted from TRSB by fitting first class seats. Renumbered from 404xx series by subtracting 200. Secondary door locks. pq. 23/–.

40204 – 40228. Lot No. 30883 Derby 1976 – 7. 36.12 t.
40231 – 40233. Lot No. 30899 Derby 1978 – 9. 36.12 t.

40204	I	SCJ	LA	40212	I	SBH	LA
40205	I	SCJ	PM	40213	I	SCJ	PM
40206	I	SCJ	PM	40221	I	SCJ	PM
40207	I	SCJ	PM	40228	I	SCJ	PM
40208	I	SCH	LA	40231	I	SCJ	LA
40209	I	SCJ	PM	40232	I	SBJ	PM
40210	I	SCJ	PM	40233	I	SBH	LA
40211	I	SBH	LA				

GK2G (TRSB)   TRAILER BUFFET STANDARD

Dia. GK202. Renumbered from 400xx series by adding 400. Secondary door locks. pq. 35/–.

40401 – 40427. Lot No. 30883 Derby 1976 – 7. 36.12 t.
40429 – 40437. Lot No. 30899 Derby 1978 – 9. 36.12 t.

40401	I	SBH	EC	40423	I	SBH	EC
40402	I	SBH	EC	40424	I	SBH	LA
40403	I	SBH	LA	40425	I	SBH	EC
40414	I	SBH	LA	40426	I	SBH	EC
40415	I	SBH	LA	40427	I	SBH	EC
40416	I	SBH	EC	40429	I	SBH	EC
40417	I	SBH	LA	40430	I	SBH	EC
40418	I	SBH	LA	40434	I	SBH	LA
40419	I	SBH	EC	40435	I	SBH	EC
40420	I	SBH	EC	40436	I	SBH	LA
40422	I	SBH	EC	40437	I	SBH	EC

GL1G (TRFK)   TRAILER KITCHEN FIRST

Dia. GL101. Reclassified from TRUK. Formerly used in "Pullman" sets, but now used as replacements for out of service TRFBs. pq. 24/–.

Lot No. 30884 Derby 1976 – 7. 37 t.

40501	d I	SBOL	ZD	40505	I	SCOL	ZC

| 40511 | I | SCOL | ZD | | 40513 d | I | SBOL | ZD |

GK1G (TRFM)   TRAILER MODULAR BUFFET FIRST

Dia. GK102. Converted to modular catering from 40719. Secondary door locks. pq. 17/–.

Lot No. 30921 Derby 1978 – 9. 38.16 t.

| 40619 | I | SBOL | ZD | |

GK1G (TRFB)   TRAILER BUFFET FIRST

Dia. GK101. These vehicles have larger kitchens than the 402xx and 404xx series vehicles, and are used in trains where full meal service is required. They have been renumbered from the 403xx series (in which the seats were unclassified) by adding 400 to previous number. Secondary door locks. pq. 17/–.

40700 – 40721. Lot No. 30921 Derby 1978 – 9. 38.16 t.
40722 – 40735. Lot No. 30940 Derby 1979 – 80. 38.16 t.
40736 – 40753. Lot No. 30948 Derby 1980 – 1. 38.16 t.
40754 – 40757. Lot No. 30966 Derby 1982. 38.16 t.

* Vehicle refurbished by ABB for Porterbrook Leasing Company.

40700	I	SBI	NL		40728	I	SBI	NL
40701	I	SBI	NL		40729	I	SBI	NL
40702	I	SBI	NL		40730	I	SBI	NL
40703	I	SCJ	LA		40731	I	SCJ	LA
40704	I	SCB	EC		40732	I	SCF	MA
40705	I	SCB	EC		40733	I	SCJ	LA
40706	I	SCB	EC		40734	I	SCJ	LA
40707	I	SCJ	LA		40735	I	SCB	EC
40708	I	SBI	NL		40736	I	SCJ	LA
40709	I	SCJ	LA		40737	I	SCB	EC
40710	I	SCJ	LA		40738	I	SCJ	LA
40711	I	SCB	EC		40739	I	SCJ	PM
40712	I	SCJ	LA		40740	I	SCB	EC
40713	I	SCJ	LA		40741	I	SBI	NL
40714	I	SCJ	PM		40742	I	SCF	MA
40715	I	SCJ	PM		40743	I	SCJ	LA
40716	I	SCJ	PM		40744	I	SCJ	PM
40717	I	SCJ	PM		40745	I	SCJ	PM
40718	I	SCJ	LA		40746	I	SBI	NL
40720	I	SCB	EC		40747	I	SCJ	PM
40721	I	SCJ	LA		40748	I	SCB	EC
40722	I	SCJ	LA		40749	I	SBI	NL
40723	I	SCF	MA		40750	I	SCB	EC
40724	I	SCJ	PM		40751	I	SBI	NL
40725	I	SCJ	LA		40752	I	SCJ	PM
40726	I	SCJ	LA		40753	I	SBI	NL
40727	I	SCJ	LA		40754 *	I	SBI	NL

40755	I	SCJ	LA	40757	I SCJ	LA
40756	I	SBI	NL			

GH1G (TF)   TRAILER FIRST

Dia. GH102. Secondary door locks. 48/- 2T.

41003 - 41056. Lot No. 30881 Derby 1976 - 7. 33.66 t.
41057 - 41120. Lot No. 30896 Derby 1977 - 8. 33.66 t.
41121 - 41148. Lot No. 30938 Derby 1979 - 80. 33.66 t.
41149 - 41166. Lot No. 30947 Derby 1980. 33.66 t.
41167 - 41169. Lot No. 30963 Derby 1982. 33.66 t.
41170. Lot No. 30967 Derby 1982. Ex prototype vehicle. 33.66 t.
41178. Lot No. 30882 Derby 1976 - 7. 33.60 t.

Note: 41170 was converted from 41001. 41178 is a prototype refurbished vehicle and has been converted from 42011 which was damaged by fire.

41003	p	I	SCJ	PM	41037	p	I SCJ	LA
41004		I	SCJ	PM	41038		I SCJ	LA
41005	p	I	SCJ	PM	41039		I SCB	EC
41006		I	SCJ	PM	41040		I SCB	EC
41007	p	I	SCJ	PM	41041	p	I SBI	NL
41008		I	SCJ	PM	41042		I SCJ	PM
41009		I	SCH	LA	41043		I SCB	EC
41010		I	SCJ	PM	41044		I SCB	EC
41011	p	I	SCJ	PM	41045		I SBH	LA
41012		I	SCJ	PM	41046		I SBI	NL
41013	p	I	SCJ	PM	41049		I SCJ	PM
41014		I	SCJ	PM	41050		I SCJ	PM
41015	p	I	SCJ	PM	41051		I SCJ	LA
41016		I	SCJ	PM	41052		I SCJ	LA
41017	p	I	SCH	LA	41055		I SCJ	LA
41018		I	SCJ	PM	41056		I SCJ	LA
41019	p	I	SCJ	PM	41057		I SBI	NL
41020		I	SCJ	PM	41058		I SBI	NL
41021	p	I	SCJ	PM	41059		I SBH	EC
41022		I	SCJ	PM	41060		I SCJ	LA
41023	p	I	SCJ	LA	41061		I SBI	NL
41024		I	SCJ	LA	41062		I SBI	NL
41025	p	I	SCF	MA	41063		I SBI	NL
41026		I	SCF	MA	41064		I SBI	NL
41027	p	I	SCJ	LA	41065		I SCJ	LA
41028		I	SCJ	LA	41066	p	I SCF	MA
41029	p	I	SCJ	LA	41067		I SBI	NL
41030		I	SCJ	LA	41068		I SBI	NL
41031	p	I	SCJ	LA	41069		I SBI	NL
41032		I	SCJ	LA	41070		I. SBI	NL
41033	p	I	SCJ	LA	41071		I SBI	NL
41034		I	SCJ	LA	41072		I SBI	NL
41035	p	I	SCF	MA	41075		I SBI	NL
41036		I	SCF	MA	41076		I SBI	NL

41077	I	SBI	NL
41078	I	SBI	NL
41079	I	SBI	NL
41080	I	SBI	NL
41081	I	SBH	EC
41082	I	SBI	NL
41083	I	SBI	NL
41084	I	SBI	NL
41085	I	SBH	EC
41086	I	SBH	EC
41087	I	SCB	EC
41088	I	SCB	EC
41089	I	SCJ	LA
41090	I	SCB	EC
41091	I	SCB	EC
41092	I	SCB	EC
41093	I	SCJ	LA
41094	I	SCJ	LA
41095	I	SBH	EC
41096	I	SBH	EC
41097	I	SCB	EC
41098	I	SCB	EC
41099	I	SCB	EC
41100	I	SCB	EC
41101	I	SCJ	LA
41102	I	SCJ	LA
41103	I	SCJ	LA
41104	I	SCJ	LA
41105	I	SCJ	PM
41106	I	SCJ	PM
41107	I	SBH	EC
41108	I	SBH	LA
41109	I	SBH	LA
41110	I	SCJ	PM
41111	I	SBI	NL
41112	I	SBI	NL
41113	I	SBI	NL
41114	I	SBH	EC
41115	I	SBI	NL
41116	I	SCJ	LA
41117	I	SBI	NL
41118	I	SCB	EC
41119	I	SBH	EC
41120	I	SCB	EC
41121 p	I	SCJ	LA
41122	I	SCJ	LA
41123 p	I	SCJ	PM
41124	I	SCJ	PM
41125	I	SCJ	PM
41126 p	I	SCJ	PM
41127 p	I	SCJ	PM
41128	I	SCJ	PM
41129 p	I	SCJ	PM
41130	I	SCJ	PM
41131 p	I	SCJ	LA
41132	I	SCJ	LA
41133 p	I	SCJ	LA
41134	I	SCJ	LA
41135 p	I	SCJ	LA
41136	I	SCJ	PM
41137 p	I	SCJ	PM
41138	I	SCJ	PM
41139 p	I	SCJ	LA
41140	I	SCJ	LA
41141 p	I	SCJ	LA
41142	I	SCJ	LA
41143 p	I	SCJ	LA
41144	I	SCJ	LA
41145 p	I	SCJ	PM
41146	I	SCJ	PM
41147	I	SBH	EC
41148	I	SBH	EC
41149	I	SBH	EC
41150	I	SCB	EC
41151	I	SCB	EC
41152	I	SCB	EC
41153	I	SBI	NL
41154	I	SBI	NL
41155	I	SBI	NL
41156	I	SBI	NL
41157	I	SCJ	LA
41158	I	SCJ	LA
41159	I	SBH	LA
41160	I	SBH	LA
41161	I	SBH	EC
41162	I	SBH	EC
41163	I	SBH	LA
41164 p	I	SCF	MA
41165	I	SBH	LA
41166	I	SBH	LA
41167	I	SBH	LA
41168	I	SBH	LA
41169	I	SBH	LA
41170	I	SCB	EC
41178	I	SCOL	PM

GH2G (TS)   TRAILER STANDARD

Dia. GH203. Secondary door locks. –/76 2T.

42003 – 42090. Lot No. 30882 Derby 1976 – 7. 33.60 t.
42091 – 42250. Lot No. 30897 Derby 1977 – 9. 33.60 t.
42251 – 42305. Lot No. 30939 Derby 1979 – 80. 33.60 t.
42306 – 42322. Lot No. 30969 Derby 1982. 33.60 t.
42323 – 42341. Lot No. 30983 Derby 1984 – 5. 33.60 t.
42342. Lot No. 30949 Derby 1982. 33.47 t. Converted from TGS.
42343/5. Lot No. 30970 Derby 1982. 33.47 t. Converted from TGS.
42344. Lot No. 30964 Derby 1982. 33.47 t. Converted from TGS.
42346/7/50/1. Lot No. 30881 Derby 1976 – 7. 33.66 t. Converted from TF.
42348/9. Lot No. 30896 Derby 1977 – 8. 33.66 t. Converted from TF.
42353/5 – 7. Lot No. 30967 Derby 1982. Ex prototype vehicles. 33.66 t.
42352/4. Lot No. 30897 Derby 1977. Were TF from 1983 to 1992. 33.66 t.

Note: 42158 was also numbered 41177 for a time.

42003	I	SCJ	PM	42036	I	SCF	MA
42004	I	SCH	LA	42037	I	SCF	MA
42005	I	SCJ	PM	42038	I	SCF	MA
42006	I	SCJ	PM	42039	I	SCJ	LA
42007	I	SCJ	PM	42040	I	SCJ	LA
42008	I	SCH	LA	42041	I	SCJ	LA
42009	I	SCJ	PM	42042	I	SCJ	LA
42010	I	SCJ	PM	42043	I	SCJ	LA
42012	I	SCH	LA	42044	I	SCJ	LA
42013	I	SCH	LA	42045	I	SCJ	LA
42014	I	SCH	LA	42046	I	SCJ	LA
42015	I	SCJ	PM	42047	I	SCJ	LA
42016	I	SCJ	PM	42048	I	SCJ	LA
42017	I	SCJ	PM	42049	I	SCJ	LA
42018	I	SCJ	PM	42050	I	SCJ	LA
42019	I	SCJ	PM	42051	I	SCF	MA
42020	I	SCJ	PM	42052	I	SCF	MA
42021	I	SCJ	PM	42053	I	SCF	MA
42022	I	SCJ	PM	42054	I	SCJ	LA
42023	I	SCJ	PM	42055	I	SCJ	LA
42024	I	SCH	LA	42056	I	SCJ	LA
42025	I	SCH	LA	42057	I	SCB	EC
42026	I	SCH	LA	42058	I	SCB	EC
42027	I	SCJ	PM	42059	I	SCB	EC
42028	I	SCJ	PM	42060	I	SCJ	PM
42029	I	SCJ	PM	42061	I	SCJ	PM
42030	I	SCJ	PM	42062	I	SCJ	LA
42031	I	SCJ	PM	42063	I	SCB	EC
42032	I	SCJ	PM	42064	I	SCB	EC
42033	I	SCJ	LA	42065	I	SCB	EC
42034	I	SCJ	LA	42066	I	SCJ	LA
42035	I	SCJ	LA	42067	I	SCJ	LA

42068	I	SCJ	LA		
42069	I	SCJ	PM		
42070	I	SCJ	PM		
42071	I	SCJ	PM		
42072	I	SCJ	PM		
42073	I	SCJ	PM		
42074	I	SCJ	PM		
42075	I	SCJ	LA		
42076	I	SCJ	LA		
42077	I	SCJ	LA		
42078	I	SCJ	LA		
42079	I	SCJ	PM		
42080	I	SCJ	PM		
42081	I	SCJ	LA		
42082	I	SCJ	LA		
42083	I	SCJ	LA		
42084	I	SBH	EC		
42085	I	SBH	EC		
42086	I	SBH	EC		
42087	I	SBH	EC		
42088	I	SBH	EC		
42089	I	SCJ	PM		
42090	I	SBH	EC		
42091	I	SBH	EC		
42092	I	SBH	LA		
42093	I	SBH	LA		
42094	I	SBH	LA		
42095	I	SBH	LA		
42096	I	SCJ	LA		
42097	I	SCJ	MA		
42098	I	SCJ	LA		
42099	I	SCJ	LA		
42100	I	SBI	NL		
42101	I	SBI	NL		
42102	I	SBI	NL		
42103	I	SBH	EC		
42104	I	SCB	EC		
42105	I	SBH	LA		
42106	I	SCB	EC		
42107	I	SCJ	LA		
42108	I	SBH	LA		
42109	I	SBH	LA		
42110	I	SBH	LA		
42111	I	SBI	NL		
42112	I	SBI	NL		
42113	I	SBI	NL		
42115	I	SBH	EC		
42116	I	SBH	EC		
42117	I	SBH	EC		
42118	I	SCJ	PM		
42119	I	SBI	NL		

42120	I	SBI	NL
42121	I	SBI	NL
42122	I	SCF	MA
42123	I	SBI	NL
42124	I	SBI	NL
42125	I	SBI	NL
42126	I	SCJ	LA
42127	I	SBH	EC
42128	I	SBH	EC
42129	I	SCJ	LA
42130	I	SBH	EC
42131	I	SBI	NL
42132	I	SBI	NL
42133	I	SBI	NL
42134	I	SCF	MA
42135	I	SBI	NL
42136	I	SBI	NL
42137	I	SBI	NL
42138	I	SCJ	PM
42139	I	SBI	NL
42140	I	SBI	NL
42141	I	SBI	NL
42143	I	SCJ	PM
42144	I	SCJ	PM
42145	I	SCJ	PM
42146	I	SCB	EC
42147	I	SBI	NL
42148	I	SBI	NL
42149	I	SBI	NL
42150	I	SCB	EC
42151	I	SBI	NL
42152	I	SBI	NL
42153	I	SBI	NL
42154	I	SCB	EC
42155	I	SBI	NL
42156	I	SBI	NL
42157	I	SBI	NL
42158	I	SCB	EC
42159	I	SBI	NL
42160	I	SBI	NL
42161	I	SBI	NL
42162	I	SBH	EC
42163	I	SBI	NL
42164	I	SBI	NL
42165	I	SBI	NL
42166	I	SBH	EC
42167	I	SBH	EC
42168	I	SBH	EC
42169	I	SBH	EC
42170	I	SBH	EC
42171	I	SCB	EC

42172	I	SCB	EC	42223	I	SBH	LA
42173	I	SBH	EC	42224	I	SBH	LA
42174	I	SBH	EC	42225	I	SBI	NL
42175	I	SBH	LA	42226	I	SCB	EC
42176	I	SBH	LA	42227	I	SBI	NL
42177	I	SBH	LA	42228	I	SBI	NL
42178	I	SBH	EC	42229	I	SBI	NL
42179	I	SCB	EC	42230	I	SBI	NL
42180	I	SCB	EC	42231	I	SBH	EC
42181	I	SCB	EC	42232	I	SBH	EC
42182	I	SCB	EC	42233	I	SBH	EC
42183	I	SCJ	LA	42234	I	SBH	EC
42184	I	SCJ	LA	42235	I	SCB	EC
42185	I	SCJ	LA	42236	I	SCJ	PM
42186	I	SCB	EC	42237	I	SBH	EC
42187	I	SBH	EC	42238	I	SBH	EC
42188	I	SBH	EC	42239	I	SBH	EC
42189	I	SBH	EC	42240	I	SCB	EC
42190	I	SCB	EC	42241	I	SCB	EC
42191	I	SCB	EC	42242	I	SCB	EC
42192	I	SCB	EC	42243	I	SCB	EC
42193	I	SCB	EC	42244	I	SCB	EC
42194	I	SBI	NL	42245	I	SCJ	LA
42195	I	SBH	EC	42246	I	SBH	EC
42196	I	SCJ	PM	42247	I	SBH	EC
42197	I	SCJ	PM	42248	I	SBH	EC
42198	I	SCB	EC	42249	I	SBH	EC
42199	I	SCB	EC	42250	I	SCJ	LA
42200	I	SCJ	LA	42251	I	SCJ	LA
42201	I	SCJ	LA	42252	I	SCJ	LA
42202	I	SCJ	LA	42253	I	SCJ	LA
42203	I	SCJ	LA	42254	I	SBH	EC
42204	I	SCJ	LA	42255	I	SCJ	PM
42205	I	SBI	NL	42256	I	SCJ	PM
42206	I	SCJ	LA	42257	I	SCJ	PM
42207	I	SCJ	LA	42258	I	SBH	EC
42208	I	SCJ	LA	42259	I	SCJ	PM
42209	I	SCJ	LA	42260	I	SCJ	PM
42210	I	SBI	NL	42261	I	SCJ	PM
42211	I	SCJ	PM	42262	I	SBH	EC
42212	I	SCJ	PM	42263	I	SCJ	PM
42213	I	SCJ	PM	42264	I	SCJ	LA
42214	I	SCJ	PM	42265	I	SCJ	LA
42215	I	SCB	EC	42266	I	SBH	EC
42216	I	SCJ	LA	42267	I	SCJ	PM
42217	I	SBH	EC	42268	I	SCJ	PM
42218	I	SBH	EC	42269	I	SCJ	PM
42219	I	SCB	EC	42270	I	SBH	EC
42220	I	SBI	NL	42271	I	SCJ	LA
42221	I	SCJ	LA	42272	I	SCJ	LA
42222	I	SBH	LA	42273	I	SCJ	LA

42274	I	SBH	EC	42308	I	SBH	LA
42275	I	SCJ	LA	42309	I	SBH	LA
42276	I	SCJ	LA	42310	I	SBH	LA
42277	I	SCJ	LA	42311	I	SBH	LA
42278	I	SBH	EC	42312	I	SBH	LA
42279	I	SCJ	LA	42313	I	SBH	LA
42280	I	SCJ	LA	42314	I	SBH	LA
42281	I	SCJ	LA	42315	I	SBH	LA
42282	I	SBH	EC	42316	I	SBH	LA
42283	I	SCJ	PM	42317	I	SBH	LA
42284	I	SCJ	PM	42318	I	SBH	LA
42285	I	SCJ	PM	42319	I	SBH	LA
42286	I	SBH	LA	42320	I	SBH	LA
42287	I	SCJ	LA	42321	I	SBH	LA
42288	I	SCJ	LA	42322	I	SBH	LA
42289	I	SCJ	LA	42323	I	SCB	EC
42290	I	SBH	LA	42324	I	SBI	NL
42291	I	SCJ	LA	42325	I	SCJ	PM
42292	I	SCJ	LA	42326	I	SBH	EC
42293	I	SCJ	LA	42327	I	SBI	NL
42294	I	SBH	LA	42328	I	SBI	NL
42295	I	SCJ	LA	42329	I	SBI	NL
42296	I	SCJ	LA	42330	I	SBH	EC
42297	I	SCJ	LA	42331	I	SBI	NL
42298	I	SBH	LA	42332	I	SCJ	PM
42299	I	SCJ	PM	42333	I	SCJ	PM
42300	I	SCJ	PM	42334	I	SBH	LA
42301	I	SCJ	PM	42335	I	SBI	NL
42302	I	SBH	LA	42336	I	SBH	EC
42303	I	SBH	LA	42337	I	SBI	NL
42304	I	SBH	LA	42338	I	SBH	EC
42305	I	SBH	LA	42339	I	SBI	NL
42306	I	SBH	LA	42340	I	SCB	EC
42307	I	SBH	LA	42341	I	SBI	NL

42342	(44082)	I	SCF	MA
42343	(44095)	I	SCJ	LA
42344	(44092)	I	SCJ	PM
42345	(44096)	I	SCJ	LA
42346	(41053)	I	SCJ	PM
42347	(41054)	I	SCJ	LA
42348	(41073)	I	SCJ	LA
42349	(41074)	I	SCJ	PM
42350	(41047)	I	SCJ	LA
42351	(41048)	I	SCJ	PM
42352	(42142, 41176)	I	SBI	NL
42353	(42001, 41171)	I	SBH	EC
42354	(42114, 41175)	I	SCB	EC
42355	(42000, 41172)	I	SCF	MA
42356	(42002, 41173)	I	SCJ	LA
42357	(41002, 41174)	I	SCF	MA

GJ2G (TGS)   TRAILER GUARD'S STANDARD

Dia. GJ205. Secondary door locks. pg. −/63 1T + tip-up seat and wheelchair space.

44000. Lot No. 30953 Derby 1980. 33.47 t.
44001 – 44090. Lot No. 30949 Derby 1980 – 2. 33.47 t.
44091 – 44094. Lot No. 30964 Derby 1982. 33.47 t.
44097 – 44101. Lot No. 30970 Derby 1982. 33.47 t.

§ Fitted with side buffers and drophead buckeye couplings.

No.		Code	Depot		No.			Code	Depot
44000	I	SBH	EC		44039	I		SCJ	LA
44001	I	SCJ	LA		44040	I		SCJ	PM
44002	I	SCJ	PM		44041	I		SBI	NL
44003	I	SCJ	PM		44042	I		SBH	EC
44004	I	SCH	LA		44043	I		SCJ	LA
44005	I	SCJ	PM		44044	I		SBI	NL
44006	I	SCJ	PM		44045	I		SCB	EC
44007	I	SCJ	PM		44046	I		SBI	NL
44008	I	SCH	LA		44047	I		SBI	NL
44009	I	SCJ	PM		44048	I		SBI	NL
44010	I	SCJ	PM		44049	I		SCJ	PM
44011	I	SCJ	LA		44050	I		SBI	NL
44012	I	SCF	MA		44051	I		SBI	NL
44013	I	SCJ	LA		44052	I		SBI	NL
44014	I	SCJ	LA		44053	I		SBI	NL
44015	I	SCJ	LA		44054	I		SBI	NL
44016	I	SCJ	LA		44055	I		SBH	EC
44017	I	SCF	MA		44056	§	I	SCB	EC
44018	I	SCJ	LA		44057	I		SBH	LA
44019	I	SCB	EC		44058	§	I	SCB	EC
44020	I	SCJ	PM		44059	§	I	SCJ	LA
44021	I	SBH	EC		44060	I		SBH	EC
44022	I	SCJ	LA		44061	I		SCB	EC
44023	I	SCJ	PM		44062	I		SBH	EC
44024	I	SCJ	PM		44063	I		SCB	EC
44025	I	SCJ	LA		44064	I		SCJ	LA
44026	I	SCJ	PM		44065	I		SBH	LA
44027	I	SBI	NL		44066	I		SCJ	LA
44028	I	SCJ	LA		44067	I		SCJ	PM
44029	I	SCJ	PM		44068	I		SBH	LA
44030	I	SCJ	PM		44069	I		SBH	EC
44031	I	SCF	MA		44070	I		SBI	NL
44032	I	SCJ	PM		44071	I		SBI	NL
44033	I	SCJ	LA		44072	I		SBH	EC
44034	I	SCJ	LA		44073	I		SBI	NL
44035	I	SCJ	LA		44074	I		SBH	EC
44036	I	SCJ	PM		44075	I		SBH	EC
44037	I	SCJ	LA		44076	I		SBH	LA
44038	I	SCJ	LA		44077	I		SCB	EC

44078	I	SBH	EC
44079	I	SBH	EC
44080	I	SCB	EC
44081	I	SBH	LA
44083	I	SBI	NL
44085	I	SBI	NL
44086 §	I	SCJ	LA
44087	I	SBH	LA
44088	I	SBH	LA
44089	I	SBH	LA

44090	I	SBH	LA
44091	I	SBH	LA
44093	I	SCJ	LA
44094	I	SCB	EC
44097 §	I	SBH	EC
44098 §	I	SCB	EC
44099	I	SCOL	LA
44100	I	SBH	EC
44101 §	I	SBH	LA

GH2G (TCSD)   TRAILER CONDUCTOR STANDARD

Dia. GH201. Converted from 44084. Guard's compartment converted to walk-through conductor's compartment with a disabled persons toilet also provided. The car is marshalled adjacent to the buffet. Secondary door locks.

45084. Lot No. 30949 Derby 1982. 33.47 t.

45084	I	SCOL	PM	I

2.4. PRE-NATIONALISATION STOCK

The following are pre-nationalisation preserved vehicles are at present passed for running on the Railtrack system. Vehicles are painted in their appropriate pre-nationalisation livery except for 902260 which is **M**. Original number is shown and other numbers may have been carried.

159	London & North Western Railway dining saloon	XSH	CJ
484	West Coast Joint Stock dining saloon	XSH	CJ
807	Great Northern Railway family saloon	XSH	CJ
9004	Great Western Railway first saloon	XRF	CS
80975	Great Western Railway inspection saloon	XRP	CM
902260	LNER General Manager's Saloon	XGS	EN

The following vehicle which had a BR freight stock number is also passed. It is in **PC** livery and carries the branding "BAGGAGE CAR No. 8".

889202	Ferry van		XVS	SL

2.5. PULLMAN CAR COMPANY STOCK

VARIOUS PULLMAN CARS

Various Pullman cars built to early designs.

* Former 'Brighton Belle' EMU vehicle now used as hauled stock.

213	MINERVA	PBF	**PC**	XVS	SL	26/−	1927	Midland
239	AGATHA	PPF	**PC**	XVSZ	SL	24/−	1928	Metro
243	LUCILLE	PKF	**PC**	XVS	SL	24/−	1928	Metro
245	IBIS	PKF	**PC**	XVS	SL	20/−	1925	BRCW
254	ZENA	PPF	**PC**	XVS	SL	24/−	1928	Metro
255	IONE	PKF	**PC**	XVS	SL	20/−	1928	Metro
261	CAR No. 83	PKS	**PC**	XVSZ	SL	−/42	1931	BRCW
280	AUDREY	PKF *	**PC**	XVS	SL	20/−	1932	Metro
281	GWEN	PKF *	**PC**	XVSZ	SL	20/−	1932	Metro
284	VERA	PKF *	**PC**	XVS	SL	20/−	1932	Metro
286	CAR No. 86	PPS *	**PC**	XVSZ	SL	−/56	1931	Metro
301	PERSEUS	PPF	**PC**	XVS	SL	32/−	1951	BRCW
302	PHOENIX	PPF	**PC**	XVS	SL	26/−	1952	Pullman Car Co.
307	CARINA	PKF	**PC**	XVSZ	SL	22/−	1951	BRCW
308	CYGNUS	PPF	**PC**	XVS	SL	32/−	1951	BRCW

PULLMAN KITCHEN FIRST

Built by Metro-Cammell 1960/1 for East Coast Main-line services. x. Commonwealth bogies. 20/− 2T. 40 t. Used in the ''Royal Scotsman'' charter train set, some of these vehicles have been modified. Names not carried.

313 FINCH	**M**	XGS	EN		319 SNIPE			**M**	XGS	EN
317 RAVEN	**M**	XGS	EN							

PULLMAN PARLOUR FIRST

Built by Metro-Cammell 1960/1 for East Coast Main-line services. x. Commonwealth bogies. 29/− 2T. 38.5 t. Used in the ''Royal Scotsman'' charter train set, some of these vehicles have been modified. Names not carried.

324 AMBER	**M**	XGS	EN		331 TOPAZ			**M**	XGS	EN
329 PEARL	**M**	XGS	EN							

PULLMAN KITCHEN SECOND

Built by Metro-Cammell 1960/1 for East Coast Main-line services. x. Commonwealth bogies. −/30 1T. 40 t.

335 CAR No. 335	**PC**	XWRZ On loan to Swanage Railway

PULLMAN PARLOUR SECOND

Built by Metro-Cammell 1960/1 for East Coast Main-line services. x. Commonwealth bogies. −/42 2T. 38.5 t.

347 CAR No. 347	**PC**	XWRZ Ferme Park CS
348 CAR No. 348	**PC**	XWRZ On loan to Swanage Railway
349 CAR No. 349	**PC**	XWRZ On loan to Kent & East Sussex Railway
350 CAR No. 350	**PC**	XWRZ BN
351 CAR No. 347	**PC**	XWRZ CP
352 CAR No. 348	**PC**	XWRZ CP
353 CAR No. 349	**PC**	XWRZ On loan to Swanage Railway

THE HADRIAN BAR

Built by Metro-Cammell 1961 for East Coast Main-line services. x. Commonwealth bogies. 24/− + bar seating 1T. 38.5 t.

354 THE HADRIAN BAR **PC** XWRZ CP

2.6. ADDITIONAL INFORMATION

The following table is presented to help readers identify vehicles which may still have their former private owner numbers painted on them. The private owner number is shown in column 1 and the number by which the vehicle is now identified is shown in column 2.

99000	4946	99321	5299	99545	80207	99723	35459
99001	4996	99322	5600	99554	92904	99782	17007
99002	5008	99323	5704	99566	3066	99818	1730
99035	35322	99324	5714	99568	3068	99821	9227
99041	35476	99325	5727	99670	546	99822	1859
99052	484	99326	4954	99671	548	99823	4832
99053	9004	99327	5044	99672	549	99824	4831
99080	21096	99328	5033	99673	550	99826	13229
99120	21236	99329	4931	99674	551	99827	3096
99121	3105	99356	21245	99675	552	99828	13230
99125	3113	99371	3128	99676	553	99829	4856
99127	3117	99405	35486	99677	586	99831	4836
99131	902260	99421	17021	99678	504	99880	159
99132	1861	99530	301	99679	506	99881	807
99141	17041	99531	302	99680	17102	99886	35407
99241	35449	99532	308	99710	25767	99887	2127
99242	35467	99534	245	99712	25893	99953	35468
99243	80975	99535	213	99713	26013	99961	324
99304	21256	99536	254	99714	16187	99962	329
99311	1882	99537	280	99716	25808	99963	331
99312	35463	99538	34991	99717	25837	99964	313
99314	25729	99539	255	99718	25862	99965	319
99315	25955	99540	3069	99719	16191	99966	34525
99316	13321	99541	243	99720	35461	99967	317
99317	3766	99542	889202	99721	25806	99993	5067
99318	4912	99543	284	99722	25756	99995	35457
99319	14168	99544	35207				

The following table lists support coaches and the locomotives which they normally support at present.

17007	35028	21236	30828	35463	48151	35476	46203
17021	777	35322	70000	35467	KR locos	35486	60009
17041	71000	35449	34027	35468	NRM locos	80220	5029
21096	4498	35457	44767				

2.7. EUROPEAN NIGHT SERVICES STOCK

In late 1996, travellers between the United Kingdom and Continental Europe via the Channel Tunnel will benefit from a new generation of overnight trains offering high quality accommodation to both business and leisure customers. At present these services are referred to as ENS, but it is probable that the word 'Nightstar' will be used as the marketing term.

This innovative venture is being developed by European Night Services Limited (ENS), a joint company established by UK-government-owned European Passenger Services (EPS), SNCF, DB and NS. The trains will operate on the following routes:

London Waterloo – Amsterdam CS.
London Waterloo – Dortmund Hbf./Frankfurt Hbf.
Glasgow/Manchester – Paris Nord.
Plymouth/Swansea – Paris Nord.

Both sleeping cars and reclining seat coaches will be used. Each train will be formed of two half-sets, London services having two reclining seat coaches, a service vehicle and five sleeping cars in each half-set to form a sixteen coach train, whilst services from the Provinces to Paris will be fourteen coaches long with each portion consisting of three sleeping cars, a service vehicle and three reclining seat coaches. The regional half-sets will be numbered 1 – 9, whilst the London half-sets will be numbered 10 – 18.

In the following lists, the UIC number for each vehicle is followed by the set number to which it belongs.

RECLINING SEAT CARS   SO End

Each car has 50 seats which are fully reclining, with generous leg space. A table is provided at each seat, and footrests will offer extra comfort. The seats are mounted on plinths, which enhance the customer's sense of personal space. Main luggage is stored beneath the seat, while hand baggage is stored in overhead lockers. Individually controlled reading lights are provided, with different levels of ambient lighting for sleeping and non-sleeping hours. Each car has three toilet compartments with washing facilities. These are designed to a high specification and include facilities such as shaver sockets and hot-air hand dryers.

61 70 20-90 001-6 *1*	61 70 20-90 007-3 *7*	61 70 20-90 013-1 *13*
61 70 20-90 002-4 *2*	61 70 20-90 008-1 *8*	61 70 20-90 014-9 *14*
61 70 20-90 003-2 *3*	61 70 20-90 009-9 *9*	61 70 20-90 015-6 *15*
61 70 20-90 004-0 *4*	61 70 20-90 010-7 *10*	61 70 20-90 016-4 *16*
61 70 20-90 005-7 *5*	61 70 20-90 011-5 *11*	61 70 20-90 017-2 *17*
61 70 20-90 006-5 *6*	61 70 20-90 012-3 *12*	61 70 20-90 018-0 *18*

RECLINING SEAT CAR   SO

Details as above, but no coupling for locomotive.

61 70 20-90 019-8 *1*	61 70 20-90 029-7 *6*	61 70 20-90 039-6 *12*
61 70 20-90 020-6 *1*	61 70 20-90 030-5 *6*	61 70 20-90 040-4 *13*
61 70 20-90 021-4 *2*	61 70 20-90 031-3 *7*	61 70 20-90 041-2 *14*
61 70 20-90 022-2 *2*	61 70 20-90 032-1 *7*	61 70 20-90 042-0 *15*
61 70 20-90 023-0 *3*	61 70 20-90 033-9 *8*	61 70 20-90 043-8 *16*
61 70 20-90 024-8 *3*	61 70 20-90 034-7 *8*	61 70 20-90 044-6 *17*
61 70 20-90 025-5 *4*	61 70 20-90 035-4 *9*	61 70 20-90 045-3 *18*
61 70 20-90 026-3 *4*	61 70 20-90 036-2 *9*	61 70 20-90 046-1 *S*
61 70 20-90 027-1 *5*	61 70 20-90 037-0 *10*	61 70 20-90 047-9 *S*
61 70 20-90 028-9 *5*	61 70 20-90 038-8 *11*	

SLEEPING CARS   SLF End

ENS sleeping cars will set high standards, with service quality and facilities akin
to those found in a good hotel. Main users are expected to be business travellers
and comfort seeking leisure travellers Each sleeping car will have 10 cabins.
Six of these will have a compact en-suite shower room, with a washbasin, toilet
and hairdryer, similar to that found on yachts. The remaining four cabins will
include en-suite toilet and washing facilities, but without the shower.

All cabins will be convertible ao that when the bunks are folded away by the
attendant after passengers have got up, two comfortable armchairs with fold-
out tables are revealed. The bunks themselves are generously sized one above
the other and will already be made up with duvets, sheets and pillows When
passengers arrive. Each cabin will have a fitted wardrobe and cupboard, together
with facilities for making hot drinks. Cabin telephones are provided for room
service.

61 70 70-90 001-5 *1*	61 70 70-90 007-2 *7*	61 70 70-90 013-0 *13*
61 70 70-90 002-3 *2*	61 70 70-90 008-0 *8*	61 70 70-90 014-8 *14*
61 70 70-90 003-1 *3*	61 70 70-90 009-8 *9*	61 70 70-90 015-5 *15*
61 70 70-90 004-9 *4*	61 70 70-90 010-6 *10*	61 70 70-90 016-3 *16*
61 70 70-90 005-6 *5*	61 70 70-90 011-4 *11*	61 70 70-90 017-1 *17*
61 70 70-90 006-4 *6*	61 70 70-90 012-2 *12*	61 70 70-90 018-9 *18*

SLEEPING CARS   SLF

Details as above, but no coupling for locomotive.

61 70 70-90 019-7 *1*	61 70 70-90 037-9 *10*	61 70 70-90 055-1 *14*
61 70 70-90 020-5 *1*	61 70 70-90 038-7 *10*	61 70 70-90 056-9 *14*
61 70 70-90 021-3 *2*	61 70 70-90 039-5 *10*	61 70 70-90 057-7 *15*
61 70 70-90 022-1 *2*	61 70 70-90 040-3 *10*	61 70 70-90 058-5 *15*
61 70 70-90 023-9 *3*	61 70 70-90 041-1 *11*	61 70 70-90 059-3 *15*
61 70 70-90 024-7 *3*	61 70 70-90 042-9 *11*	61 70 70-90 060-1 *15*
61 70 70-90 025-4 *4*	61 70 70-90 043-7 *11*	61 70 70-90 061-9 *16*
61 70 70-90 026-2 *4*	61 70 70-90 044-5 *11*	61 70 70-90 062-7 *16*
61 70 70-90 027-0 *5*	61 70 70-90 045-2 *12*	61 70 70-90 063-5 *16*
61 70 70-90 028-8 *5*	61 70 70-90 046-0 *12*	61 70 70-90 064-3 *16*
61 70 70-90 029-6 *6*	61 70 70-90 047-8 *12*	61 70 70-90 065-0 *17*
61 70 70-90 030-4 *6*	61 70 70-90 048-6 *12*	61 70 70-90 066-8 *17*
61 70 70-90 031-2 *7*	61 70 70-90 049-4 *13*	61 70 70-90 067-6 *17*
61 70 70-90 032-0 *7*	61 70 70-90 050-2 *13*	61 70 70-90 068-4 *17*
61 70 70-90 033-8 *8*	61 70 70-90 051-0 *13*	61 70 70-90 069-2 *18*
61 70 70-90 034-6 *8*	61 70 70-90 052-8 *13*	61 70 70-90 070-0 *18*
61 70 70-90 035-3 *9*	61 70 70-90 053-6 *14*	61 70 70-90 071-8 *18*
61 70 70-90 036-1 *9*	61 70 70-90 054-4 *14*	61 70 70-90 072-6 *18*

SERVICE VEHICLE/LOUNGE CAR   SV

Lounge cars are positioned in each half of the train, between the sleeping cars and the seated accommodation. These vehicles consist of of a sleeping cabin for a disabled passenger and companion with en-suite washroom, a parcels room, offices for train manager and control authority, a lounge with bar for sleeping car passengers and public telephone and a bar for seated passengers.

The vehicle also acts as a base for the sleeping car attendants and for the trolley service which will be provided for the seated passengers in the evening. There is also a seated passengers' counter so that snacks and drinks can be obtained during sleeping hours.

61 70 89-90 001-4 *1*	61 70 89-90 008-9 *8*	61 70 89-90 015-4 *15*
61 70 89-90 002-2 *2*	61 70 89-90 009-7 *9*	61 70 89-90 016-2 *16*
61 70 89-90 003-0 *3*	61 70 89-90 010-5 *10*	61 70 89-90 017-0 *17*
61 70 89-90 004-8 *4*	61 70 89-90 011-3 *11*	61 70 89-90 018-8 *18*
61 70 89-90 005-5 *5*	61 70 89-90 012-1 *12*	61 70 89-90 019-6 *S*
61 70 89-90 006-3 *6*	61 70 89-90 013-9 *13*	61 70 89-90 020-4 *S*
61 70 89-90 007-1 *7*	61 70 89-90 014-7 *14*	

3. DIESEL MULTIPLE UNITS

Diesel Multiple Unit operation on BR increased enormously since the end of the steam era, but there have been many changes in recent years. Electrification has meant the replacement of DMUs with EMUs on many routes, whilst on other services, DMUs have replaced loco-hauled trains. Very few first generation DMUs remain and most DMU services are now operated by "Pacer", "Sprinter" or other modern air-braked Express units. A few DEMUs will be found operating on the former Southern Region, but some of these now have ex-EMU centre cars. One vehicle (71634) started life as loco-hauled coach No. 4059, was converted to an EMU trailer and is now part of DEMU 205 205!

NUMBERING

Diesel mechanical and diesel hydraulic multiple unit vehicles are numbered in the series 51000-59999. All vehicles numbered in the 53000-53999 series were originally numbered in the series 50000-50999, and were renumbered by having 3000 added to their original numbers. All vehicles in the series 54000-54504 were originally numbered in the series 56000-56504, and were renumbered by having 2000 subtracted from their original numbers.

Diesel electric multiple unit vehicles are numbered in the series 60108-60918.

DESIGN CONSIDERATIONS

Unless stated otherwise, all diesel multiple unit vehicles are of BR design, or designed by contractors for BR and have buckeye couplings and tread brakes. Seating is 3 + 2 in standard class open vehicles, 2 + 2 in first class open vehicles, 12 to a non-corridor standard class compartment, 8 to a corridor standard class compartment and 6 to a corridor first class compartment. In express stock, open standards have 2 + 2 seating and open firsts have 2 + 1 seating.

VEHICLE CODES

The codes used by the BR Operating Department to describe the various different types of DMU vehicles and quoted in the class headings are as follows:

Diesel Mechanical & Diesel Hydraulic Units.

DMBC   Driving Motor Brake Composite.
DMBS   Driving Motor Brake Standard.
DMC   Driving Motor Composite
DMS   Driving Motor Standard.
DTS   Driving Trailer Standard
MS   Motor Standard.
TS   Trailer Standard.

It should be noted that as all vehicles are of an open configuration the letter 'O' is omitted for all vehicles. An 'L' suffix denotes that the vehicle is fitted with a lavatory compartment.

The letters (A) and (B) may be added to the above codes to differentiate between two cars of the same operating type which have differences between them. Note that a consistent system is used, rather than the official operator codes which are sometimes inconsistent.

A composite is a vehicle containing both First and Standard class accommodation, and vehicles are described as such even though most first class accommodation has now been declassified on most vehicles. This is done so as to differentiate between the different styles of seat provided in standard and erstwhile first class areas of a vehicle. At the time of writing no heritage units retained first class accommodation in use as such.

A brake vehicle is a vehicle containing seperate specific accommodation for the guard (as opposed to the use of spare driving cabs on second generation units).

Diesel Electric Units.

DMBSO   Driving Motor Brake Standard (Open).
DTCsoL   Driving Trailer Composite with Lavatory (Semi-Open).
DTSOL   Driving Trailer Standard with Lavatory (Open).
DTSO   Driving Trailer Standard (Open).
TSO   Trailer Standard (Open).
TSOL   Trailer Standard with Lavatory (Open).

The notes as above apply regarding composite and brake vehicles. A semi-open composite vehicle has first class accommodation in compartments with a side corridor and standard class accommodation provided in an open saloon.

WEIGHTS & DIMENSIONS

Approximate weights in working order are given in tonnes for all vehicle types in the class headings and sub headings as appropriate.

The dimensions of each type of vehicle are given in metric units, with length followed by width. All lengths quoted are over buffers (1st generation vehicles) or couplings (2nd generation vehicles). All widths quoted are maxima.

DIAGRAMS AND DESIGN CODES

For each type of vehicle, the official design code consists of a seven character code of two letters, four numbers and another letter, e.g. DP2010A. The first five characters of this are the diagram code and are given in the class heading or sub heading. These are explained as follows:

1st Letter

This is always 'D' for a diesel multiple unit vehicle.

2nd Letter

as follows for various vehicle types (DMMU or DHMU unless otherwise stated):

B   Driving motor passenger vehicles with a brake compartment (DEMU).
E   Driving trailer passenger vehicles (DEMU).
H   Trailer passenger vehicles without a brake compartment (DEMU).
P   Driving motor passenger vehicles without a brake compartment.

Q	Driving motor passenger vehicles with a brake compartment.
R	Non-Driving motor passenger vehicles.
S	Driving trailer passenger vehicles.
T	Trailer passenger vehicles without a brake compartment.
X	Parcels and Mails vehicles and single unit railcars.

1st Figure

This denotes the class of accommodation as follows:

2	Standard class accommodation (incl. declassified seats).
3	Composite accommodation.
5	No passenger accommodation.

2nd & 3rd Figures

These distinguish between the different designs of vehicle, each different design being allocated a unique two digit number.

Special Note

Where vehicles have been declassified the correct design code for a declassified vehicle is given, even though this may be at variance with official records which do not show the reality of the current position. A declassified composite is still referred to as a composite if it still retains the first class style seats in the erstwhile first class section of the vehicle. Its declassification is denoted by the fact that the first figure of the design code is a '2'.

ACCOMMODATION

This information is given in class headings and sub headings in the form F/S nT, where F & S denote the number of first class nd standard class seats followed by n which denotes the number of toilets. (e.g. 12/54 1T denotes 12 first class seats, 54 standard class seats and one toliet). In declassified vehicles, the capacity is still shown in terms of first and standard class seats to differentiate between the two physically different seat types available, although all seats followed are officially standard class in such instances.

LAYOUT

The layout in this section is as follows:
(1) Unit number.
(2) Notes (if any).
(3) Livery code.
(4) Owner code.
(5) Depot code.
(6) Individual car numbers.
(7) Name (if any).

Thus an example of the layout is as follows:

No.	Liv.	Owner	Depot	Car 1	Car 2	Name
150257	RR	SBS	NC	52257	57257	Queen Boadicea

For off-loan vehicles, the last storage location is given when known.

3.1. 'HERITAGE' DIESEL MULTIPLE UNITS

Very few first generation diesel multiple units remain. BR now refers to these as 'heritage' units. Standard features are as follows:

Brakes:

All units are vacuum braked.

Lighting:

All cars are now fitted with fluorescent lighting.

Couplings:

Screw couplings are used on all vehicles. All remaining first generation vehicles may be coupled together to work in multiple up to a maximum of 6 motor cars or 12 cars in total in a formation. First generation vehicles may not be coupled in multiple with second generation vehicles.

CLASS 101   METRO-CAMMELL

Engines: Two Leyland of 112 kW (150 hp) per power car.
Transmission: Mechanical. Cardan shaft and freewheel to a four-speed epicyclic gearbox with a further cardan shaft to the final drive, each engine driving the inner axle of one bogie.
Gangways: Midland scissors type. Within unit only.
Doors: Slam.
Bogies: DD15 (motor) and DT11 (trailer).
Dimensions: 18.49 x 2.82 m.
Seats: 3 + 2 facing (2 + 2 in first class).

51175 – 51253. DMBS. Dia. DQ202. Lot No. 30467 1958 – 59. –/52. 32.5 t.
51426 – 51463. DMBS. Dia. DQ202. Lot No. 30500 1959. –/52. (–/49 with additional luggage rack for Gatwick sets – Dia. DQ232) 32.5 t.
53164. DMBS. Dia. DQ202. Lot No. 30254 1956. –/52. 32.5 t.
53198 – 53204. DMBS. Dia. DQ202. Lot No. 30259 1957. –/52. 32.5 t.
53211 – 53228. DMBS. Dia. DQ202. Lot No. 30261 1957. –/52. 32.5 t.
53253 – 53256. DMBS. Dia. DQ202. Lot No. 30266 1957. –/52. 32.5 t.
53311 – 53314. DMBS. Dia. DQ202. Lot No. 30275 1968. –/49 with additional luggage rack for Gatwick sets – Dia. DQ232) 32.5 t.
51496 – 51533. DMCL or DMSL. Dia. DP317 or DP210. Lot No. 30501 1959. 12/46 1T with additional luggage racks. 32.5 t.
51800. DMBS. Dia. DQ202. Lot No. 30587 1956. –/52. 32.5 t.
51803. DMSL. Dia. DP210. Lot No. 30588 1959. –/72 1T. 32.5 t.
53160 – 53163. DMSL. Dia. DP214. Lot No. 30253 1956. –/72 1T. 32.5 t.
53170 – 53171. DMSL. Dia. DP214. Lot No. 30255 1957. –/72 1T. 32.5 t.
53177. DMSL. Dia. DP214. Lot No. 30256 1957. –/72 1T. 32.5 t.
53266 – 53269. DMSL. Dia. DP210. Lot No. 30267 1957. –/72 1T. 32.5 t.

53322 – 53327. DMCL. Dia. DP317. Lot No. 30276 1958. 12/46 1T with additional luggage racks. 32.5 t.
53746. DMSL. Dia. DP210. Lot No. 30271 1957. –/72 1T. 32.5 t.
54061 – 54061. DTSL. Dia. DS206. Lot No. 30260 1957. –/72 1T. 25.5 t.
54062 – 54091. DTSL. Dia. DS206. Lot No. 30262 1957. –/72 1T. 25.5 t.
54343 – 54408. DTSL. Dia. DS206. Lot No. 30468 1958. –/72 1T. 25.5 t.
59303. TSL. Dia. DT202. Lot No. 30273 1957. –/71 1T. 25.5 t.
59539. TSL. Dia. DT228. Lot No. 30502 1959. –/72 1T. 25.5 t.

Refurbished 2-car Sets. DMBS – DTSL.

101 651	RR	SCD	LO	53201	54379
101 652	RR	SCD	LO	53198	54346
101 653	RR	SCD	LO	51426	54358
101 654	RR	SCD	LO	51800	54408
101 655	RR	SCD	LO	51428	54062
101 656	RR	SCD	LO	51230	54056
101 657	RR	SCD	LO	53211	54085
101 658	RR	SCD	LO	51175	54091
101 659	RR	SCD	LO	51213	54352
101 660	RR	SCD	LO	51189	54343
101 661	RR	SCD	LO	51463	54365
101 662	RR	SCD	LO	53228	54055
101 663	RR	SCD	LO	51201	54347
101 664	RR	SCD	LO	51442	54061
101 665	RR	SCD	LO	51429	54393

Refurbished Twin Power Car and 3-Car Sets. DMBS – DMSL or DMBS – TSL – DMSL.

101 676	RR	SCD	LO	51205		51803
101 677	RR	SCD	LO	51179		51496
101 678	RR	SCD	LO	51210		53746
101 679	RR	SCD	LO	51224		51533
101 680	RR	SCD	LO	53204		53163
101 681	RR	SCD	LO	51228		51506
101 682	RR	SCD	LO	53256		51505
101 683	RR	SCD	LO	51177	59303	53269
101 684	S	SCA	CK	51187		51509
101 685	G	SCD	LO	53164	59539	53160
101 686	S	SCA	CK	51231		51500
101 687	S	SCA	CK	51247		51512
101 688	S	SCA	CK	51431		51501
101 689	S	SCA	CK	51185		51511
101 690	S	SCA	CK	51435		53177
101 691	S	SCA	CK	51253		53171
101 692	S	SCA	CK	53253		53170
101 693	S	SCA	CK	51192		53266
101 694	S	SCA	CK	51188		53268
101 695	S	SCA	CK	51226		51499

Note: At the time of publication, 101 683 and 101 685 were temporarily running as twin power car sets with the TSL removed and stored at Chester CSD.

Unrefurbished Twin Power Car Sets. DMBS – DMCL. These sets have seats removed and additional luggage racks. These modifications were carried out when they were used on Reading – Gatwick Airport services.

Note: Some units show 'L' instead of the official class prefix.

101 835	**RR**	SCD	LO	51432	51498
101 840	**N**	SCD	LO	53311	53322
101 842	**N**	SCK	PZ	53314	53327

CLASS 117   PRESSED STEEL SUBURBAN

DMBS – TSL – DMS or DMBS – DMS (DMBS – DMBS*).
Engines: Two Leyland 680/1 of 112 kW (150 hp) per power car.
Transmission: Mechanical. Cardan shaft and freewheel to a four-speed epicyclic gearbox with a further cardan shaft to the final drive, each engine driving the inner axle of one bogie.
Gangways: GWR suspension type. Within unit only.
Bogies: DD10 (motor) and DT9 (trailer).
Dimensions: 20.45 x 2.82 m.
Seats: 3 + 2 facing.

Non-standard Livery: 51368 of 117 305 is in GWR chocolate & cream whilst 51361 is in '**N**' livery.

DMBS. Dia. DQ220. Lot No. 30546 1959 – 60. – /65. 36.5 t.
TSL. Dia. DT230. Lot No. 30547 1959 – 60. – 78 2T. 30.5 t.
DMS. Dia. DP221. Lot No. 30548 1959 – 60. – /89. 36.5 t.

Note: Some SCP units show 'L' instead of the official class prefix.

117 301	f	**RR**	SCA	HA	51353	59505 51395
117 305	*	**0**	SCK	PZ	51368	51361
117 306	f	**RR**	SCA	HA	51369	59521 51411
117 308	f	**RR**	SCA	HA	51371	59509 51413
117 310	f	**RR**	SCA	HA	51373	59486 51381
117 311	f	**RR**	SCA	HA	51334	59500 51376
117 313	f	**RR**	SCA	HA	51339	59492 51382
117 314	f	**RR**	SCA	HA	51352	59489 51394
117 700		**N**	SCP	BY	51332	51374
117 701		**N**	SCP	BY	51350	51392
117 702		**N**	SCP	BY	51356	51398
117 703		**N**	SCP	BY	51359	51401
117 704		**N**	SCP	BY	51341	51383
117 705		**N**	SCP	BY	51358	51400
117 706		**N**	SCP	BY	51366	51408
117 707		**N**	SCP	BY	51335	51377
117 708		**N**	SCK	PZ	51336	51378
117 709		**N**	SCK	PZ	51344	51386
117 720		**N**	SCP	BY	51354	51396
117 721		**N**	SCP	BY	51363	51405
117 724		**N**	SCK	BY	51333	51375

CLASS 121   PRESSED STEEL SUBURBAN

DMBS.
Engines: Two Leyland 1595 of 112 kW (150 hp) per power car.
Transmission: Mechanical. Cardan shaft and freewheel to a four-speed epicylic gearbox with a further cardan shaft to the final drive, each engine driving the inner axle of one bogie.
Gangways: Non gangwayed single cars with cabs at each end.
Bogies: DD10.
Dimensions: 20.45 x 2.82 m.
Seats: 3 + 2 facing.

DMBS. Dia. DX201. Lot No. 30518 1960. – /65. 38.0 t.

Note: Some of the sets show 'L' instead of the official class prefix.

121 123	G	SCP	BY	55023
121 127	N	SCP	BY	55027
121 129	N	SCP	BY	55029
121 131	N	SCP	BY	55031

CLASS 122   GLOUCESTER SUBURBAN

DMBS.
Engines: Two AEC 220 of 112 kW (150 hp) per power car.
Transmission: Mechanical. Cardan shaft and freewheel to a four-speed epicylic gearbox with a further cardan shaft to the final drive, each engine driving the inner axle of one bogie.
Gangways: Non gangwayed single car with cabs at each end.
Bogies: DD10.
Dimensions: 20.45 x 2.82 m.
Seats: 3 + 2 facing.

DMBS. Dia. DX202. Lot No. 30419 1958. – /65. 36.5 t.

Note: This unit is used as a LoadHaul crew-training vehicle and does not carry its unit number.

122 012	LH	FD	TE	55012

3.2. SECOND GENERATION DMUS

Unit Types

There are five basic types of second generation vehicle as referred to in the class headings as follows:

● **Pacers** (Railbuses). Folding power operated exterior doors. Bus-type 3 + 2 (2 + 2 on class 141) largely unidirectional seating. Limited luggage space. Four wheel chassis. 75 mph.

● **Sprinter.** Sliding power operated exterior double doors to large entrance vestibules. High backed 3 + 2 seating. Limited luggage space. 75 mph.

● **Super Sprinter.** Sliding/sliding plug power-operated exterior doors. High backed 2 + 2 largely unidirectional seating with some tables. 75 mph.

● **Express.** Sliding plug power-operated exterior doors. Air conditioned. High backed 2 + 2 half-facing and half-unidirectional seating with some tables. 90 mph.

● **Network Turbo.** Sliding power operated exterior double doors to large entrance vestibules. 3 + 2 seating. Limited luggage space. 90 mph.

Public Address System: All vehicles are equipped with public address, with transmission equipment on driving vehicles.

Gangways: Unless stated otherwise, all vehicles have flexible diaphragm gangways.

Couplings: Unless otherwise stated all vehicles are fitted with BSI automatic couplings at their outer ends. Railbus types are fitted with bar couplings at their inner ends, but all other types have BSI couplings at their inner ends unless otherwise stated.

Brakes: All vehicles are fitted with electro-pneumatic and air brakes.

CLASS 141   LEYLAND BUS/BREL RAILBUS

DMS – DMSL. Built from Leyland National bus parts on four-wheeled under-frames.

Engines: One Leyland TL11 152 kW (205 hp) (* Cummins LT10-R) per car.
Transmission: Hydraulic. Voith T211r with Gmeinder final drive.
Gangways: Within unit only.
Doors: Folding.
Dimensions: 15.45 x 2.50 m.
Accommodation: 2 + 2 bus style.
Maximum Speed: 75 mph.

DMS. Dia. DP228 Lot No. 30977 Derby 1984. Modified by Barclay 1988 – 89.
–/50. 26.0 t.
DMSL. Dia. DP229 Lot No. 30978 Derby 1984. Modified by Barclay 1988 – 89.
–/44 1T. 26.5 t.

141 101	Y	SBC	NL	55521	55541
141 102	Y	SBC	NL	55502	55522
141 103	Y	SBOL	RFS	55503	55523
141 105	Y	SBOL	RFS	55505	55525
141 106	Y	SBOL	RFS	55506	55526
141 107	Y	SBOL	RFS	55507	55527
141 108	Y	SBOL	RFS	55508	55528
141 109	Y	SBC	NL	55509	55529
141 110	Y	SBOL	RFS	55510	55530
141 111	Y	SBC	NL	55511	55531
141 112	Y	SBOL	RFS	55512	55532
141 113	* Y	SBC	NL	55513	55533
141 114	Y	SBC	NL	55514	55534
141 115	Y	SBC	NL	55515	55535
141 116	Y	SBOL	RFS	55516	55536
141 117	Y	SBC	NL	55517	55537
141 118	Y	SBOL	RFS	55518	55538
141 119	Y	SBC	NL	55519	55539
141 120	Y	SBOL	RFS	55520	55540

CLASS 142   LEYLAND BUS/BREL RAILBUS

DMS – DMSL. Development of Class 141 with wider body and improved appearance.

Engines: One Cummins LTA10-R of 170 kW (225 h.p.) per car.
Transmission: Hydraulic. Voith T211r with Gmeinder final drive.
Gangways: Within unit only.
Doors: Folding.
Dimensions: 15.55 x 2.80 m.
Accommodation: 2 + 3 bus style.
Maximum Speed: 75 mph.
Non-Standard Livery: Chocolate & Cream.

55542 – 55591. DMS. Dia. DP234 Lot No. 31003 Derby 1985 – 6. – /62.
24.5 t.
55592 – 55641. DMSL. Dia. DP235 Lot No. 31004 Derby 1985 – 6. – /59 1T.
25.0 t.
55701 – 55746. DMS. Dia. DP234 Lot No. 31013 Derby 1986 – 7. – /62.
24.5 t.
55747 – 55792. DMSL. Dia. DP235 Lot No. 31014 Derby 1986 – 7. – /59 1T.
25.0 t.

142 001	GM	SCD	NH	55542	55592
142 002	GM	SCD	NH	55543	55593
142 003	GM	SCD	NH	55544	55594
142 004	GM	SCD	NH	55545	55595
142 005	GM	SCD	NH	55546	55596
142 006	GM	SCD	NH	55547	55597
142 007	GM	SCD	NH	55548	55598
142 008	GM	SCD	NH	55549	55599
142 009	GM	SCD	NH	55550	55600
142 010	GM	SCD	NH	55551	55601
142 011	GM	SCD	NH	55552	55602
142 012	GM	SCD	NH	55553	55603
142 013	GM	SCD	NH	55554	55604
142 014	GM	SCD	NH	55555	55605
142 015	RR	SCC	HT	55556	55606
142 016	RR	SCC	HT	55557	55607
142 017	T	SCC	HT	55558	55608
142 018	T	SCC	HT	55559	55609
142 019	T	SCC	HT	55560	55610
142 020	T	SCC	HT	55561	55611
142 021	T	SCC	HT	55562	55612
142 022	T	SCC	HT	55563	55613
142 023	RR	SCD	NH	55564	55614
142 024	O	SCC	HT	55565	55615
142 025	O	SCC	HT	55566	55616
142 026	O	SCC	HT	55567	55617
142 027	O	SCD	NH	55568	55618
142 028	GM	SCD	NH	55569	55619
142 029	GM	SCD	NH	55570	55620
142 030	GM	SCD	NH	55571	55621
142 031	GM	SCD	NH	55572	55622
142 032	GM	SCD	NH	55573	55623
142 033	RR	SCD	NH	55574	55624
142 034	PR	SCD	NH	55575	55625
142 035	PR	SCD	NH	55576	55626
142 036	RR	SCD	NH	55577	55627
142 037	PR	SCD	NH	55578	55628
142 038	PR	SCD	NH	55579	55629
142 039	PR	SCD	NH	55580	55630
142 040	PR	SCD	NH	55581	55631
142 041	PR	SCD	NH	55582	55632
142 042	PR	SCD	NH	55583	55633

142 043	PR	SCD	NH	55584	55634
142 044	RR	SCD	NH	55585	55635
142 045	PR	SCD	NH	55586	55636
142 046	PR	SCD	NH	55587	55637
142 047	RR	SCD	NH	55588	55638
142 048	RR	SCD	NH	55589	55639
142 049	PR	SCD	NH	55590	55640
142 050	PR	SCC	HT	55591	55641
142 051	MT	SCD	NH	55701	55747
142 052	MT	SCD	NH	55702	55748
142 053	MT	SCD	NH	55703	55749
142 054	MT	SCD	NH	55704	55750
142 055	MT	SCD	NH	55705	55751
142 056	MT	SCD	NH	55706	55752
142 057	MT	SCD	NH	55707	55753
142 058	MT	SCD	NH	55708	55754
142 060	PR	SCD	NH	55710	55756
142 061	PR	SCD	NH	55711	55757
142 062	PR	SCD	NH	55712	55758
142 063	PR	SCD	NH	55713	55759
142 064	PR	SCD	NH	55714	55760
142 065	PR	SCC	HT	55715	55761
142 066	PR	SCC	HT	55716	55762
142 067	GM	SCD	NH	55717	55763
142 068	GM	SCD	NH	55718	55764
142 069	GM	SCD	NH	55719	55765
142 070	PR	SCD	NH	55720	55766
142 071	PR	SCC	HT	55721	55767
142 072	RR	SCC	NL	55722	55768
142 073	RR	SCC	NL	55723	55769
142 074	RR	SCC	NL	55724	55770
142 075	RR	SCC	NL	55725	55771
142 076	PR	SCC	NL	55726	55772
142 077	PR	SCC	NL	55727	55773
142 078	PR	SCC	NL	55728	55774
142 079	PR	SCC	NL	55729	55775
142 080	PR	SCC	NL	55730	55776
142 081	PR	SCC	NL	55731	55777
142 082	PR	SCC	NL	55732	55778
142 083	PR	SCC	NL	55733	55779
142 084	PR	SCC	NL	55734	55780
142 085	PR	SCC	NL	55735	55781
142 086	PR	SCC	NL	55736	55782
142 087	PR	SCC	NL	55737	55783
142 088	PR	SCC	NL	55738	55784
142 089	PR	SCC	NL	55739	55785
142 090	PR	SCC	NL	55740	55786
142 091	RR	SCC	NL	55741	55787
142 092	RR	SCC	NL	55742	55788
142 093	RR	SCC	NL	55743	55789
142 094	RR	SCC	NL	55744	55790

| 142 095 | **RR** | SCC | NL | 55745 55791 |
| 142 096 | **RR** | SCC | NL | 55746 55792 |

CLASS 143   ALEXANDER/BARCLAY RAILBUS

DMS – DMSL. Similar design to Class 142, but bodies built by W. Alexander with Barclay underframes.

Engines: One Cummins LTA10-R of 170 kW (225 h.p.) per car.
Transmission: Hydraulic. Voith T211r with Gmeinder final drive.
Gangways: Within unit only.
Doors: Folding.
Dimensions: 15.55 x 2.70 m.
Accommodation: 2 + 3 bus style.
Maximum Speed: 75 mph.

DMS. Dia. DP236 Lot No. 31005 Andrew Barclay 1985 – 6. –/62. 24.5 t.
DMSL. Dia. DP237 Lot No. 31006 Andrew Barclay 1985 – 6. –/60 1T. 25.0 t.

Note: 143 601/10/4 are owned by Mid-Glamorgan County Council, 143 609 is owned by South Glamorgan County Council and 143 617 – 9 are owned by West Glamorgan County Council although managed by Porterbrook Leasing Company.

143 601	**RR**	SBK	CF	55642 55667	
143 602	**RR**	SBL	CF	55651 55668	
143 603	**RR**	SBL	CF	55658 55669	
143 604	**RR**	SBL	CF	55645 55670	
143 605	**RR**	SBL	CF	55646 55671	
143 606	**RR**	SBL	CF	55647 55672	
143 607	**RR**	SBL	CF	55648 55673	
143 608	**RR**	SBL	CF	55649 55674	
143 609	**RR**	SBL	CF	55650 55675	
143 610	**RR**	SBK	CF	55643 55676	
143 611	**RR**	SBL	CF	55652 55677	
143 612	**RR**	SBK	CF	55653 55678	
143 613	**RR**	SBL	CF	55654 55679	
143 614	**RR**	SBK	CF	55655 55680	
143 615	**RR**	SBL	CF	55656 55681	
143 616	**RR**	SBL	CF	55657 55682	
143 617	**RR**	SBK	CF	55644 55683	Bewick's Swan
143 618	**RR**	SBK	CF	55659 55684	
143 619	**RR**	SBK	CF	55660 55685	Whooper Swan
143 620	**RR**	SBK	CF	55661 55686	
143 621	**RR**	SBK	CF	55662 55687	
143 622	**RR**	SBK	CF	55663 55688	
143 623	**RR**	SBK	CF	55664 55689	
143 624	**RR**	SBK	CF	55665 55690	
143 625	**RR**	SBK	CF	55666 55691	

CLASS 144   ALEXANDER/BREL RAILBUS

DMS – DMSL or DMS – MS – DMSL. Similar design to Class 143, but under-frames built by BREL as subcontractor to W. Alexander.

Engines: One Cummins LTA10-R of 170 kW (225 h.p.) per car.
Transmission: Hydraulic. Voith T211r with Gmeinder final drive.
Gangways: Within unit only.
Doors: Folding.
Dimensions: 15.25 x 2.70 m.
Accommodation: 2 + 3 bus style.
Maximum Speed: 75 mph.

DMS. Dia. DP240 Lot No. 31015 Derby 1986 – 7. – /62 and wheelchair space. 24.2 t.
MS. Dia. DR205 Lot No. Derby 31037 1987. – /73. 22.6 t.
DMSL. Dia. DP241 Lot No. Derby 31016 1986 – 7. – /60 1T. 25.0 t.

Note: The centre cars of the three-car units are owned by West Yorkshire PTE, although managed by Porterbrook Leasing Company.

144 001	Y	SBC	NL	55801		55824
144 002	Y	SBC	NL	55802		55825
144 003	Y	SBC	NL	55803		55826
144 004	Y	SBC	NL	55804		55827
144 005	Y	SBC	NL	55805		55828
144 006	Y	SBC	NL	55806		55829
144 007	Y	SBC	NL	55807		55830
144 008	Y	SBC	NL	55808		55831
144 009	Y	SBC	NL	55809		55832
144 010	Y	SBC	NL	55810		55833
144 011	RR	SBC	NL	55811		55834
144 012	RR	SBC	NL	55812		55835
144 013	RR	SBC	NL	55813		55836
144 014	Y	SBC	NL	55814	55850	55837
144 015	Y	SBC	NL	55815	55851	55838
144 016	Y	SBC	NL	55816	55852	55839
144 017	Y	SBC	NL	55817	55853	55840
144 018	Y	SBC	NL	55818	55854	55841
144 019	Y	SBC	NL	55819	55855	55842
144 020	Y	SBC	NL	55820	55856	55843
144 021	Y	SBC	NL	55821	55857	55844
144 022	Y	SBC	NL	55822	55858	55845
144 023	Y	SBC	NL	55823	55859	55846

CLASS 150/0   BREL PROTOTYPE SPRINTER

DMSL – MS – DMS. Prototype Sprinter.

Engines: One Cummins NT855R5 of 210 kW (285 hp) per car.
Transmission: Hydraulic. Voith T211r with Gmeinder final drive.
Bogies: One BX8P and one BX8T.
Couplings: BSI at outer end of driving vehicles, bar non-driving ends.

Gangways: Within unit only.
Doors: Sliding.
Accommodation: 2 + 3 (mainly unidirectional).
Dimensions: 20.06 x 2.82 m (outer cars), 20.18 x 2.82 m (inner car).
Maximum Speed: 75 mph.

DMSL. Dia. DP230. Lot No. 30984 York 1984. –/72 1T. 35.8 t.
MS. Dia. DR202. Lot No. 30986 York 1984. –/92. 34.4 t.
DMS. Dia. DP231. Lot No. 30985 York 1984. –/76. 35.6 t.

Note: 150 002 was converted to 154 002 at RTC Derby in 1986, but was later converted back to a Class 150.

150 001	**CE**	SCG	TS	55200	55400	55300
150 002·	**CE**	SCG	TS	55201	55401	55301

CLASS 150/1   BREL SPRINTER

DMSL – DMS or DMSL – DMSL (Class 150/2) – DMS or DMSL – DMS (Class 150/2) – DMS.

Engines: One Cummins NT855R5 of 210 kW (285 hp) per car.
Transmission: Hydraulic. Voith T211r with Gmeinder final drive.
Bogies: One BP38 and one BT38.
Gangways: Within unit only.
Doors: Sliding.
Accommodation: 2 + 3 facing. (★ Reseated with part unidirectional seating and part facing).
Dimensions: 20.06 x 2.82 m.
Maximum Speed: 75 mph.

DMSL. Dia. DP238. Lot No. 31011 York 1985 – 6. –/68 1T (–/64 1T*, –/72 1T★). 36.5 t.
DMS. Dia. DP239. Lot No. 31012 York 1985 – 6. –/70 (–/76★, –/66§). 38.45 t.

Note: The centre cars of three-car units are Class 150/2 vehicles. For details see next Class.

150 010	r★ **CE**	SCG	TS	52110	57226	57110
150 011	r★ **CE**	SCG	TS	52111	57206	57111
150 012	r★ **CE**	SCG	TS	52112	52204	57112
150 013	r★ **CE**	SCG	TS	52113	52226	57113
150 014	r★ **CE**	SCG	TS	52114	52204	57114
150 015	r★ **CE**	SCG	TS	52115	52206	57115
150 016	r★ **CE**	SCG	TS	52116	57212	57116
150 017	r★ **CE**	SCG	TS	52117	57209	57117
150 018	r★ **CE**	SCG	TS	52118	52220	57118
150 021	r★ **CE**	SCG	TS	52121	57220	57121
150 101	r★ **CE**	SCG	TS	52101		57101
150 102	r★ **CE**	SCG	TS	52102		57102
150 103	r★ **CE**	SCG	TS	52103		57103
150 104	r★ **CE**	SCG	TS	52104		57104
150 105	r★ **CE**	SCG	TS	52105		57105

150 106	r★ CE	SCG	TS	52106	57106
150 107	r★ CE	SCG	TS	52107	57107
150 108	r★ CE	SCG	TS	52108	57108
150 109	r★ CE	SCG	TS	52109	57109
150 120	r★ CE	SCG	TS	52120	57120
150 121	r★ CE	SCG	TS	52121	57121
150 122	r★ CE	SCG	TS	52122	57122
150 123	r★ CE	SCG	TS	52123	57123
150 124	r★ CE	SCG	TS	52124	57124
150 125	r★ CE	SCG	TS	52125	57125
150 126	r★ CE	SCG	TS	52126	57126
150 127	r★ CE	SCG	TS	52127	57127
150 128	r★ CE	SCG	TS	52128	57128
150 129	r★ CE	SCG	TS	52129	57129
150 130	r★ CE	SCG	TS	52130	57130
150 131	r★ CE	SCG	TS	52131	57131
150 132	r★ CE	SCG	TS	52132	57132
150 133	r* GM	SCD	NH	52133	57133
150 134	r* GM	SCD	NH	52134	57134
150 135	r* GM	SCD	NH	52135	57135
150 136	r* GM	SCD	NH	52136	57136
150 137	r§ GM	SCD	NH	52137	57137
150 138	r* GM	SCD	NH	52138	57138
150 139	r* GM	SCD	NH	52139	57139
150 140	r* GM	SCD	NH	52140	57140
150 141	r* GM	SCD	NH	52141	57141
150 142	r GM	SCD	NH	52142	57142
150 143	r* P	SCD	NH	52143	57143
150 144	r§ P	SCD	NH	52144	57144
150 145	r§ P	SCD	NH	52145	57145
150 146	r§ RR	SCD	NH	52146	57146
150 147	r§ P	SCD	NH	52147	57147
150 148	r§ P	SCD	NH	52148	57148
150 149	r§ P	SCD	NH	52149	57149
150 150	r§ P	SCD	NH	52150	57150

CLASS 150/2   BREL SPRINTER

DMSL – DMS.

Engines: One Cummins NT855R5 of 210 kW (285 hp) per car.
Transmission: Hydraulic. Voith T211r with Gmeinder final drive.
Bogies: One BP38 and one BT38.
Gangways: Throughout.
Doors: Sliding.
Accommodation: 2 + 3 mainly unidirectional.
Dimensions: 20.06 x 2.82 m.
Maximum Speed: 75 mph.

DMSL. Dia. DP242. Lot No. 31017 York 1986 – 87. –/73 1T (– 70 1T*). 35.8 t.
DMS. Dia. DP243. Lot No. 31018 York 1986 – 7. –/76 (–/73§) and luggage

space. 34.90 t.

150 201	*	MT	SCD	NH	52201	57201	
150 202		CE	SCG	TS	52202	57202	
150 203	*	MT	SCD	NH	52203	57203	
150 205	*	MT	SCD	NH	52205	57205	
150 207	§	MT	SCD	NH	52207	57207	
150 208		RR	SBA	HA	52208	57208	
150 210		CE	SCG	TS	52210	57210	
150 211	§	MT	SCD	NH	52211	57211	
150 213		RR	SBS	NC	52213	57213	Lord Nelson
150 214		CE	SCG	TS	52214	57214	
150 215		GM	SCD	NH	52215	57215	
150 216		CE	SCG	TS	52216	57216	
150 217		RR	SBS	NC	52217	57217	
150 218	* §	GM	SCD	NH	52218	57218	
150 219		P	SBK	CF	52219	57219	
150 221		RR	SBK	CF	52221	57221	
150 222	§	GM	SCD	NH	52222	57222	
150 223	*	GM	SCD	NH	52223	57223	
150 224	*	GM	SCD	NH	52224	57224	
150 225	§	GM	SCD	NH	52225	57225	
150 227		RR	SBS	NC	52227	57227	Sir Alf Ramsey
150 228		RR	SBA	HA	52228	57228	
150 229		RR	SBS	NC	52229	57229	
150 230		RR	SBK	CF	52230	57230	
150 231		RR	SBS	NC	52231	57231	King Edmund
150 232		RR	SBK	CF	52232	57232	
150 233		RR	SBK	CF	52233	57233	
150 234		RR	SBK	CF	52234	57234	
150 235		RR	SBS	NC	52235	57235	
150 236		P	SBK	CF	52236	57236	
150 237		RR	SBS	NC	52237	57237	Hereward the Wake
150 238		P	SBK	CF	52238	57238	
150 239		RR	SBK	CF	52239	57239	
150 240		RR	SBK	CF	52240	57240	
150 241		RR	SBK	CF	52241	57241	
150 242		P	SBK	CF	52242	57242	
150 243		P	SBK	CF	52243	57243	
150 244		RR	SBK	CF	52244	57244	
150 245		RR	SBA	HA	52245	57245	
150 246		RR	SBK	CF	52246	57246	
150 247		P	SBK	CF	52247	57247	
150 248		RR	SBK	CF	52248	57248	
150 249		RR	SBK	CF	52249	57249	
150 250		RR	SBA	HA	52250	57250	
150 251		RR	SBK	CF	52251	57251	
150 252		RR	SBA	HA	52252	57252	
150 253		RR	SBK	CF	52253	57253	
150 254		P	SBK	CF	52254	57254	
150 255		RR	SBS	NC	52255	57255	Henry Blogg

150 256	RR	SBA	HA	52256	57256	
150 257	RR	SBS	NC	52257	57257	Queen Boadicea
150 258	RR	SBA	HA	52258	57258	
150 259	RR	SBA	HA	52259	57259	
150 260	RR	SBA	HA	52260	57260	
150 261	RR	SBK	CF	52261	57261	
150 262	RR	SBA	HA	52262	57262	
150 263	RR	SBK	CF	52263	57263	
150 264	RR	SBA	HA	52264	57264	
150 265	P	SBL	CF	52265	57265	
150 266	P	SBL	CF	52266	57266	
150 267	P	SBL	CF	52267	57267	
150 268	P	SBL	CF	52268	57268	
150 269	P	SBL	CF	52269	57269	
150 270	P	SBL	CF	52270	57270	
150 271	RR	SBL	CF	52271	57271	
150 272	P	SBL	CF	52272	57272	
150 273	P	SBL	CF	52273	57273	
150 274	RR	SBD	NH	52274	57274	
150 275	RR	SBL	CF	52275	57275	
150 276	RR	SBL	CF	52276	57276	
150 277	P	SBL	CF	52277	57277	
150 278	RR	SBL	CF	52278	57278	
150 279	RR	SBL	CF	52279	57279	
150 280	RR	SBL	CF	52280	57280	
150 281	RR	SBL	CF	52281	57281	
150 282	RR	SBL	CF	52282	57282	
150 283	RR	SBA	HA	52283	57283	
150 284	RR	SBA	HA	52284	57284	
150 285	RR	SBA	HA	52285	57285	

CLASS 153   LEYLAND BUS SUPER SPRINTER

DMSL. Converted by Hunslet-Barclay, Kilmarnock from Class 155 two-car units.

Engines: One Cummins NT855R5 of 213 kW (285 hp) per car.
Transmission: Hydraulic. Voith T211r with Gmeinder final drive.
Bogies: One P3-10 and one BT38.
Gangways: Throughout.
Doors: Sliding plug.
Accommodation: 2 + 2 facing/unidirectional with wheelchair space.
Dimensions: 23.21 x 2.70 m.
Maximum Speed: 75 mph.

52301 – 52335. DMSL. Dia. DX203. Lot No. 31026 1987 – 8. Converted under Lot No. 31115 1991 – 2. –/72 1TD + 3 tip-up seats. 41.2 t.
57301 – 57335. DMSL. Dia. DX203. Lot No. 31027 1987 – 8. Converted under Lot No. 31115 1991 – 2. –/72 1TD + 3 tip-up seats. 41.2 t.

Note: Cars numbered in the 573XX series have been renumbered by adding 50 to the number so that the last two digits correspond with the set number.

153 301	**RR**	SCC	HT	52301
153 302	**RR**	SCK	CF	52302
153 303	**RR**	SCK	CF	52303
153 304	**RR**	SCC	HT	52304
153 305	**RR**	SCK	CF	52305
153 306	**RR**	SBS	NC	52306	Edith Cavell
153 307	**RR**	SCC	HT	52307
153 308	**RR**	SCK	CF	52308
153 309	**RR**	SBS	NC	52309
153 310	**RR**	SBD	NH	52310
153 311	**RR**	SBS	NC	52311	John Constable
153 312	**RR**	SCK	CF	52312
153 313	**RR**	SBD	NH	52313
153 314	**RR**	SBS	NC	52314	Delia Smith
153 315	**RR**	SCC	HT	52315
153 316	**RR**	SBD	NH	52316
153 317	**RR**	SCC	HT	52317
153 318	**RR**	SCK	CF	52318
153 319	**RR**	SCC	HT	52319
153 320	**RR**	SBG	TS	52320
153 321	**RR**	SBG	TS	52321
153 322	**RR**	SBS	NC	52322	Benjamin Britten
153 323	**RR**	SBG	TS	52323
153 324	**RR**	SBD	NH	52324
153 325	**RR**	SBG	TS	52325
153 326	**RR**	SBS	NC	52326	Ted Ellis
153 327	**RR**	SCK	CF	52327
153 328	**RR**	SCC	HT	52328
153 329	**RR**	SBG	TS	52329
153 330	**RR**	SBD	NH	52330
153 331	**RR**	SCC	HT	52331
153 332	**RR**	SBD	NH	52332
153 333	**RR**	SBG	TS	52333
153 334	**RR**	SBG	TS	52334
153 335	**RR**	SBS	NC	52335
153 351	**RR**	SCC	HT	57351
153 352	**RR**	SCC	HT	57352
153 353	**RR**	SCK	CF	57353
153 354	**RR**	SBG	TS	57354
153 355	**RR**	SCK	CF	57355
153 356	**RR**	SBG	TS	57356
153 357	**RR**	SCC	HT	57357
153 358	**RR**	SBD	NH	57358
153 359	**RR**	SBD	NH	57359
153 360	**RR**	SBD	NH	57360
153 361	**RR**	SBD	NH	57361
153 362	**RR**	SCK	CF	57362
153 363	**RR**	SBD	NH	57363
153 364	**RR**	SBG	TS	57364
153 365	**RR**	SBG	TS	57365
153 366	**RR**	SBG	TS	57366

153 367	RR	SBD	NH	57367
153 368	RR	SCK	CF	57368
153 369	RR	SBG	TS	57369
153 370	RR	SCK	CF	57370
153 371	RR	SBG	TS	57371
153 372	RR	SCK	CF	57372
153 373	RR	SCK	CF	57373
153 374	RR	SCK	CF	57374
153 375	RR	SBG	TS	57375
153 376	RR	SBG	TS	57376
153 377	RR	SCK	CF	57377
153 378	RR	SCC	HT	57378
153 379	RR	SBG	TS	57379
153 380	RR	SCK	CF	57380
153 381	RR	SBG	TS	57381
153 382	RR	SCK	CF	57382
153 383	RR	SBG	TS	57383
153 384	RR	SBG	TS	57384
153 385	RR	SBG	TS	57385

CLASS 155   LEYLAND BUS SUPER SPRINTER

DMSL – DMS.

Engines: One Cummins NT855R5 of 213 kW (285 hp) per car.
Transmission: Hydraulic. Voith T211r with Gmeinder final drive.
Bogies: One P3-10 and one BT38.
Gangways: Throughout.
Doors: Sliding plug.
Accommodation: 2 + 2 facing/unidirectional with wheelchair space in DMSL.
Dimensions: 23.21 x 2.70 m.
Maximum Speed: 75 mph.

DMSL. Dia. DP248. Lot No. 31057 1988. – /80 1TD. 39.0 t.
DMS. Dia. DP249. Lot No. 31058 1988. – /80 and parcels area. 38.7 t.

Note: These units are owned by West Yorkshire PTE, although managed by Porterbrook Leasing Company.

155 341	Y	SBC	NL	52341	57341
155 342	Y	SBC	NL	52342	57342
155 343	Y	SBC	NL	52343	57343
155 344	Y	SBC	NL	52344	57344
155 345	Y	SBC	NL	52345	57345
155 346	Y	SBC	NL	52346	57346
155 347	Y	SBC	NL	52347	57347

CLASS 156   METRO-CAMMELL SUPER SPRINTER

DMSL – DMS.

Engines: One Cummins NT855R5 of 210 kW (285 hp) per car.
Transmission: Hydraulic. Voith T211r with Gmeinder final drive.

Bogies: One P3-10 and one BT38.
Gangways: Throughout.
Doors: Sliding.
Accommodation: 2 + 2 facing/unidirectional with wheelchair space in DMSL.
Dimensions: 23.03 x 2.73 m.
Maximum Speed: 75 mph.

DMSL. Dia. DP244. Lot No. 31028 1988 − 9. −/74 (−/72★) 1TD. 36.1 t.
DMS. Dia. DP245. Lot No. 31029 1987 − 9. 35.5 t. −/76 (74★) + parcels area.
Note: 156 500 − 514 are owned by Strathclyde PTE, although managed by Angel Trains Contracts.

156 401	**RE**	SBG	TS	52401	57401
156 402	**RE**	SBG	TS	52402	57402
156 403	**P**	SBG	TS	52403	57403
156 404	**P**	SBG	TS	52404	57404
156 405	**P**	SBG	TS	52405	57405
156 406	**P**	SBG	TS	52406	57406
156 407	**P**	SBG	TS	52407	57407
156 408	**P**	SBG	TS	52408	57408
156 409	**P**	SBG	TS	52409	57409
156 410	**P**	SBG	TS	52410	57410
156 411	**P**	SBG	TS	52411	57411
156 412	**P**	SBG	TS	52412	57412
156 413	**P**	SBG	TS	52413	57413
156 414	**P**	SBG	TS	52414	57414
156 415	**P**	SBG	TS	52415	57415
156 416	**P**	SBG	TS	52416	57416
156 417	**P**	SBG	TS	52417	57417
156 418	**P**	SBG	TS	52418	57418
156 419	**P**	SBG	TS	52419	57419
156 420	**RN**	SBD	NH	52420	57420
156 421	**P**	SBD	NH	52421	57421
156 422	**P**	SBG	TS	52422	57422
156 423	**P**	SBD	NH	52423	57423
156 424	**P**	SBD	NH	52424	57424
156 425	**P**	SBD	NH	52425	57425
156 426	**P**	SBD	NH	52426	57426
156 427	**P**	SBD	NH	52427	57427
156 428	**RN**	SBD	NH	52428	57428
156 429	**P**	SBD	NH	52429	57429
156 430	**P**	SCA	CK	52430	57430
156 431	**P**	SCA	CK	52431	57431
156 432	**P**	SCA	CK	52432	57432
156 433	**P**	SCA	CK	52433	57433
156 434	**P**	SCA	CK	52434	57434
156 435	**P**	SCA	HA	52435	57435
156 436	r★ **P**	SCA	CK	52436	57436
156 437	**P**	SCA	CK	52437	57437
156 438	**P**	SCC	NL	52438	57438
156 439	**P**	SCA	CK	52439	57439
156 440	**RN**	SBD	NH	52440	57440

156 441	P	SBD	NH	52441	57441	
156 442	P	SCA	CK	52442	57442	
156 443	P	SCC	HT	52443	57443	
156 444	P	SCC	HT	52444	57444	
156 445	r★ P	SCA	CK	52445	57445	
156 446	r★ P	SCA	IS	52446	57446	
156 447	r★ P	SCA	HA	52447	57447	
156 448	P	SCC	HT	52448	57448	
156 449	r★ P	SCA	CK	52449	57449	
156 450	r★ P	SCA	CK	52450	57450	
156 451	P	SCC	HT	52451	57451	
156 452	P	SBD	NH	52452	57452	
156 453	r★ P	SCA	CK	52453	57453	
156 454	P	SCC	HT	52454	57454	
156 455	P	SBD	NH	52455	57455	
156 456	r★ P	SCA	CK	52456	57456	
156 457	r★ P	SCA	IS	52457	57457	
156 458	r★ P	SCA	IS	52458	57458	
156 459	P	SBD	NH	52459	57459	
156 460	P	SBD	NH	52460	57460	
156 461	P	SBD	NH	52461	57461	
156 462	P	SCA	HA	52462	57462	
156 463	P	SCC	HT	52463	57463	
156 464	P	SBD	NH	52464	57464	
156 465	r★ P	SCA	CK	52465	57465	Bonnie Prince Charlie
156 466	P	SBD	NH	52466	57466	
156 467	P	SCA	IS	52467	57467	
156 468	P	SCC	NL	52468	57468	
156 469	P	SCC	HT	52469	57469	
156 470	P	SCC	NL	52470	57470	
156 471	P	SCC	NL	52471	57471	
156 472	P	SCC	NL	52472	57472	
156 473	P	SCC	NL	52473	57473	
156 474	r★ P	SCA	IS	52474	57474	
156 475	P	SCC	NL	52475	57475	
156 476	P	SCA	HA	52476	57476	
156 477	r★ P	SCA	IS	52477	57477	
156 478	r★ P	SCA	IS	52478	57478	
156 479	P	SCC	NL	52479	57479	
156 480	P	SCC	NL	52480	57480	
156 481	P	SCC	NL	52481	57481	
156 482	P	SCC	NL	52482	57482	
156 483	P	SCC	NL	52483	57483	
156 484	P	SCC	NL	52484	57484	
156 485	r★ P	SCA	HA	52485	57485	
156 486	P	SCC	NL	52486	57486	
156 487	P	SCC	NL	52487	57487	
156 488	P	SCC	NL	52488	57488	
156 489	P	SCC	NL	52489	57489	
156 490	P	SCC	NL	52490	57490	

156 491		P	SCC	NL	52491 57491
156 492	r★	P	SCA	CK	52492 57492
156 493	r★	P	SCA	HA	52493 57493
156 494	r★	P	SCA	HA	52494 57494
156 495	r★	P	SCA	CK	52495 57495
156 496	r★	P	SCA	CK	52496 57496
156 497		P	SCC	NL	52497 57497
156 498		P	SCC	NL	52498 57498
156 499	r★	P	SCA	IS	52499 57499
156 500	r★	P	SCA	HA	52500 57500
156 501		S	SCA	CK	52501 57501
156 502		S	SCA	CK	52502 57502
156 503		S	SCA	CK	52503 57503
156 504		S	SCA	HA	52504 57504
156 505		S	SCA	HA	52505 57505
156 506		S	SCA	CK	52506 57506
156 507		S	SCA	CK	52507 57507
156 508		S	SCA	CK	52508 57508
156 509		S	SCA	CK	52509 57509
156 510		S	SCA	CK	52510 57510
156 511		S	SCA	CK	52511 57511
156 512		S	SCA	CK	52512 57512
156 513		S	SCA	CK	52513 57513
156 514		S	SCA	CK	52514 57514

CLASS 158/0   BREL EXPRESS

DMSL (B) – DMSL (A) or DMCL – DMSL * § or DMSL (B) – MSL – DMSL (A).

Engines: One Cummins NTA855R of 260 kW (350 hp) or 300 kW (400 hp) §
(One Perkins 2006-TWH of 260 kW (350 hp) ★) per car.
Transmission: Hydraulic. Voith T211r with Gmeinder final drive.
Bogies: One BREL P4 and one BREL T4 per car.
Gangways: Throughout.
Doors: Sliding plug.
Accommodation: 2 + 2 facing/unidirectional (first & standard classes).
Dimensions: 23.21 x 2.70 m.
Maximum Speed: 90 mph.

DMSL (B).. Dia. DP252. Lot No. 31051 Derby 1990 – 2. –/68 + wheelchair
space 1TD. Public telephone and trolley space. 38.5 t.
DMCL.. Dia. DP252. Lot No. 31051 Derby 1989 – 90. 15/51*, 9/51§ +
wheelchair space 1TD. Public telephone and trolley space. 38.5 t.
MSL. Dia. DR207. Lot No. 31050 Derby 1991. 38 t. –/70 2T.
DMSL (A). Dia. DP251. Lot No. 31052 Derby 1990 – 92. –/70 1T and parcels
area. 37.8 t.

158 701	*	RE	SBA	HA	52701	57701
158 702	*	RE	SBA	HA	52702	57702
158 703	*	RE	SBA	HA	52703	57703
158 704	*	RE	SBA	HA	52704	57704
158 705	*	RE	SBA	HA	52705	57705

158 706	*	RE	SBA	HA	52706	57706
158 707	*	RE	SBA	HA	52707	57707
158 708	*	RE	SBA	HA	52708	57708
158 709	*	RE	SBA	HA	52709	57709
158 710	*	RE	SBA	HA	52710	57710
158 711	*	RE	SBA	HA	52711	57711
158 712	*	RE	SBA	HA	52712	57712
158 713	*	RE	SBA	HA	52713	57713
158 714	*	RE	SBA	HA	52714	57714
158 715	*	RE	SBA	HA	52715	57715
158 716	*	RE	SBA	HA	52716	57716
158 717	*	RE	SBA	HA	52717	57717
158 718	*	RE	SBA	HA	52718	57718
158 719	*	RE	SBA	HA	52719	57719
158 720	*	RE	SBA	HA	52720	57720
158 721	*	RE	SBA	HA	52721	57721
158 722	*	RE	SBA	HA	52722	57722
158 723	*	RE	SBA	HA	52723	57723
158 724	*	RE	SBA	HA	52724	57724
158 725	*	RE	SBA	HA	52725	57725
158 726	*	RE	SBA	HA	52726	57726
158 727	*	RE	SBA	HA	52727	57727
158 728	*	RE	SBA	HA	52728	57728
158 729	*	RE	SBA	HA	52729	57729
158 730	*	RE	SBA	HA	52730	57730
158 731	*	RE	SBA	HA	52731	57731
158 732	*	RE	SBA	HA	52732	57732
158 733	*	RE	SBA	HA	52733	57733
158 734	*	RE	SBA	HA	52734	57734
158 735	*	RE	SBA	HA	52735	57735
158 736	*	RE	SBA	HA	52736	57736
158 737	*	RE	SBA	HA	52737	57737
158 738	*	RE	SBA	HA	52738	57738
158 739	*	RE	SBA	HA	52739	57739
158 740	*	RE	SBA	HA	52740	57740
158 741	*	RE	SBA	HA	52741	57741
158 742	*	RE	SBA	HA	52742	57742
158 743	*	RE	SBA	HA	52743	57743
158 744	*	RE	SBA	HA	52744	57744
158 745	*	RE	SBA	HA	52745	57745
158 746	*	RE	SBA	HA	52746	57746
158 747	§	RE	SBH	NH	52747	57747
158 748	§	RE	SBH	NH	52748	57748
158 749	§	RE	SBH	NH	52749	57749
158 750	§	RE	SBH	NH	52750	57750
158 751	§	RE	SBH	NH	52751	57751
158 752		RE	SBD	NH	52752	57752
158 753		RE	SBD	NH	52753	57753
158 754		RE	SBD	NH	52754	57754
158 755		RE	SBD	NH	52755	57755
158 756		RE	SBD	NH	52756	57756

158 757		RE	SBD	NH	52757		57757
158 758		RE	SBD	NH	52758		57758
158 759		RE	SBD	NH	52759		57759
158 760		RE	SBC	NL	52760		57760
158 761		RE	SBC	NL	52761		57761
158 762		RE	SBC	NL	52762		57762
158 763		RE	SBC	NL	52763		57763
158 764		RE	SBC	NL	52764		57764
158 765		RE	SBC	NL	52765		57765
158 766		RE	SBC	NH	52766		57766
158 767		RE	SBC	NL	52767		57767
158 768		RE	SBC	NL	52768		57768
158 769		RE	SBC	NL	52769		57769
158 770		RE	SBC	NL	52770		57770
158 771		RE	SBC	HT	52771		57771
158 772		RE	SBC	NL	52772		57772
158 773		RE	SBC	NL	52773		57773
158 774		RE	SBC	HT	52774		57774
158 775		RE	SBC	HT	52775		57775
158 776		RE	SBC	HT	52776		57776
158 777		RE	SBC	HT	52777		57777
158 778		RE	SBC	HT	52778		57778
158 779		RE	SBC	HT	52779		57779
158 780	r	RE	SCG	NC	52780		57780
158 781	r	RE	SBC	HT	52781		57781
158 782	r	RE	SCG	NC	52782		57782
158 783	r	RE	SCG	NC	52783		57783
158 784	r	RE	SCG	NC	52784		57784
158 785	r	RE	SCG	NC	52785		57785
158 786	r	RE	SCG	NC	52786		57786
158 787	r	RE	SCG	NC	52787		57787
158 788	r	RE	SCG	NC	52788		57788
158 789	r	RE	SCG	NC	52789		57789
158 790	r	RE	SCG	NC	52790		57790
158 791	r	RE	SCG	NC	52791		57791
158 792	r	RE	SCG	NC	52792		57792
158 793	r	RE	SCG	NC	52793		57793
158 794	r	RE	SCG	NC	52794		57794
158 795	r	RE	SCG	NC	52795		57795
158 796	r	RE	SCG	NC	52796		57796
158 797	r	RE	SCG	NC	52797		57797
158 798		RE	SBC	HT	52798	58715	57798
158 799		RE	SBC	HT	52799	58716	57799
158 800		RE	SBC	HT	52800	58717	57800
158 801		RE	SBC	HT	52801	58701	57801
158 802		RE	SBC	HT	52802	58702	57802
158 803		RE	SBC	HT	52803	58703	57803
158 804		RE	SBC	HT	52804	58704	57804
158 805		RE	SBC	HT	52805	58705	57805
158 806		RE	SBC	HT	52806	58706	57806
158 807		RE	SBC	HT	52807	58707	57807

158 808		RE	SBC	HT	52808	58708 57808
158 809		RE	SBC	HT	52809	58709 57809
158 810		RE	SBC	HT	52810	58710 57810
158 811		RE	SBC	HT	52811	58711 57811
158 812		RE	SBC	HT	52812	58712 57812
158 813		RE	SBC	HT	52813	58713 57813
158 814		RE	SBC	HT	52814	58714 57814
158 815	★	RE	SCK	CF	52815	57815
158 816	★	RE	SCK	CF	52816	57816
158 817	★	RE	SCK	CF	52817	57817
158 818	★	RE	SCK	CF	52818	57818
158 819	★	RE	SCK	CF	52819	57819
158 820	★	RE	SCK	CF	52820	57820
158 821	★	RE	SCK	CF	52821	57821
158 822	★	RE	SCK	CF	52822	57822
158 823	★	RE	SCK	CF	52823	57823
158 824	★	RE	SCK	CF	52824	57824
158 825	★	RE	SCK	CF	52825	57825
158 826	★	RE	SCK	CF	52826	57826
158 827	★	RE	SCK	CF	52827	57827
158 828	★	RE	SCK	CF	52828	57828
158 829	★	RE	SCK	CF	52829	57829
158 830	★	RE	SCK	CF	52830	57830
158 831	★	RE	SCK	CF	52831	57831
158 832	★	RE	SCK	CF	52832	57832
158 833	★	RE	SCK	CF	52833	57833
158 834	★	RE	SCK	CF	52834	57834
158 835	★	RE	SCK	CF	52835	57835
158 836	★	RE	SCK	CF	52836	57836
158 837	★	RE	SCK	CF	52837	57837
158 838	★	RE	SCK	CF	52838	57838
158 839	★	RE	SCK	CF	52839	57839
158 840	★	RE	SCK	CF	52840	57840
158 841	★	RE	SCK	CF	52841	57841
158 842	★r	RE	SCK	CF	52842	57842
158 843	★r	RE	SCK	CF	52843	57843
158 844	★r	RE	SCG	NC	52844	57844
158 845	★r	RE	SCG	NC	52845	57845
158 846	★r	RE	SCG	NC	52846	57846
158 847	★r	RE	SCG	NC	52847	57847
158 848	★r	RE	SCG	NC	52848	57848
158 849	★r	RE	SCG	NC	52849	57849
158 850	★r	RE	SCG	NC	52850	57850
158 851	★r	RE	SCG	NC	52851	57851
158 852	★r	RE	SCG	NC	52852	57852
158 853	★r	RE	SCG	NC	52853	57853
158 854	★r	RE	SCG	NC	52854	57854
158 855	★r	RE	SCG	NC	52855	57855
158 856	★r	RE	SCG	NC	52856	57856
158 857	★r	RE	SCG	NC	52857	57857
158 858	★r	RE	SCG	NC	52858	57858

158 859	★r RE	SCG	NC	52859	57859
158 860	★r RE	SCG	NC	52860	57860
158 861	★r RE	SCG	NC	52861	57861
158 862	★r RE	SCG	NC	52862	57862
158 863	§ RE	SCK	CF	52863	57863
158 864	§ RE	SCK	CF	52864	57864
158 865	§ RE	SCK	CF	52865	57865
158 866	§ RE	SCK	CF	52866	57866
158 867	§ RE	SCK	CF	52867	57867
158 868	§ RE	SCK	CF	52868	57868
158 869	§ RE	SCK	CF	52869	57869
158 870	§ RE	SCK	CF	52870	57870
158 871	§ RE	SCK	CF	52871	57871
158 872	§ RE	SCK	CF	52872	57872

CLASS 158/9   BREL EXPRESS

DMSL – DMS. Units leased by West Yorkshire PTE. Details as for Class 158/0 except for seating layout and toilets.

DMSL.. Dia. DP252. Lot No. 31051 Derby 1990 – 2. –/70 + wheelchair space 1TD. Public telephone and trolley space. 38.1 t.
DMS. Dia. DP251. Lot No. 31052 Derby 1990 – 92. –/72 and parcels area. 37.8 t.

Note: Although these units are leased by West Yorkshire PTE, they are managed by Porterbrook Leasing Company.

158 901	Y	SBC	NL	52901	57901
158 902	Y	SBC	NL	52902	57902
158 903	Y	SBC	NL	52903	57903
158 904	Y	SBC	NL	52904	57904
158 905	Y	SBC	NL	52905	57905
158 906	Y	SBC	NL	52906	57906
158 907	Y	SBC	NL	52907	57907
158 908	Y	SBC	NL	52908	57908
158 909	Y	SBC	NL	52909	57909
158 910	Y	SBC	NL	52910	57910

CLASS 159   BREL EXPRESS

DMCL – MSL – DMSL. Built as Class 158 by BREL. Converted before entering passenger service to Class 159 by Rosyth Dockyard.

Engines: One Cummins NTA855R of 300 kW (400 hp) per car.
Transmission: Hydraulic. Voith T211r with Gmeinder final drive.
Bogies: One BREL P4 and one BREL T4 per car.
Gangways: Throughout.
Doors: Sliding plug.
Accommodation: 2 + 2 facing/unidirectional (standard class), 2 + 1 facing (first class).
Dimensions: 23.21 x 2.82 m.
Maximum Speed: 90 mph.

DMCL.. Dia. DP322. Lot No. 31051 Derby 1992. 24/28 1TD. 38.5 t.
MSL. Dia. DR209. Lot No. 31050 Derby 1992. 38 t. –/72 2T.
DMSL. Dia. DP260. Lot No. 31052 Derby 1992. –/72 1T and parcels area.
37.8 t.

159 001	NW SBY	SA	52873 58718 57873	CITY OF EXETER
159 002	NW SBY	SA	52874 58719 57874	CITY OF SALISBURY
159 003	NW SBY	SA	52875 58720 57875	TEMPLECOMBE
159 004	NW SBY	SA	52876 58721 57876	BASINGSTOKE
				AND DEANE
159 005	NW SBY	SA	52877 58722 57877	
159 006	NW SBY	SA	52878 58723 57878	
159 007	NW SBY	SA	52879 58724 57879	
159 008	NW SBY	SA	52880 58725 57880	
159 009	NW SBY	SA	52881 58726 57881	
159 010	NW SBY	SA	52882 58727 57882	
159 011	NW SBY	SA	52883 58728 57883	
159 012	NW SBY	SA	52884 58729 57884	
159 013	NW SBY	SA	52885 58730 57885	
159 014	NW SBY	SA	52886 58731 57886	
159 015	NW SBY	SA	52887 58732 57887	
159 016	NW SBY	SA	52888 58733 57888	
159 017	NW SBY	SA	52889 58734 57889	
159 018	NW SBY	SA	52890 58735 57890	
159 019	NW SBY	SA	52891 58736 57891	
159 020	NW SBY	SA	52892 58737 57892	
159 021	NW SBY	SA	52893 58738 57893	
159 022	NW SBY	SA	52894 58739 57894	

CLASS 165/0   BREL NETWORK TURBO

DMCL – DMS or DMCL – MS – DMS. Network SouthEast Units built for Chiltern
Line (Marylebone) services

Engines: One Perkins 2006-TWH of 260 kW (350 hp) per car.
Transmission: Hydraulic. Voith T211r with Gmeinder final drive.
Bogies: One BREL P3 and one BREL T3 per car.
Gangways: Within unit only.
Doors: Sliding plug.
Accommodation: 2 + 3 facing/unidirectional (standard class), 2 + 2 facing (first
class).
Dimensions: 23.50 x 2.85 m.
Maximum Speed: 75 mph.

58801 – 58822. **58873 – 58878. DMCL**. Dia. DP319. Lot No. 31087 York
1990. 16/72 1T. 37.0 t.
58823 – 58833. **DMCL**. Dia. DP320. Lot No. 31089 York 1991 – 1992. 24/60
1T. 37.0 t.
MS. Dia. DR208. Lot No. 31090 York 1991 – 1992. 106S. 37.0 t.
DMS. Dia. DP253. Lot No. 31088 York 1991 – 1992. 98S. 37.0 t.

165 001	NW	SCN	RG	58801		58834
165 002	NW	SCN	RG	58802		58835
165 003	NW	SCN	RG	58803		58836
165 004	NW	SCN	RG	58804		58837
165 005	NW	SCN	RG	58805		58838
165 006	NW	SCO	AL	58806		58839
165 007	NW	SCO	AL	58807		58840
165 008	NW	SCO	AL	58808		58841
165 009	NW	SCO	AL	58809		58842
165 010	NW	SCO	AL	58810		58843
165 011	NW	SCO	AL	58811		58844
165 012	NW	SCO	AL	58812		58845
165 013	NW	SCO	AL	58813		58846
165 014	NW	SCO	AL	58814		58847
165 015	NW	SCO	AL	58815		58848
165 016	NW	SCO	AL	58816		58849
165 017	NW	SCO	AL	58817		58850
165 018	NW	SCO	AL	58818		58851
165 019	NW	SCO	AL	58819		58852
165 020	NW	SCO	AL	58820		58853
165 021	NW	SCO	AL	58821		58854
165 022	NW	SCO	AL	58822		58855
165 023	NW	SCO	AL	58873		58867
165 024	NW	SCO	AL	58874		58868
165 025	NW	SCO	AL	58875		58869
165 026	NW	SCO	AL	58876		58870
165 027	NW	SCO	AL	58877		58871
165 028	NW	SCO	AL	58878		58872
165 029	NW	SCO	AL	58823	55404	58856
165 030	NW	SCO	AL	58824	55405	58857
165 031	NW	SCO	AL	58825	55406	58858
165 032	NW	SCO	AL	58826	55407	58859
165 033	NW	SCO	AL	58827	55408	58860
165 034	NW	SCO	AL	58828	55409	58861
165 035	NW	SCO	AL	58829	55410	58862
165 036	NW	SCO	AL	58830	55411	58863
165 037	NW	SCO	AL	58831	55412	58864
165 038	NW	SCO	AL	58832	55413	58865
165 039	NW	SCO	AL	58833	55414	58866

CLASS 165/1   BREL NETWORK TURBO

DMCL – DMS or DMCL – MS – DMS. Network SouthEast Units for Thames Line (Paddington) services. They now also work through to Worcester and Birmingham.

Engines: One Perkins 2006-TWH of 260 kW (350 hp) per car.
Bogies: One BREL P3 and one BREL T3 per car.

Transmission: Hydraulic. Voith T211r with Gmeinder final drive.
Gangways: Within unit only.
Doors: Sliding plug.
Accommodation: 2 + 3 facing/unidirectional (standard class), 2 + 2 facing (first class).
Dimensions: 23.50 x 2.85 m.
Maximum Speed: 90 mph.

58953 – 58969. DMCL. Dia. DP320. Lot No. 31098 York 1992. 24/60 1T. 37.0 t.
58879 – 58898. DMCL. Dia. DP319. Lot No. 31096 York 1992. 16/72 1T. 37.0 t.
MS. Dia. DR208. Lot No. 31099 York 1992. –/106. 37.0 t.
DMS. Dia. DP253. Lot No. 31097 York 1992. –/98. 37.0 t.

165 101	**NW**	SCN	RG	58916	55415	58953
165 102	**NW**	SCN	RG	58917	55416	58954
165 103	**NW**	SCN	RG	58918	55417	58955
165 104	**NW**	SCN	RG	58919	55418	58956
165 105	**NW**	SCN	RG	58920	55419	58957
165 106	**NW**	SCN	RG	58921	55420	58958
165 107	**NW**	SCN	RG	58922	55421	58959
165 108	**NW**	SCN	RG	58923	55422	58960
165 109	**NW**	SCN	RG	58924	55423	58961
165 110	**NW**	SCN	RG	58925	55424	58962
165 111	**NW**	SCN	RG	58926	55425	58963
165 112	**NW**	SCN	RG	58927	55426	58964
165 113	**NW**	SCN	RG	58928	55427	58965
165 114	**NW**	SCN	RG	58929	55428	58966
165 115	**NW**	SCN	RG	58930	55429	58967
165 116	**NW**	SCN	RG	58931	55430	58968
165 117	**NW**	SCN	RG	58932	55431	58969
165 118	**NW**	SCN	RG	58879		58933
165 119	**NW**	SCN	RG	58880		58934
165 120	**NW**	SCN	RG	58881		58935
165 121	**NW**	SCN	RG	58882		58936
165 122	**NW**	SCN	RG	58883		58937
165 123	**NW**	SCN	RG	58884		58938
165 124	**NW**	SCN	RG	58885		58939
165 125	**NW**	SCN	RG	58886		58940
165 126	**NW**	SCN	RG	58887		58941
165 127	**NW**	SCN	RG	58888		58942
165 128	**NW**	SCN	RG	58889		58943
165 129	**NW**	SCN	RG	58890		58944
165 130	**NW**	SCN	RG	58891		58945
165 131	**NW**	SCN	RG	58892		58946
165 132	**NW**	SCN	RG	58893		58947
165 133	**NW**	SCN	RG	58894		58948
165 134	**NW**	SCN	RG	58895		58949
165 135	**NW**	SCN	RG	58896		58950
165 136	**NW**	SCN	RG	58897		58951
165 137	**NW**	SCN	RG	58898		58952

CLASS 166   ABB NETWORK EXPRESS TURBO

DMCL (A) – MS – DMCL (B). Network SouthEast Units for Paddington – Oxford/ Newbury services. Air conditioned.

Engines: One Perkins 2006-TWH of 260 kW (350 hp) per car.
Bogies: One BREL P3 and one BREL T3 per car.
Transmission: Hydraulic. Voith T211r with Gmeinder final drive.
Gangways: Within unit only.
Doors: Sliding plug.
Accommodation: 2 + 3 facing/unidirectional (standard class) with 20 standard class seats in 2 + 2 format in DMCL(B), 2 + 2 facing (first class).
Dimensions: 22.91 x 2.81 m (DMCL), 22.72 x 2.81 m (MS).
Maximum Speed: 90 mph.

DMCL (A). Dia. DP321. Lot No. 31116 York 1992 – 3. 16/75 1T. 40.62 t.
MS. Dia. DR209. Lot No. 31117 York 1992 – 3. – /96. 38.04 t.
DMCL (B). Dia. DP321. Lot No. 31116 York 1992 – 3. 16/72 1T. 40.64 t.

166 201	**NW**	SCN	RG	58101	58601	58122
166 202	**NW**	SCN	RG	58102	58602	58123
166 203	**NW**	SCN	RG	58103	58603	58124
166 204	**NW**	SCN	RG	58104	58604	58125
166 205	**NW**	SCN	RG	58105	58605	58126
166 206	**NW**	SCN	RG	58106	58606	58127
166 207	**NW**	SCN	RG	58107	58607	58128
166 208	**NW**	SCN	RG	58108	58608	58129
166 209	**NW**	SCN	RG	58109	58609	58130
166 210	**NW**	SCN	RG	58110	58610	58131
166 211	**NW**	SCN	RG	58111	58611	58132
166 212	**NW**	SCN	RG	58112	58612	58133
166 213	**NW**	SCN	RG	58113	58613	58134
166 214	**NW**	SCN	RG	58114	58614	58135
166 215	**NW**	SCN	RG	58115	58615	58136
166 216	**NW**	SCN	RG	58116	58616	58137
166 217	**NW**	SCN	RG	58117	58617	58138
166 218	**NW**	SCN	RG	58118	58618	58139
166 219	**NW**	SCN	RG	58119	58619	58140
166 220	**NW**	SCN	RG	58120	58620	58141
166 221	**NW**	SCN	RG	58121	58621	58142

3.3. DIESEL ELECTRIC MULTIPLE UNITS

All SR diesel-electric multiple unit power cars have above-floor-mounted engines and all vehicles are equipped with buckeye couplings and were built at Eastleigh with frames laid at Ashford.

CLASS 205/0   3H

DMBSO – TSOL – DTCsoL.

Engine: English Electric 4SRKT engines of 450 kW (600 hp).
Transmission: Two EE 507 traction motors on the inner bogie.
Gangways: Non-gangwayed.
Dimensions: 20.28 x 2.82 m.
Maximum Speed: 75 mph.

60108 – 117/154. DMBSO. Dia DB203. Lot No. 30332 1957. –/52. 56 t.
60122 – 124. DMBSO. Dia DB203. Lot No. 30540 1958 – 59. –/52. 56 t.
60146 – 151. DMBSO. Dia DB204. Lot No. 30671 1960 – 62. –/42. 56 t.
60650 – 670. TSO. Dia DH203. Lot No. 30542 1958 – 59. –/104. 30 t.
60673 – 678. TSO. Dia DH203. Lot No. 30672 1960 – 62. –/104. 30 t.
60800 – 811. DTCsoL. Dia DE302. Lot No. 30333 1956 – 57. 19/50 2T. 32 t.
60822 – 824. DTCsoL. Dia DE302. Lot No. 30541 1958 – 59. 19/50 2T. 32 t.
60827 – 832. DTCsoL. Dia DE303. Lot No. 30673 1960 – 62. 13/62 2T. 32 t.

§ One compartment of DTCsoL converted to luggage compartment. 13/50 2T. Dia. DE301.

Notes:

60154 was renumbered from 60100.
205 023 is awaiting a decision on repair.

205 001	§	N	SBW	SU	60154	60650	60800
205 009		N	SBW	SU	60108	60658	60808
205 012		N	SBW	SU	60111	60661	60811
205 018		N	SBW	SU	60117	60674	60828
205 023		N	SBOL	ZG	60122	60668	60822
205 024	§	N	SBW	SU	60123	60669	60823
205 025	§	N	SBW	SU	60124	60670	60824
205 028		N	SBW	SU	60146	60673	60827
205 032		N	SBW	SU	60150	60677	60831
205 033		N	SBW	SU	60151	60678	60832
Spare		N	SBXZ	ZG	60664		
Spare		N	SBXZ	ZG	60665		

CLASS 205/1   3H

DMBSO – TSOL – DTSOL. Refurbished 1980. Fluorescent lighting. PA.

Engine: English Electric 4SRKT engines of 450 kW (600 hp).
Transmission: Two EE 507 traction motors on the inner bogie.

Gangways: Within unit only.
Dimensions: 20.28 x 2.82 m.
Maximum Speed: 75 mph.

DMBSO. Dia DB203. Lot No. 30332 1957. –/39. 57 t.
TSOL (ex Class 411/5 EMU). Dia. EH282. Converted from loco-hauled TSO 4059
Lot No. 30149 Ashford/Swindon 1955 – 7. –/64 2T. 33.78 t.
DTSOL. Dia DE204. Lot No. 30333 1957. –/76 2T. 32 t.

205 205	N	SBU	SU	60110 71634 60810

CLASS 207/0   2D

DMBSO – DTSO (formerly DMBSO – TCsoL – DTSO).

Engine: English Electric 4SRKT engines of 450 kW (600 hp).
Transmission: Two EE 507 traction motors on the inner bogie.
Gangways: Non-gangwayed.
Dimensions: 20.34 x 2.74 m. (DMBSO), 20.32 x 2.74 m. (DTSO), 20.34 x 2.74 m. (TCsoL).
Maximum Speed: 75 mph.

DMBSO. Dia DB205. Lot No. 30625 1962. –/42. 56 t.
TCsoL. Dia DH301. Lot No. 30626 1962. 24/42 1T. 31 t.
DTSO. Dia DE201. Lot No. 30627 1962. –/76. 32 t.

207 017	N	SBU	SU	60142	60916
Spare	N	SBOL	ZG	60138	
Spare	N	SBOL	St. Leonards	60616	

CLASS 207/1   3D

DMBSO – TSOL – DTSO.

Engine: English Electric 4SRKT engines of 450 kW (600 hp).
Transmission: Two EE 507 traction motors on the inner bogie.
Gangways: Fitted with gangways within unit.
Dimensions: 20.34 x 2.74 m. (DMBSO), 20.32 x 2.74 m. (DTS).
Maximum Speed: 75 mph.

DMBSO. Dia DB205. Lot No. 30625 1962. –/40. 56 t.
70286. TSOL (ex Class 411/5 EMU). Dia. EH282. Lot No. 30455 1958 – 9.
–/64 2T. 33.78 t.
70547/9. TSOL (ex Class 411/5 EMU). Dia. EH282. Lot No. 30620 1960 – 61
–/64 2T. 33.78 t.
DTSO. Dia DE201. Lot No. 30627 1962. –/75. 32 t.

207 201	N	SBU	SU	60129 70286 60903	Ashford Fayre
207 202	N	SBU	SU	60130 70549 60904	Brighton Royal Pavilion
207 203	N	SBU	SU	60127 70547 60901	

3.4. SERVICE DMUs

Formerly known as 'Departmental', these vehicles are owned by Railtrack or by organisations at Derby e.g. Railtest.

VARIOUS CONVERTED VEHICLES.

042222	(54342)	NL	Stores Vehicle.
RDB 975010	(79900)	ZA	Laboratory Coach 19 (Iris).
TDB 975023	(55001)	LO	Route learning car.
975025	(60755)	BM	Inspection saloon.
ADB 975042	(55019)	BY	Route learning and Sandite car. L119.
TDB 977466	(54286)	LA	Sandite car.
TDB 977486	(54285)	TS	Sandite car.
ADB 977696	(60522)	EH	Sandite car.
ADB 977722	(55020)	RG	Route learning & Sandite car. 960 002.
ADB 977723	(55021)	BY	Route learning & Sandite car. L121.
977858	(55024)	AL	Route learning & Sandite car. L124.
977859	(55025)	RG	Route learning & Sandite car. 960 011.
977860	(55028)	RG	Route learning & Sandite car. 960 014.
977866	(55030)	RG	Route learning & Sandite car. 960 013.
977873	(55022)	RG	Route learning & Sandite car. 960 012.

COMPLETE SETS (Conversions).

Ultrasonic Test Train Unit.

977391 (51433) 999602 (62483)* 977392 (53167) ZA
* Ex EMU car.

Lab 19 (Iris 2).

977693 (53222) 977694 (53338) ZA

ATP Test, Development & Training Unit.

977775 (55929) 977776 (54904) ZA

Sandite & Route Learning Units.

991	LO	977895 (53308)	977896 (53331)
992	LO	977897 (53203)	977898 (53193)
993	LO	977899 (51427)	977900 (53321)
994	LO	977901 (53200)	977902 (53231)
995	LO	977903 (53208)	977904 (53291)

Sandite Unit.

951 069 SU 977939 (60145) 977870 (60660) 977940 (60149)

NEW BUILD:

Wickham Self Propelled Laboratory. Built 1958. (4-wheeled).

RDB 999507   ZA

Railtest Track Recording unit. Built 1987. Class 150 derivative.

DB 999600   DB 999601   ZA

PLATFORM 5
EUROPEAN
RAILWAY HANDBOOKS

The Platform 5 European Railway Handbooks are the most comprehensive guides to the rolling stock of selected European railway administrations available. Each book lists all locomotives and railcars of the country concerned, giving details of number carried, livery and depot allocation, together with a wealth of technical data for each class of vehicle. Lists of preserved locos and MUs are also included, plus a guide to preservation centres. Each book is A5 size, thread sewn and includes at least 32 pages of colour photographs.

The full range of overseas titles available is as follows:

No. 1	Benelux Railways 3rd edition	£10.50
No. 2	German Railways 3rd edition	£12.50
No. 3	Austrian Railways 3rd edition	£10.50
No. 4	French Railways 2nd edition	£9.95
No. 6	Italian Railways 1st edition	£13.50
No. 7	Irish Railways 1st edition	£9.95

In addition, the following title is in preparation in 1996:

No. 5	Swiss Railways 2nd edition	£T.B.A.

Other Publishers' Overseas Titles:

TGV Handbook (Capital)	£7.95
Paris Metro Handbook (Capital)	£7.95

All these publications are available from shops, bookstalls or direct from our Mail order department (see centre pull-out for ordering details)

3.5. DMUs AWAITING DISPOSAL

The following withdrawn DMUs are awaiting disposal with the last known storage location shown.

Ex-Capital Stock

51340	ZH		55202	TS
51345	ZH		55203	TS
51364	OM		55302	TS
51406	OM		55303	TS
51410	ZD		55402	TS
51415	ZH		55403	TS
51434	TS		55709	NH
51503	TS		59117	OM
53312	ZD		59137	Chester CSD
53332	ZD		59228	Crewe Brook Sidings
53494	Chester CSD		59518	OM
54350	Crewe Brook Sidings		60200	ZG
54367	Mossend Yard		60201	ZG

Ex-Deparmental Stock

977191	(56106)	Crewe Carriage Shed
977554	(54182)	Buxton LIP
977697	(60523)	ZG
977698	(60152)	ZG
977699	(60153)	ZG
977753	(51321)	TS
977813	(52060)	LO
977814	(53926)	LO
977824	(55026)	TS
977825	(53881)	TS
977828	(55034)	TS
977829	(53093)	TS
977830	(51990)	Millerhill Yard
977831	(52030)	Millerhill Yard
977832	(52005)	Millerhill Yard
977833	(52025)	Millerhill Yard
977834	(51993)	Millerhill Yard
977835	(52012)	Millerhill Yard
977853	(53627)	ZC
977854	(51567)	ZC

4. ELECTRIC MULTIPLE UNITS

Electric Multiple Unit operation on BR has increased enormously since the end of the steam era, with most electrification schemes being carried out at 25 kV a.c. using overhead conductor wires. The notable exceptions to this are the lines of the former Southern Railway, where the existing 660-750 V d.c. third rail system has been extended, with the voltage increased to 850 V in certain areas. The other exception is the Merseyrail network, which has also been extended using the third rail system.

NUMBERING

BR design electric multiple unit vehicles are numbered in the series 61000-78999. Isle of Wight vehicles are numbered in a separate series. In this book, stock is generally listed in order of the unit or set number. The unit or set number is stated first, followed by any notes applicable to the particular set. These are followed by codes for livery, owner and depot respectively. Finally the numbers of the individual cars in the set are given, in order. Please note that reformations can and do occur.

DESIGN CONSIDERATIONS

Unless stated otherwise, all multiple unit vehicles are of BR design, or designed by contractors for BR and have buckeye couplings and tread brakes. Seating is 3 + 2 in standard class open vehicles, 2 + 2 in first class open vehicles, 8 to a corridor standard class compartment and 6 to a corridor first class compartment. In express stock, open standards have 2 + 2 seating and open firsts have 2 + 1 seating.

VEHICLE CODES

The codes used by the BR Operating Department to describe the various different types of electric multiple unit vehicles and quoted in the class headings are as follows:

M	Motor
DM	Driving Motor
BDM	Battery Driving Motor
T	Trailer
DT	Driving Trailer
BDT	Battery Driving Trailer
B	Brake, i.e. vehicle with luggage space and guards compartment.
F	First
S	Standard
C	Composite
RB	Buffet Car
RSM	Buffet Standard (Modular)
PMV	Parcels and Mails Van

H	handbrake fitted
LV	Luggage Van
K	Side corridor with lavatory
L	Open or semi-open Vehicle with lavatory
O	Open vehicle
so	Semi-open vehicle

The letters (A) and (B) may be added to the above codes to differentiate between two cars of the same operating type which have differences between them. The letter (T) denotes space for a catering trolley. Note that a consistent system is used, rather than the official operator codes which are sometimes inconsistent.

Notes:

(1) Compartment Stock (non-corridor) had no suffix.

(2) Semi-open composites generally have the first class accommodation in compartments and the standard class in open saloons.

(3) Unless stated otherwise, it is assumed that motor vehicles are fitted with pantographs. If the pantograph is on a trailer, then the trailer has the prefix 'P', e.g. PTSO - Pantograph trailer open standard.

A composite is a vehicle containing both First and Standard class accommodation.

A brake vehicle is a vehicle containing seperate specific accommodation for the guard (as opposed to the use of spare driving cabs on second generation units).

DIAGRAMS AND DESIGN CODES

For each type of vehicle, the official design code consists of a seven character code of two letters, four numbers and another letter, e.g. EC2040B. The first five characters of this are the diagram code and are given in the class heading or sub heading. These are explained as follows:

1st Letter

This is always 'E' for an electric multiple unit vehicle.

2nd Letter

as follows for various vehicle types:

A	Driving motor passenger vehicles.
B	Driving motor passenger vehicles with a brake compartment.
C	Non-Driving motor passenger vehicles.
D	Non-Driving trailer passenger vehicles with a brake compartment.
E	Driving Trailer passenger vehicles.
F	Battery Driving Trailer passenger vehicles.
G	Driving Trailer passenger vehicles with a brake compartment.
H	Trailer passenger vehicles.
I	Battery Driving Motor passenger vehicles.
J	Trailer passenger vehicles with a brake compartment.
N	Trailer passenger vehicles with a buffet compartment.
O	Battery Driving Trailer passenger vehicles with a brake compartment.

P	Trailer passenger vehicles with a handbrake.
X	Driving Motor Luggage Vans.

1st Figure

1	First class accommodation.
2	Standard class accommodation (incl. declassified seats).
3	Composite accommodation.
5	No passenger accommodation.

ACCOMMODATION

This information is given in class headings and sub headings in the form F/S nT, where F & S denote the number of first class and standard class seats followed by n which denotes the number of toilets. (e.g. 12/54 1T denotes 12 first class seats, 54 standard class seats and one toilet). In declassified vehicles, the capacity is still shown in terms of first and standard class seats to differentiate between the two physically different seat types available, although all seats are officially standard class in such instances. TD denotes a toilet suitable for a disabled person.

BUILD DETAILS

LOT NUMBERS

Each batch of vehicles is allocated a Lot (or batch) number when ordered and these are quoted in class headings and sub headings.

BUILDERS

These are shown in the class headings.Details will be found on page 335

LAYOUT

The layout in this section is as follows:

(1) Unit number.

(2) Notes (if any).
(3) Livery code.
(4) Owner code.
(5) Depot code.
(6) Individual car numbers.

Thus an example of the layout is as follows:

No.	Liv.	Owner	Depot	Car 1	Car 2	Car3	Car4
317 398	N	SC	HE	77027	62687	71604	77075

For off-loan vehicles, the last storage location is given when known.

Regional Railways liveried Class 101 No. 101 680 heads into Llandudno with the 06.43 Blaenau Ffestiniog service on 13th July 1995.
Vincent Eastwood

▲ Network SouthEast liveried Class 117 No. 117 706 is pictured at Kensal Rise on 5th October 1995 prior to working the 10.14 Willesden High Level-Clapham Junction. *Kevin Conkey*

▼ Class 121 'Bubble Car' No. L131 at Kensal Rise Junction shortly before working the 11.14 Willesden High Level-Clapham Junction service on 29th June 1995. *Kevin Conkey*

Class 142 No. 142 036 forms the 09.00 Carlisle-Whitehaven service at Parton on 29th July 1995.

Dave McAlone

▲ West Yorkshire PTE liveried Class 141 No. <u>141 111</u> passes Milford Junction on the 16th August 1995 whilst working the 11.10 Leeds-Knottingley service. *Hugh Ballantyne*

▼ The 13.45 Weston-Super-Mare-Maesteg passes East Usk on the 20th July 1995 formed of Class 143 No. 143 618. Note the modified doors now being fitted to members of the Classes 142 and 143.

Brian Denton

▲ Class 144 No. 144 017 forms the 09.13 service to Leeds at Skipton on the 28th October 1995. Most of these services are now in the hands of Class 308 units.   *Dave McAlone*

▼ Centro liveried Class 150/1 No. 150 123 stands at Birmingham Snow Hill shortly before performing a test run over point work onto the recently laid Jewellery line on 20th August 1995.   *Tony Simpson*

Greater Manchester PTE liveried Class 150/1 No. 150 141 enters Bromley Cross station with the 17.15 Blackburn-Rochdale service on 13th May 1995.

Vincent Eastwood

▲ Merseytravel liveried Class 150/2 No. 150 211 passes through the Cheshire countryside near Mouldsworth whilst working the 12.02 Southport-Chester service. The date is 2nd August 1995.

Paul D. Shannon

▼ Class 150/2 No. 150 232 runs alongside the seawall at Dawlish on 19th May 1995 whilst working the 08.57 Paignton-Exmouth service.

C.J. Marsden

With the Solway Firth and the Isle of Man in the background, Class 153s Nos. 153 363 and 153 330 pass along the Cumbrian coast with the 10.30 Barrow-in-Furness-Carlisle. The date is 17th September 1994.

Dave McAlone

Only seven units of Class 155 have not been converted into Class 153s. All of these units are operated by West Yorkshire PTE and one of them, No. 155 346, is seen here near Summit on 24th April 1995 whilst working the 14.19 Manchester Victoria-Selby service.

Vincent Eastwood

▲ Strengthened to four cars for the summer, the 08.12 Glasgow Queen Street-Mallaig service with Class 156 No. 156 492 trailing passes Kinloid on 10th August 1995. *Les Nixon*

▼ Strathclyde PTE liveried Class 156 No. 156 504 passes Carlisle Kingmoor on the 9th September 1995 as the 06.45 Girvan-Newcastle service. *Dave McAlone*

A pair of Class 158 units pass Scout Green on 13th August 1994 with the 06.02 Manchester Airport-Edinburgh service. Both units are in the Regional Railways Express livery.

Dave McAlone

▲ Class 158 903 passes near Weeton with the 15.46 York-Blackpool North on the 5th May 1995. *Brian Denton*

▼ The 10.35 London Waterloo-Paignton passes Dawlish Warren on the 9th May 1995 formed of Class 159 unit No. 159 006. *Stephen Widdowson*

▲ Class 165 'Turbo' No. 165 028 passes alongside Ruislip Gardens station on the London Underground Central line whilst working the 18.18 London Marylebone-Gerards Cross service on the 25th April 1995.
Hugh Ballantyne

▼ Class 166 No. 166 217 passes along the West of England main line at West Drayton with the 13.31 London Paddington-Bedwyn service on the 13th March 1995.
Nic Joynson

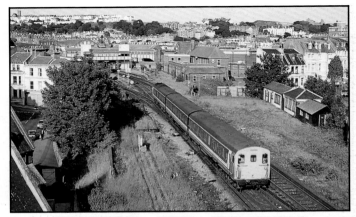

▲ Class 205/0 No. 205 033 arrives at Hastings on the 21st June 1995 with the 17.05 Brighton-Ashford service. *Brian Morrison*

▼ Class 207/2 No. 207 201 'Ashford Fayre' leaves Ashford with the 14.48 Ashford-Brighton on the 5th August 1995. This unit now has a centre car from a Class 411/5 EMU. *Chris Wilson*

Greater Manchester Metrolink cars 1023 and 1017 'ROSIE' leaving Manchester Piccadilly on an Altrincham working on 2nd April 1995. Coupled pairs were being operated for a football match at Old Trafford.

Peter Fox

▲ South Yorkshire Supertram No. 16 on West Street, Sheffield with a Malin Bridge-Halfway blue route working on 9th September 1995.

Peter Fox

▼ Modified Tyne & Wear Metro car No. 4087 at Wallsend on 4th January 1994. This car is in the same livery as that applied to Tyne & Wear PTE pacer units.

Peter Fox

NOSTALGIA CORNER . . .

STEAM DAYS ON BR 1:
THE MIDLAND LINE IN SHEFFIELD
by Peter Fox.

This first book of the series is a pictorial record of train services on the Midland Line in Sheffield during the BR steam era. The book concentrates on the wide variety of motive power in evidence at this time and the trains which they operated. Whilst primarily a pictorial account, The Midland Line in Sheffield also includes some useful reference information, including a complete allocation history for Millhouses and Grimesthorpe Motive Power Depots from 1948 to closure.

200 mm x 210 mm. Thread Sewn. 60 pages including 24 in colour. £4.95.

RAILS ALONG THE SEA WALL
by Peter Kay.

The story of the Exeter-Newton Abbot line is portrayed from the the building of the line, through the broad gauge era, right up to the present day. The development of every station on the line is described in some detail, as are the many lineside features that make this line so popular. Many colour and black & white photographs of an important historical nature are included, particularly from the BR steam era.

200 mm x 210 mm. Thread Sewn. 60 pages including 24 in colour. £4.95.

4.1. 25 kV a.c. OVERHEAD EMUs.

Note: All units are 25 kV overhead only except where stated otherwise.

CLASS 302

BDTCOL – MBSO – TSOL – DTSO. All remaining units refurbished with new seats, fluorescent lighting and pa.
Gangways: Within unit.
Traction Motors: Four EE536A 143.5 kW.
Dimensions: 19.50 x 2.82 m (outer cars), 19.36 x 2.82 m (inner cars).
Maximum Speed: 75 mph.

75085 – 75205. BDTCOL. Lot No. 30436. York/Doncaster 1958 – 59. Dia. EF303. 24/52 1T. 39.5 t. B5 bogies.
75311 – 75358. BDTCOL. Lot No. 30440. York/Doncaster 1959. Dia. EF303. 24/52 1T. 39.5 t. B5 bogies.
61060 – 61091. MBSO. Lot No. 30434. York 1958 – 59. Dia. ED216. –/76. 55.3 t. Gresley Bogies.
61122 – 61226. MBSO. Lot No. 30438. York 1960. Dia. ED216. –/76. 55.3 t. Gresley Bogies.
70060 – 70091. TSOL. Lot No. 30437. York/Doncaster 1958 – 59. Dia. EH223. –/86 1T. 34.4 t. B4 bogies.
70122 – 70226. TSOL. Lot No. 30441. York 1959 – 61. Dia. EH223. –/86 1T. 34.4 t. B4 bogies.
75033 – 75079. DTSO. Lot No. 30435. York 1958 – 59. Dia. EE219. –/88. 33.4 t. B4 or B5 bogies.
75236 – 75283. DTSO. Lot No. 30439. York 1959 – 60. Dia. EE219. –/88. 33.4 t. B4 or B5 bogies.

302 201	N	SAT	EM	75085	61060	70060	75033
302 202	N	SAT	EM	75086	61061	70061	75034
302 203	N	SAT	EM	75311	61122	70122	75236
302 204	N	SAT	EM	75088	61063	70063	75036
302 205	N	SAT	EM	75089	61064	70064	75037
302 206	N	SAT	EM	75356	61065	70224	75281
302 207	N	SAT	EM	75358	61226	70226	75283
302 209	N	SAT	EM (S)	75093	61068	70068	75041
302 210	N	SAT	EM	75094	61069	70069	75042
302 211	N	SAT	EM	75095	61070	70070	75043
302 212	N	SAT	EM	75096	61071	70071	75044
302 213	N	SAT	EM	75097	61072	70072	75060
302 214	N	SAT	EM	75352	61220	70220	75277
302 215	N	SAT	EM	75099	61074	70074	75062
302 216	N	SAT	EM	75100	61075	70075	75063
302 217	N	SAT	EM	75190	61076	70076	75064
302 218	N	SAT	EM	75191	61077	70077	75065
302 219	N	SAT	EM	75192	61078	70078	75066
302 220	N	SAT	EM	75193	61079	70079	75067
302 221	N	SAT	EM	75194	61080	70080	75068

302 222	N	SAT	EM	75195 61081 70081 75069
302 223	N	SAT	EM	75341 61209 70209 75266
302 224	N	SAT	EM	75197 61083 70083 75071
302 225	N	SAT	EM	75198 61084 70084 75072
302 226	N	SAT	EM	75199 61085 70085 75073
302 227	N	SAT	EM	75325 61193 70193 75250
302 228	N	SAT	EM	75201 61087 70087 75075
302 229	N	SAT	EM	75202 61088 70088 75076
302 230	N	SAT	EM	75205 61091 70091 75079

CLASS 303

DTSO – MBSO – BDTSO. Sliding doors.
Bogies: Gresley.
Gangways: Gangwayed within units only (non-gangwayed *).
Traction Motors: Four MV 155 kW.
Dimensions: 19.50 x 2.82 m (outer cars), 19.36 x 2.82 m (inner cars).
Maximum Speed: 75 mph.

Class 303/0. Unrefurbished set*.

DTSO. Dia. EE206. –/83. 34.4 t.
MBSO. Dia. ED201. –/70. 56.4 t.
BDTSO. Dia. EF202. –/83. 38.4 t.

Non-standard Livery: Original Glasgow 'blue train' livery.

Note: 75752 carries "75758" and 75808 carries "75814"

Class 303/1. Refurbished with 2 + 2 seating and hopper-type window vents.

DTSO. Dia. EE241. –/56. 34.4 t.
MBSO. Dia. ED220. –/48. 56.4 t.
BDTSO. Dia. EF217. –/56. 38.4 t.

75566 – 75599. DTSO. Lot No. 30579 Pressed Steel 1959 – 60.
75747 – 75801. DTSO. Lot No. 30629 Pressed Steel 1960 – 61.
61481 – 61514. MBSO. Lot No. 30580 Pressed Steel 1959 – 60.
61813 – 61867. MBSO. Lot No. 30630 Pressed Steel 1960 – 61.
75601 – 75635. BDTSO. Lot No. 30581 Pressed Steel 1959 – 60.
75803 – 75857. BDTSO. Lot No. 30631 Pressed Steel 1960 – 61.

303 001	S	SCA	GW	75566 61481 75601
303 003	S	SCA	GW	75568 61483 75603
303 004	S	SCA	GW	75569 61484 75604
303 006	S	SCA	GW	75571 61486 75606
303 008	S	SCA	GW	75573 61488 75608
303 009	S	SCA	GW	75574 61489 75609
303 010	S	SCA	GW	75575 61490 75610
303 011	S	SCA	GW	75576 61491 75611
303 012	S	SCA	GW	75577 61492 75612
303 013	S	SCA	GW	75578 61493 75613
303 014	S	SCA	GW	75579 61494 75614
303 016	S	SCA	GW	75750 61496 75616
303 019	S	SCA	GW	75584 61499 75619

303 020	S	SCA	GW	75585 61500 75620
303 021	S	SCA	GW	75586 61501 75621
303 023	S	SCA	GW	75588 61503 75623
303 024	S	SCA	GW	75589 61504 75624
303 025	S	SCA	GW	75590 61505 75625
303 027	S	SCA	GW	75592 61507 75627
303 028	S	SCA	GW	75600 61508 75635
303 032	S	SCA	GW	75597 61512 75632
303 033	S	SCA	GW	75595 61860 75817
303 034	S	SCA	GW	75599 61514 75634
303 037	S	SCA	GW	75781 61813 75803
303 040	S	SCA	GW	75581 61816 75806
303 043	S	SCA	GW	75572 61819 75809
303 045	S	SCA	GW	75755 61821 75811
303 046	S	SCOL	ZH	75756 61822 75812
303 047	S	SCA	GW	75757 61823 75813
303 048	* 0	SCA	GW (S)	75752 61824 75808
303 054	S	SCA	GW	75764 61830 75820
303 055	S	SCA	GW	75765 61831 75821
303 056	S	SCA	GW	75766 61832 75822
303 058	S	SCA	GW	75768 61834 75824
303 061	S	SCA	GW	75771 61837 75827
303 065	S	SCA	GW	75775 61841 75831
303 070	S	SCA	GW	75780 61846 75836
303 073	S	SCOL	GW	75783 61849 75839
303 077	S	SCA	GW	75787 61853 75843
303 079	S	SCA	GW	75789 61855 75845
303 080	S	SCA	GW	75790 61856 75846
303 083	S	SCA	GW	75793 61859 75849
303 085	S	SCA	GW	75795 61861 75851
303 087	S	SCA	GW	75797 61863 75853
303 088	S	SCA	GW	75798 61864 75854
303 089	S	SCA	GW	75799 61865 75855
303 090	S	SCA	GW	75800 61866 75856
303 091	S	SCA	GW	75801 61867 75857
Spare	S	SCOL		75747

CLASS 304

BDTSOL – MBSO – DTBSO. Originally 4 cars.
Bogies: Gresley.
Gangways: None.
Traction Motors: Four BTH 155 kW.
Maximum Speed: 75 mph.
Dimensions: 19.53 x 2.82 m (outer cars), 19.36 x 2.82 m (inner cars).

Class 304/1. These cars have pairs of narrow windows instead of wide windows and the MBSOs were formerly MBS and were refurbished with new seats etc.

BDTSOL. Dia. EF203. Lot No. 30429 Wolverton 1960. –/80 2T. 36.8 t.
MBSO. Dia. ED215. Lot No. 30428 Wolverton 1960. –/72. 54.5 t.

DTBSO. Dia. EG202. Lot No. 30430 Wolverton 1960. –/82. 32.5 t.

304 002		SAG	LG	75046 61046 75646
304 004		SAOL	LG	75681 61048 75648
304 005		SAOL	ZD	75049 61049 75649
304 009		SAG	LG	75053 61053 75653
304 010		SAOL	BP	75054 61054 75654
304 014		SAOL	ZD	75058 61058 75658
304 015		SAOL	BP	75059 61059 75659

Class 304/2. Standard design with wide windows.

75681 – 75697. BDTSOL. Dia. EF204. Lot No. 30610 Wolverton 1960 – 61. –/80 2T. 36.8 t.
75868 – 75872. BDTSOL. Dia. EF204. Lot No. 30645 Wolverton 1961. –/80 2T. 36.8 t.
61629 – 61645. MBSO. Dia. ED203. Lot No. 30607 Wolverton 1960 – 61. –/72. 54.5 t.
61873 – 61877. MBSO. Dia. ED203. Lot No. 30642 Wolverton 1961. –/72. 54.5 t.
75661 – 75677. DTBSO. Dia. EG203. Lot No. 30608 Wolverton 1960 – 61. –/82. 32.5 t.
75858 – 75862. DTBSO. Dia. EG203. Lot No. 30643 Wolverton 1961. –/82. 32.5 t.

304 017		SAG	LG	75048 61629 75661
304 019	RR	SAOL	Long Marston	75683 61631 75663
304 032		SAG	LG	75696 61644 75676
304 033		SAG	LG	75697 61645 75677
304 036	RR	SAOL	Long Marston	75868 61873 75858
304 037	RR	SAOL	BP	75869 61874 75859
304 040	RR	SAOL	BP	75872 61877 75862

Note: 304 004 has a Class 304/2 BDTsoL and 304 017 a Class 304/1 one.

CLASS 305/2

BDTCOL – MBSO – TSOL – DTSO or BDTCOL – MBSO – DTSO. All refurbished with fluorescent lighting, new seats and PA.
Bogies: Gresley.
Gangways: Originally non-gangwayed, but now gangwayed within unit.
Traction Motors: Four GEC WT380 of 153 kW.
Dimensions: 19.53 x 2.82 m (outer cars), 19.36 x 2.82 m (inner cars).
Maximum Speed: 75 mph.

BDTCOL. Dia. EF304. Lot No. 30566 York/Doncaster 1960. 24/52 1T. (20/40 1T*). 36.5 t.
MBSO. Dia. ED216. Lot No. 30567 York/Doncaster 1960. –/76 (–/58*). 56.5 t.
TSOL. Dia. EH223. Lot No. 30568 York/Doncaster 1960. –/86 1T. 31.5 t.
DTSO. Dia. EE220. Lot No. 30569 York/Doncaster 1960. –/88 (–/70*). 32.7 t.

305 501		RR	SCA	GW	75424	61410	70356	75443
305 502		RR	SCA	GW	75425	61421	70357	75444
305 503	*	GM	SCD	LG	75426	61412		75445
305 504		RR	SCOL	BP	75427	61413		75446

305 506	**GM** SCD	LG	75429	61415		75448
305 507	**RR** SCD	LG	75430	61416		75449
305 508	**RR** SCA	GW	75431	61417	70363	75450
305 510	**GM** SCD	LG	75433	61419		75452
305 511 *	**GM** SCD	LG	75434	61420		75453
305 513	**RR** SCOL	BP	75436	61422		75455
305 515 *	**GM** SCD	LG	75438	61424		75457
305 516 *	**GM** SCD	LG	75439	61425		75458
305 517	**RR** SCA	GW	75440	61426	70372	75459
305 518	**RR** SCD	LG	75441	61427		75460
305 519	**RR** SCA	GW	75442	61428	70374	75461
Spare	**RR** SCOL	LG		61418		
Spare	**GM** SCOL	BP			70359	
Spare	**GM** SCOL	BP			70362	

CLASS 308

BDTCOL – MBSO – DTSO. Refurbished with new seats, fluorescent lighting and pa. Originally 4-car units, but all TSOL now withdrawn.
Bogies: Gresley.
Gangways: Originally non-gangwayed, but now gangwayed within unit.
Traction Motors: Four EE 536A of 143.5 kW.
Dimensions: 19.36 x 2.82 m (outer cars), 19.35 x 2.82 m (inner cars).
Maximum Speed: 75 mph.

75879 – 75886. BDTCOL. Dia. EF304. Lot No. 30652 York 1961. 24/52 1T. 36.3 t.
75897 – 75919. BDTCOL. Dia. EF304. Lot No. 30656 York 1961. 24/52 1T. 36.3 t.
61884 – 61891. MBSO. Dia. ED216. Lot No. 30653 York 1961. -/76. 55.0 t.
61893 – 61915. MBSO. Dia. ED216. Lot No. 30657 York 1961. -/76. 55.0 t.
75888 – 75895. DTSO. Dia. EE220. Lot No. 30655 York 1961. – /88. 33 t.
75930 – 75952. DTSO. Dia. EE220. Lot No. 30659 York 1961. – /88. 33 t.

308 134	**Y** SCC	NL	75879 61884 75888
308 136	**Y** SCC	NL	75881 61886 75890
308 137	**Y** SCC	NL	75882 61887 75891
308 138	**Y** SCC	NL	75883 61888 75892
308 141	**Y** SCC	NL	75886 61891 75895
308 143	**Y** SCC	NL	75897 61893 75930
308 144	**Y** SCC	NL	75880 61894 75931
308 145	**Y** SCC	NL	75899 61895 75932
308 147	**Y** SCC	NL	75901 61897 75934
308 152	**Y** SCC	NL	75913 61902 75939
308 153	**Y** SCC	NL	75907 61903 75940
308 154	**Y** SCC	NL	75908 61904 75941
308 155	**Y** SCC	NL	75909 61905 75942
308 157	**Y** SCC	NL	75915 61907 75944
308 158	**Y** SCC	NL	75912 61908 75945
308 159	**Y** SCC	NL	75906 61909 75946
308 161	**Y** SCC	NL	75911 61911 75948
308 162	**Y** SCC	NL	75916 61912 75949

308 163	Y	SCC	NL	75917 61913 75950
308 164	Y	SCC	NL	75918 61914 75951
308 165	Y	SCC	NL	75919 61915 75952

CLASS 309/1   ESSEX EXPRESS STOCK

DMBSO(T) – TSOL – TCsoL – BDTSOL. Built 1962 – 3 as 2 car units. Made up
to four cars by the conversion of loco-hauled stock in 1973. All now refurbish-
ed with fluorescent lighting, hopper ventilators, new seating, PA.
Bogies: Commonwealth.
Gangways: Throughout.
Traction Motors: Four GEC of 210 kW.
Dimensions: 19.76 x 2.82 m (outer cars), 19.67 x 2.82 m (inner cars).
Maximum Speed: 100 mph.

DMBSO(T). Dia. EB206. Lot No. 30684 York 1962 – 63. –/44. 60 t.
TSOL. Dia. EH227. Lot No. 30871 Wolverton 1973 – 74. –/64 2T. 35 t.
TCsoL. Dia. EH309. Lot No. 30872 Wolverton 1973 – 74. 24/28 1T. 36 t.
BDTSOL. Dia. EF213. Lot No. 30683 York 1960 – 62. –/60 1T. 40 t.

309 605	N	SCOL	Long Marston	61944 71108 71113 75988
309 606	N	SCOL	Long Marston	61945 71109 71112 75989
309 607	N	SCOL	BP	61946 71107 71111 75990

Former numbers of converted hauled stock:

71107 (26203)	71109 (26196)	71112 (16249)	71113 (16244)
71108 (26189)	71111 (16246)		

CLASS 309/2   ESSEX EXPRESS STOCK

BDTCsoL – MBSOL(T) – TSO – DTSOL. Built 1962 – 3. Units 309 613 –
309 618 formerly contained griddle cars, but these were withdrawn and their
place has been taken by the conversion of loco-hauled TSOs on refurbishment.
All refurbished with fluorescent lighting, hopper ventilators, new seating, PA.
Bogies: Commonwealth.
Gangways: Throughout.
Traction Motors: Four GEC of 210 kW.
Dimensions: 19.76 x 2.82 m (outer cars), 19.67 x 2.82 m (inner cars).
Maximum Speed: 100 mph.

75639 – 44. BDTCsoL. Dia. EF301. Lot No. 30679 York 1962. 18/32 2T. 40 t.
75965 – 67. BDTCsoL. Dia. EF213. Lot No. 30675 York 1962. 18/32 2T. 40 t.
61927 – 31. MBSOL(T). Dia. ED209. Lot No. 30676 York 1962. –/44 2T. 58 t.
61934 – 39. MBSOL(T). Dia. ED209. Lot No. 30680 York 1962. –/44 2T. 58 t.
70526 – 59. TSO. Dia. EH229. Lot No. 30677 York 1962. –/68 35 t.
71756 – 61. TSO. Dia. EH228. Lot No. 31001 Wolverton 1984 – 87. –/68.
35 t.
75972 – 75. DTSOL. Dia. EF213. Lot No. 30678 York 1962. –/56 2T 37 t.
75978 – 83. DTSOL. Dia. EF213. Lot No. 30682 York 1962 – 1963. –/56 2T.
37 t.

309 613	p	NR	SCD	LG	75639	61934	71756	75978
309 616	p	NR	SCD	LG	75642	61937	71759	75981
309 617	p	N	SCD	LG	75643	61938	71760	75982
309 618	p	NR	SCOL	BP	75966	61939	71761	75983
309 623		NR	SCD	LG	75641	61927	71758	75980
309 624		N	SCD	LG	75965	61928	70256	75972
309 626		NR	SCOL	BP	75967	61930	70258	75974
309 627		N	SCD	LG	75644	61931	70259	75975

Former numbers of converted hauled stock:

71756 (5068)	71759 (5062)	71760 (5056)	71761 (5066)
71758 (5058)			

CLASS 310

Disc brakes. All facelifted. with new panels and PA.
Bogies: B4.
Gangways: Within unit.
Traction Motors: Four EE546 of 201.5 kW.
Dimensions: 19.86 x 2.82 m (outer cars), 19.93 x 2.82 m (inner cars).
Maximum Speed: 75 mph.
Non-standard Livery: Grey/light blue/white/dark blue.

BDTSOL. Dia. EF211. Lot No. 30745 Derby 1965 – 67. –/80 2T. 37.3 t.
76228. BDTSOL. Formerly a DTCOL to Lot 30748. Dia. EF210. Accomodation –/68 2T.
76998. BDTSOL. Rebuilt from TSO 70756 to Lot 30747. Dia. EF214. Accommodation –/75 2T.
MBSO. Dia. ED219. Lot No. 30746 Derby 1965 – 67. –/68. 57.2 t.
TSO. Dia. EH232. Lot No. 30747 Derby 1965 – 67. –/98. 31.7 t.
DTCOL. Dia. EE306. Lot No. 30748 Derby 1965 – 67. 25/43 2T. 34.4 t.
DTSOL (310/1). Dia. EE237. Lot No. 30748 Derby 1965 – 67. –/75 2T. 34.4 t.

Class 310/0. BDTSOL – MBSO – TSO – DTCOL.

310 046	N	SAT	EM	76130	62071	70731	76180
310 047	N	SAT	EM	76131	62072	70732	76181
310 049	N	SAT	EM	76133	62074	70734	76183
310 050	N	SAT	EM	76134	62075	70735	76184
310 051	N	SAT	EM	76135	62076	70736	76185
310 052	N	SAT	EM	76136	62077	70737	76186
310 057	N	SAT	EM	76141	62082	70742	76191
310 058	N	SAT	EM	76142	62083	70743	76192
310 059	N	SAT	EM	76143	62084	70744	76205
310 060	N	SAT	EM	76144	62085	70745	76194
310 064	N	SAT	EM	76148	62089	70749	76198
310 066	N	SAT	EM	76228	62091	70751	76200
310 067	N	SAT	EM	76151	62092	70752	76201
310 068	N	SAT	EM	76152	62093	70753	76202
310 069	N	SAT	EM	76153	62094	70754	76203
310 070	N	SAT	EM	76154	62095	70755	76204
310 074	N	SAT	EM	76145	62099	70759	76208

310 075	N	SAT	EM	76159 62100 70760 76209
310 077	N	SAT	EM	76161 62102 70762 76211
310 079	N	SAT	EM	76163 62104 70764 76222
310 080	N	SAT	EM	76164 62105 70765 76214
310 081	N	SAT	EM	76165 62106 70766 76215
310 082	N	SAT	EM	76166 62107 70767 76216
310 083	N	SAT	EM	76167 62108 70768 76217
310 084	N	SAT	EM	76168 62109 70769 76218
310 085	N	SAT	EM	76169 62110 70770 76219
310 086	N	SAT	EM	76170 62111 70771 76220
310 087	N	SAT	EM	76171 62112 70772 76221
310 088	N	SAT	EM	76172 62113 70773 76213
310 089	N	SAT	EM	76173 62114 70774 76223
310 091	N	SAT	EM	76175 62116 70776 76225
310 092	N	SAT	EM	76176 62117 70777 76226
310 093	N	SAT	EM	76177 62118 70778 76190
310 094	N	SAT	EM	76998 62119 70780 76193
310 095	N	SAT	EM	76179 62120 70779 76229
Spare	N	SAOL	ZD	76149

Name: Set 310 058 is named 'Chafford Hundred'.

Class 310/1. BDTSOL – MBSO – DTSOL (DTCOL*).

310 101	(310 073)	0	SAG	BY	76157 62098 76207
310 102	(310 055)	PM	SAG	BY	76139 62080 76189
310 103	(310 076)	RR	SAG	BY	76160 62101 76210
310 104	(310 078)	RR	SAG	BY	76162 62103 76212
310 105	(310 090)	RR	SAG	BY	76174 62115 76224
310 106	(310 072)	PM	SAG	BY	76156 62097 76206
310 107	(310 062)	PM	SAG	BY	76146 62087 76196
310 108	(310 048)	PM	SAG	BY	76132 62073 76182
310 109	(310 053)	PM	SAG	BY	76137 62078 76187
310 110	(310 054)	PM	SAG	BY	76138 62079 76188
310 111	(310 063)	PM	SAG	BY	76147 62088 76197
310 112	(310 061)	* RR	SAG	BY	76140 62086 76227
310 113	(310 056)	* RR	SAG	BY	76158 62090 76195

Spare TSO.

70733 BY	70740 TS	70748 BY	70761 ZD
70738 TS	70746 Soho	70757 Soho	70763 Soho
70739 Soho	70747 Soho	70758 TS	70775 ZN

CLASS 312

BDTSOL – MBSO – TSO – DTCOL. Disc brakes PA.
Bogies: B4.
Gangways: Within unit.
Traction Motors: Four EE546 of 201.5 kW.

Dimensions: 19.86 x 2.82 m (outer cars), 19.93 x 2.82 m (inner cars).
Maximum Speed: 90 mph.

Class 312/0. Standard design.

76994 – 97 BDTSOL. Dia. EF213. Lot No. 30891 York 1976. – /84 1T. 34.9 t.
62657 – 60 MBSO. Dia. ED214. Lot No. 30892 York 1976. – /68. 56 t.
71277 – 80 TSO. Dia. EH209. Lot No. 30893 York 1976. – /98. 30.5 t.
78045 – 48 DTCOL. Dia. EE305. Lot No. 30894 York 1976. 25/47 2T.
76949 – 74 BDTSOL. Dia. EF213. Lot No. 30863 York 1977 – 78. – /84 1T.
34.9 t.
62484 – 509 MBSO. Dia. ED212. Lot No. 30864 York 1977 – 78. – /68. 56 t.
71168 – 93 TSO. Dia. EH209. Lot No. 30865 York 1977 – 78. – /98. 30.5 t.
78000 – 25 DTCOL. Dia. EE305. Lot No. 30866 York 1977 – 78. 25/47 2T.

Notes: 312 727 – 730 were formerly numbered 312 201 – 204.

312 701	N	SCR	IL	76949 62484 71168 78000
312 702	N	SCR	IL	76950 62485 71169 78001
312 703	N	SCR	IL	76951 62486 71170 78002
312 704	N	SCR	IL	76952 62487 71171 78003
312 705	N	SCR	IL	76953 62488 71172 78004
312 706	N	SCR	IL	76954 62489 71173 78005
312 707	N	SCR	IL	76955 62490 71174 78006
312 708	N	SCR	IL	76956 62491 71175 78007
312 709	N	SCR	IL	76957 62492 71176 78008
312 710	N	SCR	IL	76958 62493 71177 78009
312 711	N	SCR	IL	76959 62494 71178 78010
312 712	N	SCR	IL	76960 62495 71179 78011
312 713	N	SCR	IL	76961 62496 71180 78012
312 714	N	SCR	IL	76962 62497 71181 78013
312 715	N	SCR	IL	76963 62498 71182 78014
312 716	N	SCR	IL	76964 62499 71183 78015
312 717	N	SCR	IL	76965 62500 71184 78016
312 718	N	SCR	IL	76966 62501 71185 78017
312 719	N	SCR	IL	76967 62502 71186 78018
312 720	N	SCR	IL	76968 62503 71187 78019
312 721	N	SCR	IL	76969 62504 71188 78020
312 722	N	SCR	IL	76970 62505 71189 78021
312 723	N	SCR	IL	76971 62506 71190 78022
312 724	N	SCR	IL	76972 62507 71191 78023
312 725	NR	SCG	LG	76973 62508 71192 78024
312 726	RR	SCG	LG	76974 62509 71193 78025
312 727	RR	SCG	LG	76994 62657 71277 78045
312 728	RR	SCG	LG	76995 62658 71278 78046
312 729	N	SCT	EM	76996 62659 71279 78047
312 730	N	SCT	EM	76997 62660 71280 78048

Class 312/1. Could also operate on 6.25 kV a.c. overhead.

BDTSOL. Dia. EF213. Lot No. 30867 York 1975 – 76. – /84 2T. 34.9 t.
MBSO. Dia. ED213. Lot No. 30868 York 1975 – 76. – /68. 56 t.
TSO. Dia. EH209. Lot No. 30869 York 1975 – 76. – /98. 30.5 t.
DTCOL. Dia. EE305. Lot No. 30870 York 1975 – 76. 25/47 2T.

312 781	N	SCT	EM	76975 62510 71194 78026
312 782	N	SCT	EM	76976 62511 71195 78027
312 783	N	SCT	EM	76977 62512 71196 78028
312 784	N	SCT	EM	76978 62513 71197 78029
312 785	N	SCT	EM	76979 62514 71198 78030
312 786	N	SCT	EM	76980 62515 71199 78031
312 787	N	SCT	EM	76981 62516 71200 78032
312 788	N	SCT	EM	76982 62517 71201 78033
312 789	N	SCT	EM	76983 62518 71202 78034
312 790	N	SCT	EM	76984 62519 71203 78035
312 791	N	SCT	EM	76985 62520 71204 78036
312 792	N	SCT	EM	76986 62521 71205 78037
312 793	N	SCT	EM	76987 62522 71206 78038
312 794	N	SCT	EM	76988 62523 71207 78039
312 795	N	SCT	EM	76989 62524 71208 78040
312 796	N	SCT	EM	76990 62525 71209 78041
312 797	N	SCT	EM	76991 62526 71210 78042
312 798	N	SCT	EM	76992 62527 71211 78043
312 799	N	SCT	EM	76993 62528 71212 78044

CLASS 313

DMSO – PTSO – BDMSO. Tightlock couplers. Sliding doors. Disc and rheostatic brakes. PA. Cab to shore radio.
System: 25 kV a.c. overhead/750 V d.c. third rail.
Bogies: BX1.
Gangways: Within unit. End doors.
Traction Motors: Four GEC G310AZ of 82.125 kW.
Dimensions: 19.80 x 2.82 m (outer cars), 19.92 x 2.82 m (inner cars).
Maximum Speed: 75 mph.

DMSO. Dia. EA204. Lot No. 30879 York 1976 – 77. – /74. 36.4 t.
PTSO. Dia. EH210. Lot No. 30880 York 1976 – 77. – /84. 30.5 t.
BDMSO. Dia. EI201. Lot No. 30885 York 1976 – 77. – /74. 37.6 t.

* – Extra shoegear for Euston – Watford and Richmond – North Woolwich line services. Class 313/1.

313 001	*	N	SAP	BY	62529 71213 62593
313 002	*	N	SAP	BY	62530 71214 62594
313 003	*	N	SAP	BY	62531 71215 62595
313 004	*	N	SAP	BY	62532 71216 62596
313 005	*	N	SAP	BY	62533 71217 62597
313 006	*	N	SAP	BY	62534 71218 62598
313 007	*	N	SAP	BY	62535 71219 62599
313 008	*	N	SAP	BY	62536 71220 62600
313 009	*	N	SAP	BY	62537 71221 62601
313 010	*	N	SAP	BY	62538 71222 62602
313 011	*	N	SAP	BY	62539 71223 62603
313 012	*	N	SAP	BY	62540 71224 62604
313 013	*	N	SAP	BY	62541 71225 62605

313 014	*	N	SAP	BY	62542 71226 62606
313 015	*	N	SAP	BY	62543 71227 62607
313 016	*	N	SAP	BY	62544 71228 62608
313 017	*	N	SAP	BY	62545 71229 62609
313 018	*	N	SAQ	HE	62546 71230 62610
313 019	*	N	SAP	BY	62547 71231 62611
313 020	*	N	SAP	BY	62548 71232 62612
313 021	*	N	SAP	BY	62549 71233 62613
313 022	*	N	SAP	BY	62550 71234 62614
313 023	*	N	SAP	BY	62551 71235 62615
313 024		N	SAQ	HE	62552 71236 62616
313 025		N	SAQ	HE	62553 71237 62617
313 026		N	SAQ	HE	62554 71238 62618
313 027		N	SAQ	HE	62555 71239 62619
313 028		N	SAQ	HE	62556 71240 62620
313 029		N	SAQ	HE	62557 71241 62621
313 030		N	SAQ	HE	62558 71242 62622
313 031		N	SAQ	HE	62559 71243 62623
313 032		N	SAQ	HE	62560 71244 62624
313 033		N	SAQ	HE	62561 71245 62625
313 034		N	SAP	BY	62562 71246 62626
313 035		N	SAQ	HE	62563 71247 62627
313 036		N	SAQ	HE	62564 71248 62628
313 037		N	SAQ	HE	62565 71249 62629
313 038		N	SAQ	HE	62566 71250 62630
313 039		N	SAQ	HE	62567 71251 62631
313 040		N	SAQ	HE	62568 71252 62632
313 041		N	SAQ	HE	62569 71253 62633
313 042		N	SAQ	HE	62570 71254 62634
313 043		N	SAQ	HE	62571 71255 62635
313 044		N	SAQ	HE	62572 71256 62636
313 045		N	SAQ	HE	62573 71257 62637
313 046		N	SAQ	HE	62574 71258 62638
313 047		N	SAQ	HE	62575 71259 62639
313 048		N	SAQ	HE	62576 71260 62640
313 049		N	SAQ	HE	62577 71261 62641
313 050		N	SAQ	HE	62578 71262 62649
313 051		N	SAQ	HE	62579 71263 62643
313 052		N	SAQ	HE	62580 71264 62644
313 053		N	SAQ	HE	62581 71265 62645
313 054		N	SAQ	HE	62582 71266 62646
313 055		N	SAQ	HE	62583 71267 62647
313 056		N	SAQ	HE	62584 71268 62648
313 057		N	SAQ	HE	62585 71269 62642
313 058		N	SAQ	HE	62586 71270 62650
313 059		N	SAQ	HE	62587 71271 62651
313 060		N	SAQ	HE	62588 71272 62652
313 061		N	SAQ	HE	62589 71273 62653
313 062		N	SAQ	HE	62590 71274 62654
313 063		N	SAQ	HE	62591 71275 62655
313 064		N	SAQ	HE	62592 71276 62656

CLASS 314

DMSO – PTSO – DMSO. Thyristor control. Tightlock couplers. Sliding doors. Disc and rheostatic brakes. PA. Cab to shore radio.
Bogies: BX1.
Gangways: Within unit. End doors.
Traction Motors: Four GEC G310AZ (Brush TM61-53*) of 82.125 kW.
Dimensions: 19.80 x 2.82 m (outer cars), 19.92 x 2.82 m (inner cars).
Maximum Speed: 75 mph.

64583 – 64614. DMSO. Dia. EA206. Lot No. 30912 York 1979. – /68. 34.5 t.
64588". DMSO. Dia. EA202. Lot No. 30908 York 1978 – 80. – /74. 35.63 t.
Converted from Class 507 No. 64426. The original 64588 has been scrapped.
PTSO. Dia. EH211. Lot No. 30913 York 1979. – /76. 33.0 t.

Note: TCOL No. 71452 of set 314 203 is named 'European Union'.

314 201	*	S	SCA	GW	64583	71450 64584
314 202	*	S	SCA	GW	64585	71451 64586
314 203	*	S	SCA	GW	64587	71452 64588"
314 204	*	S	SCA	GW	64589	71453 64590
314 205	*	S	SCA	GW	64591	71454 64592
314 206	*	S	SCA	GW	64593	71455 64594
314 207		S	SCA	GW	64595	71456 64596
314 208		S	SCA	GW	64597	71457 64598
314 209		S	SCA	GW	64599	71458 64600
314 210		S	SCA	GW	64601	71459 64602
314 211		S	SCA	GW	64603	71460 64604
314 212		S	SCA	GW	64605	71461 64606
314 213		S	SCA	GW	64607	71462 64608
314 214		S	SCA	GW	64609	71463 64610
314 215		S	SCA	GW	64611	71464 64612
314 216		S	SCA	GW	64613	71465 64614

CLASS 315

DMSO – TSO – PTSO – DMSO. Thyristor control. Tightlock couplers. Sliding doors. Disc and rheostatic brakes. PA.
Bogies: BX1.
Gangways: Within unit. End doors.
Traction Motors: Four Brush TM61-53 (GEC G310AZ*) of 82.125 kW.
Dimensions: 19.80 x 2.82 m (outer cars), 19.92 x 2.82 m (inner cars).
Maximum Speed: 75 mph.

64461 – 64582. DMSO. Dia. EA207. Lot No. 30902 York 1980 – 81. – /74. 35 t.
71281 – 71341. TSO. Dia. EH216. Lot No. 30904 York 1980 – 81. – /86. 25.5 t.
71389 – 71449. PTSO. Dia. EH217. Lot No. 30903 York 1980 – 81. – /84. 32 t.

315 801	N	SAR	IL	64461 71281 71389 64462

315 802		N	SAR	IL	64463	71282	71390	64464
315 803		N	SAR	IL	64465	71283	71391	64466
315 804		N	SAR	IL	64467	71284	71392	64468
315 805		N	SAR	IL	64469	71285	71393	64470
315 806		N	SAR	IL	64471	71286	71394	64472
315 807		N	SAR	IL	64473	71287	71395	64474
315 808		N	SAR	IL	64475	71288	71396	64476
315 809		N	SAR	IL	64477	71289	71397	64478
315 810		N	SAR	IL	64479	71290	71398	64480
315 811		N	SAR	IL	64481	71291	71399	64482
315 812		N	SAR	IL	64483	71292	71400	64484
315 813		N	SAR	IL	64485	71293	71401	64486
315 814		N	SAR	IL	64487	71294	71402	64488
315 815		N	SAR	IL	64489	71295	71403	64490
315 816		N	SAR	IL	64491	71296	71404	64492
315 817		N	SAR	IL	64493	71297	71405	64494
315 818		N	SAR	IL	64495	71298	71406	64496
315 819		N	SAR	IL	64497	71299	71407	64498
315 820		N	SAR	IL	64499	71300	71408	64500
315 821		N	SAR	IL	64501	71301	71409	64502
315 822		N	SAR	IL	64503	71302	71410	64504
315 823		N	SAR	IL	64505	71303	71411	64506
315 824		N	SAR	IL	64507	71304	71412	64508
315 825		N	SAR	IL	64509	71305	71413	64510
315 826		N	SAR	IL	64511	71306	71414	64512
315 827		N	SAR	IL	64513	71307	71415	64514
315 828		N	SAR	IL	64515	71308	71416	64516
315 829		N	SAR	IL	64517	71309	71417	64518
315 830		N	SAR	IL	64519	71310	71418	64520
315 831		N	SAR	IL	64521	71311	71419	64522
315 832		N	SAR	IL	64523	71312	71420	64524
315 833		N	SAR	IL	64525	71313	71421	64526
315 834		N	SAR	IL	64527	71314	71422	64528
315 835		N	SAR	IL	64529	71315	71423	64530
315 836		N	SAR	IL	64531	71316	71424	64532
315 837		N	SAR	IL	64533	71317	71425	64534
315 838		N	SAR	IL	64535	71318	71426	64536
315 839		N	SAR	IL	64537	71319	71427	64538
315 840		N	SAR	IL	64539	71320	71428	64540
315 841		N	SAR	IL	64541	71321	71429	64542
315 842	*	N	SAR	IL	64543	71322	71430	64544
315 843	*	N	SAR	IL	64545	71323	71431	64546
315 844	*	N	SAR	IL	64547	71324	71432	64548
315 845	*	N	SAR	IL	64549	71325	71433	64550
315 846	*	N	SAQ	HE	64551	71326	71434	64552
315 847	*	N	SAQ	HE	64553	71327	71435	64554
315 848	*	N	SAQ	HE	64555	71328	71436	64556
315 849	*	N	SAQ	HE	64557	71329	71437	64558
315 850	*	N	SAQ	HE	64559	71330	71438	64560
315 851	*	N	SAQ	HE	64561	71331	71439	64562
315 852	*	N	SAQ	HE	64563	71332	71440	64564

315 853	*	N	SAQ	HE	64565	71333	71441	64566
315 854	*	N	SAQ	HE	64567	71334	71442	64568
315 855	*	N	SAQ	HE	64569	71335	71443	64570
315 856	*	N	SAQ	HE	64571	71336	71444	64572
315 857	*	N	SAQ	HE	64573	71337	71445	64574
315 858	*	N	SAQ	HE	64575	71338	71446	64576
315 859	*	N	SAQ	HE	64577	71339	71447	64578
315 860	*	N	SAQ	HE	64579	71340	71448	64580
315 861	*	N	SAQ	HE	64581	71341	71449	64582

CLASS 317

DTSO(A) – MSO – TCOL – DTSO(B). Thyristor control. Tightlock couplers.
Sliding doors. Disc brakes. PA.
Bogies: BP20 (MSO), BT13 (others).
Gangways: Throughout.
Traction Motors: Four GEC G315BZ of 247.5 kW.
Dimensions: 19.83 x 2.82 m (outer cars), 19.92 x 2.82 m (inner cars).
Maximum Speed: 100 mph.

Class 317/1. Pressure ventilated.

DTSO(A) Dia. EE216. Lot No. 30955 York 1981 – 82. –/74. 29.44 t.
MSO. Dia. EC202. Lot No. 30958 York 1981 – 82. –/79. 49.76 t.
TCOL. Dia. EH307. Lot No. 30957 Derby 1981 – 82. 22/46 2T. 28.80 t. Controlled emission toilets (but decommisioned).
DTSO(B) Dia. EE235 (EE232★). Lot No. 30956 York 1981 – 82. –/70.
(–/71★). 29.28 t.

317 301	N	SCQ	HE	77024	62661	71577	77048
317 302	N	SCQ	HE	77001	62662	71578	77049
317 303	N	SCQ	HE	77002	62663	71579	77050
317 304	N	SCQ	HE	77003	62664	71580	77051
317 305	N	SCQ	HE	77004	62665	71581	77052
317 306	N	SCQ	HE	77005	62666	71582	77053
317 307	N	SCQ	HE	77006	62667	71583	77054
317 308	N	SCQ	HE	77007	62668	71584	77055
317 309	N	SCQ	HE	77008	62669	71585	77056
317 310	N	SCQ	HE	77009	62670	71586	77057
317 311	N	SCQ	HE	77010	62697	71587	77058
317 312	N	SCQ	HE	77011	62672	71588	77059
317 313	N	SCQ	HE	77012	62673	71589	77060
317 314	N	SCQ	HE	77013	62674	71590	77061
317 315	N	SCQ	HE	77014	62675	71591	77062
317 316	N	SCQ	HE	77015	62676	71592	77063
317 317	N	SCQ	HE	77016	62677	71593	77064
317 318	N	SCQ	HE	77017	62678	71594	77065
317 319	N	SCQ	HE	77018	62679	71595	77066
317 320	N	SCQ	HE	77019	62680	71596	77067
317 321	N	SCQ	HE	77020	62681	71597	77068
317 329	N	SCQ	HE	77028	62689	71605	77076
317 330	N	SCQ	HE	77029	62690	71606	77077

317 331		N	SCQ	HE	77030 62691 71607 77078
317 332		N	SCQ	HE	77031 62692 71608 77079
317 333		N	SCQ	HE	77032 62693 71609 77080
317 334		N	SCQ	HE	77033 62694 71610 77081
317 335		N	SCQ	HE	77034 62695 71611 77082
317 336		N	SCQ	HE	77035 62696 71612 77083
317 337	★	N	SCQ	HE	77036 62671 71613 77084
317 338	★	N	SCQ	HE	77037 62698 71614 77085
317 339	★	N	SCQ	HE	77038 62699 71615 77086
317 340	★	N	SCQ	HE	77039 62700 71616 77087
317 341	★	N	SCQ	HE	77040 62701 71617 77088
317 342	★	N	SCQ	HE	77041 62702 71618 77089
317 343	★	N	SCQ	HE	77042 62703 71619 77090
317 344	★	N	SCQ	HE	77043 62704 71620 77091
317 345	★	N	SCQ	HE	77044 62705 71621 77092
317 346	★	N	SCQ	HE	77045 62706 71622 77093
317 347	★	N	SCQ	HE	77046 62707 71623 77094
317 348	★	N	SCQ	HE	77047 62708 71624 77095

Class 317/2. Convection heating.

77200 – 19. DTSO(A). Dia. EE224. Lot No. 30994 York 1985 – 86. –/74. 29.31 t.

77280 – 83. DTSO(A). Dia. EE224. Lot No. 31007 York 1987. –/74. 29.31 t.

62846 – 65. MSO. Dia. EC205. Lot No. 30996 York 1985 – 86. –/79. 50.08 t.

62886 – 89. MSO. Dia. EC205. Lot No. 31009 York 1987. –/79. 50.08 t.

71734 – 53. TCOL. Dia. EH308. Lot No. 30997 York 1985 – 86. 22/46 2T. 28.28 t.

71762 – 65. TCOL. Dia. EH308. Lot No. 31010 York 1987. 22/46 2T. 28.28 t.

77220 – 39. DTSO(B). Dia. EE225. Lot No. 30995 York 1985 – 86. 29.28 t. –/71.

77284 – 87. DTSO(B). Dia. EE225. Lot No. 31008 York 1987. 29.28 t. –/71.

317 349	N	SCQ	HE	77200 62846 71734 77220
317 350	N	SCQ	HE	77201 62847 71735 77221
317 351	N	SCQ	HE	77202 62848 71736 77222
317 352	N	SCQ	HE	77203 62849 71739 77223
317 353	N	SCQ	HE	77204 62850 71738 77224
317 354	N	SCQ	HE	77205 62851 71737 77225
317 355	N	SCQ	HE	77206 62852 71740 77226
317 356	N	SCQ	HE	77207 62853 71742 77227
317 357	N	SCQ	HE	77208 62854 71741 77228
317 358	N	SCQ	HE	77209 62855 71743 77229
317 359	N	SCQ	HE	77210 62856 71744 77230
317 360	N	SCQ	HE	77211 62857 71745 77231
317 361	N	SCQ	HE	77212 62858 71746 77232
317 362	N	SCQ	HE	77213 62859 71747 77233
317 363	N	SCQ	HE	77214 62860 71748 77234
317 364	N	SCQ	HE	77215 62861 71749 77235
317 365	N	SCQ	HE	77216 62862 71750 77236
317 366	N	SCQ	HE	77217 62863 71752 77237
317 367	N	SCQ	HE	77218 62864 71751 77238

317 368	N	SCQ	HE	77219 62865 71753 77239
317 369	N	SCQ	HE	77280 62886 71762 77284
317 370	N	SCQ	HE	77281 62887 71763 77285
317 371	N	SCQ	HE	77282 62888 71764 77286
317 372	N	SCQ	HE	77283 62889 71765 77287

Class 317/0. As Class 317/1, but TCOL has first class seating declassified.

317 392	N	SCQ	HE	77021 62681 71598 77069
317 393	N	SCQ	HE	77022 62682 71599 77070
317 394	N	SCQ	HE	77023 62683 71600 77071
317 395	N	SCQ	HE	77000 62684 71601 77072
317 396	N	SCQ	HE	77025 62685 71602 77073
317 397	N	SCQ	HE	77026 62686 71603 77074
317 398	N	SCQ	HE	77027 62687 71604 77075

Names:

TCOL No. 71746 of set 317 361 is named 'Kings Lynn Festival'.
TCOL No. 71765 of set 317 372 is named 'Welwyn Garden City'.

CLASS 318

DTSOL – MSO – DTSO. Thyristor control. Tightlock couplers. Sliding doors. Disc brakes. PA. Cab to shore radio.
Bogies: BP20 (MSO), BT13 (others).
Gangways: Throughout.
Traction Motors: Four Brush TM 2141 of 268 kW.
Dimensions: 19.83 x 2.82 m (outer cars), 19.92 x 2.82 m (inner cars).
Maximum Speed: 90 mph.

77240 – 59. DTSOL. Dia. EE227. Lot No. 30999 York 1985 – 86. – /66 1T. 30.01 t.
77288. DTSOL. Dia. EE227. Lot No. 31020 York 1986 – 87. – /66 1T. 30.01 t.
62866 – 85. MSO. Dia. EC207. Lot No. 30998 York 1985 – 86. – /79. 50.90 t.
62890. MSO. Dia. EC207. Lot No. 31019 York 1987. – /79. 50.90 t.
77260 – 79. DTSO. Dia. EE228. Lot No. 31000 York 1985 – 86. – /71. 26.60 t.
77289. DTSO. Dia. EE228. Lot No. 31021 York 1987. – /71. 26.60 t.

318 250	S	SAA	GW	77260 62866 77240
318 251	S	SAA	GW	77261 62867 77241
318 252	S	SAA	GW	77262 62868 77242
318 253	S	SAA	GW	77263 62869 77243
318 254	S	SAA	GW	77264 62870 77244
318 255	S	SAA	GW	77265 62871 77245
318 256	S	SAA	GW	77266 62872 77246
318 257	S	SAA	GW	77267 62873 77247
318 258	S	SAA	GW	77268 62874 77248
318 259	S	SAA	GW	77269 62875 77249
318 260	S	SAA	GW	77270 62876 77250
318 261	S	SAA	GW	77271 62877 77251
318 262	S	SAA	GW	77272 62878 77252
318 263	S	SAA	GW	77273 62879 77253
318 264	S	SAA	GW	77274 62880 77254

318 265	S	SAA	GW	77275 62881 77255
318 266	S	SAA	GW	77276 62882 77256
318 267	S	SAA	GW	77277 62883 77257
318 268	S	SAA	GW	77278 62884 77258
318 269	S	SAA	GW	77279 62885 77259
318 270	S	SAA	GW	77289 62890 77288

Names:

DTSOL No. 77240 of set 318 250 is named 'GEOFF SHAW'.
DTSOL No. 77256 of set 318 266 is named 'STRATHCLYDER'.

CLASS 319

Thyristor control. Tightlock couplers. Sliding doors. Disc brakes. PA. Cab to shore radio.
System: 25 kV a.c. overhead/750 V d.c. third rail.
Bogies: P7-4 (MSO), T3-7 (others).
Gangways: Within unit. End doors.
Traction Motors: Four GEC G315BZ of 268 kW.
Dimensions: 19.83 x 2.82 m (outer cars), 19.92 x 2.82 m (inner cars).
Maximum Speed: 100 mph.

Class 319/0. DTSO – MSO – TSOL – DTSO.

77291 – 381. DTSO. Dia. EE233. Lot No. 31022 (odd nos.) York 1987 – 8. – /82. 30 t.
77431 – 457. DTSO. Dia. EE233. Lot No. 31038 (odd nos.) York 1988. – /82. 30 t.
62891 – 936. MSO. Dia. EC209. Lot No. 31023 York 1987 – 8. – /82. 51 t.
62961 – 974. MSO. Dia. EC209. Lot No. 31039 York 1988. – /82. 51 t.
71772 – 817. TSOL. Dia. EH234. Lot No. 31024 York 1987 – 8. – /77 2T. 51 t.
71866 – 879. TSOL. Dia. EH234. Lot No. 31040 York 1988. – /77 2T. 51 t.
77290 – 380. DTSO. Dia. EE234. Lot No. 31025 (even nos.) York 1987 – 8. – /78. 30 t.
77430 – 456. DTSO. Dia. EE234. Lot No. 31041 (even nos.) York 1988. – /78. 30 t.

319 001	N	SBW	SU	77291 62891 71772 77290
319 002	N	SBW	SU	77293 62892 71773 77292
319 003	N	SBW	SU	77295 62893 71774 77294
319 004	N	SBW	SU	77297 62894 71775 77296
319 005	N	SBW	SU	77299 62895 71776 77298
319 006	N	SBW	SU	77301 62896 71777 77300
319 007	N	SBW	SU	77303 62897 71778 77302
319 008	N	SBW	SU	77305 62898 71779 77304
319 009	N	SBW	SU	77307 62899 71780 77306
319 010	N	SBW	SU	77309 62900 71781 77308
319 011	N	SBW	SU	77311 62901 71782 77310
319 012	N	SBW	SU	77313 62902 71783 77312
319 013	N	SBW	SU	77315 62903 71784 77314
319 014	N	SBW	SU	77317 62904 71785 77316
319 015	N	SBW	SU	77319 62905 71786 77318
319 016	N	SBW	SU	77321 62906 71787 77320
319 017	N	SBW	SU	77323 62907 71788 77322
319 018	N	SBW	SU	77325 62908 71789 77324

319 019	N	SBW	SU	77327	62909	71790	77326
319 020	N	SBW	SU	77329	62910	71791	77328
319 021	N	SBX	SU	77331	62911	71792	77330
319 022	TL	SBX	SU	77333	62912	71793	77332
319 023	TL	SBX	SU	77335	62913	71794	77334
319 024	N	SBX	SU	77337	62914	71795	77336
319 025	N	SBX	SU	77339	62915	71796	77338
319 026	N	SBX	SU	77341	62916	71797	77340
319 027	TL	SBX	SU	77343	62917	71798	77342
319 028	TL	SBX	SU	77345	62918	71799	77344
319 029	TL	SBX	SU	77347	62919	71800	77346
319 030	TL	SBX	SU	77349	62920	71801	77348
319 031	TL	SBX	SU	77351	62921	71802	77350
319 032	TL	SBX	SU	77353	62922	71803	77352
319 033	TL	SBX	SU	77355	62923	71804	77354
319 034	TL	SBX	SU	77357	62924	71805	77356
319 035	TL	SBX	SU	77359	62925	71806	77358
319 036	TL	SBX	SU	77361	62926	71807	77360
319 037	TL	SBX	SU	77363	62927	71808	77362
319 038	TL	SBX	SU	77365	62928	71809	77364
319 039	TL	SBX	SU	77367	62929	71810	77366
319 040	TL	SBX	SU	77369	62930	71811	77368
319 041	TL	SBX	SU	77371	62931	71812	77370
319 042	TL	SBX	SU	77373	62932	71813	77372
319 043	TL	SBX	SU	77375	62933	71814	77374
319 044	TL	SBX	SU	77377	62934	71815	77376
319 045	TL	SBX	SU	77379	62935	71816	77378
319 046	TL	SBX	SU	77381	62936	71817	77380
319 047	TL	SBX	SU	77431	62961	71866	77430
319 048	TL	SBX	SU	77433	62962	71867	77432
319 049	TL	SBX	SU	77435	62963	71868	77434
319 050	TL	SBX	SU	77437	62964	71869	77436
319 051	TL	SBX	SU	77439	62965	71870	77438
319 052	TL	SBX	SU	77441	62966	71871	77440
319 053	TL	SBX	SU	77443	62967	71872	77442
319 054	TL	SBX	SU	77445	62968	71873	77444
319 055	TL	SBX	SU	77447	62969	71874	77446
319 056	TL	SBX	SU	77449	62970	71875	77448
319 057	N	SBX	SU	77451	62971	71876	77450
319 058	N	SBX	SU	77453	62972	71877	77452
319 059	N	SBX	SU	77455	62973	71878	77454
319 060	N	SBX	SU	77457	62974	71879	77456

Names:

TSOL 71776 of set 319 005 is named 'Partnership For Progress'.
TSOL 71779 of set 319 008 is named 'Cheriton'.
TSOL 71780 of set 319 009 is named 'Coquelles'.
TSOL 71801 of set 319 030 is named 'Harlington Festival'.

Class 319/1. DTCO – MSO – TSOL – DTSO.

DTCO. Dia. EE310. Lot No. 31063 York 1990. 16/54. 29 t.
MSO. Dia. EC214. Lot No. 31064 York 1990. –/79. 50.6 t.

TSOL. Dia. EH238. Lot No. 31065 York 1990. –/74 2T. 31 t.
DTSO. Dia. EE240. Lot No. 31066 York 1990. –/78. 29.7 t.

319 161	NW	SBX	SU	77459 63043 71929 77458
319 162	NW	SBX	SU	77461 63044 71930 77460
319 163	NW	SBX	SU	77463 63045 71931 77462
319 164	NW	SBX	SU	77465 63046 71932 77464
319 165	NW	SBX	SU	77467 63047 71933 77466
319 166	NW	SBX	SU	77469 63048 71934 77468
319 167	NW	SBX	SU	77471 63049 71935 77470
319 168	NW	SBX	SU	77473 63050 71936 77472
319 169	NW	SBX	SU	77475 63051 71937 77474
319 170	NW	SBX	SU	77477 63052 71938 77476
319 171	NW	SBX	SU	77479 63053 71939 77478
319 172	NW	SBX	SU	77481 63054 71940 77480
319 173	NW	SBX	SU	77483 63055 71941 77482
319 174	NW	SBX	SU	77485 63056 71942 77484
319 175	NW	SBX	SU	77487 63057 71943 77486
319 176	NW	SBX	SU	77489 63058 71944 77488
319 177	NW	SBX	SU	77491 63059 71945 77490
319 178	NW	SBX	SU	77493 63060 71946 77492
319 179	NW	SBX	SU	77495 63061 71947 77494
319 180	NW	SBX	SU	77497 63062 71948 77496
319 181	NW	SBX	SU	77973 63093 71979 77974
319 182	NW	SBX	SU	77975 63094 71980 77976
319 183	NW	SBX	SU	77977 63095 71981 77978
319 184	NW	SBX	SU	77979 63096 71982 77980
319 185	NW	SBX	SU	77981 63097 71983 77982
319 186	NW	SBX	SU	77983 63098 71984 77984

CLASS 320

DTSO(A) – MSO – DTSO(B). Thyristor control. Tightlock couplers. Sliding doors.
Disc brakes. PA.
Bogies: P7-4 (MSO), T3-7 (others).
Gangways: Within unit.
Traction Motors: Brush TM2141B of 268 kW.
Dimensions: 19.83 x 2.82 m (outer cars), 19.92 x 2.82 m (inner car).
Maximum Speed: 75 mph.

DTSO (A). Dia. EE238. Lot No. 31060 York 1990. –/77. 30.7 t.
MSO. Dia. EC212. Lot No. 31062 York 1990. –/77. 52.1 t.
DTSO (B). Dia. EE239. Lot No. 31061 York 1990. –/76 31.7 t.

Names:
MSO 63025 of set 320 305 is named GLASGOW SCHOOL OF ART.
MSO 63042 of set 320 322 is named FESTIVE GLASGOW ORCHID.

320 301	S	SAA	GW	77899 63021 77921
320 302	S	SAA	GW	77900 63022 77922
320 303	S	SAA	GW	77901 63023 77923
320 304	S	SAA	GW	77902 63024 77924
320 305	S	SAA	GW	77903 63025 77925

320 306	S	SAA	GW	77904 63026 77926
320 307	S	SAA	GW	77905 63027 77927
320 308	S	SAA	GW	77906 63028 77928
320 309	S	SAA	GW	77907 63029 77929
320 310	S	SAA	GW	77908 63030 77930
320 311	S	SAA	GW	77909 63031 77931
320 312	S	SAA	GW	77910 63032 77932
320 313	S	SAA	GW	77911 63033 77933
320 314	S	SAA	GW	77912 63034 77934
320 315	S	SAA	GW	77913 63035 77935
320 316	S	SAA	GW	77914 63036 77936
320 317	S	SAA	GW	77915 63037 77937
320 318	S	SAA	GW	77916 63038 77938
320 319	S	SAA	GW	77917 63039 77939
320 320	S	SAA	GW	77918 63040 77940
320 321	S	SAA	GW	77919 63041 77941
320 322	S	SAA	GW	77920 63042 77942

CLASS 321

DTCO (DTSO on Class 321/9) – MSO – TSOL – DTSO. Thyristor control. Tightlock couplers. Sliding doors. Disc brakes. PA.
Bogies: P7-4 (MSO), T3-7 (others).
Gangways: Within unit.
Traction Motors: Brush TM2141C of 268 kW.
Dimensions: 19.83 x 2.82 m (outer cars), 19.92 x 2.82 m (inner cars).
Maximum Speed: 100 mph.
Non-Standard Livery: NS (Netherlands Railways) Intercity livery (yellow and deep blue).

Note: Lot numbers and diagrams were officially changed on 09/02/90.

Class 321/3. Units built for Liverpool Street workings.

DTCO. Dia. EE308. Lot No. 31053 York 1988 – 90. 12/56. 29.3 t.
MSO. Dia. EC210. Lot No. 31054 York 1988 – 90. –/79. 51.5 t.
TSOL. Dia. EH235. Lot No. 31055 York 1988 – 90. –/74 2T. 28 t.
DTSO. Dia. EE236. Lot No. 31056 York 1988 – 90. –/78. 29.1 t.

321 301	NW	SAR	IL	78049 62975 71880 77853
321 302	NW	SAR	IL	78050 62976 71881 77854
321 303	NW	SAR	IL	78051 62977 71882 77855
321 304	NW	SAR	IL	78052 62978 71883 77856
321 305	NW	SAR	IL	78053 62979 71884 77857
321 306	NW	SAR	IL	78054 62980 71885 77858
321 307	NW	SAR	IL	78055 62981 71886 77859
321 308	A	SAR	IL	78056 62982 71887 77860
321 309	NW	SAR	IL	78057 62983 71888 77861
321 310	NW	SAR	IL	78058 62984 71889 77862
321 311	NW	SAR	IL	78059 62985 71890 77863
321 312	NW	SAR	IL	78060 62986 71891 77864
321 313	NW	SAR	IL	78061 62987 71892 77865
321 314	NW	SAR	IL	78062 62988 71893 77866

321 315	NW	SAR	IL	78063 62989 71894 77867
321 316	NW	SAR	IL	78064 62990 71895 77868
321 317	NW	SAR	IL	78065 62991 71896 77869
321 318	NW	SAR	IL	78066 62992 71897 77870
321 319	NW	SAR	IL	78067 62993 71898 77871
321 320	NW	SAR	IL	78068 62994 71899 77872
321 321	NW	SAR	IL	78069 62995 71900 77873
321 322	NW	SAR	IL	78070 62996 71901 77874
321 323	NW	SAR	IL	78071 62997 71902 77875
321 324	NW	SAR	IL	78072 62998 71903 77876
321 325	NW	SAR	IL	78073 62999 71904 77877
321 326	NW	SAR	IL	78074 63000 71905 77878
321 327	NW	SAR	IL	78075 63001 71906 77879
321 328	NW	SAR	IL	78076 63002 71907 77880
321 329	NW	SAR	IL	78077 63003 71908 77881
321 330	NW	SAR	IL	78078 63004 71909 77882
321 331	NW	SAR	IL	78079 63005 71910 77883
321 332	NW	SAR	IL	78080 63006 71911 77884
321 333	NW	SAR	IL	78081 63007 71912 77885
321 334	0	SAR	IL	78082 63008 71913 77886
321 335	NW	SAR	IL	78083 63009 71914 77887
321 336	NW	SAR	IL	78084 63010 71915 77888
321 337	NW	SAR	IL	78085 63011 71916 77889
321 338	NW	SAR	IL	78086 63012 71917 77890
321 339	NW	SAR	IL	78087 63013 71918 77891
321 340	NW	SAR	IL	78088 63014 71919 77892
321 341	NW	SAR	IL	78089 63015 71920 77893
321 342	NW	SAR	IL	78090 63016 71921 77894
321 343	NW	SAR	IL	78091 63017 71922 77895
321 344	NW	SAR	IL	78092 63018 71923 77896
321 345	NW	SAR	IL	78093 63019 71924 77897
321 346	NW	SAR	IL	78094 63020 71925 77898
321 347	NW	SAR	IL	78131 63105 71991 78280
321 348	NW	SAR	IL	78132 63106 71992 78281
321 349	NW	SAR	IL	78133 63107 71993 78282
321 350	NW	SAR	IL	78134 63108 71994 78283
321 351	NW	SAR	IL	78135 63109 71995 78284
321 352	NW	SAR	IL	78136 63110 71996 78285
321 353	NW	SAR	IL	78137 63111 71997 78286
321 354	NW	SAR	IL	78138 63112 71998 78287
321 355	NW	SAR	IL	78139 63113 71999 78288
321 356	NW	SAR	IL	78140 63114 72000 78289
321 357	NW	SAR	IL	78141 63115 72001 78290
321 358	NW	SAR	IL	78142 63116 72002 78291
321 359	NW	SAR	IL	78143 63117 72003 78292
321 360	NW	SAR	IL	78144 63118 72004 78293
321 361	NW	SAR	IL	78145 63119 72005 78294
321 362	NW	SAR	IL	78146 63120 72006 78295
321 363	NW	SAR	IL	78147 63121 72007 78296
321 364	NW	SAR	IL	78148 63122 72008 78297
321 365	NW	SAR	IL	78149 63123 72009 78298

321 366 **NW** SAR   IL   78150 63124 72010 78299

Names:

DTSOL No. 71891 of set 321 312 is named 'Southend-on-Sea'.
DTSOL No. 71913 of set 321 334 is named 'Amsterdam'.
DTSOL No. 71915 of set 321 336 is named 'Geoffrey Freeman Allen'.

Class 321/4. Units built for WCML workings.

DTCO. Dia. EE309. Lot No. 31067 York 1989 – 90. 28/40. 29.3 t.
MSO. Dia. EC210. Lot No. 31068 York 1989 – 90. –/79. 51.5 t.
TSOL. Dia. EH235. Lot No. 31069 York 1989 – 90. –/74 2T. 28 t.
DTSO. Dia. EE236. Lot No. 31070 York 1989 – 90. –/78. 29.1 t.

Note: The DTCOs of sets allocated to IL have 12 First Class seats declassified.

321 401	**NW**	SAP	BY	78095	63063	71949	77943
321 402	**NW**	SAP	BY	78096	63064	71950	77944
321 403	**NW**	SAP	BY	78097	63065	71951	77945
321 404	**NW**	SAP	BY	78098	63066	71952	77946
321 405	**NW**	SAP	BY	78099	63067	71953	77947
321 406	**NW**	SAP	BY	78100	63068	71954	77948
321 407	**NW**	SAP	BY	78101	63069	71955	77949
321 408	**NW**	SAP	BY	78102	63070	71956	77950
321 409	**NW**	SAP	BY	78103	63071	71957	77951
321 410	**NW**	SAP	BY	78104	63072	71958	77952
321 411	**NW**	SAP	BY	78105	63073	71959	77953
321 412	**NW**	SAP	BY	78106	63074	71960	77954
321 413	**NW**	SAP	BY	78107	63075	71961	77955
321 414	**NW**	SAP	BY	78108	63076	71962	77956
321 415	**NW**	SAP	BY	78109	63077	71963	77957
321 416	**NW**	SAP	BY	78110	63078	71964	77958
321 417	**NW**	SAP	BY	78111	63079	71965	77959
321 418	**NW**	SAP	BY	78112	63080	71966	77960
321 419	**NW**	SAP	BY	78113	63081	71967	77961
321 420	**NW**	SAP	BY	78114	63082	71968	77962
321 421	**NW**	SAP	BY	78115	63083	71969	77963
321 422	**NW**	SAP	BY	78116	63084	71970	77964
321 423	**NW**	SAP	BY	78117	63085	71971	77965
321 424	**NW**	SAP	BY	78118	63086	71972	77966
321 425	**NW**	SAP	BY	78119	63087	71973	77967
321 426	**NW**	SAP	BY	78120	63088	71974	77968
321 427	**NW**	SAP	BY	78121	63089	71975	77969
321 428	**NW**	SAP	BY	78122	63090	71976	77970
321 429	**NW**	SAP	BY	78123	63091	71977	77971
321 430	**NW**	SAP	BY	78124	63092	71978	77972
321 431	**NW**	SAP	BY	78151	63125	72011	78300
321 432	**NW**	SAP	BY	78152	63126	72012	78301
321 433	**NW**	SAP	BY	78153	63127	72013	78302
321 434	**NW**	SAP	BY	78154	63128	72014	78303
321 435	**NW**	SAP	BY	78155	63129	72015	78304
321 436	**NW**	SAP	BY	78156	63130	72016	78305
321 437	**NW**	SAP	BY	78157	63131	72017	78306

321 438	NW	SAR	IL	78158 63132 72018 78307
321 439	NW	SAR	IL	78159 63133 72019 78308
321 440	NW	SAR	IL	78160 63134 72020 78309
321 441	NW	SAR	IL	78161 63135 72021 78310
321 442	NW	SAR	IL	78162 63136 72022 78311
321 443	NW	SAR	IL	78125 63099 71985 78274
321 444	NW	SAR	IL	78126 63100 71986 78275
321 445	NW	SAR	IL	78127 63101 71987 78276
321 446	NW	SAR	IL	78128 63102 71988 78277
321 447	NW	SAR	IL	78129 63103 71989 78278
321 448	NW	SAR	IL	78130 63104 71990 78279

Class 321/9. Units owned by West Yorkshire PTE although managed by Eversholt Train Leasing. DTSO(A) – MSO – TSOL – DTSO(B).

DTSO (A). Dia. EE277. Lot No. 31108 York 1991. – /77. 29.3 t.
MSO. Dia. EC216. Lot No. 31109 York 1991. – /79. 51.5 t.
TSOL. Dia. EH240. Lot No. 31110 York 1991. – /74 2T. 28 t.
DTSO (B). Dia. EE277. Lot No. 31111 York 1991. – /77. 29.1 t.

321 901	Y	SAC	NL	77990 63153 72128 77993
321 902	Y	SAC	NL	77991 63154 72129 77994
321 903	Y	SAC	NL	77992 63155 72130 77995

CLASS 322   STANSTED EXPRESS STOCK

DTCO – MSO – TSOL – DTSO. Units dedicated for use on Stansted Airport services. Thyristor control. Tightlock couplers. Sliding doors. Disc brakes. PA.
Bogies: P7-4 (MSO), T3-7 (others).
Gangways: Within unit.
Traction Motors: Brush TM2141C of 268 kW.
Dimensions: 19.83 x 2.82 m (outer cars), 19.92 x 2.82 m (inner cars).
Maximum Speed: 100 mph.
Non-Standard Livery: Light grey with broad green band and narrow white and dark grey bands. White at cantrail level and on outer ends of end cars. 'Stansted Express' lettering.

DTCO. Dia. EE313. Lot No. 31094 York 1990. 35/22. 30.43 t.
MSO. Dia. EC215. Lot No. 31092 York 1990. – /70. 52.27 t.
TSOL. Dia. EH239. Lot No. 31093 York 1990. – /60 2T. 29.51 t.
DTSO. Dia. EE242. Lot No. 31091 York 1990. – /65. 29.77 t.

322 481	O	SAG	HE	78163 63137 72023 77985
322 482	O	SAG	HE	78164 63138 72024 77986
322 483	O	SAG	HE	78165 63139 72025 77987
322 484	O	SAG	HE	78166 63140 72026 77988
322 485	O	SAG	HE	78167 63141 72027 77989

CLASS 323

DMSO(A) – TSOL – DMSO(B). Aluminium alloy bodies. Thyristor control. Tightlock couplers. Sliding doors. Disc brakes. PA.

Bogies: RFS BP62 (power cars) and BT52 (trailer car).
Gangways: Within unit.
Traction Motors: Four Holec DMKT 52/24 of 146 kW per car.
Dimensions: 23.37 x 2.80 m (outer cars), 23.44 x 2.80 m (inner cars).
Maximum Speed: 75 mph.

DMSO (A). Dia. EA272. Lot No. 31112 Hunslet 1992 – 3. –/98 (–/82*).
41.0 t.
TSOL. Dia. EH296. Lot No. 31113 Hunslet 1992 – 3. –/88 1T (–/80 1T*).
39.4 t.
DMSO (B). Dia. EA272. Lot No. 31114 Hunslet 1992 – 3. –/98 (–/82*).
23.37 t.

323 201	CE	SBG	BY	64001	72201	65001
323 202	CE	SBG	BY	64002	72202	65002
323 203	CE	SBG	BY	64003	72203	65005
323 204	CE	SBG	BY	64004	72204	65004
323 205	CE	SBG	BY	64005	72205	65003
323 206	CE	SBG	BY	64006	72206	65006
323 207	CE	SBG	BY	64007	72207	65007
323 208	CE	SBG	BY	64008	72208	65008
323 209	CE	SBG	BY	64009	72209	65009
323 210	CE	SBG	BY	64010	72210	65010
323 211	CE	SBG	BY	64011	72211	65011
323 212	CE	SBG	BY	64012	72212	65012
323 213	CE	SBG	BY	64013	72213	65013
323 214	CE	SBG	BY	64014	72214	65014
323 215	CE	SBG	BY	64015	72215	65015
323 216	CE	SBG	BY	64016	72216	65016
323 217	CE	SBG	BY	64017	72217	65017
323 218	CE	SBG	BY	64018	72218	65018
323 219	CE	SBG	BY	64019	72219	65019
323 220	CE	SBG	BY	64020	72220	65020
323 221	CE	SBG	BY	64021	72221	65021
323 222	CE	SBG	BY	64022	72222	65022
323 223	* GM	SBD	LG	64023	72223	65023
323 224	* GM	SBD	LG	64024	72224	65024
323 225	* GM	SBD	LG	64025	72225	65025
323 226	GM	SBD	LG	64026	72226	65026
323 227	GM	SBD	LG	64027	72227	65027
323 228	GM	SBD	LG	64028	72228	65028
323 229	GM	SBD	LG	64029	72229	65029
323 230	GM	SBD	LG	64030	72230	65030
323 231	GM	SBD	LG	64031	72231	65031
323 232	GM	SBD	LG	64032	72232	65032
323 233	GM	SBD	LG	64033	72233	65033
323 234	GM	SBD	LG	64034	72234	65034
323 235	GM	SBD	LG	64035	72235	65035
323 236	GM	SBD	LG	64036	72236	65036
323 237	GM	SBD	LG	64037	72237	65037
323 238	GM	SBD	LG	64038	72238	65038
323 239	GM	SBD	LG	64039	72239	65039

323 240	**CE**	SBG	BY	64040 72340 65040
323 241	**CE**	SBG	BY	64041 72341 65041
323 242	**CE**	SBG	BY	64042 72342 65042
323 243	**CE**	SBG	BY	64043 72343 65043

CLASS 325

DTPMV(A) – MPMV – TPMV – DTPMV(B). New parcels units for Rail Express Systems. based on Class 319. Roller shutter doors and compatibility with diesel locomotive haulage. Cab to shore radio.

System: 25 kV a.c. overhead/750 V d.c. third rail.
Bogies: P7-4 (MSO), T3-7 (others).
Gangways: Within unit.
Traction Motors: Four GEC G315BZ of 247.5 kW.
Dimensions: 19.83 x 2.82 m (outer cars), 19.92 x 2.82 m (inner cars).
Maximum Speed: 100 mph.

68300 – 68330 (even Nos). DTPMV(A). Dia. EE501. Lot No. 31144. ABB Derby 1995.
MPMV. Dia. EC501. Lot No. 31145. ABB Derby 1995.
TPMV. Dia. EH501. Lot No. 31146. ABB Derby 1995.
68301 – 68331 (odd Nos). DTPMV(B). Dia. EE501. Lot No. 31147. ABB Derby 1995.

325 001	**RM**	MP	CE	68300 68340 68360 68301
325 002	**RM**	MP	CE	68302 68341 68361 68303
325 003	**RM**	MP	CE	68304 68342 68362 68305
325 004	**RM**	MP	CE	68306 68343 68363 68307
325 005	**RM**	MP	CE	68308 68344 68364 68309
325 006	**RM**	MP	CE	68310 68345 68365 68311
325 007	**RM**	MP	CE	68312 68346 68366 68313
325 008	**RM**	MP	CE	68314 68347 68367 68315
325 009	**RM**	MP	CE	68316 68348 68368 68317
325 010	**RM**	MP	CE	68318 68349 68369 68319
325 011	**RM**	MP	CE	68320 68350 68370 68321
325 012	**RM**	MP	CE	68322 68351 68371 68323
325 013	**RM**	MP	CE	68324 68352 68372 68325
325 014	**RM**	MP	CE	68326 68353 68373 68327
325 015	**RM**	MP	CE	68328 68354 68374 68329
325 016	**RM**	MP	CE	68330 68355 68375 68331

Name: 325 008 is named 'Peter Howarth O.B.E.'

CLASS 365   NETWORKER EXPRESS

DMCO – TSOL – PTSOL – DMSO. New units with Aluminium bodies. GTO thyristor control. Tightlock couplers. Sliding doors. Disc, rheostatic and regenerative brakes. PA.

System: 25 kV a.c. overhead/750 V d.c. third rail.
Electrical Equipment: Networker.
Bogies: P3 (Power cars), T3 (trailers).

Gangways: Within set.
Traction Motors: Four Brush three-phase induction motors per car.
Dimensions: 20.89 x 2.81 m (outer cars), 20.06 x 2.81 m (inner cars).
Maximum Speed: 100 mph.

DMCO. Dia. EA301. Lot No. 31??? ABB York 1994 – 5. 12/56. 46.70 t.
TSOL. Dia. EH298. Lot No. 31??? ABB York 1994 – 5. –/59 (+ 5 tip-up) 1TD. 32.90 t.
PTSOL. Dia. EH298. Lot No. 31??? ABB York 1994 – 5. –/68 1T. 34.60 t.

365 501	NW	SA		65894	72241	72240	65935
365 502	NW	SA		65895	72243	72242	65936
365 503	NW	SA		65896	72245	72244	65937
365 504	NW	SA		65897	72247	72246	65938
365 505	NW	SA		65898	72249	72248	65939
365 506	NW	SA		65899	72251	72250	65940
365 507	NW	SA		65900	72253	72252	65941
365 508	NW	SA		65901	72255	72254	65942
365 509	NW	SA		65902	72257	72256	65943
365 510	NW	SA		65903	72259	72258	65944
365 511	NW	SA		65904	72261	72260	65945
365 512	NW	SA		65905	72263	72262	65946
365 513	NW	SA		65906	72265	72264	65947
365 514	NW	SA		65907	72267	72266	65948
365 515	NW	SA		65908	72269	72268	65949
365 516	NW	SA		65909	72271	72270	65950
365 517	NW	SA		65910	72273	72272	65951
365 518	NW	SA		65911	72275	72274	65952
365 519	NW	SA		65912	72277	72276	65953
365 520	NW	SA		65913	72279	72278	65954
365 521	NW	SA		65914	72281	72280	65955
365 522	NW	SA		65915	72283	72282	65956
365 523	NW	SA		65916	72285	72284	65957
365 524	NW	SA		65917	72287	72286	65958
365 525	NW	SA		65918	72289	72288	65959
365 526	NW	SA		65919	72291	72290	65960
365 527	NW	SA		65920	72293	72292	65961
365 528	NW	SA		65921	72295	72294	65962
365 529	NW	SA		65922	72297	72296	65963
365 530	NW	SA		65923	72299	72298	65964
365 531	NW	SA		65924	72301	72300	65965
365 532	NW	SA		65925	72303	72302	65966
365 533	NW	SA		65926	72305	72304	65967
365 534	NW	SA		65927	72307	72306	65968
365 535	NW	SA		65928	72309	72308	65969
365 536	NW	SA		65929	72311	72310	65970
365 537	NW	SA		65930	72313	72312	65971
365 538	NW	SA		65931	72315	72314	65972
365 539	NW	SA		65932	72317	72316	65973
365 540	NW	SA		65933	72319	72318	65974
365 541	NW	SA		65934	72321	72320	65975

4.2. FORMER SOUTHERN REGION d.c. EMUs

These classes are all allocated to the former Southern Region and operate on the third rail system at 750 – 850 V d.c. Except where stated otherwise, all multiple units can run in multiple with one another. Buffet cars have electric cooking. In addition to the class number, the old SR designations e.g. 4 Cig are quoted. Outer couplings are buckeyes on units built befored 1982 with bar couplings within units. Newer units have tightlock outer couplings.

CLASS 438   4 TC

DTSO – TFK – TBSK – DTSO. Converted from loco-hauled stock. Unpowered units which worked push & pull with class 431/2 tractor units and class 33/1 and 73 locos. Express stock.

Electrical Equipment: 1966-type.
Bogies: B5 (SR) bogies.
Gangways: Throughout.
Dimensions: 19.66 x 2.82 m.
Maximum Speed: 90 mph.

DTSO. Dia. EE266. Lot No. 30764 York 1966 – 67. –/64. 32 t.
TFK. Dia. EH160. Lot No. 30766 York 1966 – 67. 42/– 2T. 33.5 t.
TBSK. Dia. EJ260. Lot No. 30765 York 1966 – 67. 32S 1T. 35.5 t.

Renumbered from 8010/8017. Formerly class 491.

Units off loan

Two units remain and regained their original numbers for use on charter and special services. They are at present stored.

410	**B**	SBOL	Kineton	76288	70859*	70812	76287
417	**B**	SBOL	Kineton	76302	70860*	70826	76301
Spare	**N**	SBOL	ZG	76327			* at ZG

Former numbers of vehicles converted from hauled stock:

70812 (34987)	70860 (13019)	76288 (4391)	76302 (4382)
70826 (34980)	76287 (4379)	76301 (4375)	76327 (4018)
70859 (13040)		

CLASS 421/5   'GREYHOUND' 4 Cig (PHASE 2)

DTCsoL (A) – MBSO – TSO – DTCsoL (B). Express stock. All facelifted with new trim, fluorescent lighting in saloons, PA.

Note: The following details apply to all Class 421 (phase 2) sets.

Diagram Numbers: EE369, ED264, EH287, EE369.
Electrical Equipment: 1963-type.
Bogies: Two Mk. 6 motor bogies (MBSO). B5 (SR) bogies (trailer cars).
Gangways: Throughout.

Traction Motors: Four EE507 of 185 kW.
Dimensions: 19.75 x 2.82 m.
Maximum Speed: 90 mph.

76561 – 76567. DTCsoL(A). Lot No. 30802 York 1970. 18/36 2T. 35.5 t.
76581 – 76610. DTCsoL(A). Lot No. 30806 York 1970. 18/36 2T. 35.5 t.
76717 – 76787. DTCsoL(A). Lot No. 30814 York 1970 – 72. 18/36 2T. 35.5 t.
76859. DTCsoL(A). Lot No. 30827 York 1972. 18/36 2T. 35.5 t.
62277 – 62283. MBSO. Lot No. 30804 York 1970. –/56. 49t.
62287 – 62316. MBSO. Lot No. 30808 York 1970. –/56. 49t.
62355 – 62425. MBSO. Lot No. 30816 York 1970. –/56. 49t.
62430. MBSO. Lot No. 30829 York 1972. –/56. 49t.
70967 – 70996. TSO. Lot No. 30809 York 1970 – 71. –/72. 31.5t.
71035 – 71105. TSO. Lot No. 30817 York 1970. –/72. 31.5t.
71106. TSO. Lot No. 30830 York 1972. –/72. 31.5t.
71926 – 71928. TSO. Lot No. 30805 York 1970. –/72. 31.5t.
76571 – 76577. DTCsoL(B). Lot No. 30803 York 1970. 24/28 2T. 35 t.
76611 – 76640. DTCsoL(B). Lot No. 30807 York 1970. 24/28 2T. 35 t.
76788 – 76858. DTCsoL(B). Lot No. 30815 York 1970 – 72. 24/28 2T. 35 t.
76859. DTCsoL(B). Lot No. 30828 York 1972. 18/36 2T. 35 t.

These sets are known as 'Greyhound' units and are fitted with an additional stage of field weakening to improve the maximum attainable speed. This term is traditional on the lines of the former London & South Western Railway, as it was formerly applied to their Class T9 4 – 4 – 0 steam locomotives.

1301	N	SAY	FR	76595	62301	70981	76625
1302	N	SAY	FR	76584	62290	70970	76614
1303	N	SAY	FR	76581	62287	70967	76611
1304	N	SAY	FR	76583	62289	70969	76613
1305	N	SAY	FR	76717	62355	71035	76788
1306	N	SAY	FR	76723	62361	71041	76794
1307	N	SAY	FR	76586	62292	70972	76616
1308	N	SAY	FR	76627	62298	70978	76622
1309	N	SAY	FR	76594	62300	70980	76624
1310	N	SAY	FR	76567	62283	71926	76577
1311	N	SAY	FR	76561	62277	71927	76571
1312	N	SAY	FR	76562	62278	71928	76572
1313	N	SAY	FR	76596	62302	70982	76626
1314	N	SAY	FR	76588	62294	70974	76618
1315	N	SAY	FR	76608	62314	70994	76638
1316	N	SAY	FR	76585	62291	70971	76615
1317	N	SAY	FR	76597	62303	70983	76592
1318	N	SAY	FR	76590	62296	70976	76620
1319	N	SAY	FR	76591	62297	70977	76621
1320	N	SAY	FR	76593	62299	70979	76623
1321	N	SAY	FR	76589	62295	70975	76619
1322	N	SAY	FR	76587	62293	70973	76617

Former numbers of converted buffet cars:

71926 (69315) |71927 (69330) |71928 (69331) |

Note: No new Lot Nos were issued for the above conversions.

CLASS 411/5

4 Cep

DMSO (A) – TBCK – TSOL – DMSO (B). Kent Coast Express Stock. Refurbished and renumbered from the 71/72xx series. Fitted with hopper ventilators, Inter-City 70 seats, fluorescent lighting and PA.

Electrical Equipment: 1957-type.
Bogies: One Mk. 4 (Mk 3B§) motor bogie (DMSO). Commonwealth trailer bogies.
Gangways: Throughout.
Traction Motors: Two EE507 of 185 kW.
Dimensions: 19.75 x 2.82 m.
Maximum Speed: 90 mph.

★ – 70345 is a TBFK with one compartment declassified. It is from the original refurbished unit (1500), has a different interior colour scheme and does not have hopper ventilators.

DMSO (A). Dia. EA263. –/64. 44.15 t.
TBCK. Dia. EJ361. 24/6 2T. 36.17 t.
TSOL. Dia. EH282. –/64 2T. 33.78 t.
DMSO (B). Dia. EA264. –/64. 43.54 t.

Lot numbers are as follows, all cars being built at Ashford/Eastleigh:

61229 – 61240. 30449 1958.	70241. 30640 1961.
61306 – 61409. 30454 1958 – 59.	70261 – 70302. 30455 1958 – 59.
61694 – 61811. 30619 1960 – 61.	70304 – 70355. 30456 1958 – 59.
61868 – 61869. 30638 1960 – 61.	70503 – 70551. 30620 1960 – 61.
61948 – 61959. 30708 1963.	70552 – 70610. 30621 1960 – 61.
70043 – 70044. 30639 1961.	70653 – 70657. 30709 1963.
70229 – 70234. 30450 1958.	70660 – 70664. 30710 1963.
70235 – 70239. 30451 1958.	

(T) – Used as secondary door locking test train.

1507	N	SBU	RE	61363	70332	70289	61362
1509	N	SBU	RE	61335	70318	70275	61334
1510	N	SBU	RE	61365	70333	70290	61364
1511	N	SBU	RE	61367	70334	70291	61366
1512	N	SBU	RE	61321	70311	70268	61320
1515	N	SBU	RE	61345	70323	70280	61344
1517	N	SBU	RE	61317	70309	70266	61316
1518	N	SBU	RE	61333	70317	70274	61332
1519	N	SBU	RE	61403	70352	70516	61402
1520	N	SBU	RE	61343	70327	70284	61380
1523	N	SBU	RE	61383	70342	70299	61382
1524	N	SBU	RE	61309	70305	70262	61308
1527	N	SBU	RE	61237	70239	70233	61238
1530	N	SBU	RE	61331	70316	70273	61330
1531	N	SBU	RE	61233	70237	70231	61234
1532	N	SBU	RE	61391	70346	71626	61390
1533	N	SBU	RE	61393	70347	71627	61385
1534	N	SBU	RE	61405	70353	71628	61404

1535		N	SBU	RE	61397	70349	71629	61396
1536		N	SBU	RE	61399	70350	71631	61398
1537		N	SBU	RE	61229	70235	70229	61230
1538		N	SBU	RE	61307	70304	70261	61306
1539		N	SBU	RE	61401	70351	71632	61400
1540		N	SBOL	Ludgershall	61355	70343	70300	61384
1541		N	SBU	RE	61409	70355	71633	61408
1543		N	SBU	RE	61323	70312	70297	61322
1544		N	SBU	RE	61315	70308	70265	61349
1545		N	SBOL	AF	61359	70330	70287	61358
1547	★	N	SBU	RE	61329	70345	70272	61328
1548		N	SBU	RE	61375	70338	70295	61374
1549		N	SBU	RE	61339	70320	70277	61338
1550		N	SBU	RE	61313	70307	70264	61312
1551		N	SBU	RE	61325	70313	70270	61324
1552		N	SBOL	Ludgershall	61373	70337	70294	61372
1553		N	SBU	RE	61728	70306	70263	61350
1554		N	SBU	RE	61369	70335	70292	61368
1555		N	SBU	RE	61311	70326	70283	61310
1556		N	SBU	RE	61371	70336	70293	61370
1557		N	SBU	RE	61337	70331	70288	61360
1559		N	SBU	RE	61377	70339	70296	61376
1560		N	SBU	RE	61387	70344	70301	61386
1561		N	SBU	RE	61231	70604	70230	61232
1562		N	SBU	RE	61407	70236	70241	61406
1563	§	N	SBU	RE	61740	70575	70526	61741
1564	§	N	SBU	RE	61788	70599	70550	61789
1565	§	N	SBU	RE	61762	70586	71711	61763
1566	§	N	SBU	RE	61722	70566	70517	61723
1568	§	N	SBOL	Ludgershall	61766	70588	70539	61767
1570	§	N	SBU	RE	61738	70574	70525	61739
1571	§	N	SBU	RE	61806	70608	71636	61807
1572	§	N	SBU	RE	61734	70572	70523	61735
1573	§	N	SBU	RE	61726	70568	70519	61727
1574	§	N	SBU	RE	61792	70601	71635	61793
1575	§	N	SBU	RE	61768	70589	70540	61769
1576	§	N	SBU	RE	61770	70590	70541	61771
1577	§	N	SBU	RE	61718	70564	70515	61719
1578	§	N	SBU	RE	61700	70555	70506	61701
1579	§	N	SBOL	AF	61772	70591	70281	61773
1580	§	N	SBU	RE	61756	70589	70534	61757
1581	§	N	SBU	RE	61784	70597	70548	61785
1582	§	N	SBU	RE	61748	70603	71630	61797
1583	§	N	SBOL	Ludgershall	61746	70578	70529	61747
1584	§	N	SBU	RE	61752	70581	70532	61753
1585	§	N	SBU	RE	61710	70560	70511	61711
1586	§	N	SBU	RE	61714	70562	70513	61715
1587	§	N	SBU	RE	61764	70587	71625	61765
1588	§	N	SBU	RE	61720	70044	70520	61721
1589	§	N	SBOL	Ludgershall	61742	70576	70527	61743
1590	§	N	SBU	RE	61696	70553	70504	61697

1591	§	N	SBU	RE		61790	70600	70551	61791
1592	§	N	SBU	RE		61778	70594	70545	61779
1593	§	N	SBU	RE		61730	70570	70521	61731
1594	§	N	SBU	RE		61754	70582	70533	61755
1595	§	N	SBU	RE		61704	70557	70508	61705
1596	§	N	SBU	RE		61716	70563	70514	61717
1597	§	N	SBU	RE		61708	70559	70510	61709
1598	§	N	SBU	RE		61780	70595	70546	61781
1599	§	N	SBU	RE		61706	70558	70509	61707
1600	§	N	SBU	RE		61724	70567	70518	61725
1601	§	N	SBOL	Ludgershall		61776	70593	70544	61777
1602	§	N	SBU	RE		61958	70565	70279	61959
1603	§	N	SBOL	AF		61351	70569	70298	61729
1604	§	N	SBOL	AF		61732	70571	70522	61733
1605	§	N	SBOL	ZG		61712	70561	70512	61713
1606	§	N	SBOL	AF		61694	70552	70503	61695
1607	§	N	SBU	RE		61698	70554	70505	61699
1609	§	N	SBU	RE		61744	70577	70528	61745
1610	§	N	SBU	RE		61750	70580	70531	61751
1611	§	N	SBU	RE		61758	70584	70537	61759
1612	§	N	SBU	RE		61794	70602	70535	61795
1613	§	N	SBU	RE		61760	70585	70536	61761
1614	§	N	SBU	RE		61702	70556	70507	61703
1615	§	N	SBU	RE		61956	70657	70664	61957
1616	§	N	SBU	RE		61950	70654	70543	61951
1617	§	N	SBU	RE		61800	70605	70661	61801
1618	§	N	SBU	RE		61868	70043	70663	61869
1619	§	N	SBU	RE		61952	70655	70662	61953
1620	§	N	SBXZ	EH (T)		61948	70653	70660	61949

Former numbers of converted hauled stock:

71625 (4381)	71628 (3844)	71631 (4436)	71635 (3990)
71626 (3916)	71629 (3992)	71632 (4063)	71636 (4065)
71627 (3921)	71630 (3988)	71633 (4072)	71711 (3994)

Note: No new lot numbers were issued for the above conversions.

CLASS 421/3   4 Cig (PHASE 1)

DTCsoL – MBSO – TSO – DTCsoL. Express stock. Fitted with electric parking brake. Facelifted with new trim, fluorescent lighting in saloons, PA.

Electrical Equipment: 1963-type.
Bogies: Two Mk. 4 motor bogies (MBSO). B5 (SR) bogies (trailer cars).
Gangways: Throughout.
Traction Motors: Four EE507 of 185 kW.
Dimensions: 19.75 x 2.82 m.
Maximum Speed: 90 mph.

DTCsoL(A). Dia. EE364. Lot No. 30741 York 1964 – 65. 18/36 2T. 35.5 t.
MBSO. Dia. ED260. Lot No. 30742 York 1964 – 65. –/56. 49 t.

70695 – 70730. TSO. Dia. EH275. Lot No. 30734 York 1964 – 65. –/72. 31.5 t.
71044 – 71097. TSO. Dia. EH275. Lot No. 30817 York 1970. –/72. 31.5 t.
71766 – 71770. TSO. Dia. EH275. Lot No. 30784 York 1964 – 65. –/72. 31.5 t.
DTCsoL(B). Dia. EE363. Lot No. 30740 York 1964 – 65. 24/28 2T.

* Units reformed from Class 422 to enable all Class 422 power cars to have Mk. 6 motor bogies. Phase 1 units with phase 2 TSOs.

1701	N	SCW	BI	76087	62028	70706	76033
1702	N	SCW	BI	76101	62042	70720	76047
1703	N	SCW	BI	76097	62038	70716	76043
1704	N	SCW	BI	76092	62033	70711	76038
1705	N	SCW	BI	76076	62017	70695	76022
1706	N	SCW	BI	76094	62035	70713	76040
1707	N	SCW	BI	76084	62025	70703	76030
1708	N	SCW	BI	76110	62051	70729	76056
1709	N	SCW	BI	76103	62044	70722	76049
1710	N	SCW	BI	76078	62019	70697	76024
1711	N	SCW	BI	76114	62055	71766	76060
1712	N	SCW	BI	76079	62020	70698	76025
1713	N	SCW	BI	76128	62069	71767	76074
1714	N	SCW	BI	76077	62018	70696	76023
1717	N	SCW	BI	76083	62024	70702	76029
1719	N	SCW	BI	76116	62057	70719	76062
1720	N	SCW	BI	76098	62039	71769	76044
1721	N	SCW	BI	76090	62031	70709	76036
1722	N	SCW	BI	76106	62047	70725	76052
1724	N	SCW	BI	76120	62061	71770	76066
1725	N	SCW	BI	76088	62029	70707	76034
1726	N	SCW	BI	76109	62050	70728	76055
1727	N	SCW	BI	76111	62052	70730	76057
1731	N	SCW	BI	76095	62036	70714	76041
1733 *	N	SCW	BI	76122	62063	71047	76068
1734 *	N	SCW	BI	76063	62054	71044	76059
1735 *	N	SCW	BI	76117	62058	71050	76051
1736 *	N	SCW	BI	76124	62065	71052	76070
1737 *	N	SCW	BI	76121	62062	71048	76067
1738 *	N	SCW	BI	76129	62064	71046	76069
1739 *	N	SCW	BI	76123	62070	71066	76075
1740 *	N	SCOL	Ludgershall	76126	62067	71097	76072
1741	N	SCOL	Ludgershall	76089	62030	70708	76035
1742	N	SCW	BI	76086	62027	70705	76032
1743 *	N	SCOL	Ludgershall	76118	62059	71065	76064
1744 *	N	SCOL	Ludgershall	76127	62068	71064	76073
1745	N	SCW	BI	76085	62026	70704	76031
1746	N	SCW	BI	76091	62032	70710	76037
1747	N	SCW	BI	76026	62034	70712	76093
1748 *	N	SCW	BI	76115	62056	71067	76061
1749 *	N	SCW	BI	76112	62053	71068	76058
1750	N	SCW	BI	76080	62021	70699	76039
1751	N	SCW	BI	76125	62066	71051	76071

1752		N	SCW	Bl	76119 62060 70717 76065
1753		N	SCW	Bl	76102 62043 70721 76048

Former numbers of converted buffet cars:

71766 (69303)	71768 (69317)	71769 (69305)	71770 (69308)
71767 (69314)			

Note: No new Lot Nos were issued for the above conversions.

CLASS 421/4   4 Cig (PHASE 2)

DTCsoL – MBSO – TSO – DTCsoL. Express stock. Facelifted with new trim, fluorescent lighting in saloons, PA. For details see Class 421/5.

1803	(7430)	N	SCW	Bl	76780 62418 71098 76851
1804	(7428)	N	SCW	Bl	76778 62416 71096 76849
1805	(7432)	N	SCW	Bl	76782 62420 71100 76853
1806	(7433)	N	SAU	RE	76783 62421 71101 76854
1807	(7434)	N	SAU	RE	76784 62422 71102 76855
1808	(7435)	N	SAU	RE	76785 62423 71103 76856
1809	(7436)	N	SAU	RE	76786 62424 71104 76857
1810	(7437)	N	SAU	RE	76787 62425 71105 76858
1811	(7431)	N	SAU	RE	76781 62419 71099 76852
1812	(7407)	N	SAU	RE	76757 62395 71075 76828
1813	(7438)	N	SAU	RE	76859 62430 71106 76860
1831	(1254)	N	SCW	Bl	76598 62304 70984 76628
1832	(1269)	N	SCW	Bl	76719 62357 71037 76790
1833	(1238)	N	SCW	Bl	76582 62288 70968 76612
1834	(1258)	N	SCW	Bl	76566 62282 70988 76576
1835	(1257)	N	SCW	Bl	76601 62307 70987 76631
1837	(1272)	N	SCW	Bl	76722 62360 71040 76793
1839	(1263)	N	SAU	RE	76607 62313 70993 76637
1840	(1274)	N	SAU	RE	76724 62362 71042 76795
1841	(1259)	N	SAU	RE	76603 62309 70989 76633
1842	(1275)	N	SAU	RE	76725 62363 71043 76796
1843	(1281)	N	SAU	RE	76731 62369 71049 76802
1845	(1255)	N	SCW	Bl	76599 62305 70985 76629
1846	(1287)	N	SCW	Bl	76737 62375 71055 76808
1847	(1256)	N	SCW	Bl	76600 62306 70986 76630
1848	(1261)	N	SCW	Bl	76605 62311 70991 76635
1850	(1268)	N	SCW	Bl	76718 62356 71036 76789
1851	(1271)	N	SCW	Bl	76721 62359 71039 76792
1853	(1262)	N	SCW	Bl	76606 62312 70992 76636
1854	(1288)	N	SCW	Bl	76738 62376 71056 76809
1855	(1270)	N	SCW	Bl	76720 62358 71038 76791
1856	(1289)	N	SCW	Bl	76739 62377 71057 76810
1857	(1266)	N	SCW	Bl	76610 62316 70996 76640
1858	(1260)	N	SCW	Bl	76604 62310 70990 76634
1859	(1277)	N	SCW	Bl	76727 62365 71045 76798
1860	(1202)	N	SCW	Bl	76752 62390 71070 76823
1861	(1285)	N	SCW	Bl	76735 62373 71053 76806
1862	(1286)	N	SCW	Bl	76736 62374 71054 76807

1863	(1292)	N	SCW	BI	76742	62380	71060	76813
1864	(1291)	N	SCW	BI	76741	62379	71059	76812
1865	(1295)	N	SCW	BI	76745	62383	71063	76639
1866	(1293)	N	SCW	BI	76743	62381	71061	76814
1867	(1294)	N	SCW	BI	76744	62382	71062	76815
1868	(1201)	N	SCW	BI	76751	62389	71069	76822
1869	(1203)	N	SCW	BI	76753	62391	71071	76804
1870	(1221)	N	SAU	RE	76108	62409	71089	76842
1871	(1206)	N	SAU	RE	76756	62394	71074	76827
1872	(1208)	N	SAU	RE	76771	62396	71076	76829
1873	(1209)	N	SAU	RE	76759	62397	71077	76830
1874	(1205)	N	SCW	BI	76755	62393	71073	76826
1876	(1211)	N	SAU	RE	76761	62399	71079	76832
1877	(1213)	N	SAU	RE	76763	62401	71081	76834
1878	(1218)	N	SAU	RE	76768	62406	71086	76839
1879	(1210)	N	SAU	RE	76760	62398	71078	76831
1880	(1220)	N	SAY	FR	76770	62408	71088	76841
1881	(1212)	N	SAY	FR	76762	62400	71080	76833
1882	(1215)	N	SAY	FR	76765	62403	71083	76836
1883	(1214)	N	SAY	FR	76764	62402	71082	76835
1884	(1217)	N	SAY	FR	76767	62405	71085	76838
1885	(1219)	N	SAY	FR	76769	62407	71087	76840
1886	(1222)	N	SAY	FR	76772	62410	71090	76843
1887	(1216)	N	SAY	FR	76766	62404	71084	76837
1888	(1223)	N	SAY	FR	76773	62411	71091	76844
1889	(1224)	N	SAY	FR	76774	62412	71092	76845
1890	(1225)	N	SAY	FR	76775	62413	71093	76846
1891	(1226)	N	SAY	FR	76776	62414	71094	76847
Spare		N	SCOL	ZG			70995	

CLASS 421/9   4 Cig (PHASE 1)

DTCsoL – MBSO – TSO – DTCsoL. Express stock. Fitted with electric parking brake. Facelifted with new trim, fluorescent lighting in saloons, PA. For details see Class 421/3. These units are fitted with ex-Class 432 Mark 6 motor bogies.

1903	N	SCW	BI	76081	62022	70700	76027
1904	N	SCW	BI	76107	62048	70726	76053
1905	N	SCW	BI	76099	62040	70718	76045
1906	N	SCW	BI	76105	62046	70724	76113
1907	N	SCW	BI	76104	62045	70723	76050
1908	N	SCW	BI	76096	62037	70715	76042

CLASS 422/0   8 Dig

New 8 car units with Class 432 motor bogies formed from one Class 421 and one Class 422 unit. For details see Classes 421 & 422.

2001	(1875)	N	SBW	BI	76779	62392	69333	76825
	(2262)				76754	62417	71072	76850
2002	(1716)	N	SBW	BI	76100	62041	71768	76046
	(2254)				76732	62370	69306	76803

2003	(1801)	N	SBW	BI	76777	62415	71095	76848
	(2255)				76740	62378	69310	76811
2004	(1715)	N	SBW	BI	76082	62023	70701	76028
	(2259)				76748	62386	69318	76819

CLASS 422/2   4 Big (PHASE 2)

DTCsoL (A) – MBSO – TSRB – DTCsoL (B). Express stock.

Diagram Numbers: EE369, ED264, EN260, EE369.
Electrical Equipment: 1963-type.
Bogies: Two Mk. 6 motor bogies (MBSO). B5 (SR) bogies (trailer cars).
Gangways: Throughout.
Traction Motors: Four EE507 of 185 kW.
Dimensions: 19.75 x 2.82 m.
Maximum Speed: 90 mph.

76563 – 76570. DTCsoL(A). Lot No. 30802 York 1970. 18/36 2T. 35.5 t.
76602. DTCsoL(A). Lot No. 30806 York 1970. 18/36 2T. 35.5 t.
62279 – 62286. MBSO. Lot No. 30804 York 1970. –/56. 49t.
62308. MBSO. Lot No. 30808 York 1970. –/56. 49t.
69332 – 69339. TSRB. Lot No. 30805 York 1970. –/40. 35 t.
76573 – 76580. DTCsoL(B). Lot No. 30803 York 1970. 24/28 2T. 35 t.
76632. DTCsoL(B). Lot No. 30807 York 1970. 24/28 2T. 35 t.

2203	N	SBW	BI	76563	62279	69332	76573
2204	N	SBW	BI	76564	62280	69336	76574
2205	N	SBW	BI	76565	62281	69339	76575
2206	N	SBW	BI	76602	62308	69338	76632
2208	N	SBW	BI	76568	62284	69334	76578
2209	N	SBW	BI	76569	62285	69335	76579
2210	N	SBW	BI	76570	62286	69337	76580

CLASS 422/3   Facelifted 4 Big (PHASE 2/1)

DTCsoL (A) – MBSO – TSRB – DTCsoL (B). Express stock. Units reformed from
Class 421 to ensure that all Class 422 power cars have Mk. 6 motor bogies.
Phase 2 units with phase 1 TSRBs. For other details see Class 421/5.

Diagram Numbers: EE369, ED264, EN260, EE369.
Electrical Equipment: 1963-type.
Bogies: Two Mk. 6 motor bogies (MBSO). B5 (SR) bogies (trailer cars).
Gangways: Throughout.
Traction Motors: Four EE507 of 185 kW.
Dimensions: 19.75 x 2.82 m.
Maximum Speed: 90 mph.

69301 – 69318. TSRB. Lot No. 30744 York 1966. 40S. 35 t.

2251	N	SBW	BI	76726	62364	69302	76797
2252	N	SBW	BI	76728	62366	69312	76799
2253	N	SBW	BI	76734	62372	69313	76805
2256	N	SBW	BI	76747	62385	69307	76818
2257	N	SBW	BI	76800	62367	69311	76729

2258,	N	SBW	Bl	76746 62384 69316 76817
2260	N	SBW	Bl	76749 62387 69304 76820
2261	N	SBW	Bl	76750 62388 69301 76821

CLASS 412   REFURBISHED 4 Bep

DMSO (A) – TBCK – TRB – DMSO (B). Kent Coast Express Stock. Refurbished and renumbered from the 70xx series. Fitted with hopper ventilators, Inter-City 70 seats, fluorescent lighting and PA.

Electrical Equipment: 1957-type.
Bogies: Mk 6 motor bogies and B5(SR) trailer bogies.
Gangways: Throughout.
Traction Motors: Four EE507 of 185 kW.
Dimensions: 19.75 x 2.82 m.
Maximum Speed: 90 mph.

DMSO (A). Dia. EA263. –/64. 44.15 t.
TBCK. Dia. EJ361. 24/6 2T. 36.17 t.
TRSB. Dia. EN261. –/24 1T + 9 longitudinal buffet chairs. 35.5 t.
DMSO (B). Dia. EA264. –/64. 43.54 t.
Lot numbers are as follows, all cars being built at Ashford/Eastleigh:

61736 – 61809. 30619 1960 – 61.	70354. 30456 1959.
61954 – 61955. 30708 1963.	70573 – 70609. 30621 1960 – 61.
69341 – 69347. 30622 1961.	70656. 30709 1963.

2301	N	SBY	FR	61804 70607 69341 61805
2302	N	SBY	FR	61774 70592 69342 61809
2303	N	SBY	FR	61954 70656 69347 61955
2304	N	SBY	FR	61736 70573 69344 61737
2305	N	SBY	FR	61798 70354 69345 61799
2306	N	SBY	FR	61808 70609 69346 61775
2307	N	SBY	FR	61802 70606 69343 61803

Former numbers of converted buffet cars:

| 69341 (69014) | 69343 (69018) | 69345 (69013) | 69347 (69015) |
| 69342 (69019) | 69344 (69012) | 69346 (69016) | |

Note: No new lot numbers were issued for the above conversions.

CLASS 442   WESSEX EXPRESS STOCK

DTFsoL – TSOL(A) – MBRSM – TSOL(B) – DTSOL. Express stock built for Waterloo – Bournemouth – Weymouth service. Now also used on certain Portsmouth Harbour services. Air conditioned (heat pump system). Power-operated sliding plug doors. PA. Can be hauled and heated by any BR ETH fitted locomotive. Multiple working with class 33/1 and 73 locomotives.

Electrical Equipment: 1986-type.
Bogies: Mk 6 motor bogies (MBRSM). T4 trailer bogies.
Gangways: Throughout.
Traction Motors: Four EE546 of 300 kW recovered from class 432.
Dimensions: 23.00 x 2.74 m (inner cars), 23.15 x 2.74 m (outer cars).

Maximum Speed: 100 mph.

DTFsoL. Dia. EE160. Lot No. 31030 Derby 1988 – 89. 50/ – 1T. (36 in six compartments and 14 2 + 2 in one saloon). Public Telephone. 39.06 t.
TSOL (A). Dia. EH288. Lot No. 31032 Derby 1988 – 89. – /80 2T. 35.26 t.
MBRSM. Dia. ED265. Lot No. 31034 Derby 1988 – 89. – /14. 54.10 t.
TSOL (B). Dia. EH289. Lot No. 31033 Derby 1988 – 89. – /76 2T + wheelchair space. + 2 tip-up seats. 35.36 t.
DTSOL. Dia. EE273. Lot No. 31031 Derby 1988 – 89. – /78 1T. 39.06 t.

2401	NW	SAY	BM	77382	71818	62937	71842	77406
2402	NW	SAY	BM	77383	71819	62938	71843	77407
2403	NW	SAY	BM	77384	71820	62941	71844	77408
2404	NW	SAY	BM	77385	71821	62939	71845	77409
2405	NW	SAY	BM	77386	71822	62944	71846	77410
2406	NW	SAY	BM	77389	71823	62942	71847	77411
2407	NW	SAY	BM	77388	71824	62943	71848	77412
2408	NW	SAY	BM	77387	71825	62945	71849	77413
2409	NW	SAY	BM	77390	71826	62946	71850	77414
2410	NW	SAY	BM	77391	71827	62948	71851	77415
2411	NW	SAY	BM	77392	71828	62940	71858	77422
2412	NW	SAY	BM	77393	71829	62947	71853	77417
2413	NW	SAY	BM	77394	71830	62949	71854	77418
2414	NW	SAY	BM	77395	71831	62950	71855	77419
2415	NW	SAY	BM	77396	71832	62951	71856	77420
2416	NW	SAY	BM	77397	71833	62952	71857	77421
2417	NW	SAY	BM	77398	71834	62953	71852	77416
2418	NW	SAY	BM	77399	71835	62954	71859	77423
2419	NW	SAY	BM	77400	71836	62955	71860	77424
2420	NW	SAY	BM	77401	71837	62956	71861	77425
2421	NW	SAY	BM	77402	71838	62957	71862	77426
2422	NW	SAY	BM	77403	71839	62958	71863	77427
2423	NW	SAY	BM	77404	71840	62959	71864	77428
2424	NW	SAY	BM	77405	71841	62960	71865	77429

Names:

62937 BEAULIEU	62946 BOURNEMOUTH ORCHESTRAS
62938 COUNTY OF HAMPSHIRE	62948 MERIDIAN TONIGHT
62939 BOROUGH OF WOKING	62951 MARY ROSE
62941 THE NEW FOREST	62954 WESSEX CANCER TRUST
62942 VICTORY	62955 BBC SOUTH TODAY
62943 THOMAS HARDY	62956 CITY OF SOUTHAMPTON
62944 CITY OF PORTSMOUTH	62958 OPERATION OVERLORD
62945 COUNTY OF DORSET	62959 COUNTY OF SURREY

CLASS 423/0   4 Vep

DTCsoL – MBSO – TSO – DTCsoL. Outer suburban stock. Facelifted with fluorescent lighting, PA.

Electrical Equipment: 1963-type.
Bogies: Two Mk. 4 motor bogies (MBSO). B5 (SR) bogies (trailer cars).

Gangways: Throughout.
Traction Motors: Four EE507 of 185 kW.
Dimensions: 19.75 x 2.82 m.
Maximum Speed: 90 mph.

62121 – 40. MBSO. Dia. ED266. Lot No. 30760 Derby 1967. –/76. 49 t.
62182 – 216. MBSO. Dia. ED266. Lot No. 30773 York 1967 – 68. –/76. 49 t.
62217 – 66. MBSO. Dia. ED266. Lot No. 30794 York 1968 – 69. –/76. 49 t.
62267 – 76. MBSO. Dia. ED266. Lot No. 30800 York 1970. –/76. 49 t.
62317 – 54. MBSO. Dia. ED266. Lot No. 30813 York 1970 – 73. –/76. 49 t.
62435 – 75. MBSO. Dia. ED266. Lot No. 30851 York 1973 – 74. –/76. 49 t.
70781 – 800. TSO. Dia. EH291. Lot No. 30759 Derby 1967. –/98. 31.5 t.
70872 – 906. TSO. Dia. EH291. Lot No. 30772 York 1967 – 68. –/98. 31.5 t.
70907 – 56. TSO. Dia. EH291. Lot No. 30793 York 1968 – 69. –/98. 31.5 t.
70957 – 66. TSO. Dia. EH291. Lot No. 30801 York 1970. –/98. 31.5 t.
70997 – 71034. TSO. Dia. EH291. Lot No. 30812 York 1970 – 73. –/98. 31.5 t.
71115 – 55. TSO. Dia. EH291. Lot No. 30852 York 1973 – 74. –/98. 31.5 t.
76230 – 69. DTCsoL. Dia. EE373. Lot No. 30758 York 1967. 18/46 1T. 35 t.
76275. DTSO (Class 438). Dia. EE266. Lot No. 30764 York 1966. –/64. 32 t. (Converted from hauled TSO 3929).
76333 – 402. DTCsoL. Dia. EE373. Lot No. 30771 York 1967 – 68. 18/46 1T. 35 t.
76441 – 540. DTCsoL. Dia. EE373. Lot No. 30792 York 1968 – 69. 18/46 1T. 35 t.
76541 – 60. DTCsoL. Dia. EE373. Lot No. 30799 York 1970. 18/46 1T. 35 t.
76641 – 716. DTCsoL. Dia. EE373. Lot No. 30811 York 1970 – 73. 18/46 1T. 35 t.
76861 – 942. DTCsoL. Dia. EE373. Lot No. 30853 York 1973 – 74. 18/46 1T. 35 t.

Note: Porterbrook units allocated to South Eastern Trains have been renumbered in the 3800 series to differentiate them from the Angel Trains units operating on the same services.

3401	(3001)	**N**	SAY	WD	76230	62276	70781	76231
3402	(3002)	**N**	SAY	WD	76233	62123	70782	76232
3403	(3003)	**N**	SAY	WD	76234	62254	70783	76235
3404	(3441)	**N**	SAY	WD	76378	62261	70894	76236
3405	(3005)	**N**	SAY	WD	76239	62271	70785	76238
3406	(3006)	**N**	SAY	WD	76241	62130	70786	76240
3407	(3007)	**N**	SAY	WD	76243	62348	70787	76242
3408	(3008)	**N**	SAY	WD	76244	62435	70788	76245
3409	(3009)	**N**	SAY	WD	76246	62239	70789	76247
3410	(3010)	**N**	SAY	WD	76369	62442	70790	76249
3411	(3011)	**N**	SAY	WD	76251	62342	70791	76250
3412	(3012)	**N**	SCU	RE	76252	62340	70792	76253
3413	(3013)	**N**	SAY	WD	76255	62441	70793	76254
3414	(3014)	**N**	SAY	WD	76257	62446	70794	76248
3415	(3015)	**N**	SAY	WD	76258	62462	70795	76259
3416	(3016)	**N**	SCU	RE	76261	62451	70796	76260
3417	(3017)	**N**	SAY	WD	76262	62236	70797	76263
3418	(3018)	**N**	SAY	WD	76265	62133	70875	76264

3419	(3019)	N	SAY	WD	76267	62354	70799	76266
3420	(3020)	N	SAY	WD	76269	62349	70800	76268
3421	(3168)	N	SCU	RE	76889	62449	71129	76890
3422	(3040)	N	SCU	RE	76372	62201	70891	76371
3423	(3061)	N	SCU	RE	76452	62222	70912	76451
3424	(3031)	N	SCU	RE	76354	62185	70882	76353
3425	(3023)	N	SAY	WD	76338	62192	70874	76358
3426	(3047)	N	SAY	WD	76386	62208	70898	76385
3427	(3041)	N	SAY	WD	76374	62184	70892	76373
3428	(3062)	N	SAY	WD	76454	62223	70913	76453
3429	(3021)	N	SAY	WD	76334	62202	70872	76333
3430	(3028)	N	SAY	WD	76348	62189	70879	76347
3431	(3064)	N	SAY	WD	76458	62182	70915	76457
3432	(3054)	N	SAY	WD	76400	62225	70905	76399
3433	(3057)	N	SAY	WD	76444	62215	70908	76443
3434	(3066)	N	SAY	WD	76462	62218	70917	76461
3435	(3025)	N	SBW	BI	76342	62228	70876	76341
3436	(3029)	N	SBW	BI	76350	62190	70880	76349
3437	(3027)	N	SBW	BI	76346	62186	70878	76345
3438	(3100)	N	SBW	BI	76530	62262	70951	76529
3439	(3055)	N	SBW	BI	76402	62227	70906	76401
3442	(3081)	N	SBW	BI	76492	62216	70932	76491
3445	(3060)	N	SCU	RE	76450	62242	70911	76449
3446	(3101)	N	SCU	RE	76532	62243	70952	76531
3447	(3044)	N	SCU	RE	76380	62199	70895	76379
3448	(3042)	N	SCU	RE	76376	62221	70886	76375
3449	(3022)	N	SCU	RE	76336	62205	70873	76335
3450	(3060)	N	SCU	RE	76460	62204	70916	76459
3451	(3079)	N	SCU	RE	76488	62240	70930	76487
3452		N	SCU	RE	76340	62183	71021	76690
3453	(3045)	N	SCU	RE	76382	62226	70896	76381
3454		N	SCU	RE	76390	62200	70798	76389
3455	(3048)	N	SAY	WD	76388	62206	70899	76387
3456	(3063)	N	SAY	WD	76456	62210	70914	76455
3457	(3050)	N	SAY	WD	76392	62197	70901	76391
3458	(3051)	N	SAY	WD	76394	62209	70902	76393
3459	(3052)	N	SAY	WD	76396	62224	70903	76395
3462	(3103)	N	SBW	BI	76536	62213	70954	76535
3463	(3053)	N	SBW	BI	76398	62266	70904	76397
3464	(3056)	N	SBW	BI	76442	62265	70907	76441
3466	(3067)	N	SAY	WD	76464	62214	70918	76463
3467	(3058)	N	SAY	WD	76446	62217	70909	76445
3468	(3059)	N	SAY	WD	76448	62267	70910	76447
3469	(3108)	N	SAY	WD	76546	62219	70959	76545
3470	(3083)	N	SAY	WD	76496	62220	70934	76495
3471	(3084)	N	SCU	RE	76498	62269	70935	76497
3472	(3085)	N	SCU	RE	76500	62244	70936	76499
3473	(3086)	N	SCU	RE	76502	62245	70937	76339
3474	(3087)	N	SCU	RE	76504	62246	70938	76503
3475	(3111)	N	SCU	RE	76552	62270	70962	76551
3476	(3109)	N	SBW	BI	76548	62247	70960	76547

3478	(3122)	N	SBW	BI	76653	62125	71003	76654
3479	(3123)	N	SAY	WD	76655	62272	71004	76656
3480	(3072)	N	SAY	WD	76474	62323	70923	76473
3481	(3119)	N	SAY	WD	76648	62324	70900	76647
3482	(3124)	N	SAY	WD	76657	62320	71005	76658
3483	(3126)	N	SAY	WD	76661	62233	71007	76662
3484	(3073)	N	SAY	WD	76476	62325	70924	76475
3485	(3089)	N	SAY	WD	76508	62327	70940	76507
3486	(3074)	N	SAY	WD	76478	62234	70925	76477
3487	(3090)	N	SCU	RE	76645	62250	70941	76509
3488	(3127)	N	SAY	WD	76663	62235	71008	76664
3489	(3128)	N	SAY	WD	76665	62251	71009	76666
3490	(3143)	N	SAY	WD	76695	62328	71024	76696
3491	(3076)	N	SCU	RE	76337	62436	70927	76481
3492	(3129)	N	SCU	RE	76667	62344	71010	76668
3493	(3130)	N	SCU	RE	76669	62237	71011	76670
3494	(3133)	N	SCU	RE	76675	62330	71014	76676
3495	(3145)	N	SCU	RE	76699	62331	71026	76700
3496	(3132)	N	SCU	RE	76673	62334	71013	76674
3497	(3131)	N	SCU	RE	76671	62346	71012	76672
3498	(3146)	N	SCU	RE	76701	62333	71027	76702
3499	(3174)	N	SCU	RE	76901	62347	71135	76902
3500	(3070)	N	SCU	RE	76470	62455	70921	76469
3501	(3091)	N	SBW	BI	76512	62332	70942	76511
3502	(3150)	N	SBW	BI	76709	62252	71031	76710
3503	(3136)	N	SBW	BI	76681	62231	71017	76682
3504	(3151)	N	SBW	BI	76711	62351	71032	76712
3505	(3071)	N	SBW	BI	76472	62352	70922	76471
3506	(3112)	N	SBW	BI	76554	62317	70963	76553
3507	(3114)	N	SBW	BI	76558	62232	70965	76557
3508	(3117)	N	SAY	WD	76643	62273	70998	76644
3509	(3115)	N	SAY	WD	76560	62275	70966	76559
3510	(3116)	N	SAY	WD	76641	62274	70997	76642
3511	(3118)	N	SCU	RE	76893	62135	70999	76646
3512	(3135)	N	SBW	BI	76679	62337	71016	76680
3513	(3141)	N	SBW	BI	76691	62336	71022	76692
3514	(3137)	N	SBW	BI	76683	62136	71018	76684
3515	(3107)	N	SBW	BI	76544	62319	70958	76543
3516	(3142)	N	SAY	WD	76693	62268	71023	76694
3517	(3138)	N	SBW	BI	76685	62338	71019	76686
3518	(3140)	N	SBW	BI	76689	62343	70887	76363
3519	(3113)	N	SAY	WD	76556	62274	70964	76555
3520	(3144)	N	SAY	WD	76697	62131	71025	76698
3521	(3077)	N	SCU	RE	76484	62345	70928	76483
3522	(3148)	N	SBW	BI	76705	62341	71029	76706
3523	(3121)	N	SAY	WD	76651	62139	71002	76652
3524	(3068)	N	SAY	WD	76466	62322	70919	76370
3526	(3097)	N	SBW	BI	76524	62255	70948	76523
3527	(3095)	N	SBW	BI	76520	62326	70946	76519
3528	(3094)	N	SBW	BI	76518	62258	70945	76517
3529	(3125)	N	SAY	WD	76659	62257	71006	76660

3530	(3069)	N	SAY	WD	76468	62256	70920	76467
3531	(3120)	N	SAY	WD	76649	62230	71001	76650
3532	(3099)	N	SBW	BI	76528	62321	70950	76527
3533	(3098)	N	SBW	BI	76364	62260	70949	76525
3534	(3088)	N	SBW	BI	76506	62259	70939	76505
3535	(3134)	N	SBW	BI	76677	62335	71015	76678
3536	(3046)	N	SAY	WD	76384	62207	70897	76383
3537	(3092)	N	SBW	BI	76514	62249	70943	76513
3538	(3093)	N	SBW	BI	76516	62253	70944	76515
3539	(3154)	N	SAY	WD	76861	62122	71115	76862
3540	(3155)	N	SAY	WD	76863	62128	71116	76864
3541	(3147)	N	SBW	BI	76703	62238	71028	76704
3542	(3075)	N	SAY	WD	76480	62127	70926	76479
3543	(3173)	N	SCU	RE	76899	62137	71134	76900
3544	(3170)	N	SCU	RE	76892	62434	71131	76894
3545	(3161)	N	SCU	RE	76875	62121	71122	76876
3546	(3139)	N	SBW	BI	76687	62339	71020	76688
3547	(3171)	N	SCU	RE	76895	62126	71132	76896
3548	(3175)	N	SCU	RE	76903	62452	71136	76904
3549	(3149)	N	SBW	BI	76707	62132	71030	76708
3550	(3080)	N	SBW	BI	76490	62350	70931	76489
3551	(3152)	N	SBW	BI	76465	62456	71033	76714
3552	(3153)	N	SAY	WD	76715	62353	71034	76716
3553	(3180)	N	SCU	RE	76913	62241	71141	76914
3554	(3176)	N	SCU	RE	76905	62461	71137	76906
3555	(3156)	N	SAY	WD	76865	62140	71117	76866
3556	(3166)	N	SCU	RE	76885	62457	71127	76886
3557	(3158)	N	SAY	WD	76869	62437	71119	76870
3558	(3030)	N	SAY	WD	76352	62447	70881	76351
3559	(3078)	N	SAY	WD	76486	62239	70929	76485
3560	(3172)	N	SCU	RE	76897	62191	71133	76898
3561	(3157)	N	SAY	WD	76867	62453	71118	76868
3562	(3177)	N	SCU	RE	76907	62129	71138	76908
3563	(3160)	N	SAY	WD	76873	62438	71121	76874
3564	(3165)	N	SCU	RE	76883	62458	71126	76884
3565	(3162)	N	SCU	RE	76877	62134	71123	76878
3566	(3181)	N	SCU	RE	76915	62443	71142	76916
3567	(3159)	N	SAY	WD	76871	62138	71120	76872
3568	(3167)	N	SCU	RE	76887	62440	71128	76888
3569	(3026)	N	SAY	WD	76344	62448	70877	76343
3570	(3178)	N	SCU	RE	76909	62187	71139	76910
3571	(3187)	N	SCU	RE	76927	62463	71148	76928
3572	(3163)	N	SCU	RE	76879	62468	71124	76880
3573	(3183)	N	SCU	RE	76919	62444	71144	76920
3574	(3188)	N	SCU	RE	76929	62464	71149	76930
3575	(3189)	N	SCU	RE	76931	62469	71150	76932
3576	(3035)	N	SAY	WD	76362	62196	70890	76361
3577	(3190)	N	SCU	RE	76933	62470	71151	76934
3578	(3032)	N	SAY	WD	76356	62193	70883	76355
3579	(3191)	N	SCU	RE	76935	62471	71152	76936
3580	(3034)	N	SAY	WD	76360	62195	70885	76359

3581	(3037)	N	SAY	WD	76366 62198 70888 76365
3582	(3169)	N	SCU	RE	76891 62472 71130 76275
3583	(3192)	N	SCU	RE	76937 62450 71153 76938
3584	(3164)	N	SCU	RE	76881 62473 71125 76882
3585	(3193)	N	SCU	RE	76939 62445 71154 76940
3586	(3184)	N	SCU	RE	76921 62474 71145 76922
3587	(3186)	N	SCU	RE	76925 62465 71147 76926
3588	(3185)	N	SCU	RE	76923 62467 71146 76924
3589	(3179)	N	SCU	RE	76911 62466 71140 76912
3590	(3194)	N	SCU	RE	76941 62460 71155 76942
3591	(3182)	N	SCU	RE	76917 62475 71143 76918
3801	(3525)	N	SBU	RE	76522 62229 70947 76521
3802	(3440)	N	SBU	RE	76534 62188 70953 76533
3803	(3443)	N	SBU	RE	76494 62263 70933 76493
3804	(3444)	N	SBU	RE	76368 62204 70889 76367
3805	(3460)	N	SBU	RE	76540 62211 70956 76539
3806	(3461)	N	SBU	RE	76538 62212 70955 76537
3807	(3465)	N	SBU	RE	76542 62264 70957 76541
3808	(3477)	N	SBU	RE	76550 62248 70961 76549
Spare		N	SBOL	ZG	62459
Spare			SCOL	ZG	76510

CLASS 455/7

DTSO − MSO − TSO − DTSO. Sliding doors. Disc brakes. Fluorescent lighting.
PA. Second series with TSOs originally in Class 508. Pressure ventilation.

Bogies: BT13 (DTSO), BP27 (MSO), BX1 (TSO).
Gangways: Through gangwayed.
Traction Motors: Four EE507 of 185 kW.
Dimensions: 19.83 x 2.82 m. (outer cars), 19.92 x 2.82 m (inner cars).
Maximum Speed: 75 mph.

DTSO. Dia. EE218. Lot No. 30976 York 1984 − 85. −/74. 29.5 t.
MSO. Dia. EC203. Lot No. 30975 York 1984 − 85. −/84. 45 t.
TSO. Dia. EH219. Lot No. 30944 York 1977 − 80. −/86. 25.48 t.

Note: 5750 was renumberd from 5743 as a gimmick (BS 5750 is the quality
assurance standard).

5701	N	SBY	WD	77727 62783 71545 77728
5702	N	SBY	WD	77729 62784 71547 77730
5703	N	SBY	WD	77731 62785 71540 77732
5704	N	SBY	WD	77733 62786 71548 77734
5705	N	SBY	WD	77735 62787 71565 77736
5706	N	SBY	WD	77737 62788 71534 77738
5707	N	SBY	WD	77739 62789 71536 77740
5708	N	SBY	WD	77741 62790 71560 77742
5709	N	SBY	WD	77743 62791 71532 77744
5710	N	SBY	WD	77745 62792 71566 77746
5711	N	SBY	WD	77747 62793 71542 77748
5712	N	SBY	WD	77749 62794 71546 77750
5713	N	SBY	WD	77751 62795 71567 77752

5714	N	SBY	WD	77753 62796 71539 77754
5715	N	SBY	WD	77755 62797 71535 77756
5716	N	SBY	WD	77757 62798 71564 77758
5717	N	SBY	WD	77759 62799 71528 77760
5718	N	SBY	WD	77761 62800 71557 77762
5719	N	SBY	WD	77763 62801 71558 77764
5720	N	SBY	WD	77765 62802 71568 77766
5721	N	SBY	WD	77767 62803 71553 77768
5722	N	SBY	WD	77769 62804 71533 77770
5723	N	SBY	WD	77771 62805 71526 77772
5724	N	SBY	WD	77773 62806 71561 77774
5725	N	SBY	WD	77775 62807 71541 77776
5726	N	SBY	WD	77777 62808 71556 77778
5727	N	SBY	WD	77779 62809 71562 77780
5728	N	SBY	WD	77781 62810 71527 77782
5729	N	SBY	WD	77783 62811 71550 77784
5730	N	SBY	WD	77785 62812 71551 77786
5731	N	SBY	WD	77787 62813 71555 77788
5732	N	SBY	WD	77789 62814 71552 77790
5733	N	SBY	WD	77791 62815 71549 77792
5734	N	SBY	WD	77793 62816 71531 77794
5735	N	SBY	WD	77795 62817 71563 77796
5736	N	SBY	WD	77797 62818 71554 77798
5737	N	SBY	WD	77799 62819 71544 77800
5738	N	SBY	WD	77801 62820 71529 77802
5739	N	SBY	WD	77803 62821 71537 77804
5740	N	SBY	WD	77805 62822 71530 77806
5741	N	SBY	WD	77807 62823 71559 77808
5742	N	SBY	WD	77809 62824 71543 77810
5750	N	SBY	WD	77811 62825 71538 77812

Names:

5735   The Royal Borough of Kingston
5750   Wimbledon Train Care

CLASS 455/8

DTSO − MSO − TSO − DTSO. Sliding doors. Disc brakes. Fluorescent lighting. PA. First series. Pressure ventilation.

Bogies: BP20 (MSO), BT13 (trailer cars).
Gangways: Through gangwayed.
Traction Motors: Four EE507 of 185 kW.
Dimensions: 19.83 x 2.82 m. (outer cars), 19.92 x 2.82 m (inner cars).
Maximum Speed: 75 mph.

DTSO. Dia. EE218. Lot No. 30972 York 1982 − 84. −/74. 29.5 t.
MSO. Dia. EC203. Lot No. 30973 York 1982 − 84. −/84. 45.6 t.
TSO. Dia. EH221. Lot No. 30974 York 1982 − 84. −/84. 27.1 t.

5801	N	SAW	SU	77579	62709	71637	77580
5802	N	SAW	SU	77581	62710	71664	77582
5803	N	SAW	SU	77583	62711	71639	77584
5804	N	SAW	SU	77585	62712	71640	77586
5805	N	SAW	SU	77587	62713	71641	77588
5806	N	SAW	SU	77589	62714	71642	77590
5807	N	SAW	SU	77591	62715	71643	77592
5808	N	SAW	SU	77593	62716	71644	77594
5809	N	SAW	SU	77595	62717	71645	77596
5810	N	SAW	SU	77597	62718	71646	77598
5811	N	SAW	SU	77599	62719	71647	77600
5812	N	SAW	SU	77601	62720	71648	77602
5813	N	SAW	SU	77603	62721	71649	77604
5814	N	SAW	SU	77605	62722	71650	77606
5815	N	SAW	SU	77607	62723	71651	77608
5816	N	SAW	SU	77609	62724	71652	77633
5817	N	SAW	SU	77611	62725	71653	77612
5818	N	SAW	SU	77613	62726	71654	77614
5819	N	SAW	SU	77615	62727	71655	77616
5820	N	SAW	SU	77617	62728	71656	77618
5821	N	SAW	SU	77619	62729	71657	77620
5822	N	SAW	SU	77621	62730	71658	77622
5823	N	SAW	SU	77623	62731	71659	77624
5824	N	SAW	SU	77637	62732	71660	77626
5825	N	SAW	SU	77627	62733	71661	77628
5826	N	SAW	SU	77629	62734	71662	77630
5827	N	SAW	SU	77610	62735	71663	77632
5828	N	SAW	SU	77634	62736	71638	77631
5829	N	SAW	SU	77635	62737	71665	77636
5830	N	SAW	SU	77625	62743	71666	77638
5831	N	SAW	SU	77639	62739	71667	77640
5832	N	SAW	SU	77641	62740	71668	77642
5833	N	SAW	SU	77643	62741	71669	77644
5834	N	SAW	SU	77645	62742	71670	77646
5835	N	SAW	SU	77647	62738	71671	77648
5836	N	SAW	SU	77649	62744	71672	77650
5837	N	SAW	SU	77651	62745	71673	77652
5838	N	SAW	SU	77653	62746	71674	77654
5839	N	SAW	SU	77655	62747	71675	77656
5840	N	SAW	SU	77657	62748	71676	77658
5841	N	SAW	SU	77659	62749	71677	77660
5842	N	SAW	SU	77661	62750	71678	77662
5843	N	SAW	SU	77663	62751	71679	77664
5844	N	SAW	SU	77665	62752	71680	77666
5845	N	SAW	SU	77667	62753	71681	77668
5846	N	SAW	SU	77669	62754	71682	77670
5847	N	SBY	WD	77671	62755	71683	77672
5848	N	SBY	WD	77673	62756	71684	77674
5849	N	SBY	WD	77675	62757	71685	77676
5850	N	SBY	WD	77677	62758	71686	77678
5851	N	SBY	WD	77679	62759	71687	77680

5852	N	SBY	WD	77681 62760 71688 77682
5853	N	SBY	WD	77683 62761 71689 77684
5854	N	SBY	WD	77685 62762 71690 77686
5855	N	SBY	WD	77687 62763 71691 77688
5856	N	SBY	WD	77689 62764 71692 77690
5857	N	SBY	WD	77691 62765 71693 77692
5858	N	SBY	WD	77693 62766 71694 77694
5859	N	SBY	WD	77695 62767 71695 77696
5860	N	SBY	WD	77697 62768 71696 77698
5861	N	SBY	WD	77699 62769 71697 77700
5862	N	SBY	WD	77701 62770 71698 77702
5863	N	SBY	WD	77703 62771 71699 77704
5864	N	SBY	WD	77705 62772 71700 77706
5865	N	SBY	WD	77707 62773 71701 77708
5866	N	SBY	WD	77709 62774 71702 77710
5867	N	SBY	WD	77711 62775 71703 77712
5868	N	SBY	WD	77713 62776 71704 77714
5869	N	SBY	WD	77715 62777 71705 77716
5870	N	SBY	WD	77717 62778 71706 77718
5871	N	SBY	WD	77719 62779 71707 77720
5872	N	SBY	WD	77721 62780 71708 77722
5873	N	SBY	WD	77723 62781 71709 77724
5874	N	SBY	WD	77725 62782 71710 77726

CLASS 455/9

DTSO – MSO – TSO – DTSO. Sliding doors. Disc brakes. Fluorescent lighting.
PA. Third series. Convection heating.

Bogies: BP20 (MSO), BT13 (trailer cars).
Gangways: Through gangwayed.
Traction Motors: Four EE507 of 185 kW.
Dimensions: 19.83 x 2.82 m. (outer cars), 19.92 x 2.82 m (inner cars).
Maximum Speed: 75 mph.

DTSO. Dia. EE226. Lot No. 30991 York 1985. –/74. 29.5 t.
MSO. Dia. EC206. Lot No. 30992 York 1985. –/84. 45.6 t.
TSO. Dia. EH224. Lot No. 30993 York 1985. –/84. 27.1 t.
TSO n. Dia. EH224. Lot No. 30932 Derby 1981. –/84. 27.1 t.

* Chopper control.
§ Tread brakes.
c "Crossrail" interiors.
n Prototype vehicle converted from a Class 210 DMU.

5901		N	SBY	WD	77813 62826 71714 77814
5902		N	SBY	WD	77815 62827 71715 77816
5903		N	SBY	WD	77817 62828 71716 77818
5904		N	SBY	WD	77819 62829 71717 77820
5905	c	N	SBY	WD	77821 62830 71731 77822
5906		N	SBY	WD	77823 62831 71719 77824
5907		N	SBY	WD	77825 62832 71720 77826
5908		N	SBY	WD	77827 62833 71721 77828

5909		N	SBY	WD	77829 62834 71722 77830
5910		N	SBY	WD	77831 62835 71723 77832
5911		N	SBY	WD	77833 62836 71724 77834
5912	*	N	SBY	WD	77835 62837 71725 77836
5913	§	N	SBY	WD	77837 62838 71726 77838
5914	§	N	SBY	WD	77839 62839 71727 77840
5915	§	N	SBY	WD	77841 62840 71728 77842
5916	*	N	SBY	WD	77843 62841 71729 77844
5917	*	N	SBY	WD	77845 62842 71730 77846
5918	*c	N	SBY	WD	77847 62843 71732 77848
5919	*	N	SBY	WD	77849 62844 71718 77850
5920	*	N	SBY	WD	77851 62845 71733 77852
Spare n		N	SBY	WD	67400

CLASS 488   VICTORIA – GATWICK TRAILER SETS

TFOLH – TSOL (Class 488/3 only) – TSOLH. Converted 1983 – 84 from loco-hauled Mk. 2F FOs and TSOs for Victoria – Gatwick service. Express stock. Air conditioned. Fluorescent lighting. PA. Conversion consisted of a modified seating layout and the removal of one toilet to provide additional luggage space.

Bogies: B4.
Gangways: Throughout.
Dimensions: 20.12 x 2.82 m.
Maximum Speed: 90 mph.

72500 – 72509. TFOLH. Dia. EP101. Lot No. 30859 Derby 1973 – 74. 41/–
1T. 35 t.
72602 – 14/6 – 8/20 – 44/46/7. TSOLH. Dia. EP201. Lot No. 30860 Derby
1973 – 74. –/48 1T. 35 t.
72615/19/45. TSOLH. Dia. EP201. Lot No. 30846 Derby 1973. –/48 1T. 35 t.
72701 – 72718. TSOL. Dia. EH285. Lot No. 30860 Derby 1973 – 74. –/48
1T. 35 t.

CLASS 488/2. Note: TFOLH fitted with public telephone.

8201	GE	SBV	SL	72500 (3413)	72638 (6068)
8202	GE	SBV	SL	72501 (3382)	72617 (6086)
8203	GE	SBV	SL	72502 (3321)	72640 (6097)
8204	GE	SBV	SL	72503 (3407)	72641 (6079)
8205	GE	SBV	SL	72504 (3406)	72628 (6058)
8206	GE	SBV	SL	72505 (3415)	72629 (6048)
8207	GE	SBV	SL	72506 (3335)	72642 (6076)
8208	GE	SBV	SL	72507 (3412)	72643 (6040)
8209	GE	SBV	SL	72508 (3409)	72644 (6039)
8210	GE	SBV	SL	72509 (3398)	72635 (6128)

CLASS 488/3. TSOLH – TSOL – TSOLH.

8302	GE	SBV	SL	72602 (6130)	72701 (6088)	72604 (6087)
8303	GE	SBV	SL	72603 (6093)	72702 (6099)	72608 (6077)
8304	GE	SBV	SL	72606 (6084)	72703 (6075)	72611 (6083)
8305	GE	SBV	SL	72605 (6082)	72704 (6132)	72609 (6080)

8306	GE	SBV	SL	72607	(6020)	72705	(6032)	72610	(6074)
8307	GE	SBV	SL	72612	(6156)	72706	(6143)	72613	(6126)
8308	GE	SBV	SL	72614	(6090)	72707	(6127)	72615	(5938)
8309	GE	SBV	SL	72616	(6007)	72708	(6095)	72639	(6070)
8310	GE	SBV	SL	72618	(6044)	72709	(5982)	72619	(5909)
8311	GE	SBV	SL	72620	(6140)	72710	(6003)	72621	(6108)
8312	GE	SBV	SL	72622	(6004)	72711	(6109)	72623	(6118)
8313	GE	SBV	SL	72624	(5972)	72712	(6091)	72625	(6085)
8314	GE	SBV	SL	72626	(6017)	72713	(6023)	72627	(5974)
8315	GE	SBV	SL	72636	(6071)	72714	(6092)	72645	(5942)
8316	GE	SBV	SL	72630	(6094)	72715	(6019)	72631	(6096)
8317	GE	SBV	SL	72632	(6072)	72716	(6114)	72633	(6129)
8318	GE	SBV	SL	72634	(6089)	72717	(6069)	72637	(6098)
8319	GE	SBV	SL	72646	(6078)	72718	(5979)	72647	(6081)

CLASS 489   VICTORIA – GATWICK GLV

Converted 1983 – 84 from class 414/3 (2 Hap) DMBSOs to work with class 488.

Bogies: Mk 4.
Gangways: Gangwayed at inner end only.
Traction Motors: Two EE507 of 185 kW.
Dimensions: 19.49 x 2.82 m.
Maximum Speed: 90 mph.

DMLV. Dia. EX561. Lot No. 30452 Ashford/Eastleigh 1959. 40.5 t.

9101	GE	SBV	SL	68500	(61269)
9102	GE	SBV	SL	68501	(61281)
9103	GE	SBV	SL	68502	(61274)
9104	GE	SBV	SL	68503	(61277)
9105	GE	SBV	SL	68504	(61286)
9106	GE	SBV	SL	68505	(61299)
9107	GE	SBV	SL	68506	(61292)
9108	GE	SBV	SL	68507	(61267)
9109	GE	SBV	SL	68508	(61272)
9110	GE	SBV	SL	68509	(61280)

CLASS 456

DMSO – DTSO. Sliding doors. Disc brakes. Fluorescent lighting. PA.

Bogies: P7 (motor) and T3 trailer.
Gangways: Within set.
Traction Motors: Two EE507 of 185 kW.
Dimensions: 19.83 x 2.82 m.
Maximum Speed: 75 mph.

DMSO. Dia. EA267. Lot No. 31073 York 1990 – 1. –/79. 41.1 t.
DTSO. Dia. EE276. Lot No. 31074 York 1990 – 1. –/51. 31.4 t.

456 001	N	SBW	SU	64735	78250
456 002	N	SBW	SU	64736	78251
456 003	N	SBW	SU	64737	78252

456 004	N	SBW	SU	64738 78253
456 005	N	SBW	SU	64739 78254
456 006	N	SBW	SU	64740 78255
456 007	N	SBW	SU	64741 78256
456 008	N	SBW	SU	64742 78257
456 009	N	SBW	SU	64743 78258
456 010	N	SBW	SU	64744 78259
456 011	N	SBW	SU	64745 78260
456 012	N	SBW	SU	64746 78261
456 013	N	SBW	SU	64747 78262
456 014	N	SBW	SU	64748 78263
456 015	N	SBW	SU	64749 78264
456 016	N	SBW	SU	64750 78265
456 017	N	SBW	SU	64751 78266
456 018	N	SBW	SU	64752 78267
456 019	N	SBW	SU	64753 78268
456 020	N	SBW	SU	64754 78269
456 021	N	SBW	SU	64755 78270
456 022	N	SBW	SU	64756 78271
456 023	N	SBW	SU	64757 78272
456 024	N	SBW	SU	64758 78273

CLASS 465   NETWORKER

DMSO – TSO – TSOL – DMSO. New units with Aluminium bodies. Sliding doors. Disc, rheostatic and regenerative brakes. PA.

Electrical Equipment: Networker.
Bogies: P3 (Power cars), T3 (trailers).
Gangways: Within set.
Traction Motors: Four Brush three-phase induction motors per car.
Dimensions: 20.89 x 2.81 m (outer cars), 20.06 x 2.81 m (inner cars).
Maximum Speed: 75 mph.

64759 – 64808. DMSO(A). Dia. EA268. Lot No. 31100 BREL York 1991 – 3. – /86. 38.9 t.
64809 – 64858. DMSO(B). Dia. EA268. Lot No. 31100 BREL York 1991 – 3. – /86. 39 t.
65700 – 65749. DMSO(A). Dia. EA269. Lot No. 31103 Metro-Cammell 1991 – 3. – /86. 38.8 t.
65750 – 65799. DMSO(B). Dia. EA269. Lot No. 31103 Metro-Cammell 1991 – 3. – /86. 38.9 t.
65800 – 65846. DMSO(A). Dia. EA268. Lot No. 31130 ABB York 1993 – 4. – /86.   t.
65847 – 65893. DMSO(A). Dia. EA268. Lot No. 31130 ABB York 1993 – 4. – /86.   t.
72028 – 72126 (even Nos.). TSO. Dia. EH293. Lot No. 31102 BREL York 1991 – 3. – /86. 29.5 t.
72029 – 72127 (odd Nos.). TSOL. Dia. EH292. Lot No. 31101 BREL York 1991 – 3. – /86. 28.6 t.
72719 – 72817 (odd Nos.). TSOL. Dia. EH294. Lot No. 31104 Metro-Cammell 1991 – 3. – /86. 30.2 t.

72720 – 72818 (even Nos.). TSO. Dia. EH295. Lot No. 31105 Metro-Cammell 1991 – 3. – /86. 29.1 t.
72900 – 72992 (even Nos.). TSO. Dia. EH293. Lot No. 31102 ABB York 1993 – 4. – /86. t.
72901 – 72993 (odd Nos.). TSOL. Dia. EH292. Lot No. 31101 ABB York 1993 – 4. – /86. t.

Class 465/0. Built by ABB.

465 001	**NW** SAU	SG	64759	72028	72029	64809
465 002	**NW** SAU	SG	64760	72030	72031	64810
465 003	**NW** SAU	SG	64761	72032	72033	64811
465 004	**NW** SAU	SG	64762	72034	72035	64812
465 005	**NW** SAU	SG	64763	72036	72037	64813
465 006	**NW** SAU	SG	64764	72038	72039	64814
465 007	**NW** SAU	SG	64765	72040	72041	64815
465 008	**NW** SAU	SG	64766	72042	72043	64816
465 009	**NW** SAU	SG	64767	72044	72045	64817
465 010	**NW** SAU	SG	64768	72046	72047	64818
465 011	**NW** SAU	SG	64769	72048	72049	64819
465 012	**NW** SAU	SG	64770	72050	72051	64820
465 013	**NW** SAU	SG	64771	72052	72053	64821
465 014	**NW** SAU	SG	64772	72054	72055	64822
465 015	**NW** SAU	SG	64773	72056	72057	64823
465 016	**NW** SAU	SG	64774	72058	72059	64824
465 017	**NW** SAU	SG	64775	72060	72061	64825
465 018	**NW** SAU	SG	64776	72062	72063	64826
465 019	**NW** SAU	SG	64777	72064	72065	64827
465 020	**NW** SAU	SG	64778	72066	72067	64828
465 021	**NW** SAU	SG	64779	72068	72069	64829
465 022	**NW** SAU	SG	64780	72070	72071	64830
465 023	**NW** SAU	SG	64781	72072	72073	64831
465 024	**NW** SAU	SG	64782	72074	72075	64832
465 025	**NW** SAU	SG	64783	72076	72077	64833
465 026	**NW** SAU	SG	64784	72078	72079	64834
465 027	**NW** SAU	SG	64785	72080	72081	64835
465 028	**NW** SAU	SG	64786	72082	72083	64836
465 029	**NW** SAU	SG	64787	72084	72085	64837
465 030	**NW** SAU	SG	64788	72086	72087	64838
465 031	**NW** SAU	SG	64789	72088	72089	64839
465 032	**NW** SAU	SG	64790	72090	72091	64840
465 033	**NW** SAU	SG	64791	72092	72093	64841
465 034	**NW** SAU	SG	64792	72094	72095	64842
465 035	**NW** SAU	SG	64793	72096	72097	64843
465 036	**NW** SAU	SG	64794	72098	72099	64844
465 037	**NW** SAU	SG	64795	72100	72101	64845
465 038	**NW** SAU	SG	64796	72102	72103	64846
465 039	**NW** SAU	SG	64797	72104	72105	64847
465 040	**NW** SAU	SG	64798	72106	72107	64848
465 041	**NW** SAU	SG	64799	72108	72109	64849
465 042	**NW** SAU	SG	64800	72110	72111	64850
465 043	**NW** SAU	SG	64801	72112	72113	64851

465 044	NW SAU	SG	64802 72114 72115 64852
465 045	NW SAU	SG	64803 72116 72117 64853
465 046	NW SAU	SG	64804 72118 72119 64854
465 047	NW SAU	SG	64805 72120 72121 64855
465 048	NW SAU	SG	64806 72122 72123 64856
465 049	NW SAU	SG	64807 72124 72125 64857
465 050	NW SAU	SG	64808 72126 72127 64858

Class 465/1. Built by ABB. As Class 465/0 but with detail differences.

465 151	NW SAU	SG	65800 72900 72901 65847
465 152	NW SAU	SG	65801 72902 72903 65848
465 153	NW SAU	SG	65802 72904 72905 65849
465 154	NW SAU	SG	65803 72906 72907 65850
465 155	NW SAU	SG	65804 72908 72909 65851
465 156	NW SAU	SG	65805 72910 72911 65852
465 157	NW SAU	SG	65806 72912 72913 65853
465 158	NW SAU	SG	65807 72914 72915 65854
465 159	NW SAU	SG	65808 72916 72917 65855
465 160	NW SAU	SG	65809 72918 72919 65856
465 161	NW SAU	SG	65810 72920 72921 65857
465 162	NW SAU	SG	65811 72922 72923 65858
465 163	NW SAU	SG	65812 72924 72925 65859
465 164	NW SAU	SG	65813 72926 72927 65860
465 165	NW SAU	SG	65814 72928 72929 65861
465 166	NW SAU	SG	65815 72930 72931 65862
465 167	NW SAU	SG	65816 72932 72933 65863
465 168	NW SAU	SG	65817 72934 72935 65864
465 169	NW SAU	SG	65818 72936 72937 65865
465 170	NW SAU	SG	65819 72938 72939 65866
465 171	NW SAU	SG	65820 72940 72941 65867
465 172	NW SAU	SG	65821 72942 72943 65868
465 173	NW SAU	SG	65822 72944 72945 65869
465 174	NW SAU	SG	65823 72946 72947 65870
465 175	NW SAU	SG	65824 72948 72949 65871
465 176	NW SAU	SG	65825 72950 72951 65872
465 177	NW SAU	SG	65826 72952 72953 65873
465 178	NW SAU	SG	65827 72954 72955 65874
465 179	NW SAU	SG	65828 72956 72957 65875
465 180	NW SAU	SG	65829 72958 72959 65876
465 181	NW SAU	SG	65830 72960 72961 65877
465 182	NW SAU	SG	65831 72962 72963 65878
465 183	NW SAU	SG	65832 72964 72965 65879
465 184	NW SAU	SG	65833 72966 72967 65880
465 185	NW SAU	SG	65834 72968 72969 65881
465 186	NW SAU	SG	65835 72970 72971 65882
465 187	NW SAU	SG	65836 72972 72973 65883
465 188	NW SAU	SG	65837 72974 72975 65884
465 189	NW SAU	SG	65838 72976 72977 65885
465 190	NW SAU	SG	65839 72978 72979 65886
465 191	NW SAU	SG	65840 72980 72981 65887
465 192	NW SAU	SG	65841 72982 72983 65888

465 193	NW SAU	SG	65842 72984 72985 65889
465 194	NW SAU	SG	65843 72986 72987 65890
465 195	NW SAU	SG	65844 72988 72989 65891
465 196	NW SAU	SG	65845 72990 72991 65892
465 197	NW SAU	SG	65846 72992 72993 65893

Class 465/2. Built by Metro-Cammell.

465 201	NW SAU	SG	65700 72719 72720 65750
465 202	NW SAU	SG	65701 72721 72722 65751
465 203	NW SAU	SG	65702 72723 72724 65752
465 204	NW SAU	SG	65703 72725 72726 65753
465 205	NW SAU	SG	65704 72727 72728 65754
465 206	NW SAU	SG	65705 72729 72730 65755
465 207	NW SAU	SG	65706 72731 72732 65756
465 208	NW SAU	SG	65707 72733 72734 65757
465 209	NW SAU	SG	65708 72735 72736 65758
465 210	NW SAU	SG	65709 72737 72738 65759
465 211	NW SAU	SG	65710 72739 72740 65760
465 212	NW SAU	SG	65711 72741 72742 65761
465 213	NW SAU	SG	65712 72743 72744 65762
465 214	NW SAU	SG	65713 72745 72746 65763
465 215	NW SAU	SG	65714 72747 72748 65764
465 216	NW SAU	SG	65715 72749 72750 65765
465 217	NW SAU	SG	65716 72751 72752 65766
465 218	NW SAU	SG	65717 72753 72754 65767
465 219	NW SAU	SG	65718 72755 72756 65768
465 220	NW SAU	SG	65719 72757 72758 65769
465 221	NW SAU	SG	65720 72759 72760 65770
465 222	NW SAU	SG	65721 72761 72762 65771
465 223	NW SAU	SG	65722 72763 72764 65772
465 224	NW SAU	SG	65723 72765 72766 65773
465 225	NW SAU	SG	65724 72767 72768 65774
465 226	NW SAU	SG	65725 72769 72770 65775
465 227	NW SAU	SG	65726 72771 72772 65776
465 228	NW SAU	SG	65727 72773 72774 65777
465 229	NW SAU	SG	65728 72775 72776 65778
465 230	NW SAU	SG	65729 72777 72778 65779
465 231	NW SAU	SG	65730 72779 72780 65780
465 232	NW SAU	SG	65731 72781 72782 65781
465 233	NW SAU	SG	65732 72783 72784 65782
465 234	NW SAU	SG	65733 72785 72786 65783
465 235	NW SAU	SG	65734 72787 72788 65784
465 236	NW SAU	SG	65735 72789 72790 65785
465 237	NW SAU	SG	65736 72791 72792 65786
465 238	NW SAU	SG	65737 72793 72794 65787
465 239	NW SAU	SG	65738 72795 72796 65788
465 240	NW SAU	SG	65739 72797 72798 65789
465 241	NW SAU	SG	65740 72799 72800 65790
465 242	NW SAU	SG	65741 72801 72802 65791
465 243	NW SAU	SG	65742 72803 72804 65792
465 244	NW SAU	SG	65743 72805 72806 65793

465 245	**NW** SAU	SG	65744	72807 72808	65794
465 246	**NW** SAU	SG	65745	72809 72810	65795
465 247	**NW** SAU	SG	65746	72811 72812	65796
465 248	**NW** SAU	SG	65747	72813 72814	65797
465 249	**NW** SAU	SG	65748	72815 72816	65798
465 250	**NW** SAU	SG	65749	72817 72818	65799

CLASS 466   NETWORKER

DMSO – DTSO. New units with Aluminium bodies. Sliding doors. Disc, rheostatic and regenerative brakes. PA.

Electrical Equipment: Networker.
Bogies: P3 (Power car), T3 (trailer).
Gangways: Within set.
Traction Motors: Four Brush three-phase induction motors.
Dimensions: 20.89 x 2.81 m.
Maximum Speed: 75 mph.

DMSO. Dia. EA271. Lot No. 31128 Metro-Cammell 1992 – 3. – /86. 39.2 t.
DTSO. Dia. EE279. Lot No. 31129 Metro-Cammell 1991 – 2. – /82. 33.2 t.

466 001	**NW** SAU	SG	64860	78312
466 002	**NW** SAU	SG	64861	78313
466 003	**NW** SAU	SG	64862	78314
466 004	**NW** SAU	SG	64863	78315
466 005	**NW** SAU	SG	64864	78316
466 006	**NW** SAU	SG	64865	78317
466 007	**NW** SAU	SG	64866	78318
466 008	**NW** SAU	SG	64867	78319
466 009	**NW** SAU	SG	64868	78320
466 010	**NW** SAU	SG	64869	78321
466 011	**NW** SAU	SG	64870	78322
466 012	**NW** SAU	SG	64871	78323
466 013	**NW** SAU	SG	64872	78324
466 014	**NW** SAU	SG	64873	78325
466 015	**NW** SAU	SG	64874	78326
466 016	**NW** SAU	SG	64875	78327
466 017	**NW** SAU	SG	64876	78328
466 018	**NW** SAU	SG	64877	78329
466 019	**NW** SAU	SG	64878	78330
466 020	**NW** SAU	SG	64879	78331
466 021	**NW** SAU	SG	64880	78332
466 022	**NW** SAU	SG	64881	78333
466 023	**NW** SAU	SG	64882	78334
466 024	**NW** SAU	SG	64883	78335
466 025	**NW** SAU	SG	64884	78336
466 026	**NW** SAU	SG	64885	78337
466 027	**NW** SAU	SG	64886	78338
466 028	**NW** SAU	SG	64887	78339
466 029	**NW** SAU	SG	64888	78340
466 030	**NW** SAU	SG	64889	78341

466 031	**NW** SAU	SG	64890 78342
466 032	**NW** SAU	SG	64891 78343
466 033	**NW** SAU	SG	64892 78344
466 034	**NW** SAU	SG	64893 78345
466 035	**NW** SAU	SG	64894 78346
466 036	**NW** SAU	SG	64895 78347
466 037	**NW** SAU	SG	64896 78348
466 038	**NW** SAU	SG	64897 78349
466 039	**NW** SAU	SG	64898 78350
466 040	**NW** SAU	SG	64899 78351
466 041	**NW** SAU	SG	64900 78352
466 042	**NW** SAU	SG	64901 78353
466 043	**NW** SAU	SG	64902 78354

CLASS 483   'NEW' ISLE OF WIGHT STOCK

DMBSO(A) – DMBSO(B). Tube stock. Built 1938 onwards for LTE. Converted 1989 – 90 for Isle of Wight Line. Sliding doors. End doors. dg. pa. Former London Underground numbers are shown in parentheses.

System: 660 V d.c. third rail.
Gangways: Non-gangwayed.
Traction Motors: Two of 130 kW.
Dimensions: 15.95 x 2.69 m.
Maximum Speed: 45 mph.

DMSO (A). Lot No. 31071. Dia. EA265. –/42. 27.5 t.
DMSO (B). Lot No. 31072. Dia. EA266. –/42. 27.5 t.

483 001	**NW**	SAZ	RY	121	(10184)	225	(11142)
483 002	**NW**	SAZ	RY	122	(10221)	222	(11221)
483 003	**NW**	SAZ	RY	123	(10116)	221	(11184)
483 004	**NW**	SAZ	RY	124	(10205)	224	(11205)
483 005	**NW**	SAZ	RY	125	(10142)	223	(11116)
483 006	**NW**	SAZ	RY	126	(10297)	226	(11297)
483 007	**NW**	SAZ	RY	127	(10291)	227	(11291)
483 008	**NW**	SAZ	RY	128	(10255)	228	(11255)
483 009	**NW**	SAZ	RY	129	(10289)	229	(11229)

4.3. MERSEYRAIL 750 V d.c. EMUs

CLASS 507

BDMSO – TSO – DMSO. Tightlock couplers. Sliding doors. Disc and rheostatic brakes. PA.

System: 750 V d.c. third rail.
Bogies: BX1.
Gangways: Gangwayed within unit. End doors.
Traction Motors: Four GEC G310AZ of 82.125 kW.
Dimensions: 19.80 x 2.82 m (outer cars), 19.92 x 2.82 m (inner cars).
Maximum Speed: 75 mph.

BDMSO. Dia. EI202. Lot No. 30906 York 1978 − 80. − /74 (− /68*). 37.06 t.
TSO. Dia. EH205. Lot No. 30907 York 1978 − 80. − /82 (− /86*). 25.60 t.
DMSO. Dia. EA201. Lot No. 30908 York 1978 − 80. − /74 (− /68*). 35.62 t.

507 001		**MT** SCE	HR	64367	71342	64405
507 002		**MT** SCE	HR	64368	71343	64406
507 003		**MT** SCE	HR	64369	71344	64407
507 004		SCE	HR	64388	71345	64408
507 005		**MT** SCE	HR	64371	71346	64409
507 006	*	**MT** SCE	HR	64372	71347	64410
507 007		**MT** SCE	HR	64373	71348	64411
507 008		**MT** SCE	HR	64374	71349	64412
507 009		**MT** SCE	HR	64375	71350	64413
507 010		**MT** SCE	HR	64376	71351	64414
507 011		**MT** SCE	HR	64377	71352	64415
507 012		SCE	HR	64378	71353	64416
507 013		**MT** SCE	HR	64379	71354	64417
507 014		**MT** SCE	HR	64380	71355	64418
507 015		**MT** SCE	HR	64381	71356	64419
507 016		**MT** SCE	HR	64382	71357	64420
507 017	*	**MT** SCE	HR	64383	71358	64421
507 018		**MT** SCE	HR	64384	71359	64422
507 019		**MT** SCE	HR	64385	71360	64423
507 020		**MT** SCE	HR	64386	71361	64424
507 021		**MT** SCE	HR	64387	71362	64425
507 023		**MT** SCE	HR	64389	71364	64427
507 024	*	**MT** SCE	HR	64390	71365	64428
507 025		SCE	HR	64391	71366	64429
507 026		**MT** SCE	HR	64392	71367	64430
507 027		**MT** SCE	HR	64393	71368	64431
507 028		**MT** SCE	HR	64394	71369	64432
507 029		**MT** SCE	HR	64395	71370	64433
507 030		SCE	HR	64396	71371	64434
507 031		SCE	HR	64397	71372	64435
507 032		SCE	HR	64398	71373	64436
507 033		SCE	HR	64399	71374	64437

Spare	SCOL	ZH	64370	
Spare	SCXZ			71363

CLASS 508

DMSO – TSO – BDMSO. Tightlock couplers. Sliding doors. Disc and rheostatic brakes. PA. Originally built as four car units and numbered 508 001 – 043. One trailer removed and used for class 455/7 on transfer from the SR.

System: 750 V d.c. third rail.
Bogies: BX1.
Gangways: Gangwayed within unit. End doors.
Traction Motors: Four GEC G310AZ of 82.125 kW.
Dimensions: 19.80 x 2.82 m (outer cars), 19.92 x 2.82 m (inner cars).
Maximum Speed: 75 mph.

64649 – 64691. DMSO. Dia. EA208. Lot No. 30979 York 1979 – 80. –/74. 36.15 t.
71483 – 71525. TSO. Dia. EH218. Lot No. 30980 York 1979 – 80. –/82. 26.72 t.
64692 – 64734. BDMSO. Dia. EI203. Lot No. 30981 York 1979 – 80. –/74. 36.61 t.

508 101		SCOL	Kineton	64649 71483 64692
508 102	MT	SCE	BD	64650 71484 64693
508 103	MT	SCE	BD	64651 71485 64694
508 104	MT	SCOL		64652 71486 64695
508 105		SCE	BD	64653 71487 64696
508 106		SCOL	Kineton	64654 71488 64697
508 107		SCOL	Kineton	64655 71489 64698
508 108		SCE	BD	64656 71490 64699
508 109		SCOL	Kineton	64657 71491 64700
508 110	MT	SCE	BD	64658 71492 64701
508 111	MT	SCE	BD	64659 71493 64702
508 112		SCE	BD	64660 71494 64703
508 113		SCOL	Kineton	64661 71495 64704
508 114	MT	SCE	BD	64662 71496 64705
508 115		SCE	BD	64663 71497 64706
508 116		SCOL	Kineton	64664 71498 64707
508 117		SCE	BD	64665 71499 64708
508 118		SCE	BD	64666 71500 64709
508 119		SCE	BD	64667 71501 64710
508 120	MT	SCE	BD	64668 71502 64711
508 121		SCOL	Southport C.S.	64669 71503 64712
508 122		SCE	BD	64670 71504 64713
508 123	MT	SCE	BD	64671 71505 64714
508 124		SCE	BD	64672 71506 64715
508 125		SCOL		64673 71507 64716
508 126		SCE	BD	64674 71508 64717
508 127		SCE	BD	64675 71509 64718
508 128		SCOL		64676 71510 64719
508 129		SCOL	Southport C.S.	64677 71511 64720

508 130		SCE	BD	64678	71512	64721
508 131	**MT**	SCE	BD	64679	71513	64722
508 132		SCOL	Southport C.S.	64680	71514	64723
508 133		SCE	BD	64681	71515	64724
508 134		SCE	BD	64682	71516	64725
508 135	**MT**	SCE	BD	64683	71517	64726
508 136		SCE	BD	64684	71518	64727
508 137		SCE	BD	64685	71519	64728
508 138		SCE	BD	64686	71520	64729
508 139		SCE	HR	64687	71521	64730
508 140	**MT**	SCE	HR	64688	71522	64731
508 141		SCE	HR	64689	71523	64732
508 142		SCE	HR	64690	71524	64733
508 143	**MT**	SCE	HR	64691	71525	64734

HIGH SPEED IN EUROPE

by David Haydock

High Speed in Europe is a comprehensive review of the progress made to date in implementing high speed rail travel. Each country is addressed in turn with new trains and new infrastructure examined in detail, including Eurostar, and the Channel Tunnel Rail Link. There are features on the new High Speed trains and routes in Germany, France, Spain, Italy and Sweden including TGV, ICE, X 2000, AVE etc. Also includes Appendices of European High Speed Line Statistics and High Speed Train Numbering. **A4 size. Thread Sewn. 80 pages including 38 in full colour. £9.95.**

4.4. EUROSTAR SETS (CLASS 373)

The Eurostar sets, formerly known as Trans-Manche Super Trains (TMSTs) work services through the Channel Tunnel between London and Paris and Brussels. They are based on the French TGV design concept, and the individual cars are numbered like French TGVs.

Each train consists of two 9-coach sets back-to-back with a power car at the outer end. BR sets are allocated to North Pole (London), Belgian Railways (SNCB/NMBS) sets are allocated to Bruxelles Forest/Brussel Vorst and French Railways (SNCF) sets are allocated to Le Landy (Paris). In addition, trains for North of London consisting of two 7-coach half-sets are being delivered.

All sets are articulated with an extra motor bogie on the coach next to the power car. Coaches are numbered R1 – R9 (and in traffic R10 – R18 in the second set). Coaches R18 – R10 are identical to R1 – R9.

BR Sets:

3001	F15	PI	3730010 3730011 3730012 3730013
3002	F15	PI	3730020 3730021 3730022 3730023
3003	UK3	PI	3730030 3730031 3730032 3730033
3004	UK3	PI	3730040 3730041 3730042 3730043
3005	UK4	PI	3730050 3730051 3730052 3730053
3006	UK4	PI	3730060 3730061 3730062 3730063
3007	UK5	PI	3730070 3730071 3730072 3730073
3008	UK5	PI	3730080 3730081 3730082 3730083
3009	UK8	PI	3730090 3730091 3730092 3730093
3010	UK8	PI	3730100 3730101 3730102 3730103
3011	UK9	PI	3730110 3730111 3730112 3730113
3012	UK9	PI	3730120 3730121 3730122 3730123
3013	UK10	PI	3730130 3730131 3730132 3730133
3014	UK10	PI	3730140 3730141 3730142 3730143
3015	UK11	PI	3730150 3730151 3730152 3730153
3016	UK11	PI	3730160 3730161 3730162 3730163
3017	UK12	PI	3730170 3730171 3730172 3730173
3018	UK12	PI	3730180 3730181 3730182 3730183
3019	UK14	PI	3730190 3730191 3730192 3730193
3020	UK14	PI	3730200 3730201 3730202 3730203
3021	UK15	PI	3730210 3730211 3730212 3730213
3022	UK15	PI	3730220 3730221 3730222 3730223

SNCB/NMBS Sets:

3101	UK1	FF	3731010 3731011 3731012 3731013
3102	UK1	FF	3731020 3731021 3731022 3731023
3103	UK2	FF	3731030 3731031 3731032 3731033
3104	UK2	FF	3731040 3731041 3731042 3731043
3105	UK6	FF	3731050 3731051 3731052 3731053
3106	UK6	FF	3731060 3731061 3731062 3731063
3107	UK7	FF	3731070 3731071 3731072 3731073
3108	UK7	FF	3731080 3731081 3731082 3731083

Systems: 25 kV a.c. overhead, 3000 V d.c. overhead and 750 V d.c. third rail.

Built: 1992 – 3 by GEC Alsthom at various works.
Wheel Arrangement: Bo – Bo + Bo – 2 – 2 – 2 – 2 – 2 – 2 – 2 – 2 – 2
Traction Motors: 6
Length: 22.15 + 21.845 + (7 x 18.70) + 21.845 m.
Max. Speed: 300 km/h (187.5 mph).
Livery: White with dark blue window band roof and yellow bodysides.
Details:

Car Type		Seats	Lot No.	Car Type		Seats	Lot No.
M	DM		31118	R5	TSOL	–/60 2T	31123
R1	MSOL	–/52 1T	31119	R6	Kitchen/bar		31124
R2	TSOL	–/60 1T	31120	R7	TFOL	39/– 1T	31125
R3	TSOL	–/60 2T	31121	R8	TFOL	39/– 1T	31126
R4	TSOL	–/60 1T	31122	R9	TBFOL	27/– 1T	31127

Note: The pairs of sets are also known by designations as follows: F/FN – Assembled in France, UK/UN – Assembled in the UK.

3730014	3730015	3730016	3730017	3730018	3730019
3730024	3730025	3730026	3730027	3730028	3730029
3730034	3730035	3730036	3730037	3730038	3730039
3730044	3730045	3730046	3730047	3730048	3730049
3730054	3730055	3730056	3730057	3730058	3730059
3730064	3730065	3730066	3730067	3730068	3730069
3730074	3730075	3730076	3730077	3730078	3730079
3730084	3730085	3730086	3730087	3730088	3730089
3730094	3730095	3730096	3730097	3730098	3730099
3730104	3730105	3730106	3730107	3730108	3730109
3730114	3730115	3730116	3730117	3730118	3730119
3730124	3730125	3730126	3730127	3730128	3730129
3730134	3730135	3730136	3730137	3730138	3730139
3730144	3730145	3730146	3730147	3730148	3730149
3730154	3730155	3730156	3730157	3730158	3730159
3730164	3730165	3730166	3730167	3730168	3730169
3730174	3730175	3730176	3730177	3730178	3730179
3730184	3730185	3730186	3730187	3730188	3730189
3730194	3730195	3730196	3730197	3730198	3730199
3730204	3730205	3730206	3730207	3730208	3730209
3730214	3730215	3730216	3730217	3730218	3730219
3730224	3730225	3730226	3730227	3730228	3730229

3731014	3731015	3731016	3731017	3731018	3731019
3731024	3731025	3731026	3731027	3731028	3731029
3731034	3731035	3731036	3731037	3731038	3731039
3731044	3731045	3731046	3731047	3731048	3731049
3731054	3731055	3731056	3731057	3731058	3731059
3731064	3731065	3731066	3731067	3731068	3731069
3731074	3731075	3731076	3731077	3731078	3731079
3731084	3731085	3731086	3731087	3731088	3731089

SNCF Sets:

3201	F16	LY	3732010	3732011	3732012	3732013
3202	F16	LY	3732020	3732021	3732022	3732023
3203	F1	LY	3732030	3732031	3732032	3732033
3204	F1	LY	3732040	3732041	3732042	3732043
3205	F2	LY	3732050	3732051	3732052	3732053
3206	F2	LY	3732060	3732061	3732062	3732063
3207	F3	LY	3732070	3732071	3732072	3732073
3208	F3	LY	3732080	3732081	3732082	3732083
3209	F4	LY	3732090	3732091	3732092	3732093
3210	F4	LY	3732100	3732101	3732102	3732103
3211	F5	LY	3732110	3732111	3732112	3732113
3212	F5	LY	3732120	3732121	3732122	3732123
3213	F6	LY	3732130	3732131	3732132	3732133
3214	F6	LY	3732140	3732141	3732142	3732143
3215	F7	LY	3732150	3732151	3732152	3732153
3216	F7	LY	3732160	3732161	3732162	3732163
3217	F8	LY	3732170	3732171	3732172	3732173
3218	F8	LY	3732180	3732181	3732182	3732183
3219	F9	LY	3732190	3732191	3732192	3732193
3220	F9	LY	3732200	3732201	3732202	3732203
3221	F10	LY	3732210	3732211	3732212	3732213
3222	F10	LY	3732220	3732221	3732222	3732223
3223	F11	LY	3732230	3732231	3732232	3732233
3224	F11	LY	3732240	3732241	3732242	3732243
3225	F12	LY	3732250	3732251	3732252	3732253
3226	F12	LY	3732260	3732261	3732262	3732263
3227	F13	LY	3732270	3732271	3732272	3732273
3228	F13	LY	3732280	3732281	3732282	3732283
3229	F14	LY	3732290	3732291	3732292	3732293
3230	F14	LY	3732300	3732301	3732302	3732303
3231	UK13	LY	3732310	3732311	3732312	3732313
3232	UK13	LY	3732320	3732321	3732322	3732323

'Regional Eurostar' Sets for services from the North of England & Scotland:

These are 7 coach sets consisting of PC + R1/3/2/5/6/7/9 only.

3301	FN1	PI	3733010	3733011	3733013	3733012
3302	FN1	PI	3733020	3733021	3733023	3733022
3303	FN2		3733030	3733031	3733033	3733032
3304	FN2		3733040	3733041	3733043	3733042
3305	UN1		3733050	3733051	3733053	3733052
3306	UN1		3733060	3733061	3733063	3733062
3307	UN2		3733070	3733071	3733073	3733072
3308	UN2		3733080	3733081	3733083	3733082
3309	UN3		3733090	3733091	3733093	3733092
3310	UN3		3733100	3733101	3733103	3733102
3311	UN4		3733110	3733111	3733113	3733112
3312	UN4		3733120	3733121	3733123	3733122
3313	UN5		3733130	3733131	3733133	3733132
3314	UN5		3733140	3733141	3733143	3733142

3732014 3732015 3732016 3732017 3732018 3732019
3732024 3732025 3732026 3732027 3732028 3732029
3732034 3732035 3732036 3732037 3732038 3732039
3732044 3732045 3732046 3732047 3732048 3732049
3732054 3732055 3732056 3732057 3732058 3732059
3732064 3732065 3732066 3732067 3732068 3732069
3732074 3732075 3732076 3732077 3732078 3732079
3732084 3732085 3732086 3732087 3732088 3732089
3732094 3732095 3732096 3732097 3732098 3732099
3732104 3732105 3732106 3732107 3732108 3732109
3732114 3732115 3732116 3732117 3732118 3732119
3732124 3732125 3732126 3732127 3732128 3732129
3732134 3732135 3732136 3732137 3732138 3732139
3732144 3732145 3732146 3732147 3732148 3732149
3732154 3732155 3732156 3732157 3732158 3732159
3732164 3732165 3732166 3732167 3732168 3732169
3732174 3732175 3732176 3732177 3732178 3732179
3732184 3732185 3732186 3732187 3732188 3732189
3732194 3732195 3732196 3732197 3732198 3732199
3732204 3732205 3732206 3732207 3732208 3732209
3732214 3732215 3732216 3732217 3732218 3732219
3732224 3732225 3732226 3732227 3732228 3732229
3732234 3732235 3732236 3732237 3732238 3732239
3732244 3732245 3732246 3732247 3732248 3732249
3732254 3732255 3732256 3732257 3732258 3732259
3732264 3732265 3732266 3732267 3732268 3732269
3732274 3732275 3732276 3732277 3732278 3732279
3732284 3732285 3732286 3732287 3732288 3732289
3732294 3732295 3732296 3732297 3732298 3732299
3732304 3732305 3732306 3732307 3732308 3732309
3732314 3732315 3732316 3732317 3732318 3732319
3732324 3732325 3732326 3732327 3732328 3732329

3733015 3733016 3733017 3733019
3733025 3733026 3733027 3733029
3733035 3733036 3733037 3733039
3733045 3733046 3733047 3733049
3733055 3733056 3733057 3733059
3733065 3733066 3733067 3733069
3733075 3733076 3733077 3733079
3733085 3733086 3733087 3733089
3733095 3733096 3733097 3733099
3733105 3733106 3733107 3733109
3733115 3733116 3733117 3733119
3733125 3733126 3733127 3733129
3733135 3733136 3733137 3733139
3733145 3733146 3733147 3733149

4.5. SERVICE EMUs

Formerly known as 'Departmental', these vehicles are owned by Railtrack or by organisations at Derby e.g. Railtest.

INDIVIDUAL VEHICLES.

ADB 975032	(75165)	SH	Class 932 experimental stock. 'Mars'.
DB 977335	(76277)	ZA	MTA Pool Generator coach for DB999550.
ADB 977364	(10400)	RE	Class 930 deicing trailer.
ADB 977385	(61148)	SH	Depot pilot.
ADB 977578	(77101)	HE	Sandite car (930 078).
			(works with Class 313/317).
ADB 977579	(77109)	SU	Sandite car (930 079).
			(works with Class 319).

COMPLETE UNITS

Note: Most service units do not carry '93x' numbers.

Class 930. 750 V d.c. De-icing and Sandite units.

930 003	SU	ADB	975594 (12658)	ADB 975595 (10904)
930 004	FR	ADB	975586 (10907)	ADB 975587 (10908)
930 005	WD	ADB	975588 (10981)	ADB 975589 (10982)
930 006	WD	ADB	975590 (10833)	ADB 975591 (10834)
930 007	GI	ADB	975592 (10933)	ADB 975593 (12659)
930 008	AF	ADB	975596 (10844)	ADB 975597 (10987)
930 009	BI	ADB	975598 (10989)	ADB 975599 (10990)
930 010	BI	ADB	975600 (10988)	ADB 975601 (10843)
930 011	RE	ADB	975602 (10991)	ADB 975603 (10992)
930 012	FR	ADB	975604 (10939)	ADB 975605 (10940)
930 013	RE	ADB	975896 (11387)	ADB 975897 (11388)
930 014	WD	ADB	977609 (65414)	ADB 977207 (61658)
930 016	FR	ADB	977533 (14273)	ADB 977534 (14384)
930 017	BM	ADB	977566 (65312)	ADB 977567 (65314)
930 030	FR		977804 (65336)	977805 (65357)
930 031	SU		977864 (65341)	977865 (65355)
930 032	RE		977874 (65302)	977875 (65304)
930 033	RE		977871 (65353)	977872 (65367)
930 034	WD		977924 (65382)	977925 (65379)

Class 930. 750 V d.c. Route learning unit.

930 082	SU	ADB	977861 (61044)	ADB 977862 (70039)
		ADB	977863 (61038)	

Class 931. 750 V d.c. Route learning Unit.

931 001	SL	ADB	977857 (65346)	ADB 977856 (77531)
931 002	RE		977917 (65331)	977918 (77516)

▲ Class 302 No. 302 215, in Network SouthEast livery, forms the lead unit of the 10.30 London Fenchurch Street-Shoeburyness at Shadwell on 11 July 1994.
Kevin Conkey

▼ Class 303 No. 303 047, in Strathclyde PTE livery, at Glasgow Central on 11th August 1995 prior to working the 08.35 service to Newton.
Hugh Ballantyne

▲ Blue and Grey liveried Class 304 No. 304 033 calls at Smethwick Galton Bridge on 28th September 1995 whilst forming the 13.22 Wolverhampton-Coventry service. *Chris Morrison*

▼ Greater Manchester PTE liveried Class 305 No. 305 503 arrives at Manchester Airport on 29th March 1994 with the 13.10 from Manchester Piccadilly. *Hugh Ballantyne*

▲ Class 308 No. 308 158, in West Yorkshire PTE livery, leaves Leeds with the 13.04 departure for Skipton on 28th October 1995.

Dave McAlone

▼ Carrying a modified form of Network SouthEast livery (the red stripe having been painted light blue), Class 309 No. 309 623 passes Slindon, Staffordshire with the 17.16 Manchester Piccadilly-Birmingham New Street on 9th August 1995.

Alex Dasi-Sutton

▲ Class 310 No. 310 092 is pictured at Shadwell on 23rd September 1995 with an unidentified Shoeburyness-London Fenchurch Street service. *Kevin Conkey*

▼ Regional Railways liveried Class 312 No. 312 728 passes Dudley Port with the 13.51 Birmingham New Street-Liverpool Lime Street service on 2nd November 1995. *Chris Morrison*

▲ The 15.28 Moorgate-Welwyn Garden City, formed of Class 313s Nos. 313 052 and 049, is pictured leaving Hadley Wood North Tunnel on 20th June 1994. *Brian Morrison*

▼ Class 315 No. 315 853 enters Bethnal Green station on 13th August 1994 whilst forming the 11.02 London Liverpool Street-Enfield Town. *Kevin Conkey*

▲ Class 317 No. <u>317 392</u> passes Hertford East signal box on 21st May 1995 with a local service from Broxbourne. *Hugh Ballantyne*

▼ Strathclyde PTE liveried Class 318 No. <u>318 263</u> passes non-stop through Hillingdon East with a Glasgow Central bound train on 11th August 1995. *Hugh Ballantyne*

▲ Carrying the recently introduced Thameslink livery, Class 319 No. 319 040 leaves Kentish Town with the 12.35 St Albans-Sutton service. The date is 26th June 1995.　　　　　　　　　　　　　　*Kevin Conkey*

▼ Class 321 No. 321 308, carrying 3M advertising livery, pauses at Manningtree whilst working the 11.00 London Liverpool Street-Ipswich service on 25th July 1995.　　　　　　　　　　　　　　*C.J. Marsden*

▲ Class 322 units are dedicated for use on Stansted Airport-London Liverpool Street services and all members of the class also carry a special livery. Unit 322 485 is pictured here passing through Hackney Downs with the 14.00 Stansted-London Liverpool Street on 2nd September 1995. *Kevin Conkey*

▼ Centro liveried Class 323 No. 323 217 passes Shallowford, Norton Bridge on 13th August 1994 whilst forming the 08.35 Stoke-on-Trent-Stafford. *Hugh Ballantyne*

Royal Mail liveried Class 325 postal units are now under construction. The first of the class, No. 325 001 is pictured here approaching Low Gill on 13th July 1995 with a Preston-Carlisle test train.   *Kevin Conkey*

Class 373 'Eurostar' units Nos. 3013 & 3014 pass Sevington, near Ashford, with the 12.53 London Waterloo-Paris Gare du Nord. The date is 5th August 1995.

Alex Dasi-Sutton

▲ A trio of units with Class 411/5 (4 Cep) No. 1530 leading form the 10.00 London Charing Cross-Ramsgate near Otford Junction on 14th April 1995. *Chris Wilson*

▼ Class 422/2 (4 Big) No. 2205 and Class 421/3 (4 Cig) No. 1714 depart from Lewes on 30th June 1995 with the 09.43 London Victoria-Hastings. *Chris Wilson*

▲ Class 412 (4 Bep) No. 2304 approaches Eastleigh with the 08.36 Poole-London Waterloo on 17th August 1995. *David Brown*

▼ Class 442 unit No. 2418 forms the 11.41 Poole-Eastleigh service near Southampton on 21st July 1995. *Nic Joynson*

▲ Class 423/1 (4 Vep) leads a pair of units past five Oak Green, near Paddock Wood on 25th July 1995. *Nic Joynson*

▼ Class 455 EMUs Nos. 5905 & 5741 run into Surbiton on 11th August 1995 with the 17.14 London Waterloo-Guildford via Cobham service. The second vehicle in the lead unit, No. 71731, has experimental plug-doors. *David Brown*

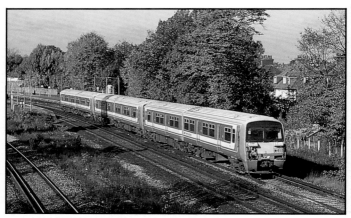

▲ An ECS formed of Class 456 units Nos. 456 002, 456 016 & 456 006 pass Norbury on 28th October 1994.   *Alex Dasi-Sutton*

▼ Class 465 No. 465 028 leads a similar unit of Class 466 at Penge East on 9th December 1994 whilst working an ECS to Orpington.
          Chris Wilson

▲ Class 466 'Networker' No. 466 042 runs into Chatham station whilst forming the front portion of the 11.27 London Charing Cross-Gillingham service. The date is 22nd July 1995.   *David Brown*

▼ Class 483 Isle of Wight unit No. 483 004 waits at Shanklin with 16.44 service to Ryde Pier Head on 21st July 1995.   *Martyn Hilbert*

▲ Gatwick Express liveried Class 489 GLV No. 9101 passes Redhill with the diverted 09.50 Gatwick Airport-London Victoria on 23rd July 1995.
Chris Wilson

▼ Merseytravel liveried Class 507 No. 507 007 forms a Southport-Hunts Cross service at Birkdale on 9th July 1995. *Martyn Hilbert*

Class 932. 750 V d.c. Test Units.

| 932 053 | SH | ADB | 977505 (65321) | ADB 977508 (77112) |
| 932 054 | SH | ADB | 977506 (65323) | ADB 977296 (65319) |

Class 936. Merseyrail 750 V d.c. Sandite Unit.

| 936 003 | BD | ADB | 977349 (61183) | ADB 977350 (75183) |

Class 936. 25 kV a.c. three-car Sandite Units (ex Class 311).

936 103	GW		977844 (76414)	977845 (62174)
			977846 (76433)	
936 104	GW		977847 (76415)	977848 (62175)
			977849 (76434)	

Class 937. Miscellaneous 25 kV a.c. Sandite Units and tractor units.

937 908	IL	ADB	977741 (75469)	ADB 977742 (61436)
		ADB	977743 (75521)	
937 990	EM		977876 (75905)	977877 (61901)
			977878 (75938)	
937 991	IL		977926 (75900)	977927 (61896)
			977928 (75933)	
937 996	IL	ADB	977598 (75080)	ADB 977599 (61073)
		ADB	977600 (75061)	
937 998	IL	ADB	977604 (75077)	ADB 977605 (61062)
		ADB	977606 (75070)	

Test unit.

| 303 999 | GW | TDB | 977711 (75759) | TDB 977712 (61825) |
| | | TDB | 977713 (75815) | |

Class 316. Test Unit (secondary door locks). Works with 1620.

| 316 997 | EH | ADB | 977708 (75118) | ADB 977709 (61018) |
| | | ADB | 977710 (75018) | |

Service numbers not carried.

CLASS 931 (Formerly 419) 1957 type MLV

DMLV. Built 1959 – 61. Dual braked. These units are now officially in service stock, but they retain their capital stock side numbers.

Electrical Equipment: 1957-type.
Bogies: Mk 3B.
Gangways: Non-gangwayed.
Traction Motors: Two EE507 of 185 kW.
Dimensions: 19.64 x 2.82 m.
Maximum Speed: 90 mph.

68001. DMLV. Dia. EX560. Lot No. 30458 Ashford/Eastleigh. 1959. 45.5 t.
68003 – 10. DMLV. Dia. EX560. Lot No. 30623 Ashford./Eastleigh. 1960 – 61. 45.5 t.

931 090	(9010)	J	SBU	RE	68010
931 091	(9001)	N	SBU	RE	68001
931 093	(9003)	B	SBU	RE	68003
931 094	(9004)	N	SBU	RE	68004
931 095	(9005)	N	SBU	RE	68005
931 097	(9007)	N	SBU	RE	68007
931 098	(9008)	N	SBU	RE	68008
931 099	(9009)	J	SBU	RE	68009

4.6. EMUs AWAITING DISPOSAL

The following withdrawn DMUs are awaiting disposal with the last known storage location shown.

Former Capital Stock Units

304 003	Crewe Brook Sidings	75047	61047	75647
304 006	Stafford Salop Sidings	75050	61050	75650
304 008	CP	75052	61052	75652
304 013	Stafford Salop Sidings	75057	61057	75657
304 021	Crewe Brook Sidings	75685	61633	75665
304 024	Crewe Brook Sidings	75688	61636	75668
304 027	Crewe Brook Sidings	75691	61639	75671
304 029	Crewe Brook Sidings	75693	61641	75673
304 030	Crewe Brook Sidings	75694	61642	75674
304 042	BP	75874	61879	75864
304 043	TS	75875	61880	75865
305 401	BP	75471	61429	75514
305 403	LG	75506	61473	75558
305 410	BP	75462	61438	75523
305 420	BP	75481	61448	75533
306 017	IL	65217	65417	65617
308 142	NL	75929	61892	75896
4309	SH	61276	75396	
4311	SH	61287	75407	
4732	BI	12795	10239	12354 12796
5001	SH	14001	15207	15101 14002
5176	SH	14352	15396	15354 14351
6213	SH	65327	77512	
6259	SH	65373	77558	
6307	SH	14573	16117	
6308	SH	14564	16108	
6309	SH	14562	16106	
6402	SH	65362	77547	
6417	Basingstoke	65366	77551	
7001	ZG	67300	67401	67301

Former Service Stock Vehicles

977304	(65317)	WD	977684	(76282)	ZG
977305	(65322)	WD	977685	(70818)	ZG
977345	(61180)	BD	977686	(70850)	ZG
977347	(61178)	BD	977687	(76281)	ZG
977639	(75548)	Southall ECD	977763	(70871)	ZG
977640	(61463)	Southall ECD	977764	(70866)	ZG
977641	(75214)	Southall ECD			

Loose Cars

61433 LG   75773 Yoker
70612 70621 70622 70631 70640 Crewe Brook Sidings

5. NON-PASSENGER-CARRYING COACHING STOCK

The notes shown for locomotive-hauled passenger stock generally apply also to non-passenger-carrying coaching stock (often abbreviated to NPCCS).

TOPS CODES

TOPS codes for NPCCS are made up as follows:

(1) Two letters denoting the type of the vehicle:

NA Propelling control vehicle.
NB High security gangwayed brake van (90 mph).
NC Gangwayed brake van modified for newspaper conveyance (100 mph).
ND Gangwayed brake van (90 mph).
NE Gangwayed brake van (100 mph).
NF Gangwayed brake van with guard's safety equipment removed.
NG Motorail loading wagon.
NH Gangwayed brake van (110 mph).
NJ General utility van (90 mph).
NK General utility van (100 mph modified).
NL Newspaper van.
NM Newspaper van.
NN Courier vehicle.
NO General utility van (100 mph e.t.h. wired).
NP General utility van for Post Office use or Motorail van (110 mph).
NR BAA Container van (100 mph).
NS Post office sorting van.
NT Post office stowage van.
NU Brake post office stowage van.
NX Motorail van (100 mph).
NY Exhibition van.
NZ Driving brake van (also known as driving van trailer).

A third letter denoting the brake type:

A   Air braked
V   Vacuum braked
X   Dual braked

OPERATOR CODES

The normal operator codes are given in brackets after the TOPS codes. These are as follows:

BG   Gangwayed brake van.
BPOT   Brake post office stowage van.
DLV   Driving brake van (also known as driving van trailer — DVT).
GUV   General utility van.
POS   Post office sorting van.
POT   Post office stowage van.

AK51 (RK)   KITCHEN CAR

Dia. AK503. Mark 1. Gas cooking. Converted from RBR. Fluorescent lighting.
x*. ETH 2X.

Note: Kitchen cars have traditionally been numbered in the NPCCS series, but
have passenger coach diagram numbers!

Lot No. 30628 Pressed Steel 1960 – 61. 39 t.

80041 (1690)   I   XWR

NN   COURIER VEHICLE

Dia. NN504. Converted 1986 – 7 from Mark 1 BSKs. One compartment retained for courier use. Roller shutter doors. xd. ETH 2.
Non-Standard Livery: GWR plain brown.

80207. Lot No. 30721 Wolverton 1963. 37 t.
80211 – 6/23. Lot No. 30699 Wolverton 1962. Commonwealth bogies. 37 t.
80220/4. Lot No. 30573 Gloucester 1960. B4 bogies. 33 t.

80207 (35466)	PC	XVR	SL
80211 (35296)	RY	XWRS	Ferme Park
80212 (35307)	RM	MPOZ	NC
80213 (35316)	CH	XRP	CO
80214 (35323)	RY	XWRS	Ferme Park
80216 (35295)	RM	MPOZ	NC
80220 (35276)	O	XRT	CO
80223 (35331)	RY	XWRS	Ferme Park
80224 (35291)	RY	XRPS	CO

NPX   POST OFFICE GUV

Dia. NP502. Converted 1991 onwards from newspaper vans. Mark 1. Short
frames (57'). Originally converted from GUV. Fluorescent lighting, toilets and
gangways fitted. Load 14 t. ETH 3X. e. B5 bogies.

Lot No. 30922 Wolverton or Doncaster 1977 – 8. e. 31 t.

80250 (86838, 94008)	a	RM	MP		BK
80251 (86467, 94017)	x	RM	MP		EN
80252 (86718, 94022)	a	RM	MP		EN
80253 (86170, 94018)	a	RM	MP		EN
80254 (86082, 94012)	x	RM	MP		EN
80255 (86098, 94019)	x	RM	MP		EN
80256 (86408, 94013)	x	RM	MP		EN
80257 (86221, 94023)	x	RM	MP		EN
80258 (86651, 94002)	a	RM	MP		EN
80259 (86845, 94005)	x	RM	MP		BK

NS (POS)   POST OFFICE SORTING VAN

Used in travelling post office (TPO) trains. Mark 1. Various diagrams.

The following lots are v and have Mark 1 bogies except * – B5 bogies. x. (subtract 2 t from weight).

80300 – 80305. Lot No. 30486 Wolverton 1959. Dia. NS501. Originally built with nets for collecting mail bags in motion. Equipment now removed. ETH 3X. 36 t.

80306 – 80308. Lot No. 30487 Wolverton 1959. Dia. NS502. ETH 3. 36 t.
80309 – 80314. Lot No. 30661 Wolverton 1961. Dia. NS501. ETH 3. 37 t.
80315 – 80316. Lot No. 30662 Wolverton 1961. Dia. NS501. ETH 3X. 36 t.
80318. Lot No. 30663 Wolverton 1961. Dia. NS501. ETH 3X. 35 t.

80300	**RM MZ**	DY		80310	**RM MZ**	CA
80301	**RM MZ**	DY		80312	**RM MZ**	CA
80303 *	**RM MPOZ**	CA		80313	**RM MZ**	ZH
80305	**RM MZ**	CA		80314 *	**RM MPOZ**	NC
80306	**RM MPOZ**	NC		80315	**RM MZ**	CA
80308 *	**RM MPOZ**	CA		80316 *	**RM MPOZ**	NC
80309 *	**RM MPOZ**	CA		80318 *	**RM MPOZ**	NC

The following lots are pressure ventilated and have B5 bogies.

80319 – 80327. Dia. NS504. Lot No. 30778 York 1968 – 9.   ETH 4. 35 t.
80328 – 80338. Dia. NS505. Lot No. 30779 York 1968 – 9.   ETH 4. 35 t.
80339 – 80355. Dia. NS506. Lot No. 30780 York 1968 – 9.   ETH 4. 35 t.

80319 x	**RM MPOZ**	CA		80338 x	**RM MPOZ**	HT
80320 x	**RM MPOZ**	CA		80339 a	**RM MPOZ**	EN
80321 a	**RM MPOZ**	CA		80340 a	**RM MPOZ**	DY
80322 a	**RM MPOZ**	CA		80341 a	**RM MPOZ**	EN
80323 x	**RM MPOZ**	CA		80342 x	**RM MPOZ**	EN
80324 x	**RM MPOZ**	CA		80343 x	**RM MPOZ**	DY
80325 x	**RM MPOZ**	DY		80344 a	**RM MPOZ**	DY
80326 a	**RM MPOZ**	DY		80345 a	**RM MPOZ**	BK
80327 a	**RM MPOZ**	PZ		80346 a	**RM MPOZ**	CA
80328 x	**RM MPOZ**	EN		80347 x	**RM MPOZ**	CA
80329 a	**RM MPOZ**	DY		80348 x	**RM MPOZ**	HT
80330 a	**RM MPOZ**	CA		80349 a	**RM MPOZ**	BK
80331 a	**RM MPOZ**	EN		80350 x	**RM MPOZ**	EN
80332 x	**RM MPOZ**	CA		80351 x	**RM MPOZ**	PZ
80333 a	**RM MPOZ**	CA		80352 x	**RM MPOZ**	HT
80334 x	**RM MPOZ**	DY		80353 x	**RM MPOZ**	EN
80335 x	**RM MPOZ**	EN		80354 a	**RM MPOZ**	EN
80336 x	**RM MPOZ**	HT		80355 a	**RM MPOZ**	DY
80337 a	**RM MPOZ**	HT				

Name: 80320 The Borders Mail

80356 – 80380. Lot No. 30839 York 1972 – 3. Dia. NS501. Pressure ventilated. Fluorescent lighting. B5 bogies. ETH 4X. 37 t.

80356 a	**RM MPOZ**	EN		80363 a	**RM MPOZ**	EN
80357 x	**RM MPOZ**	EN		80364 x	**RM MPOZ**	CA
80358	**RM MPOZ**	CA		80365 x	**RM MPOZ**	CA
80359 a	**RM MPOZ**	HT		80366 a	**RM MPOZ**	EN
80360 a	**RM MPOZ**	NC		80367 a	**RM MPOZ**	EN
80361 x	**RM MPOZ**	CA		80368 a	**RM MPOZ**	EN
80362 x	**RM MPOZ**	CA		80369 a	**RM MPOZ**	CA

80370	a	**RM** MPOZ	EN
80371	a	**RM** MPOZ	EN
80372	a	**RM** MPOZ	EN
80373	a	**RM** MPOZ	EN
80374	a	**RM** MPOZ	DY
80375	a	**RM** MPOZ	BK

80376	a	**RM** MPOZ	EN
80377	a	**RM** MPOZ	EN
80378	a	**RM** MPOZ	EN
80379	a	**RM** MPOZ	EN
80380	x	**RM** MPOZ	PZ

Name: 80367 M.G. Berry

80381 – 80395. Lot No. 30900 Wolverton 1977. Dia NS531. Converted from SK. Pressure ventilated. Fluorescent lighting. B5 bogies. ETH 4X. 38 t.

80381	(25112)	a	**RM** MPOZ	EN
80382	(25109)	a	**RM** MPOZ	EN
80383	(25033)	a	**RM** MPOZ	EN
80384	(25078)	a	**RM** MPOZ	EN
80385	(25083)	a	**RM** MPOZ	EN
80386	(25099)	a	**RM** MPOZ	EN
80387	(25045)	x	**RM** MPOZ	EN
80388	(25088)	a	**RM** MPOZ	EN

80389	(25103)	a	**RM** MPOZ	EN
80390	(25047)	a	**RM** MPOZ	EN
80391	(25089)	x	**RM** MPOZ	EN
80392	(25082)	a	**RM** MPOZ	EN
80393	(25118)	a	**RM** MPOZ	EN
80394	(25156)	a	**RM** MPOZ	EN
80395	(25056)	x	**RM** MPOZ	DY

NT (POT)   POST OFFICE STOWAGE VAN

Mark 1. Open vans used for stowage of mail bags in conjunction with POS. Various diagrams.

Lot No. 30488 Wolverton 1959. Dia. NT502. Originally built with nets for collecting mail bags in motion. Equipment now removed. B5 bogies. ETH 3. 35 t.

80400	a	**RM** MPOZ	EN
80401	x	**RM** MPOZ	EN

80402	x	**RM** MPOZ	EN

The following eight vehicles were converted at York from BSK to lot 30143 (80403) and 30229 (80404 – 80414). No new lot number was issued. Dia. NT503. B5 bogies. 35 t. (*dia. NT501 BR2 bogies 38 t. ETH 3 (3X*).

80403	(34361)	x	**RM** MPOZ	DY
80404	(35014)	a	**RM** MPOZ	DY
80405	(35009)	x	**RM** MPOZ	DY
80406	(35022)	x	**RM** MPOZ	DY

80411	(35003)	x*	**RM** MPOZ	CA
80412	(35002)	x*	**RM** MPOZ	CA
80413	(35004)	x*	**RM** MPOZ	CA
80414	(35005)	x*	**RM** MPOZ	DY

Lot No. 30781 York 1968. Dia. NT505. Pressure ventilated. B5 bogies. ETH 4. 34 t.

80415	a	**RM** MPOZ	EN
80416	x	**RM** MPOZ	EN
80417	a	**RM** MPOZ	EN
80418	a	**RM** MPOZ	EN
80419	x	**RM** MPOZ	EN

80420	x	**RM** MPOZ	HT
80421	a	**RM** MPOZ	CA
80422	x	**RM** MPOZ	CA
80423	a	**RM** MPOZ	EN
80424	x	**RM** MPOZ	EN

Lot No. 30840 York 1973. Dia. NT504. Pressure ventilated. fluorescent lighting. B5 bogies. ETH 4X. 35 t.

80425	a	**RM** MPOZ	EN
80426	a	**RM** MPOZ	CA
80427	x	**RM** MPOZ	HT

80428	a	**RM** MPOZ	EN
80429	a	**RM** MPOZ	EN
80430	a	**RM** MPOZ	BN

Lot No. 30901 Wolverton 1977. converted from SK. Dia. NT521. Pressure ventilated. Fluorescent lighting. B5 bogies. ETH 4X. 35 t.

80431	(25104) x	**RM**	MPOZ	PZ	80432	(25071) x	**RM**	MPOZ	HT
80433	(25150) a	**RM**	MPOZ	HT	80437	(25068) a	**RM**	MPOZ	EN
80434	(25119) a	**RM**	MPOZ	CA	80438	(25139) x	**RM**	MPOZ	PZ
80435	(25117) a	**RM**	MPOZ	EN	80439	(25127) x	**RM**	MPOZ	DY
80436	(25077) x	**RM**	MPOZ	EN					

NU (BPOT)   BRAKE POST OFFICE STOWAGE VAN

As NT but with brake. Mark 1.

Lot No. 30782 York 1968. Dia. NU502. Pressure ventilated. B5 bogies. ETH 4. 36 t.

80456	a	**RM**	MPOZ	EN	80458	x	**RM**	MPOZ	EN
80457	a	**RM**	MPOZ	EN					

NZ (DLV)   DRIVING BRAKE VAN (110 mph)

Dia. NZ501. Mark 3B. Air conditioned. T4 bogies. a. dg. Cab to shore communication. ETH 5X.

Lot No. 31042 Derby 1988. 45.18 t.

82101	I	SBF	PC	82127	I	SBF	PC
82102	I	SBF	OY	82128	I	SBF	OY
82103	I	SBF	OY	82129	I	SBF	OY
82104	I	SBF	PC	82130	I	SBF	MA
82105	I	SBF	MA	82131	I	SBF	PC
82106	I	SBF	OY	82132	I	SBF	OY
82107	I	SBF	PC	82133	I	SBF	OY
82108	I	SBF	MA	82134	I	SBF	PC
82109	I	SBF	MA	82135	I	SBF	PC
82110	I	SBF	PC	82136	I	SBF	MA
82111	I	SBF	PC	82137	I	SBF	PC
82112	I	SBF	MA	82138	I	SBF	PC
82113	I	SBF	OY	82139	I	SBF	MA
82114	I	SBF	PC	82140	I	SBF	PC
82115	I	SBF	PC	82141	I	SBF	MA
82116	I	SBF	MA	82142	I	SBF	PC
82117	I	SBF	PC	82143	I	SBF	OY
82118	I	SBF	OY	82144	I	SBF	OY
82119	I	SBF	MA	82145	I	SBF	OY
82120	I	SBF	MA	82146	I	SBF	PC
82121	I	SBF	MA	82147	I	SBF	MA
82122	I	SBF	OY	82148	I	SBF	OY
82123	I	SBF	PC	82149	I	SBF	MA
82124	I	SBF	PC	82150	I	SBF	MA
82125	I	SBF	OY	82151	I	SBF	OY
82126	I	SBF	PC	82152	I	SBF	OY

NZ (DLV)   DRIVING BRAKE VAN (140 mph)

Dia. NZ502. Mark 4. Air conditioned. Swiss-built (SIG) bogies. a dg. Cab to shore communication. ETH 6X.

Lot No. 31043 Metro-Cammell 1988. 45.18 t.

82200	I	SAB	BN	82216	I SAB	BN
82201	I	SAB	BN	82217	I SAB	BN
82202	I	SAB	BN	82218	I SAB	BN
82203	I	SAB	BN	82219	I SAB	BN
82204	I	SAB	BN	82220	I SAB	BN
82205	I	SAB	BN	82221	I SAB	BN
82206	I	SAB	BN	82222	I SAB	BN
82207	I	SAB	BN	82223	I SAB	BN
82208	I	SAB	BN	82224	I SAB	BN
82209	I	SAB	BN	82225	I SAB	BN
82210	I	SAB	BN	82226	I SAB	BN
82211	I	SAB	BN	82227	I SAB	BN
82212	I	SAB	BN	82228	I SAB	BN
82213	I	SAB	BN	82229	I SAB	BN
82214	I	SAB	BN	82230	I SAB	BN
82215	I	SAB	BN	82231	I SAB	BN

ND (BG)   GANGWAYED BRAKE VAN (90 mph)

Dia. ND501. These vans are built on short frames (57'). Load 10t. BR1 bogies. vd. ETH 1. The full lot number list is listed here for reference purposes with renumbered vehicles.

b – (Dia. NB501). High security letter mail van. Converted at WB from BG 1985. Gangways removed. x.

80525. Lot No. 30009 Derby 1952 – 3. 31 t.
80561. Lot No. 30039 Derby 1954. 31 t.
80620 – 80621. Lot No. 30046 York 1954. 31.5 t.
80700 – 80703. Lot No. 30136 Metro-Cammell 1955. 31.5 t.
80731 – 80791. Lot No. 30140 BRCW 1955 – 6. 31.5 t.
80805 – 80848. Lot No. 30144 Cravens 1955. 31.5 t.
80855 – 80962. Lot No. 30162 Pressed Steel 1956 – 7. 32 t.
80971 – 81014. Lot No. 30173 York 1956. 31.5 t.
81019 – 81051. Lot No. 30224 Cravens 1956. 31.5 t.
81055 – 81179. Lot No. 30228 Metro-Cammell 1957 – 8. 31.5 t.
81182 – 81200. Lot No. 30234 Cravens 1956 – 7. 31.5 t.
81205 – 81265. Lot No. 30163 Pressed Steel 1957. 31.5 t.
81266 – 81309. Lot No. 30323 Pressed Steel 1957. 32 t.
81313 – 81497. Lot No. 30400 Pressed Steel 1957 – 8. 32 t.
81498 – 81568. Lot No. 30484 Pressed Steel 1958. 32 t.
81588 – 81590. Lot No. 30715 Gloucester 1962. 31 t.
81598 – 81610. Lot No. 30716 Gloucester 1962. 31 t.

Note: All 84xxx vehicles were renumbered from the 81xxx series by adding 3000 to the original number.

84025 (81025)		**M**	XRFZ	CS
84197 (81197)			MP	DY
84382 (81382, 80460)	b	**RX**	MPXT	CA
84387 (81387, 80461)	b	**B**	MPXT	CA
84477 (81477, 80463)	b	**B**	MPXT	CA
84519 (81519)			MPXX	Crewe Coal Sdgs.

84197 is kept at Shrewsbury Road Sidings, Sheffield for use when the station lifts are out of order.

NE/NH (BG) 100/110 mph GANGWAYED BRAKE VAN

As ND but rebogied with B4 bogies suitable for 100 mph – NE (110 mph with special maintenance – NH). d. ETH 1 (1X* and NHA). For lot numbers refer to original number series. Deduct 1.5t from weights. All NHA are a*pg.

92067 (81243)	a to **I**		MPXX	Doncaster West Yd.
92100 (81391)	a to **I**		XWRS	BN
92105 (81405)	a	**RY**	MP	CA
92110 (81426)	a*	**RX**	MP	EN
92111 (81432)	NHA **I**		SAXZ	Long Marston
92112 (81440)	x	**RY**	MP	EN
92114 (81443)	NHA **I**		SAXZ	Longtown
92116 (81450)	a to **I**		XWRS	Crewe South Yard
92121 (81457)	x*	**RX**	MP	BK
92122 (81459)	x*to **RY**		MP	CA
92125 (81470)	a to **I**		SCM	OY
92146 (81498)	NHA **I**		SAOL	Longtown
92155 (81525)	a*pg **I**		SCM	LA
92159 (81534)	NHA **I**		SAA	IS
92172 (81562)	a pg **I**		MP	BK
92174 (81567)	NHA **I**		SAA	IS
92175 (81568)	a pg **I**		SAJ	LA
92188 (81598)	a to **I**		SCM	LA
92193 (81604)	a pg **I**		MP	HT
92194 (81606)	a to **I**		SAJ	LA
92197 (81610)	a to **I**		SCM	LA
92198 (81613)	a to **I**		MP	HT
92211 (81267)	x	**R**	MP	CA
92229 (80902)	x	**RY**	MP	EN
92230 (81423)	a	**RY**	MP	CA
92234 (81336, 80460)	a	**RX**	MP	BK
92238 (81563, 84563)	a	**RY**	MP	CA
92243 (81489, 84489)	a	**RY**	MP	EN
92252 (80959)	x	**RY**	MP	BK
92258 (81346, 84346)	a	**RY**	MP	CA
92259 (81313, 84313)	x	**RY**	MP	EN
92260 (81104, 84104)	x	**RY**	MPXX	BK
92261 (80988)	x*	**RY**	MP	BK
92265 (80945)	x	**RY**	MP	EN
92267 (81404, 84404)	x		MP	BK
92271 (80962)	x*	**R**	MP	BK

NE (BG)   100 mph GANGWAYED BRAKE VAN

As ND but rebogied with Commonwealth bogies suitable for 100 mph. x. ETH 1
(1X*). For lot numbers refer to original number series. Add 1.5 t to weights to
allow for the increased weight of the Commonwealth bogies.

92302 (81501, 84501)	a	RX	MP	CA
92303 (81427, 84427)	a	RX	MP	BK
92306 (81217, 84217)	a*	RY	MP	CA
92307 (80805)	a*		MP	BK
92309 (81043, 84043)	x*	RX	MP	CA
92311 (81453, 84453)	x	RY	MP	BK
92312 (81548, 84548)	a	RX	MP	EN
92314 (80777)	x*	RY	MP	EN
92316 (80980)	x*	RY	MP	BK
92319 (81055, 84055)	x*	RY	MP	PZ
92321 (81566, 84566)	a	RY	MP	EN
92323 (80832)	a*	R	MP	EN
92324 (81087, 84087)	a	RY	MP	EN
92325 (80791)	x	RY	MP	DY
92328 (80999)	x*	RY	MP	EN
92329 (81001, 84001)	a*	RY	MP	EN
92330 (80995)	x*	RY	MP	BK
92332 (80845)	a*	RX	MP	CA
92333 (80982)	a*	RY	MP	CA
92334 (80983)	x*	R	MP	BK
92337 (81140, 84140)	a*	RX	MP	CA
92340 (81059, 84059)	a*	RY	MP	DY
92341 (81316, 84316)	x	RY	MP	CA
92343 (81505, 84505)	x	R	MP	EN
92344 (81154, 84154)	a*	RY	MP	EN
92345 (81083, 84083)	x*	RY	MP	BK
92346 (81091, 84091)	a	RY	MP	EN
92347 (81326, 84326)	a	RX	MP	EN
92348 (81075, 84075)	x*	R	MP	BK
92350 (81049, 84049)	a*	RY	MP	BK
92351 (81174, 84174)	x	RX	MP	BK
92353 (81323, 84323)	a	R	MP	EN
92355 (81517, 84517)	x	RX	MP	BK
92356 (81535, 84535)	x		MP	BK
92357 (81136, 84136)	x	RX	MP	BK
92362 (81188, 84188)	x	RY	MP	DY
92363 (81294, 84294)	x	RY	MP	CA
92364 (81030, 84030)	x*	R	MP	BK
92365 (81122, 84122)	a	RX	MP	EN
92366 (81551, 84551)	a	RX	MP	CA
92369 (80960)	x*		MP	CA
92370 (81324, 84324)	a		MP	BK
92371 (80856)	x*		MPXX	ABB Crewe
92377 (80928)	a*	RX	MP	HT

92379 (80914)	a*	RX	MP	CA
92380 (81247, 84247)	a*	R	MP	EN
92381 (81476, 84476)	a	RX	MP	CA
92382 (81561, 84561)	a	RX	MP	BK
92384 (80893)	a	RY	MP	CA
92385 (81261, 84261)	x*	RY	MP	PZ
92387 (81380, 84380)	x		MP	BK
92389 (81026, 84026)	a	RY	MP	PZ
92390 (80834)	a*		MP	CA
92392 (80861)	a*	RY	MP	EN
92395 (81274, 84274)	a		MP	CA
92398 (80859)	x*	RY	MP	EN
92399 (80781)	x*	RY	MP	BK
92400 (81211, 84211)	a*		MP	BK
92401 (81280, 84280)	x	RX	MP	BK
92402 (81099, 84099)	a*	RY	MP	DY
92403 (81273, 84273)	x	RY	MP	EN
92404 (81051, 84051)	x*		MP	BK
92406 (81475, 84475)	x	RY	MP	DY
92409 (81370, 84370)	x*		MP	BK
92410 (81469, 84469)	x		MP	BK
92411 (81252, 84252)	x*	RY	MP	BK
92412 (81354, 84354)	x	RY	MP	BK
92413 (81472, 84472)	x	RY	MP	DY
92414 (81458, 84458)	x		MP	BK
92415 (81388, 84388)	a	RX	MP	EN
92416 (81250, 84250)	a*	RY	MP	CA
92417 (80885)	a*	RX	MP	CA
92418 (81512, 84512)	a	RX	MP	EN

92369 is kept at Doncaster West Yard for use when Doncaster station lifts are out of order.

NF (BG)   100/110 mph GANGWAYED BRAKE VAN

As NE but with emergency equipment removed. For details and lot numbers refer to original number series. 92503 – 92755 have B4 bogies whilst 92800 – 92897 have Commonwealth bogies

b – (Dia. NB501). High security letter mail van. Converted at WB from BG 1985. Gangways removed.

92503 (80864, 92903)	x*	RY	MP	BK
92505 (80876, 92905)	x*	I	MP	BK
92509 (80897, 92909)	x*	RX	MP	DY
92510 (80900, 92910)	x*	RX	MP	EN
92513 (80916, 92913)	x*	RX	MP	EN
92518 (80941, 92918)	x*	RX	MP	CA
92521 (80956, 92921)	x*	I	MP	BK
92530 (81461, 84461)	xb	RX	MP	CA
92542 (81207, 92942)	a	RX	MP	BK
92547 (81216, 92947)	a	RX	MP	CA

92550 (81220, 92950)	a	**RX**	MP		EN
92555 (81225, 92955)	a	**RX**	MP		CA
92558 (81228, 92958)	a	**RX**	MP		CA
92562 (81232, 92962)	a	**RX**	MP		EN
92566 (81238, 92966)	a	**RX**	MP		BK
92568 (81244, 92968)	a	**RX**	MP		CA
92576 (81257, 92976)	a	**RX**	MP		CA
92577 (81258, 92977)	a	**RX**	MP		BK
92582 (81265, 92982)	a	**RY**	MP		PZ
92606 (81409, 92106)	x	**RY**	MP		EN
92607 (81410, 92107)	x	**RX**	MP		EN
92609 (81413, 92109)	a	**RX**	MP		CA
92617 (81451, 92117)	x	**RY**	MP		PZ
92644 (81496, 92144)	a	**RY**	MP		CA
92649 (81509, 92149)	x		MP		BK
92650 (81514, 92150)	a to	**RY**	MP		EN
92709 (80873, 92209)	x	**RX**	MP		CA
92714 (81504, 92214)	x	**RX**	MP		CA
92716 (81376, 92216)	x	**RY**	MP		EN
92717 (80877, 92217)	x	**RY**	MP		CA
92718 (81314, 92218)	a	**RY**	MP		BK
92720 (80924, 92220)	x	**RX**	MP		CA
92721 (80888, 92221)	x	**RY**	MP		BK
92722 (80887, 92222)	x	**RX**	MP		BK
92725 (80891, 92225)	a	**RX**	MP		CA
92728 (80921, 92228)	x	**RX**	MP		EN
92740 (80703, 92240)	x	**RY**	MP		EN
92748 (80935, 92248)	a	**RX**	MP		CA
92750 (81235, 92250)	x	**RX**	MP		EN
92753 (80936, 92253)	x	**RY**	MP		BK
92755 (80871, 92255)	x	**RX**	MP		CA
92800 (81200, 92300)	x	**RX**	MP		BK
92804 (81339, 92304)	x	**RX**	MP		HT
92805 (81590, 92305)	x	**RX**	MP		EN
92808 (80784, 92308)	x*	**RX**	MP		EN
92810 (81105, 92310)	a	**RX**	MP		EN
92815 (80848, 92315)	a*	**RX**	MP		EN
92817 (80836, 92317)	x*	**RX**	MP		BK
92820 (81166, 92320)	x		MP		BK
92822 (80771, 92322)	x*	**RX**	MP		CA
92827 (80842, 92327)	x*	**RX**	MP		EN
92831 (81365, 92331)	a	**RX**	MP		EN
92842 (81397, 92342)	x	**RY**	MP		CA
92852 (81182, 92352)	a	**RX**	MP		BK
92854 (81353, 92354)	x	**RX**	MP		EN
92858 (84393, 92358)	x	**RX**	MP		CA
92859 (81275, 92359)	a	**RX**	MP		CA
92860 (81431, 92360)	x	**RX**	MP		EN
92861 (81463, 92361)	a	**R**	MP		EN
92867 (81293, 92367)	x	**RX**	MP		EN
92872 (81362, 92372)	x	**RY**	MP		EN

92873 (81528, 92373)	a	**RX**	MP	EN
92875 (81335, 92375)	x		MPXX	ABB Crewe
92876 (81374, 92376)	a	**RX**	MP	EN
92883 (81429, 92383)	a	**RX**	MP	EN
92886 (80843, 92386)	x*	**RX**	MP	EN
92888 (80868, 92388)	a*	**RX**	MP	EN
92893 (80701, 92393)	x	**RX**	MP	EN
92894 (81322, 92394)	x	**RX**	MP	CA
92897 (80700, 92397)	x*	**RY**	MP	EN

NE/NH (BG)   100/110 mph GANGWAYED BRAKE VAN

Renumbered from 920xx series by adding 900 to number to avoid conflict with Class 92 locos. Class continued from 92271.

92901 (80855, 92001)	NHA	**I**		SAA	IS
92904 (80867, 92004)	a*pg	**G**		XVS	SL
92907 (80880, 92007)	a*pg	**RX**		MP	CA
92908 (80895, 92008)	NHA	**I**		SAA	IS
92912 (80910, 92012)	a*pg	**I**		SAOL	Long Marston
92916 (80930, 92016)	x*pg	**RY**		MP	CA
92917 (80940, 92017)	a*to	**RX**		MP	EN
92919 (80944, 92019)	a*pg	**I**		MP	BK
92920 (80950, 92020)	x*pg	**I**		MP	BK
92922 (80958, 92022)	x*pg	**RX**		MP	EN
92923 (80971, 92023)	a*pg	**I**		SAOL	Longtown
92926 (81060, 92026)	NHA	**I**		SAXZ	Longtown
92927 (81061, 92027)	NHA	**I**		SAXZ	Longtown
92928 (81064, 92028)	NHA	**I**		SAXZ	Longtown
92929 (81077, 92029)	NHA	**I**		SAXZ	Long Marston
92931 (81102, 92031)	NHA	**I**		SAA	IS
92932 (81117, 92032)	NHA	**I**		SAA	IS
92933 (81123, 92033)	NHA	**I**		SAXZ	Long Marston
92934 (81142, 92034)	NHA	**I**		SAOL	Longtown
92935 (81150, 92035)	a*pg	**I**		SAA	IS
92936 (81158, 92036)	NHA	**I**		SAA	IS
92937 (81165, 92037)	NHA	**I**		SAA	IS
92938 (81173, 92038)	NHA	**I**		SAA	IS
92939 (81175, 92039)	NHA	**I**		SAOL	Long Marston
92940 (81186, 92040)	a pg	**I**		SAJ	LA
92946 (81214, 92046)	NHA	**I**		SAA	IS
92948 (81218, 92048)	NHA	**I**		SAA	IS
92957 (81227, 92057)	a to	**I**		XWRS	BN
92961 (81231, 92061)	a	**I**		SAXZ	Longtown
92972 (81253, 92072)	a to	**I**		MPXX	BK
92973 (81254, 92073)	a to	**RY**		MP	CA
92986 (81282, 92086)	a to	**I**		SAXZ	Long Marston
92988 (81284, 92088)	a to	**I**		SAOL	Longtown
92989 (81303, 92089)	a to	**I**		SCM	LA
92991 (81308, 92091)	a to	**I**		SAXZ	Longtown
92998 (81381, 92098)	NHA	**I**		SAOL	Longtown

NJ (GUV)   GENERAL UTILITY VAN

Mark 1. NJ501. Short frames. Load 14 t. Screw couplings. Dia. NJ501. All vehicles have BR Mark 2 bogies. vr. ETH 0 or OX*. These vehicles were originally numbered in the 86xxx series, and 7000 was added to the original numbers to avoid confusion with Class 86. The full lot number list is listed here for reference purposes with renumbered vehicles.

86081 – 86499. Lot No. 30417 Pressed Steel 1958 – 9. 30 t.
86508 – 86518. Lot No. 30343 York 1957. 30 t.
86521 – 86651. Lot No. 30403 York/Glasgow 1958 – 60. 30 t.
86656 – 86834. Lot No. 30565 Pressed Steel 1959. 30 t.
86836 – 86980. Lot No. 30616 Pressed Steel 1959 – 60. 30 t.

93267	vr*	**RY**	MPXX	CA		93717	vy	**B**	MPXX	CA
93446	vr	**R**	MPXX	Crewe S. Yard		93952	vr*	**B**	MP	EN
93701	vr*	**B**	MPXX	CA		93979	vr*	**B**	MP	EN

NL   NEWSPAPER VAN

Dia. NL501. Mark 1. Short frames (57'). Converted from NJ (GUV). Fluorescent lighting, toilets and gangways fitted. Load 14 t. ETH 3X. Not now used for News traffic. B5 bogies except § – BR Mark 1 bogies.

Lot No. 30922 Wolverton or Doncaster 1977 – 8. e. 31 t (33 t§).

94003	(86281, 93999)	x	**RX**		CA
94004	(86156, 55504)	x	**RY**		BK
94006	(86202, 55506)	a	**RY**		BK
94007	(86572, 55507)	a	**B**		BK
94009	(86144, 55509)	a	**RY**		EN
94010	(86151, 55510)	x §	**RX**		CA
94011	(86437, 55511)	a	**RX**		BK
94015	(86484, 55515)	x	**B**		BK
94016	(86317, 55516)	x	**B**		BK
94020	(86220, 55520)	x	**RY**		EN
94021	(86204, 55521)	x	**B**		BK
94024	(86106, 55524)	a	**B**		BK
94025	(86377, 55525)	a	**RY**		EN
94026	(86703, 55526)	x	**RY**		EN
94027	(86732, 55527)	a §	**R**		BK
94028	(86733, 55528)	x §	**RX**		BK
94029	(86740, 55529)	x	**RY**		BK
94030	(86746, 55530)	x	**B**		BK
94031	(86747, 55531)	x	**B**		BK
94032	(86730, 55532)	a	**B**		BK
94033	(86731, 55533)	x	**RY**		EN

NMV   NEWSPAPER VAN

Dia. NM501/2. Mark 1. Standard NJs (GUVs) modified as newspaper vans. vd*.

ETH 3X. For lot numbers see 93xxx series. Formerly NLV. Not now used for News traffic.

94058 (86530, 93530)	**B**	MPXX	CA
94062 (86803, 93803)	**B**	MPXX	Crewe South Yard

NKA   SUPER GENERAL UTILITY VAN

Dia. NK501. ay. ETH 0X. Commonwealth bogies. For lot Nos. see 93xxx series. Add 2 t to weight. These vehicles are GUVs further modified with new floors, roller shutter doors and the end doors removed.

94100 (86668, 95100)	**RX**	MP	EN
94101 (86142, 95101)	**RX**	MP	BK
94102 (86762, 95102)	**RX**	MP	BK
94103 (86956, 95103)	**RX**	MP	BK
94104 (86942, 95104)	**RX**	MP	BK
94105 (,)			
94106 (86353, 95106)	**RX**	MP	BK
94107 (86576, 95107)	**RX**	MP	BK
94108 (86600, 95108)	**RX**	MP	BK
94109 (,)			
94110 (86393, 95110)	**RX**	MP	EN
94111 (86578, 95111)	**RX**	MP	EN
94112 (86673, 95112)	**RX**	MP	EN
94113 (86235, 95113)	**RX**	MP	BK
94114 (86081, 95114)	**RX**	MP	BK
94115 (,)			
94116 (,)			
94117 (86534, 95117)	**RX**	MP	BK
94118 (86675, 95118)	**RX**	MP	NC
94119 (86167, 95119)	**RX**	MP	BK
94120 (,)			
94121 (86518, 95121)	**RX**	MP	BK
94123 (86376, 95123)	**RX**	MP	BK
94124 (,)			
94125 (,)			
94126 (86692, 95126)	**B**	MP	NC
94127 (,)			
94128 (,)			
94129 (,)			
94130 (,)			
94131 (,)			
94132 (86607, 95132)	**RX**	MP	EN
94133 (,)			
94134 (,)			
94135 (,)			
94136 (,)			
94137 (86610, 95137)	**RX**	MP	CA
94138 (86212, 95138)	**RX**	MP	NC
94139 (,)			
94140 (86571, 95140)	**RX**	MP	BK

94141 (,)			
94142 (,)			
94143 (,)			
94144 (,)			
94145 (,)			
94146 (86648, 95146)	**RX**	MP	CA
94147 (86091, 95147)	**RX**	MP	BK
94148 (86416, 95148)	**RX**	MP	BK
94149 (,)			
94150 (86560, 95150)	**RX**	**MP**	BK
94151 (,)			
94152 (,)			
94153 (,)			
94154 (,)			
94155 (86520, 95155)	**RX**	MP	NC
94156 (,)			
94157 (86523, 95157)	**RX**	MP	CA
94158 (,)			
94159 (,)			
94160 (86581, 95160)	**RX**	MP	CA
94161 (,)			
94162 (,)			
94163 (,)			
94164 (86104, 95164)	**RX**	MP	BK
94165 (,)			
94166 (86112, 95166)	**RX**	MP	BK
94167 (,)			
94168 (86914, 95168)	**RX**	MP	BK
94169 (,)			
94170 (86395, 95170)	**RX**	MP	BK
94171 (,)			
94172 (86429, 95172)	**RX**	MP	CA
94173 (,)			
94174 (86852, 95174)	**RX**	MP	BK
94175 (86521, 95175)	**RX**	MP	CA
94176 (86210, 95176)	**RX**	MP	BK
94177 (86411, 95177)	**RX**	MP	CA
94178 (,)			
94179 (,)			
94180 (86362, 95141)	**RX**	MP	BK
94181 (,)			
94182 (86710, 95182)	**RY**	MP	BK
94183 (,)			
94184 (,)			
94185 (,)			
94186 (,)			
94187 (,)			
94188 (,)			
94189 (,)			
94190 (86624, 95350)	**RX**	MP	CA
94191 (86596, 95351)	**RX**	MP	EN

94192 (86727, 95352)	**RX**	MP		BK
94193 (86514, 95353)	**RX**	MP		BK
94195 (86375, 95355)	**RX**	MP		BK
94196 (86478, 95356)	**RX**	MP		CA
94197 (86508, 95357)	**RX**	MP		BK
94198 (86195, 95358)	**RX**	MP		CA
94199 (86854, 95359)	**RX**	MP		BK
94200 (86207, 95360)	**RX**	MP		EN
94201 (,)				
94202 (86563, 95362)	**RX**	MP		NC
94203 (86345, 95363)	**RX**	MP		BK
94204 (86715, 95364)	**RX**	MP		BK
94205 (86857, 95365)	**RX**	MP		BK
94207 (86529, 95367)	**RX**	MP		BK
94208 (86656, 95368)	**RX**	MP		BK
94209 (86390, 95369)	**RX**	MP		BK
94210 (,)				
94211 (86713, 95371)	**RX**	MP		BK
94212 (86728, 95372)	**RX**	MP		NC
94213 (86258, 95373)	**RX**	MP		CA
94214 (86367, 95374)	**RX**	MP		CA
94215 (86862, 94077)	**RX**	MP		BK
94216 (86711, 93711)	**RX**	MP		BK
94217 (86131, 93131)	**RX**	MP		BK
94218 (86541, 93541)	**RX**	MP		BK
94221 (86905, 93905)	**RX**	MP		CA
94222 (86474, 93474)	**RX**	MP		BK
94223 (86660, 93660)	**RX**	MP		CA
94224 (86273, 93273)	**RX**	MP		BK
94225 (86849, 93849)	**RX**	MP		CA
94226 (86525, 93525)	**RX**	MP		BK
94227 (86585, 93585)	**RX**	MP		BK
94228 (86511, 93511)	**RX**	MP		BK
94229 (86720, 93720)	**RX**	MP		EN

NAA   PROPELLING CONTROL VEHICLE

Dia. NA508. (PCV) Mark 1. Class 307 driving trailers converted for use in propelling parcels trains out of termini. Fitted with roller shutter doors. Equipment fitted for communication between cab of PCV and locomotive. ae.

Lot No. 30206 Ashford/Eastleigh 1.954 – 6. Converted at Hunslet-Barclay, Kilmarnock 1994 onwards (RTC, Derby 1993*).

Note: 92327 – 92342 are to be converted from vehicles selected from 75002/3/5/7/8/10 – 2/5 – 7/9/20/2 – 6/8 – 32, 75116.

94300 (75114) *	**RX**	MP	EN	94304 (75107)	**RX**	MP	
94301 (75102) *	**RX**	MP	EN	94305 (75104)	**RX**	MP	
94302 (75124)	**RX**	MP		94306 (75112)	**RX**	MP	
94303 (75131)	**RX**	MP		94307 (75127)	**RX**	MP	

94308 (75125)	**RX**	MP	
94309 (75130)	**RX**	MP	
94310 (75119)	**RX**	MP	
94311 (75105)	**RX**	MP	
94312 (75126)	**RX**	MP	
94313 (75129)	**RX**	MP	
94314 (75109)	**RX**	MP	
94315 (75132)	**RX**	MP	
94316 (75108)	**RX**	MP	
94317 (75117)	**RX**	MP	
94318 (75115)	**RX**	MP	
94319 (75128)	**RX**	MP	
94320 (75120)	**RX**	MP	
94321 (75122)	**RX**	MP	
94322 (75111)	**RX**	MP	
94323 (75110)	**RX**	MP	
94324 (75103)	**RX**	MP	
94325 (75113)	**RX**	MP	
94326 (75123)	**RX**	MP	
94327 (75)	**RX**	MP	
94328 (75)	**RX**	MP	
94329 (75)	**RX**	MP	
94330 (75)	**RX**	MP	
94331 (75)	**RX**	MP	
94332 (75)	**RX**	MP	
94333 (75)	**RX**	MP	
94334 (75)	**RX**	MP	
94335 (75)	**RX**	MP	
94336 (75)	**RX**	MP	
94337 (75)	**RX**	MP	
94338 (75)			
94339 (75)			
94340 (75)			
94341 (75)			
94342 (75)			
94343 (75027)	**RX**	MP	
94344 (75014)	**RX**	MP	
94345 (75004)	**RX**	MP	

NBA   SUPER BRAKE VAN

Dia. NB501. ae. ETH 1X. B4 bogies. For lot Nos. refer to original number series. These vehicles are NEs further modified with new floors & roller shutter doors.

94400 (81224, 92954)	**RX**	MP	BK
94401 (81277, 92224)	**RX**	MP	EN
94403 (81479, 92629)	**RX**	MP	BK
94404 (81486, 92135)	**RX**	MP	CA
94405 (80890, 92233)	**RX**	MP	BK
94406 (81226, 92956)	**RX**	MP	BK
94407 (81223, 92553)	**RX**	MP	HT
94408 (81264, 92981)	**RX**	MP	BK
94409 (81511, 92249)	**RX**	MP	BK
94410 (81205, 92941)	**RX**	MP	BK
94411 (81378, 92997)	**RX**	MP	CA
94412 (81210, 92945)	**RX**	MP	BK
94413 (80909, 92236)	**RX**	MP	BK
94414 (81377, 92996)	**RX**	MP	HT
94415 (81309, 92992)	**RX**	MP	BK
94416 (80929, 92746)	**RX**	MP	BK
94417 (,)			
94418 (81248, 92244)	**RX**	MP	BK
94419 (80858, 92902)	**RX**	MP	BK
94420 (81325, 92263)	**RX**	MP	BK
94421 (81230, 92960)	**RX**	MP	BK
94422 (81516, 92651)	**RX**	MP	CA
94423 (80923, 92914)	**RX**	MP	BK
94424 (81400, 92103)	**RX**	MP	CA
94425 (80937, 92212)	**RX**	MP	BK
94426 (81283, 92987)	**RX**	MP	BK
94427 (80894, 92754)	**RX**	MP	BK

94428 (81550, 92166)	**RX**	MP	BK
94429 (80870, 92232)	**RX**	MP	HT
94430 (80908, 92235)	**RX**	MP	HT
94431 (81401, 92604)	**RX**	MP	BK
94432 (81383, 92999)	**RX**	MP	BK
94433 (81495, 92643)	**RX**	MP	BK
94434 (81268, 92584)	**RX**	MP	HT
94435 (81485, 92134)	**RX**	MP	BK
94436 (81237, 92565)	**RX**	MP	BK
94437 (81403, 92208)	**RX**	MP	BK
94438 (81425, 92251)	**RX**	MP	BK
94439 (81480, 92130)	**RX**	MP	BK
94440 (81497, 92645)	**RX**	MP	BK
94441 (81492, 92140)	**RX**	MP	BK
94442 (80932, 92723)	**RX**	MP	BK
94443 (81473, 92127)	**RX**	MP	BK
94444 (81484, 92133)	**RX**	MP	BK
94445 (81444, 92615)	**RX**	MP	BK
94446 (80857, 92242)	**RX**	MP	BK
94447 (81515, 92266)	**RX**	MP	CA
94448 (81541, 92664)	**RX**	MP	BK
94449 (81536, 92747)	**RX**	MP	CA
94450 (80927, 92915)	**RX**	MP	CA
94451 (80955, 92257)	**RX**	MP	BK
94452 (81394, 92602)	**RX**	MP	BK
94453 (81170, 92239)	**RX**	MP	BK
94454 (81465, 92124)	**RX**	MP	CA
94455 (81239, 92264)	**RX**	MP	EN
94456 (80879, 92226)	**RX**	MP	BK
94457 (81454, 92119)	**RX**	MP	BK
94458 (81255, 92974)	**RX**	MP	BK
94459 (81490, 92138)	**RX**	MP	CA
94460 (81266, 92983)	**RX**	MP	BK
94461 (81487, 92136)	**RX**	MP	BK
94462 (81289, 92270)	**RX**	MP	BK
94463 (81375, 92995)	**RX**	MP	CA
94464 (81240, 92262)	**RX**	MP	BK
94465 (81481, 92131)	**RX**	MP	BK
94466 (81236, 92964)	**RX**	MP	CA
94467 (81245, 92969)	**RX**	MP	BK
94468 (81259, 92978)	**RX**	MP	BK
94469 (81260, 92979)	**RX**	MP	BK
94470 (81442, 92113)	**RX**	MP	BK
94471 (81518, 92152)	**RX**	MP	HT
94472 (81526, 92975)	**RX**	MP	DY
94473 (81262, 92272)	**RX**	MP	EN
94474 (81452, 92618)	**RX**	MP	BK
94475 (81208, 92943)	**RX**	MP	BK
94476 (81209, 92944)	**RX**	MP	BK
94477 (81494, 92642)	**RX**	MP	BK
94478 (81488, 92637)	**RX**	MP	BK

94479 (81482, 92132)		**RX**	MP		BK
94480 (81411, 92608)		**RX**	MP		EN
94481 (81493, 92641)		**RX**	MP		EN
94482 (81491, 92639)		**RX**	MP		CA
94483 (81500, 92647)		**RX**	MP		CA
94484 (,)					
94485 (,)					
94486 (,)					
94487 (,)					

NOX (GUV)   GENERAL UTILITY VAN (100 MPH ETH WIRED)

Dia. NO513. xy. ETH OX. Commonwealth bogies except where shown otherwise. For lot Nos. see 93xxx series. Add 2 t to weight (Subtract 2 t for B4).

95105 (86126, 93126)	a	**RX**	MP	EN
95109 (86269, 93269)	x	**B**	MP	CA
95115 (86174, 93174)	x	**B**	MP	BK
95116 (86426, 93426)	x	**B**	MP	BK
95120 (86468, 93468)	x	**RY**	MP	CA
95124 (86836, 93836)	x	**R**	MP	BK
95125 (86143, 93143)	x	**RY**	MP	BK
95127 (86323, 93323)	x	**RY**	MP	CA
95128 (86764, 93764)	x	**RY**	MP	EN
95129 (86347, 93347)	x	**RY**	MP	EN
95130 (86263, 93263)	x	**RY**	MP	EN
95131 (86860, 93860)	a	**RX**	MP	CA
95133 (86604, 93604)	x	**RX**	MP	CA
95134 (86462, 93462)	x	**RX**	MP	EN
95135 (86249, 93249)	x	**RY**	MP	EN
95136 (86396, 93396)	x	**RX**	MP	EN
95139 (86172, 93172)	x	**RY**	MP	EN
95142 (86844, 93844)	x	**RX**	MP	BK
95143 (86485, 93485)	x	**RX**	MP	CA
95144 (86165, 93165)	x	**RY**	MP	BK
95145 (86293, 93293)	x	**RX**	MP	BK
95149 (86265, 93265)	x	**RY**	MP	EN
95151 (86606, 93606)	x	**RX**	MP	CA
95152 (86969, 93969)	x	**RY**	MP	BK
95153 (86798, 93798)	x	**RY**	MP	EN
95154 (86897, 93897)	x	**RY**	MP	BK
95156 (86160, 93160)	x	**RX**	MP	EN
95158 (86499, 93499)	x	**RX**	MP	CA
95159 (86084, 93084)	x	**RX**	MP	EN
95161 (86205, 93205)	x	**RX**	MP	EN
95162 (86122, 93122)	x	**RX**	MP	EN
95163 (86407, 93407)	x	**RX**	MP	EN
95165 (86262, 93262)	x	**RX**	MP	BK
95167 (86255, 93255)	x	**RX**	MP	EN
95169 (86277, 93277)	x	**RX**	MP	EN
95171 (86110, 93110)	x	**RX**	MP	CA

95173 (86842, 94076)	x	**RX**	MP	CA
95181 (86971, 95361)	x	**B**	MP	CA
95190 (86643, 95393)	x B4	**RY**	MP	BK
95191 (86278, 95391)	x B4	**B**	MP	BK
95192 (86495, 95392)	x B4		MP	BK
95193 (86694, 93694)	x B4	**RX**	MP	BK
95194 (86192, 93192)	x B4	**RX**	MP	EN
95195 (86539, 93539)	x B4	**RX**	MP	EN
95196 (86775, 93775)	x B4	**RX**	MP	CA
95197 (86590, 93590)	x B4	**RX**	MP	CA
95198 (86134, 93134)	x B4	**RX**	MP	CA
95199 (86141, 93141)	x B4	**RX**	MP	EN

NCX   NEWSPAPER VAN (100 mph)

Dia. NC501. BGs modified to carry newspapers. xe. ETH 3 (3X*). Commonwealth bogies. For lot Nos. see BG section. Add 2 t to weight. Not now used for News traffic.

95200 (81019, 84019)	*	**RY**	MP	CA
95201 (80875)		**RY**	MP	EN
95204 (80947)	*	**RX**	MP	BK
95205 (80620)	*	**B**	MPXX	BK
95206 (80561)		**RY**	MP	NC
95209 (81047, 84047)		**RX**	MP	CA
95210 (80731)		**RX**	MP	BK
95211 (80949)		**RX**	MP	NC
95212 (81179, 84179)		**B**	MPXX	BK
95217 (81385, 84385)		**B**	MP	EN
95222 (80774)		**RX**	MP	EN
95223 (80933)	*	**RY**	MP	EN
95227 (81292, 95310)		**RX**	MP	NC
95228 (81014, 95332)		**RX**	MP	EN
95229 (81341, 95329)		**RX**	MP	BK
95230 (80525, 95321)		**RX**	MP	EN

NOV   GENERAL UTILITY VAN (100 mph ETH WIRED)

Dia. NO513. vy. ETH 0X. Commonwealth bogies. For lot Nos. see 93xxx section. Add 2 t to weight.

95366 (86251, 93251)	**B**	MP		BK

NRX   BAA CONTAINER VAN (100 mph)

Dia. NR503. Modified for carriage of British Airports Authority containers with roller shutter doors and roller floors and gangways removed. xe. ETH 3 (3X*). Commonwealth bogies. For lot Nos. see original number series. Add 2 t to weight.

95400 (80621, 95203)	**RX**	MP	DY
95410 (80826, 95213)	**RX**	MP	DY

NX (GUV)   MOTORAIL VAN (100 mph)

Mark 1. Dia. NX501. Renumbered from 93xxx series. For details and lot numbers see 93xxx series. ETH 0 (0X*). 100 mph.

96100 (86734, 93734)	a*B5I	SAOL	Kineton
96101 (86741, 93741)	a*B5I	SAOL	Kineton
96103 (86744, 93744)	a*B5I	SAOL	Kineton
96110 (86738, 93738)	a*C I	SAOL	Kineton
96111 (86742, 93742)	a*C I	SAOL	Kineton
96112 (86750, 93750)	a*C I	SAOL	Longtown
96130 (86736, 93736)	a*C I	SAOL	Kineton
96131 (86737, 93737)	a*C I	SAOL	Kineton
96132 (86754, 93754)	a*C I	SAOL	Longtown
96133 (86685, 93685)	a C I	SAOL	Longtown
96134 (86691, 93691)	a C I	SAOL	Longtown
96135 (86755, 93755)	a C I	SAOL	Long Marston
96136 (86735, 93735)	a C I	SAOL	Longtown
96137 (86748, 93748)	a C I	SAOL	ZN
96138 (86749, 93749)	a C I	SAXZ	Longtown
96139 (86751, 93751)	a C I	SAOL	Long Marston
96141 (86753, 93753)	a C B	SAOL	Longtown
96150 (86097, 93097)	a*B5I	SAOL	Kineton
96155 (86334, 93334)	a*B5I	SAOL	Kineton
96156 (86337, 93337)	a*B5I	SAOL	Kineton
96157 (86344, 93344)	a*B5I	SAOL	Kineton
96162 (86647, 93647)	a*C I	SAOL	Longtown
96163 (86646, 93646)	a*C I	SAOL	Kineton
96164 (86880, 93880)	a*C I	SAOL	Longtown
96165 (86784, 93784)	a*C I	SAOL	Kineton
96166 (86834, 93834)	a*C I	SAOL	Kineton
96167 (86756, 93756)	a*C I	SAOL	Kineton
96168 (86978, 93978)	a*C I	SAOL	Kineton
96169 (86937, 93937)	a*C I	SAOL	Longtown
96170 (86159, 93159)	x*C I	SAOL	Kineton
96171 (86326, 93326)	x*C I	SAOL	Longtown
96172 (86363, 93363)	x*C I	SAOL	Kineton
96173 (86440, 93440)	x*C I	SAOL	Kineton
96174 (86453, 93453)	x*C I	SAOL	Longtown
96175 (86628, 93628)	x*C I	SAOL	Kineton
96176 (86641, 93641)	x*C I	SAOL	Kineton
96177 (86980, 93980)	a*C I	SAOL	Kineton
96178 (86782, 93782)	a*C I	SAOL	Kineton
96179 (86910, 93910)	a*C I	SAOL	Longtown
96181 (86875, 93875)	a*C I	SAOL	Longtown
96182 (86944, 93944)	a*C I	SAOL	Long Marston
96185 (86083, 93083)	x*C I	SAOL	Longtown
96186 (86087, 93087)	x*C I	SAOL	Longtown
96187 (86168, 93168)	x*C I	SAOL	Longtown
96188 (86320, 93320)	x*C I	SAOL	Longtown

96189 (86447, 93447)	x*C I	SAOL	Longtown
96190 (86448, 93448)	x*C I	SAOL	Longtown
96191 (86665, 93665)	x*C I	SAOL	Kineton
96192 (86669, 93669)	x*C I	SAOL	Kineton
96193 (86874, 93874)	x*C I	SAOL	Longtown
96194 (86949, 93949)	x*C I	SAOL	Longtown
96195 (86958, 93958)	x*C I	SAOL	Longtown

NP (GUV)   MOTORAIL VAN (110 mph)

Mark 1. Dia. NP503. Vehicles modified with concertina end doors. For details
and lot numbers see 93xxx series. B5 Bogies. ay. ETH 0X*.

96210 (86355, 96159)	I	SAOL	Longtown
96211 (86745, 96104)	I	SAOL	Kineton
96212 (86443, 96161)	I	SAOL	Longtown
96213 (86324, 96152)	I	SAOL	Kineton
96214 (86331, 96154)	I	SAOL	Kineton
96215 (86351, 96158)	I	SAOL	Kineton
96216 (86385, 96160)	I	SAOL	Kineton
96217 (86327, 96153)	I	SAOL	Kineton
96218 (86286, 96151)	I	SAOL	Longtown

NG (MRCF)   MOTORAIL LOADING WAGON

Dia. NG503. These vehicles have been renumbered from weltrol wagons and
are used for loading purposes.

Built Swindon 1960. wagon Lot No. 3102 (3192*).

96450 (B900920)		SAOL	WB
96451 (B900912)		SAOL	WB
96452 (B900917)		SAOL	Longtown
96453 (B900926)	*	SAOL	PC
96454 (B900938)	*	SAOL	ZH

NY   EXHIBITION VAN

Various interiors. Converted from various vehicle types. Electric heating from
shore supply. In some cases new lot numbers were issued for conversions, but
not always. Non-standard livery – varies according to job being undertaken.

Lot 30842 Swindon 1972 – 3. Dia. NY503. Converted from BSK to Lot No.
30156 Wolverton 1955.

99621 (34697) x BR1	**0**	MPNW	Ferme Park	Exhibition Coach.
99625 (34693) x Mk4	**0**	MPNW	Ferme Park	Generator Van.

Converted Salisbury 1981 from RB to Lot No. 30636 Pressed Steel 1962. Dia
NY523/4 respectively.

99645 (1765) v C	**0**	MPNW	Ferme Park	Club Car.
99646 (1766) v C	**0**	MPNW	Ferme Park	Club Car.

Note: Mk4 denotes a Southern Region Mark 4 EMU trailer bogie.

6. EUROTUNNEL STOCK

This section presents the complete rolling stock of Eurotunnel, the operator of the Channel Tunnel. Whilst through rail passengers travel in the 'Eurostar' sets motorised passengers travel in special car and lorry-carring vehicles.

Car passengers travel in special double deck car carrying vehicles. Coaches, campervans, caravans and light goods vehicles are accommodated in single deck carriers of similar design. Up to three motorbikes can be carried in each double deck loader. Cars with roof loads over 1.65 m must travel in the single deck stock. The double deck loaders have side sliding roof mechanism.

The system is drive-on – drive-off and car passengers are normally expected to remain in their vehicles, although it is possible to walk along the coach to a toilet or snack machine. The vehicles are well lit with information displays giving anticipated arrival times during the journey. All tourists are able to use a motorway service station style rest area before lining up for allocation. The platform to platform transit is about 35 minutes with 25 of that spent in the Tunnel.

For heavy goods vehicles (HGVs), drivers will not remain in their vehicles, but will travel in separate 'club' cars. An at seat meal service will be provided for the drivers.

The Tunnel itself consists of twin 50.5 km (31.4 mile) long large diameter tunnels up to 126 metres (413 ft.) below sea level. There is also a service tunnel between the two running tunnels. All 'Le Shuttle' workings have two locomotives.

EUROTUNNEL LOCOMOTIVES

CLASS 0   MaK   Bo – Bo

These general purpose diesel locomotives are the same basic design as the Netherlands Railways 6400 Class.
Built: 1992 – 3 by Krupp-MaK/ABB at Kiel, Germany. (Type DE1004)
Engine: MaK 940 kW (1280 hp) at 1800 r.p.m.
Traction Motor: Four ABB three-phase traction motors.
Max. Tractive Effort: 305 kN.
Continuous Tractive Effort: 140 kN at 20 m.p.h.
Power at Rail: 750 kW.
Brake Force: 120 kN.   **Length over Couplers:** 16.50 m.
Weight: 84 tonnes   **Wheel Diameter:** 1000 mm.
Max. Speed: 120 (75 km/h)   **Train Brakes:** Air.
Communication Equipment: Cab to shore radio.
Couplings: High and Low level Sharfenberg plus UIC screw.
Cab Signalling: TVM 430.
Livery: Standard NS grey and yellow (Netherlands Railways).

0001	CQ
0002	CQ
0003	CQ
0004	CQ
0005	CQ

CLASS 0   B

Schöma rebuilds of Hunslet 900 mm gauge locos.
Built: 1989 – 90. Rebuilt 1993 – 4.
Engine: Deutz 270 kW (200 hp).
Transmission: Mechanical.
Max. Speed: 30 mph (120 km/h when gears disengaged).
Train Brakes: Air.

0031	CQ
0032	CQ
0033	CQ
0034	CQ
0035	CQ
0036	CQ
0037	CQ
0038	CQ
0039	CQ
0040	CQ

CLASS 9   BRUSH EUROSHUTTLE   Bo – Bo – Bo

A.C. electric locomotives which will be used on the Eurotunnel shuttle trains between Cheriton and Coquelles.
Built: 1992 – 4 by Brush/ABB at Loughborough.
Supply System: 25 kV a.c. from overhead equipment.
Traction Motors: 6 x ABB 6PH.
Control System: GTO thyristor.
Max. Tractive Effort: 400 kN (90 000 lbf).
Continuous Rating: 5760 kW (7725 hp) giving a tractive effort of 310 kN at 65 km/h.
Brake Force: 50 t.   **Length over Buffers:** 22.00 m.
Design Speed: 175 km/h (110 mph). **Weight:** 132 t.
Max. Speed: 160 km/h (100 mph).   **RA:** Channel Tunnel only.
ETH Index: **Wheel Diameter:** 1090 mm.
Train Brakes: Air.   **Electric Brake:** Regenerative.
Multiple Working: Time division multiplex system. RC232 data bus
Couplings: High level Sharfenburg plus UIC screw links.
Communication Equipment: Cab to shore radio and in-train system.
Cab Signalling: TVM 430.
Livery: Two-tone grey and white with green, blue bands.

9001	CQ		9020	CQ
9002	CQ		9021	CQ
9003	CQ		9022	CQ
9004	CQ		9023	CQ
9005	CQ		9024	CQ
9006	CQ		9025	CQ
9007	CQ		9026	CQ
9008	CQ		9027	CQ
9009	CQ		9028	CQ
9010	CQ		9029	CQ
9011	CQ		9030	CQ
9012	CQ		9031	CQ
9013	CQ		9032	CQ
9014	CQ		9033	CQ
9015	CQ		9034	CQ
9016	CQ		9035	CQ
9017	CQ		9036	CQ
9018	CQ		9037	CQ
9019	CQ		9038	CQ

'LE SHUTTLE' PASSENGER FLEET'

DOUBLE DECK CARRIER WAGON · DDCa

Builder: Bombardier (Canada)/ANF, Crespin, France.
Weight: 62 t.
Height: 5.575 m.
Length: 26.00 m.
Width: 4.1 m.
Couplings: Automatic Scharfenburg at one end, semi-automatic Scharfenburg at the other.

1001	1013	1025	1201	1213	1225
1002	1014	1026	1202	1214	1226
1003	1015	1027	1203	1215	1227
1004	1016	1028	1204	1216	1228
1005	1017	1029	1205	1217	1229
1006	1018	1030	1206	1218	1230
1007	1019	1031	1207	1219	1231
1008	1020	1032	1208	1220	1232
1009	1021	1033	1209	1221	1233
1010	1022	1034	1210	1222	1234
1011	1023	1035	1211	1223	1235
1012	1024	1036	1212	1224	1236

DOUBLE DECK CARRIER WAGON · DDCs

These vehicles have a toilet and stairs.

Builder: Bombardier (Canada)/ANF, Crespin, France.
Weight: 62 t.
Height: 5.575 m.
Length: 26.000 m.
Width: 4.1 m.
Couplings: Semi-automatic Scharfenburg at both ends.

1401	1407	1413	1419	1425	1431
1402	1408	1414	1420	1426	1432
1403	1409	1415	1421	1427	1433
1404	1410	1416	1422	1428	1434
1405	1411	1417	1423	1429	1435
1406	1412	1418	1424	1430	1436

DOUBLE DECK LOADER WAGON · DDL

Builder: Bombardier, Canada.
Weight: 64 t.
Height: 5.575 m.
Length: 27.25 m.
Width: 4.1 m.

Couplings: Low level Scharfenburg electro-pneumatic auto couplers.

1801	1805	1808	1811	1814	1817
1802	1806	1809	1812	1815	1818
1803	1807	1810	1813	1816	1819
1804					

Formations:

Formations are as follows:

Set 1 is 1801 + 1001 – 1401 – 1201 + 1002 – 1402 – 1202 + 1003 – 1403 – 1203 + 1004 – 1404 – 1204 + 1802 with other sets being in sequence.

SINGLE DECK CARRIER WAGON   SDCa

Builder: Bombardier BN, Brugge, Belgium.
Weight: 62.5 t.   **Length:** 26.00 m.
Height: 5.575 m.   **Width:** 4.1 m.
Couplings: Low level Scharfenburg electro-pneumatic auto coupler at one end and semi-auto Scharfenburg at other

3001	3013	3025	3201	3213	3225
3002	3014	3026	3202	3214	3226
3003	3015	3027	3203	3215	3227
3004	3016	3028	3204	3216	3228
3005	3017	3029	3205	3217	3229
3006	3018	3030	3206	3218	3230
3007	3019	3031	3207	3219	3231
3008	3020	3032	3208	3220	3232
3009	3021	3033	3209	3221	3233
3010	3022	3034	3210	3222	3234
3011	3023	3035	3211	3223	3235
3012	3024	3036	3212	3224	3236

SINGLE DECK CARRIER WAGON   SDCs

With toilet

Builder: Bombardier BN, Brugge, Belgium.
Weight: 63 t.
Height: 5.575 m.
Length: 26.000 m.
Width: 4.1 m.
Couplings: Low level semi-automatic Scharfenburg electro-pneumatic at both ends.

3401	3407	3413	3419	3425	3431
3402	3408	3414	3420	3426	3432
3403	3409	3415	3421	3427	3433
3404	3410	3416	3422	3428	3434
3405	3411	3417	3423	3429	3435
3406	3412	3418	3424	3430	3436

SINGLE DECK LOADER WAGON · SDL

Builder: Fiat, Savigliano, Italy.
Weight: 61 t.
Height: 5.570 m.
Length: 26.000 m.
Width: 4.1 m.
Couplings: Low level Scharfenburg electro-pneumatic auto couplers.

3801	3804	3807	3810	3813	3816
3802	3805	3808	3811	3814	3817
3803	3806	3809	3812	3815	3818

Formations:

Formations are as follows:

Set 1 is 3801 + 3001 – 3401 – 3201 + 3002 – 3402 – 3202 + 3003 – 3403 – 3203 + 3004 – 3404 – 3204 + 3802 with other sets being in sequence.

'LE SHUTTLE' HGV FLEET

LIGHT HGV CARRIER WAGON · LHGVC

Length: 20.506 m.
Height: 5.595 m.
Width: 4.1 m.
Weight: 34 t.
Builders: OMECA, Reggio, Calabria, Italy (110), Ferrosud, Materia, Italy (70) and Imesi, Palermo, Italy (48).

5001	5115	5201	5219	5305	5323
5002	5116	5202	5220	5306	5324
5003	5117	5203	5221	5307	5325
5004	5118	5204	5222	5308	5326
5101	5119	5205	5223	5309	5327
5102	5120	5206	5224	5310	5328
5103	5121	5207	5225	5311	5329
5104	5122	5208	5226	5312	5330
5105	5123	5209	5227	5313	5331
5106	5124	5210	5228	5314	5332
5107	5125	5211	5229	5315	5401
5108	5126	5212	5230	5316	5402
5109	5127	5213	5231	5317	5403
5110	5128	5214	5232	5318	5404
5111	5129	5215	5301	5319	5405
5112	5130	5216	5302	5320	5406
5113	5131	5217	5303	5321	5407
5114	5132	5218	5304	5322	5408

5409	5429	5517	5605	5625	5713
5410	5430	5518	5606	5626	5714
5411	5431	5519	5607	5627	5715
5412	5432	5520	5608	5628	5716
5413	5501	5521	5609	5629	5717
5414	5502	5522	5610	5630	5718
5415	5503	5523	5611	5631	5719
5416	5504	5524	5612	5632	5720
5417	5505	5525	5613	5701	5721
5418	5506	5526	5614	5702	5722
5419	5507	5527	5615	5703	5723
5420	5508	5528	5616	5704	5724
5421	5509	5529	5617	5705	5725
5422	5510	5530	5618	5706	5726
5423	5511	5531	5619	5707	5727
5424	5512	5532	5620	5708	5728
5425	5513	5601	5621	5709	5729
5426	5514	5602	5622	5710	5730
5427	5515	5603	5623	5711	5731
5428	5516	5604	5624	5712	5732

LIGHT HGV LOADER WAGON   LHGVL

Length: 25.100 m.
Height: 3.490 m.
Width: 4.1 m.
Weight: 45 t.
Builder: Fiat, Savigliano, Italy.

5801	5807	5813	5819	5824	5829
5802	5808	5814	5820	5825	5830
5803	5809	5815	5821	5826	5831
5804	5810	5816	5822	5827	5832
5805	5811	5817	5823	5828	5833
5806	5812	5818			

LIGHT AMENITY COACH-CLUB CAR   LAMC

Length: 25.720 m.
Height: 3.950 m.
Width: 3 m.
Weight: 45 t.
Builders: OMECA, Calabria, Italy (8) and Breda, Sisloia, Italy (1).

5901	5903	5905	5907	5908	5909
5902	5904	5906			

7. CODES

7.1. LIVERY CODES

LOCOMOTIVES

All locomotives are blue unless otherwise indicated. The colour of the lower half of the bodyside is stated first. Minor variations to these liveries are ignored.

BR   Revised blue (large numbers and full height BR logo).

BS   Blue with red solebar stripe.

C   Civil Engineers (grey and yellow).

CS   Central services (grey and red).

CT   Civil Engineers livery with Transrail markings.

D   Departmental (plain grey with black cab doors).

E   European Passenger Services - As 'F' with blue roof and Channel Tunnel markings.

F   New Railfreight (two-tone grey sides with sub-sector markings).

FA   Trainload Construction - As 'F' with construction markings (blue blocks on a yellow background).

FC   Trainload Coal - As 'F' with coal markings (black diamonds on a yellow background).

FD   Old Railfreight Distribution - As 'F' with Railfreight Distribution markings (red diamonds on a yellow background).

FL   New Railfreight Livery with LoadHaul markings.

FE   New Railfreight Distribution - Two-tone grey with blue roof and Railfreight Distribution lettering and markings (red diamonds on a yellow background).

FF   Freightliner - As 'F' with Freightliner lettering and markings (red diagonal stripes behind right hand cab door).

FM   New Railfreight Livery with Mainline markings.

FO   Old Railfreight (grey sides, yellow cabsides, red bufferbeams and full height BR logo).

FP   Trainload Petroleum - As 'F' with Trainload Petroleum markings (blue waves on a yellow background).

FR   As 'FO' but with red solebar stripe.

FS   Trainload Metals - As 'F' with metals markings (blue chevrons on a yellow background).

FT   New Railfreight Livery with Transrail markings.

G   BR or GWR green.

GE   Gatwick Express (white and dark grey with claret stripe and Gatwick Express lettering and motif).

I   InterCity (white and dark grey with red stripe and yellow lower cab sides).

IO   Old InterCity (light grey and dark grey with red stripe and yellow lower cab sides).

LH   LoadHaul (black with orange cabsides and Loadhaul markings).

M   Mainline (as old InterCity but without the yellow cabsides).

MD   Merseyrail Departmental (dark grey and yellow with Merseyrail logo and lettering).

ML   Mainline Freight company livery (blue with silver body stripe and Mainline markings).

N   Network SouthEast (grey/white/red/white/blue/white).

O   Other livery (non-Standard - refer to text).

R   Parcels (post office red and dark grey).

RR   Regional Railways (grey/light blue/white/dark blue).
RX   Rail Express Systems (post office red with Res blue & black markings).
T   Racal-BRT (two-tone grey with green markings).
W   Waterman Railways (black with cream & red lining).

Note: Trainload Freight sub-sector markings are gradually being withdrawn.

COACHING STOCK AND MULTIPLE UNITS

Coaching stock vehicles are in the old blue & grey livery unless otherwise indicated. The colour of the lower half of the bodyside is stated first.

A	Advertising Livery
B	Plain Blue
CC	BR Carmine & Cream ("Blood & Custard")
CE	Centro (WMPTE) (grey/light blue/white/green)
CH	BR/GWR Chocolate & Cream
E	European Passenger Services (two-tone grey).
G	Southern Region or DMU Green
GE	Gatwick Express (white and dark grey with claret stripe and Gatwick Express lettering and motif)
GM	New Greater Manchester PTE (dark grey/red/white/light grey)
H	LNER Tourist Green and Cream ("Highland Heritage")
I	InterCity (light grey (white on DVTs)/red stripe/dark grey)
J	Jaffacake livery (grey/dark brown with orange stripe)
M	BR Maroon
MT	Merseytravel (yellow/blue/white/yellow)
N	Network SouthEast (grey/white/red/white/blue/white)
NR	Network SouthEast livery with the red stripe repainted blue.
NW	Network SouthEast (white/red/white/blue/white)
O	Other livery (non-standard - refer to text)
P	Provincial services (grey/light blue/white/dark blue)
PC	Pullman Car Company (umber & cream).
PL	Porterbrook Leasing (purple and grey)
PM	Provincial Midline. As 'P' but with grey and cream stripes
R	Plain Red.
RE	Regional Railways Express (buff/light grey/dark grey/light grey/buff, with dark blue, white and light blue stripes)
RM	Red with Yellow stripes above solebar with Royal Mail insignia or "Royal Mail Travelling Post Office" markings
RR	Regional Railways (grey/light blue/white/dark blue with three black and white stripes at end of each light blue band under cabs)
RX	Rail Express Systems (Red and grey with blue/black markings)
RY	Red with yellow stripes above solebar and BR logo
S	Strathclyde PTE (orange and black)
TL	Thameslink (grey with orange and blue logos)
W	Waterman Railways (maroon with cream stripes)
WV	Waterman Railways (West Coast Joint Stock lined purple lake)
Y	West Yorkshire PTE (red and cream)

7.2. LOCOMOTIVE POOL CODES

Central Services

CDJD   Derby Etches Park Class 08 (Research)

Railfreight Distribution

DAAN   Allerton Class 08
DAEC   Crewe Electric Class 92 (Not in Traffic)
DAET   Tinsley Class 47 (Channel Tunnel/Automotive)
DAIC   Crewe Electric Class 92 (Operational Fleet)
DAMC   Crewe Electric Class 87/1 & 90
DANC   Crewe Electric Class 86/6
DAST   Tinsley Class 47
DASY   Tinsley Class 08 (Saltley)
DATI   Tinsley Class 08
DAWE   Allerton Class 08/09 (Wembley/Dagenham/Southampton)
DAYX   Stored Locos

Freightliner (1995) Ltd.

DFLC   Crewe Electric Class 90/1
DFLS   Allerton & Tinsley Class 08
DFLT   Crewe Class 47
DFNC   Crewe Electric Class 86/6

Mainline Freight Ltd.

ENAN   Toton Class 60
ENBN   Toton Class 58
ENRN   Stratford Class 47
ENSN   Toton Class 08/09 (Toton/Peterborough)
ENSX   Toton Class 08 (Stored)
ENTN   Toton Class 31/37 (Infrastructure North)
ENXX   Stored Locos
ENZX   Locos for Withdrawal
ESAB   Stewarts Lane Class 60
ESBB   Stewarts Lane Class 37/7
EWCN   Toton Class 37 (GW Infrastructure)
EWDB   Stewarts Lane Class 33/37 (Chiltern & Heathrow Infrastructure)
EWDS   Stratford Class 37 (Anglia Infrastructure)
EWEB   Stewarts Lane Class 73 (Infrastructure)
EWEH   Eastleigh Class 08
EWHB   Stewarts Lane Class 73 (For Hire)
EWHG   Stewarts Lane Class 09
EWOC   Old Oak Common Class 08/09/97
EWRB   Stewarts Lane Class 33/37/73 (Restricted)
EWSF   Stratford Class 08/09
EWSU   Selhurst Class 08/09
EWSX   Stratford Class 08 (Stored)

Loadhaul Ltd.

FDAI   Immingham Class 60

FDBI	Immingham Class 56 (Humberside)
FDBK	Immingham Class 56 (Aire Valley)
FDCI	Immingham Class 37 (Humberside)
FDDI	Immingham Class 37/47 (North East Infrastructure)
FDKI	Immingham Class 37/56 (Control Contingency)
FDRI	Immingham Class 37 (Restricted)
FDSD	Doncaster Class 08
FDSI	Immingham Class 08
FDSK	Knottingley Class 08/09
FDSX	Stored Shunters
FDYX	Stored Locos
FEPS	Immingham Class 37/5 (For EPS)
FMAY	Thornaby Class 60
FMBY	Thornaby Class 56
FMSY	Thornaby Class 08/09

European Passenger Services Ltd.

GPSN	Stewarts Lane Class 73 (North Pole)
GPSS	Old Oak Common Class 08 (North Pole)
GPSV	St Philips Marsh Class 37/6

Passenger Train Operating Company Shunters

HASS	ScotRail - Inverness Class 08
HBSH	InterCity East Coast Ltd. - Bounds Green/Edinburgh Craigentinny Class 08
HEBD	Merseyrail Electrics - Birkenhead North Class 73/0
HFSL	InterCity West Coast Ltd. - Longsight Class 08
HFSN	InterCity West Coast Ltd. - Willesden Class 08
HGSS	Central Trains Ltd. - Tyseley Class 08
HISE	Cross Country Trains Ltd. - Derby Etches Park Class 08
HISL	Midland Main Line Ltd. - Neville Hill Class 08
HJSE	Great Western Trains Co. Ltd. - Landore Class 08
HJSL	Great Western Trains Co. Ltd. - Laira Class 08
HJXX	Great Western Trains Co. Ltd. - Old Oak Common/St Phillips Marsh Class 08
HLSV	Cardiff Railway Co. Ltd. - Cardiff Canton Class 08
HSSN	Anglia Railways - Norwich Crown Point Class 08
HWSU	Network SouthCentral Ltd. - Selhurst Class 09
HYSB	South West Trains ltd. - Bournemouth Class 73/1
HZSH	Island Line - Ryde Class 03

Intercity Train Operating Companies

IANA	Anglia Railways - Norwich Crown Point Class 86/2 (SA)
ICCA	Cross Country Trains Ltd. - Longsight Class 86/2 (SA)
ICCP	Cross Country Trains Ltd. - Laira Class 43 (SB)
ICCS	Cross Country Trains Ltd. - Edinburgh Craigentinny Class 43 (SB)
IECA	InterCity East Coast Ltd. - Bounds Green Class 91 (SA)
IECP	InterCity East Coast Ltd. - Edinburgh Craigentinny/Neville Hill Class 43 (SC)
ILRA	Cross Country Trains Ltd. - Crewe Diesel Class 47/4 (SB)
IMLP	Midland Main Line Ltd. - Neville Hill Class 43 (SB)
IVGA	Gatwick Express Ltd. - Stewarts Lane Class 73 (SB)
IWBR	Great Western Trains Co. Ltd. - St Phillips Marsh Class 47/4 (SB)
IWCA	InterCity West Coast Ltd. - Willesden Class 87/90 (SB)

IWCP   InterCity West Coast Ltd. - Manchester Longsight Class 43 (SC)
IWPA   InterCity West Coast Ltd. - Willesden Class 86 (SA)
IWRP   Great Western Trains Co. Ltd. - Laira/St Phillips Marsh Class 43 (SC)

Works Shunters

KCSI   ADTranz Ilford Works Class 08
KDSD   ADTranz Doncaster Works Class 08
KESE   Wessex Traincare Eastleigh Works Class 08
KGSS   Railcare Springburn Works Class 08
KWSW   Railcare Wolverton Works Class 08

Transrail Freight Ltd.

LBBS   Bescot Class 08/09
LBCB   Bescot Class 47 (Infrastructure)
LBDB   Bescot Class 31 (Infrastructure)
LBLB   Bescot Class 37 (Infrastructure)
LGAM   Motherwell Class 56
LGBM   Motherwell Class 37
LGHM   Motherwell Class 37/4 (West Highland)
LGML   Motherwell Class 08/09
LGPM   Motherwell Class 37 HGR
LNAK   Cardiff Canton Class 60 (South Wales)
LNBK   Cardiff Canton Class 56 (South Wales)
LNCF   Cardiff Canton Class 08/09/97
LNCK   Cardiff Canton Class 37/7 (Wales)
LNDK   Cardiff Canton Class 37 (Infrastructure)
LNHK   Cardiff Canton Class 37/9
LNLK   Cardiff Canton Class 37 (St Blazey)
LNSK   Cardiff Canton Class 37 (Sandite Fitted)
LNWX   Strategic Reserve Pool
LNXX   Stored Locos
LWAK   Cardiff Canton Class 60 (North West)
LWBK   Cardiff Canton Class 56 (Midlands & North West)
LWCC   Springs Branch Class 37 (North West)
LWCK   Cardiff Canton Class 60 (Peak Forest)
LWDC   Springs Branch Class 31 (Infrastructure)
LWMC   Crewe Diesel Class 37/4 (North West Passenger)
LWNC   Springs Branch Class 31 (Freight)
LWSP   Springs Branch Class 08

Carriage & Traction Co. Ltd. Ltd.

PWLO   Cardiff Canton/Crewe Diesel Class 47

Rail Express Systems Ltd.

PXLA   Crewe Electric Class 90
PXLB   Crewe Diesel Class 47 (Extended Range)
PXLC   Crewe Diesel Class 47
PXLD   Crewe Diesel Class 47 (Reserve)
PXLE   Crewe Electric Class 86
PXLG   Crewe Diesel Class 47 (Charters)
PXLH   Crewe Diesel Class 47 (75 mph maximum)

PXLK   Crewe Diesel Class 47/9
PXLS   Cambridge/Crewe Diesel/Heaton/Willesden Class 08
PXLT   Cambridge/Crewe Diesel Class 08 (Freight owned/Res maintained)
PXXA   Crewe Diesel/Springs Branch Class 08

Eversholt Holdings

SAXL   Eversholt Off Lease

Porterbrook Leasing Co. Ltd.

SBXL   Porterbrook Off Lease

Racal-BRT

TAKB   Bescot Class 20
TAKX   Stored Locos

Other Privately Owned Locos

XHSD   Direct Rail Services Class 20/3
XYPA   ARC Class 59/1
XYPD   Hunslet Barclay Class 20/9
XYPN   National Power Class 59/2
XYPO   Foster Yeoman Class 59/0

7.3. COACHING STOCK OWNER CODES

Owner codes for loco-hauled coaching stock and multiple unit vehicles consist of three parts as follows:

The first letter denotes the type of owner. These are 'M' for Rail Express Systems, 'Q' for Railtrack, 'S' for leasing companies and 'X' for vehicles owned by private companies which were not part of BR.

The second component denotes the particular leasing company or private owner. This component consists of one letter for the leasing companies, Rail Express Systems or Railtrack and two letters for the private owners.

The third component is either one letter which represents the operating company on which the vehicle or unit is in service or two letters which represent the status of a vehicle not in service.

First and Second Components

Rail Express Systems

MP   Parcels & mail traffic.

Leasing Companies

SA   Eversholt Holdings.
SB   Porterbrook Leasing Co. Ltd..
SC   Great Rolling Stock Co. (formerly Angel Trains Contracts).

Vehicles belonging to companies not formerly part of BR

This section gives the code for the company plus the correspondence addres

XBC   75014 Locomotive Operators Group c/o B. Cooke, 129 The Mount, York.
XBL   Britannia locomotive Society, c/o Mr A.A. Lawson, Gaylands, 9 Bennett Drive, Myton Grange, Warwick, CV34 6QJ.
XCI   Chell Instruments, Tudor House, Grammar School Road, North Walsham, Norfolk.
XCR   West Coast Railway Co. c/o W.D. Smith, Steamtown Railway Museum, Carnforth, Lancs, LA5 9HX.
XWR   Flying Scotsman Railways, P.O. Box 6000, Derby.
XGS   Great Scottish & Western Railway Co. Ltd., c/o L & R leisure plc, 46a Constitution Street, Leith, Edinburgh, EH6 6RS.
XHL   Humberside Locomotive Preservation Group, 19 Wilson Street, Anlaby, Hull, HU10 7AN.
XJB   J.B. Cameron, Balbuthie Farm, Kilconquhar, Fife.
XMA   Manchester Pullman Co. Ltd., 2nd Floor, Yorkshire Bank Chambers, St. James Street, Accrington, Lancs, BB5 1LY.
XMR   B.P. Ewart, The Holmestead, Yeldersley Lane, Bradley, Ashbourne, DE6 1PJ.
XMN   Merchant Navy Preservation Society Ltd., c/o R.F. Abercrombie, 12 Inglewood Avenue, Heatherside, Camberley, Surrey, GU15 1RJ.
XNR   National Railway Museum, Leeman Road, York.
XRF   Railfilms Ltd., Mr. N. Dobson, 26 Regent Street, Altrincham, Cheshire,

WA14 1RP.

XRP	RPR Trains Ltd., c/o C.J. Paget, 11 Weston Close, Dorridge, Solihull, B93 8BL.
XSC	Scottish Railway Preservation Society, Macland, Maddiston Road, Brightons, Falkirk, FK2 0JP.
XSH	Scottish Highland Railway Co. Ltd., Mills Road, Aylesford, Maidstone, Kent, ME20 7NW.
XSN	A4 Locomotive Society, Lloyd's Bank Chambers, Hastlergate, Bradford, BD1 1UQ.
XST	44767 George Stephenson, c/o Mr I.L. Storey, 13 Felton Close, Stobhill Farm, Morpeth, Northumberland NE61 2TG.
XSV	Severn Valley Railway, Bewdley Station, Bewdley, Worcestershire.
XTS	Titanstar Ltd., c/o C.J. Paget, 11 Weston Close, Dorridge, Solihull, B93 8BL.
XVS	Venice Simplon Orient Express Ltd., 1 Hanover Square, London, W1R 9RD.

Third Component

Rail Express Systems

NW	Vehicles belonging to the former Charter train unit that were not wanted by Waterman railways
OZ	Royal Mail traffic
XX	Stored vehicles

Train Operating Companies

A	ScotRail
B	Inter City East Coast Ltd.
C	Regional Railways North East Ltd.
D	North West Regional Railways Ltd.
E	Merseyrail Electrics
F	Inter City West Coast Ltd.
G	Central Trains Ltd.
H	Cross Country Trains Ltd.
I	Midland Main Line Ltd.
J	Great Western Train Co. Ltd.
K	Regional Railways South Wales and West
L	Cardiff Railway Co. Ltd.
N	Thames Trains
O	Chiltern Railways.
P	North London Railways.
Q	West Anglia Great Northern Railway Train Operating Unit.
R	Great Eastern Railway.
S	Anglia Railways.
T	LTS Rail (London Tilbury & Southend Train Operating Company).
U	The South Eastern Train Co. Ltd.
V	Gatwick Express Ltd.
W	Network South Central Ltd.
X	Thameslink Rail Ltd.
Y	South West Trains Ltd.
Z	Island Line Train Operating Unit.

Other Codes

M   denotes leasing company vehicles used for movement purposes.
         (Note that Porterbrook Leasing use 'OL' for this use.)
OL   denotes off-loan vehicles.
XZ   denotes stored vehicles.

Unofficial Codes

V   Privately-owned vehicles on hire to VSOE.
Z   Privately-owned vehicles not at present registered to run on Railtrack
         metals.

Railtrack

Vehicles owned by Railtrack have codes beginning with QA with the last letter
denoting the type of vehicle.

7.4. DEPOT & WORKS CODES

Depot Codes

Note: This list includes various locations which are not necessarily official operating company maintenance depots.

AF	Ashford Chart Leacon TMD
AL	Aylesbury TMD
AN	Allerton TMD (Liverpool)
AY	Ayr TMD
BD	Birkenhead North T&RSMD
BI	Brighton T&RSMD
BK	Bristol Barton Hill CWMD
BM	Bournemouth T&RSMD
BN	Bounds Green T&RSMD (London)
BO	Bo'Ness & Kinneil Railway, Bo'Ness Station, West Lothian.
BP	Blackpool Carriage Sidings
BQ	East Lancashire Railway, Bury, Greater Manchester.
BR	Bristol Bath Road TMD
BS	Bescot TMD (Walsall)
BY	Bletchley TMD
BZ	St. Blazey TMD (Par)
CA	Cambridge T&RSMD
CD	Crewe TMD (D)
CE	Crewe International TMD (E)
CF	Cardiff Canton T&RSMD
CJ	Clapham Yard CSD, London.
CK	Corkerhill SD (Glasgow)
CL	Carlisle Upperby CWMD
CO	West Somerset Railway, Cranmore, Somerset.
CP	Crewe Carriage Shed
CQ	Coquelles (France)
DI	Great Western Society, Didcot Railway Centre, Didcot, Oxon.
DR	Doncaster TMD
CS	West Coast Railway Co., Steamtown, Carnforth
DY	Derby Etches Park T&RSMD
EC	Craigentinny T&RSMD (Edinburgh)
EH	Eastleigh T&RSMD
EM	East Ham EMUD (London)
EN	Euston Downside CARMD (London)
FB	Ferrybridge (National Power)
FF	Bruxelles Forest/Brussel Vorst
FR	Fratton (Portsmouth)
GI	Gillingham EMUD
GT	North Yorkshire Moors Railway, Grosmont, North Yorkshire.
GW	Glasgow Shields TMD
HA	Haymarket TMD (Edinburgh)
HB	Kilmarnock (Hunslet__Barclay)
HE	Hornsey TMD (London)

HR	Hall Road EMUD (Merseyside)
HT	Heaton T&RSMD (Newcastle)
IL	Ilford T&RSMD (London)
IM	Immingham TMD (South Humberside)
IS	Inverness T&RSMD
KR	Severn Valley Railway, Kidderminster, Worcestershire.
KY	Knottingley TMD
LA	Laira T&RSMD (Plymouth)
LE	Landore T&RSMD (Swansea)
LG	Longsight TMD (E) (Manchester)
LL	Liverpool Edge Hill CARMD
LO	Longsight TMD (D) (Manchester)
LY	Le Landy (Paris)
MA	Manchester Longsight CARMD
MD	Merehead (Foster Yeoman)
MK	Markinch Goods Shed, Markinch, Fife.
ML	Motherwell TMD
NC	Norwich Crown Point T&RSMD
NH	Newton Heath T&RSMD (Manchester)
NL	Neville Hill T&RSMD (Leeds)
OC	Old Oak Common TMD (D)
OM	Old Oak Common CARMD (London)
OO	Old Oak Common TMD (HST) (London)
OY	Oxley CARMD (Wolverhampton)
PC	Polmadie CARMD (Glasgow)
PI	North Pole International (London)
PM	St. Phillips Marsh T&RSMD (Bristol)
PZ	Penzance T&RSMD
RE	Ramsgate T&RSMD
RG	Reading TMD
RY	Ryde (Isle of Wight) T&RSMD
SA	Salisbury TMD
SF	Stratford TMD (London)
SG	Slade Green T&RSMD
SH	Strawberry Hill EMUD (London)
SK	Midland Railway Centre, Swanwick Junction, Derbyshire.
SL	Stewarts Lane T&RSMD (London)
SO	Southall Railway Centre, Southall Depot, Southall, Gtr. London
SP	Springs Branch TMD (Wigan)
SU	Selhurst TMD (London)
TE	Thornaby TMD
TI	Tinsley TMD (Sheffield)
TO	Toton TMD (Notts)
TS	Tyseley TMD (Birmingham)
WB	Wembley InterCity CARMD (London)
WD	East Wimbledon EMUD (London)
WH	Whatley (ARC Limited)
WN	Willesden TMD (London)
YM	National Railway Museum, Leeman Road, York, North Yorkshire.

Works Codes

RFS	RFS Engineering, Doncaster
ZA	Railway Technical Centre (Derby)
ZC	ABB Crewe Locomotive Works.
ZD	ABB Derby Carriage Works.
ZF	ABB Customer Support Lt., Doncaster Works.
ZG	Wessex Traincare Ltd., Eastleigh Works.
ZH	Railcare Ltd., Springburn Works, Glasgow.
ZI	ABB Customer Support Ltd., Ilford Works.
ZK	Hunslet-Barclay Kilmarnock Works
ZN	Railcare Ltd., Wolverton Works.

Depot Type Codes

CARMD	Carriage Maintenance depot.
CSD	Carriage Servicing depot.
CWMD	Carriage and wagon maintenance depot.
EMUD	Electric Multiple Unit Depot.
SD	Servicing depot.
TMD	Traction Maintenance Depot.
TMD (D)	Traction Maintenance Depot (Diesel).
TMD (E)	Traction Maintenance Depot (Electric).
TMD (HST)	HST Maintenance Depot.
T&RSMD	Traction and rolling stock maintenance depot.
WRD	Wagon Repair Depot.

Storage Locations

Storage locations without codes are shown for certain coaches, DMUs and EMUs. The places "Kineton", "Long Marston", "Longtown" and "Ludgershall" refer to the Ministry of Defence establishments at those points

7.5. GENERAL ABBREVIATIONS

BR	British Railways
GWR	Great Western Railway
LNER	London & North Eastern Railway
LMS	London Midland & Scottish Railway
SR	Southern Railway
EPS	European Passenger Services Ltd.
NMBS	Nationale Maatschappij Belgische Spoorwegen*
SNCB	Société Nationale des Chemins de Fer Belges*
SNCF	Société Nationale des Chemins de Fer Francais§
DEMU	diesel electric multiple unit.
DHMU	diesel hydraulic multiple unit.
DMMU	diesel mechanical multiple unit.
DMU	diesel multiple unit (general term).
EMU	Electric Multiple Unit
h.p.	horsepower.
kW	Kilowatts.
T	Toilets.
TD	Toilets (suitable for disabled passengers).
m	metres.
mph	miles per hour.
r	Fitted with radio electronic token block apparatus.
t	tons.
(S)	Stored servicable.
(U)	Stored unserviceable

* Belgian Railways in Dutch and French respectively
§ French Railways.

7.6. BUILDERS

These are shown in class headings where the following abbreviations are used:

Alexander	Walter Alexander Ltd., Falkirk.
ABB Derby	ABB Transportation Ltd., Derby Carriegae Works
ABB York	ABB Transportation Ltd., York Works
AEI	Associated Electrical Industries Ltd.
Barclay	Andrew Barclay Ltd., Kilmarnock.
Brush	Brush Traction Ltd., Loughborough
BRCW	The Birmingham Railway Carriage & Wagon Co. Ltd.
BTH	The British Thomson Houston Co. Ltd.
Cravens	Cravens Ltd., Sheffield
CP	Crompton-Parkinson Ltd.
EE	The English Electric Co. Ltd.
GEC	The General Electric Company Ltd. (Now GEC Alsthom).
Gloucester	The Gloucester Railway Carriage and Wagon Co. Ltd.
Hunslet	Hunslet Transportation Projects Ltd.
Leyland Bus	Leyland Bus Ltd., Workington.
Metro	The Metropolitan Railway Carriage and Wagon Co. Ltd., Birmingham.
Metro-Cammell	The Metropolitan Cammell Railway Carriage and Wagon Co. Ltd., Birmingham.
Midland	The Midland Railway Carriage and Wagon Co. Ltd., Oldbury, Worcs.
Pressed Steel	Pressed Steel Ltd., Swindon

This list generally excludes BR/BREL workshops which are denoted in the text by their town/city. Where a dual BR works builder is shown (e.g. Ashford/Eastleigh) the first named built the underframe and the last named built the body and assembled the vehicle. For second generation vehicles, the first name is that of the main contractor with the second name being the underframe and final assembly sub-contractor.

8. UK LIGHT RAIL SYSTEMS & METROS

Details are given in this section of the rolling stock of the various Metros and Light Rail systems of the UK. London Underground is not included but details can be found in "London Underground Rolling Stock" (13th edition) published by Capital Transport Publishing at £8.95 and available from our mail order department (see centre pull-out for details of how to order).

8.1. BLACKPOOL & FLEETWOOD TRAMWAY

System: 660 V d.c. overhead. **Depot:** Rigby Road.
Livery: Cream and green. (many in advertising livery).
Note: Numbers in brackets are pre-1968 numbers.

ONE-MAN CAR

Rebuilt 1972 – 76 from English Electric railcoaches built 1934 – 5. Radio fitted. 13 converted (1 – 13), but only one remains.
Seats: 48U.
Traction Motors: Two EE305 of 40 kW.

Note: First number in brackets is post 1968 number prior to conversion.

11 (615, 268)(U)

OPEN BOAT CARS

Built 1934 – 5 by English Electric. 12 built (225 – 236).
Seats: 56U.
Traction Motors: Two EE327 of 30 kW.

600	(225)	*	604	(230)	§	606	(235)	b
602	(227)	★	605	(233)		607	(236)	

* On loan to Heaton Park Tramway, Manchester.
★ Yellow and black livery.
§ Red and white livery.
b Blue & yellow livery.

REPLICA VANGUARD

Built 1987 on underframe of one man car No. 7.(619 – 282).
Seats: U.
Traction Motors: Two EE327 of 30 kW.

619

BRUSH RAILCOACHES

Built 1937 by Brush. 20 built (284 – 303).
Seats: 48U.
Traction Motors: Two EE305 of 40 kW. (EE327 of 30 kW*).

621	(284)	627	(290)	633	(296)
622	(285) *	630	(293)	634	(297)
623	(286)	631	(294)	635	(299)
625	(288)	632	(295)	637	(300)
626	(289)				

CENTENARY CLASS

Built 1984 – 7. Body by East Lancs. Coachbuilders, Blackburn. One man operated. Radio fitted.
Seats: 52U.
Traction Motors: Two EE305 of 40 kW.

* Rebuilt from GEC car 651.

641	644	647
642	645	648*
643	646	

CORONATION CLASS

Built 1953 by Charles Roberts & Co. Resilient wheels. 25 built (304 – 328).
Seats: 56U.
Traction motors: Four Crompton-Parkinson 92 of 34 kW.

660   (324)

PROGRESS TWIN CARS

Motor cars (671 – 677) rebuilt 1958 – 60 from English Electric railcoaches.
Seats: 53U.
Traction Motors: Two EE305 of 40 kW.
Driving trailers (681 – 687) built 1960 by Metro-Cammell.
Seats: 53U.

671 + 681 (281 + T1)	674 + 684 (284 + T4)	676 + 686 (286 + T6)
672 + 682 (282 + T2)	675 + 685 (285 + T5)	677 + 687 (287 + T7)
673 + 683 (283 + T1)		

SINGLE CARS

Rebuilt 1958 – 60 from English Electric railcoaches. Originally ran with trailers.
Seats: 48U.
Traction Motors: Two EE305 of 40 kW.

678 (278)	679 (279)	680 (280)

"BALLOON" DOUBLE DECKERS

Built 1934 – 5 by English Electric. 700 – 712 were originally built with open tops, and 706 has now reverted to that condition and is named 'PRINCESS ALICE'. 719 is being rebuilt with new cabs.
Seats: 94U.

Traction Motors: Two EE305 of 40 kW.

G Wartime green livery with cream stripe.
R Red and white livery.

701	(238)	**R**	710	(247)	719	(256)
702	(239)		711	(248)	720	(257)
703	(240)	**G**	712	(249)	721	(258)
704	(241)		713	(250)	722	(259)
706	(243)		715	(252)	723	(260)
707	(244)	(U)	716	(253)	724	(261)
708	(245)		717	(254)	726	(263)
709	(246)		718	(255)		

ILLUMINATED CARS

732	(168)	Rocket	Seats: 47U
733	(209)	Western Train loco. & tender	Seats: 35U
734	(174)	Western Train coach	Seats: 60U
735	(222)	Hovertram	Seats: 99U
736	(170)	HMS Blackpool	Seats: 71U

WORKS CARS

259	(748, 624)	PW gang towing car.
260	(751, 628, 291)	Crane car and rail carrier.
749	(S)	Tower wagon trailer.
750		Cable drum trailer.
752	(2, 1)	Rail grinder and snowplough.
754		New works car (unnumbered).

JUBILEE CLASS DOUBLE DECKERS

Rebuilt 1979/82 from Balloon cars. Standard bus ends, thyristor control and stairs at each end. 761 has one door per side whereas 762 has two. Radio fitted.
Seats: 100U.
Traction Motors: Two EE305 of 40 kW.

761 (725, 262) |762 (714, 251)

PRESERVED CARS

Blackpool & Fleetwood 40	Box car. Bogie single decker built 1914
Bolton 66	Bogie double-decker built 1901

8.2. DOCKLANDS LIGHT RAILWAY

This is a light rail line running in London's East End from Bank, Tower Gateway and Stratford to Island Gardens. It is being extended to Beckton and Lewisham. Originally owned by London Transport, it is now owned by the London Docklands Development Corporation.

System: 750 V d.c. third rail (bottom contact).
Depots: Poplar, Beckton.

CLASS P89   B – 2 – B

Built 1990 by BREL Ltd. York Works. 28.80 x 2.65 m. Sliding doors. Chopper control. Scharfenberg Couplers.

Weight: 39 t.
Seats: 84U.
Traction Motors: Two GEC of 185 kW.
Max. Speed: 80 km/h.
Electric Brake: Rheostatic.

12	15	18	20
13	16	19	21
14	17		

CLASS B90   B – 2 – B

Built 1991 – 2 by BN Construction, Brugge, Belgium. (now Bombardier BN). 28.80 x 2.65 m. Sliding doors. End doors for staff use. Chopper control. Scharfenberg Couplers. These units are to be converted for Seltrack signalling.

Weight: 36 t.
Seats: 66U + 4 tip-up.
Traction Motors: Two Brush of 140 kW.
Max. Speed: 80 km/h.
Electric Brake: Rheostatic.

22	28	34	40	46
23	29	35	41	
24	30	36	42	
25	31	37	43	
26	32	38	44	
27	33	39	45	

CLASS B92   B – 2 – B

Built 1992 – 5 by BN Construction, Brugge, Belgium. (now Bombardier BN).
28.80 x 2.65 m. Sliding doors. End doors for staff use. Chopper control.
Scharfenberg Couplers. Fitted with Seltrack signalling.

Weight: 36 t.
Seats: 66U + 4 tip-up.
Traction Motors: Two Brush of 140 kW.
Max. Speed: 80 km/h.
Electric Brake: Rheostatic.

48	60	72	84
49	61	73	85
50	62	74	86
51	63	75	87
52	64	76	88
53	65	77	89
54	66	78	90
55	67	79	91
56	68	80	92
57	69	81	93
58	70	82	94
59	71	83	

Note:

The **Docklands Light Rail Official Handbook**, published by Capital Transport
Publishing is available from our Mail Order Department, price £7.95 plus postage.

8.3. GREATER MANCHESTER METROLINK

This new light rail system runs from Bury to Altrincham through the streets of Manchester, with a spur to Piccadilly Station.

System: 750 V d.c. overhead.
Depot: Queens Road.

SIX-AXLE ARTICULATED CARS   Bo – 2 – Bo

Built 1991 – 2 by Firema, Italy. Power operated sliding doors. Chopper control. Scharfenberg Couplers.

Weight: 45 t.
Seats: 82U (74U*).
Dimensions: 29.00 x 2.65 m.
Traction Motors: Four GEC of 130 kW.
Braking: Rheostatic, regenerative, disc and emergency track brakes.

1001		CHILDREN'S HOSPITALS APPEAL I
1002		MANCHESTER ARNDALE VOYAGER
1003		CHILDREN'S HOSPITALS APPEAL II
1004		THE ROBERT OWEN
1005		GREATER ALTRINCHAM ENTERPRISE
1006		
1007		THE GUINNESS RECORD BREAKER
1008		MANCHESTER AIRPORT
1009		CO-OPERATIVE INSURANCE
1010		MANCHESTER CHAMPION
1011		SPONSORED BY TESCO
1012		KERRY
1013		THE FUSILIER
1014		THE CITY OF DRAMA
1015		SPARKY
1016		
1017		ROSIE
1018		SIR MATT BUSBY
1019		THE ERIC BLACK
1020		THE DAVID GRAHAM CBE
1021		THE GREATER MANCHESTER RADIO
1022	*	THE MANCHESTER EVENING NEWS
1023		
1024		THE JOHN GREENWOOD
1025		
1026		THE POWER

SPECIAL PURPOSE VEHICLE

Built 1991 by RFS Industries, Kilnhurst and Brown Root. Used for shunting and track maintenance. Includes a crane.

Unnumbered.

LIGHT RAIL REVIEW

Over the past 15 years light rail transit has advanced considerably in the UK with the introduction of schemes like Manchester Metrolink and South Yorkshire Supertram, and further important developments are in the pipeline. Light Rail Review takes a comprehensive look at current and future light rail schemes. The editorial content consists of topical articles by recognised authorities in the light rail field, concentrating both on UK and overseas advances. Much use is made of illustrations, a high proportion of which are in colour making Light Rail Review an informative source of reference which will appeal to both enthusiasts and transport professionals alike. *Each book is A4 size. and Thread sewn.*

Light Rail Review 3 .... £7.50
Light Rail Review 4 .... £7.50
Light Rail Review 5 .... £7.50
Light Rail Review 6 .... £7.50
Light Rail Review 7 **MARCH 1996** £8.95

TRAM TO SUPERTRAM

Peter Fox, Paul Jackson & Roger Benton.
The official publication to commemorate the opening of Sheffield's new Supertram light rail system, is a pictorial account of Sheffield's tramway development. *Printed in colour throughout,* the book illustrates the old street tramway which finally died out in October 1960 and contrasts this with the construction, development and operation of the new modern tramway network.
A4. 48 pages. Saddle Stitched. £4.95.

A further more comprehensive publication covering the Supertram system, to accompany 'UK Light Rail Systems No.1: Manchester Metrolink', will be published in late 1996 or early 1997.

8.4. SOUTH YORKSHIRE SUPERTRAM

The final phase of this new light rail system opened on 23rd October 1995. There are three lines radiating from Sheffield City Centre to Meadowhall, Halfway/Herdings Park and Middlewood/Malin Bridge. Because of the severe gradients in Sheffield (up to 1 in 10), all axles are powered on these vehicles.

System: 750 V d.c. overhead.
Depot: Nunnery.

EIGHT-AXLE ARTICULATED UNITS   B – B – B – B

Built 1993 – 4 by Siemens-Duewag, Düsseldorf, Germany.

Weight: 52 t.
Seats: 82U.
Dimensions: 34.75 x 2.65 m.
Traction Motors: Four 260 kW monomotors.
Braking: Rheostatic, regenerative, disc and emergency track brakes.

01	08	14	20
02	09	15	21
03	10	16	22
04	11	17	23
05	12	18	24
06	13	19	25
07			

Note: The No. 1 body sections have been exchanged between cars 02 and 11 after accident damage.

8.5. STRATHCLYDE PTE UNDERGROUND

This circular 4' gauge underground line in Glasgow is generally referred to as the "Subway".

System: 750 V d.c. third rail.
Depot: Broomloan.

SINGLE CARS   Bo – Bo

Built 1978 – 9 by Metro-Cammell. Power-operated sliding doors. 12.58 x 2.34 m.

Seats: 36U.
Traction Motors: Two GEC G312AZ.

101	110	118	126
102	111	119	127
103	112	120	128
104	113	121	129
105	114	122	130
106	115	123	131
107	116	124	132
108	117	125	133
109			

INTERMEDIATE TRAILERS   2 – 2

Built 1992 by Metro-Cammell. Power-operated sliding doors. 12.58 x 2.34 m. No details available.

201	203	205	207
202	204	206	208

8.6. TYNE AND WEAR METRO

System: 1500 V d.c. overhead.
Depot: South Gosforth.

BATTERY/OVERHEAD ELECTRIC LOCOS

Built: 1989 – 80 by Hunslet, Leeds. BSI couplers.
Traction Motors: Hunslet-Greenbat T9-4P.
Weight: 26 t.

BL1	BL2	BL3

SIX-AXLE ARTICULATED UNITS   B – 2 – B

Built 1976, 1978 – 81 by Metro-Cammell. 27.80 x 2.65m. BSI couplers.
Weight: 39 t.
Seats: 84U (68U r, 72U p).
Traction Motors: Two 187 kW monomotor bogies.

p Prototype refurbished car with revised cab and seating layout.
r Refurbished cars with revised cab and seating layout.

4001	4019	4037	4055 r R	4073
4002	4020	4038	4056	4074
4003	4021 r R	4039 r T	4057	4075
4004 r G	4022	4040	4058	4076
4005 r R	4023	4041	4059	4077
4006	4024	4042	4060	4078
4007 r R	4025	4043	4061 r G	4079
4008	4026 r A	4044 r R	4062	4080
4009	4027 r R	4045 r T	4063	4081
4010	4028	4046	4064 r R	4082 r G
4011	4029	4047	4065 r R	4083
4012	4030 r R	4048 r B	4066	4084
4013	4031	4049	4067	4085
4014	4032	4050	4068	4086 r B
4015	4033	4051 r R	4069	4087 p T
4016	4034	4052	4070	4088
4017	4035	4053	4071	4089
4018	4036 r G	4054	4072	4090

Names:

4041	HARRY COWANS	4065	Catherine Cookson

Standard livery is yellow and white.

A	Advertising livery.
B	Blue livery.
G	Green livery.
R	Red livery.
T	'T' livery (see page 75).

PLATFORM 5 PUBLISHING LIMITED

MAIL ORDER CATALOGUE

**Mail Order Dept., Platform 5 Publishing Ltd.,
3 Wyvern House, Sark Road, SHEFFIELD, S2 4HG.**

NEW TITLES

	Price
British Railways Locomotives & Coaching Stock 1996	8.95
BR Pocket Book No.1: Locomotives	2.25
BR Pocket Book No.2: Coaching Stock	2.25
BR Pocket Book No.3: DMUs & Light Rail Systems	2.25
BR Pocket Book No.4: Electric Multiple Units	2.25
High Speed in Europe	9.95
European Handbook No. 6: Italian Railways 1st ed.	13.50
European Handbook No. 7: Irish Railways 1st ed. *END FEB*	9.95
Light Rail Review 7 *MARCH*	8.95
Light Rail in Europe (Capital)	9.95
The 1996 Stagecoach Bus Handbook (British Bus)	9.95
The Lancashire, Cumbria & Manchester Bus Handbook (British Bus) *MARCH*	9.95
The Merseyside & Cheshire Bus Handbook (British Bus) *MARCH*	9.95
Power Railway Signalling Part 1B (Kay)	9.95
Railway Track Diagrams No. 6: Ireland (Quail)	5.50
London Transport Railway Track Map (Quail)	1.75
Ukraine Belarus Moldova Railway Atlas (Quail)	7.95
Harz Smalspurbahn Track Diagram (Quail)	0.60
Locomotives & Railcars of Bord Na Mona (Midland)	4.99

Modern British Railway Titles

Preserved Locomotives of British Railways 9th ed.	7.95
Preserved Coaching Stock Part 1: BR Design Stock	7.95
Diesel & Electric Loco Register 3rd edition	7.95
Today's Railways Review of the Year Volume 1	11.95
Today's Railways Review of the Year Volume 2	11.95
Today's Railways Review of the Year Volume 3	13.95
Today's Railways Review of the Year Volume 4	14.95
London Underground Rolling Stock 13th edition (Capital)	8.95
Docklands Light Rail Official Handbook (Capital)	7.95

Underground Official Handbook (Capital)	7.95
Underground Train Overhaul (Capital)	5.95
Blood, Sweat and Fifties (Class 50 Society)	2.95
Air Braked Series Wagon Fleet (SCTP)	7.95
Departmental Coaching Stock 5th edition (SCTP)	6.95
On-Track Plant on British Railways 5th edition (SCTP)	7.95
Engineers Series Wagon Fleet 970000-999999 (SCTP)	6.95
British Rail Wagon Fleet - B-Prefix Series (SCTP)	6.95
British Rail Internal Users (SCTP)	7.95
RIV Wagon Fleet (SCTP)	5.95
Thomas The Privatised Tank Engine (Midland)	4.99
Class 20s In Colour (Midland)	9.99
Miles & Chains Volume 2 - London Midland (Milepost)	1.60
Miles & Chains Volume 3 - Scottish (Milepost)	1.60
Miles & Chains Volume 5 - Southern (Milepost)	1.60
Class Fifty Factfile (Class 50 Society)	2.95

Overseas Railways

European Handbook No. 1: Benelux Railways 3rd ed.	10.50
European Handbook No. 2: German Railways Locomotives & MUs 3rd ed	12.50
European Handbook No. 3: Austrian Railways 3rd ed.	10.50
European Handbook No. 4: French Railways/Chemins de fer Francais 2nd ed	9.95
Railways of Southern Africa Loco Guide 1994 (Beyer-Garrett)	4.25
Industrial Locomotives of South Africa 1991 (Beyer/Garrett)	7.95
TGV Handbook (Capital)	7.95
Paris Metro Handbook (Capital)	7.95
Irish Narrow Gauge - Pictorial History Part 1 (Midland)	15.99
Irish Narrow Gauge - Pictorial History Part 2 (Midland)	15.99
Irish Railways In Colour: From Steam to Diesel 1955-1967 (Midland)	16.99
Irish Railways In Colour: A Second Glance 1947-1970 (Midland)	19.99

Historical Railway Titles

6203 'Princess Margaret Rose'	19.95
Steam Days on BR 1 - The Midland Line in Sheffield	4.95
Rails along the Sea Wall (Dawlish-Teignmouth Pictorial)	4.95
The Rolling Rivers	6.95
British Baltic Tanks	6.95
The Railways of Winchester	6.95
Register of Closed Railways 1948-91 (Milepost)	5.95

LNWR Branch Lines of West Leics & East Warwicks (Milepost)	7.95
Steam Alive (Friends of the NRM)	2.95
Railways South East - The Album (Capital)	9.95
Rails Through The Clay (Capital)	25.00
The 1938 Tube Stock (Capital)	9.95
Metropolitan Steam Locomotives (Capital)	9.95
Going Green (Capital)	5.95
An Illustrated History of the Cheshire Lines Committee	10.95
Private Owner Wagons Volume 1 (Headstock)	8.95
Private Owner Wagons Volume 2 (Headstock)	9.95
Private Owner Wagons Volume 3 (Headstock)	7.95
Private Owner Wagons Volume 4 (Headstock)	7.95
Totley & The Tunnel	4.95
Scottish Colliery Pugs in the Seventies	4.95
Railway Signal Engineering - Mechanical (Kay)	12.50
Bradshaw's Guide 1850 (Kay)	7.95
Power Railway Signalling Part 2 (Kay)	15.95

Rambling

Rambles by Rail 1 - The Hope Valley Line	1.95
Rambles by Rail 2 - Liskeard-Looe	1.95
Rambles by Rail 4 - The New Forest	1.95
Buxton Spa Line Rail Rambles	1.20

Light Rail Transit & Trams

Tram to Supertram	4.95
Light Rail Review 3	7.50
Light Rail Review 4	7.50
Light Rail Review 5	7.50
Light Rail Review 6	7.50
Manx Electric	8.95
Blackpool & Fleetwood By Tram	7.50
Tramtracks & Trolleybooms (Headstock)	3.95
On The Trams (Gill)	4.95

Cars + Buses

Greater Manchester Buses (Capital)	19.95
London Trolleybus Routes (Capital)	18.95

Routemaster Volume Two 1970-1989 (Capital)	19.95
South West Buses (Capital)	10.95
London Bus Handbook Part 1 (Capital)	9.95
London Bus Handbook Part 2 (Capital)	9.95
Premier Travel (Capital)	9.95
South East Buses (Capital)	9.95
DMS Handbook (Capital)	9.95
London Coach Handbook (Capital)	10.95
The Last Years of the General (Capital)	16.95
Metrobus - The Company's First Ten Years (Capital)	7.95
The Eastern Bus Handbook (British Bus)	9.95
The Firstbus Bus Handbook (British Bus)	9.95
The Leyland Lynx Bus Handbook (British Bus)	8.95
The Fire Brigade Handbook (British Bus)	8.95
The Model Bus Handbook (British Bus)	9.95
The North East Bus Handbook (British Bus)	9.95
The Yorkshire Bus Handbook (British Bus)	9.95
The Scottish Bus Handbook (British Bus)	9.95
The East Midlands Bus Handbook (British Bus)	8.95
The Welsh Bus Handbook (British Bus)	9.95
The South Midlands Bus Handbook (British Bus)	8.95
The North Midlands Bus Handbook (British Bus)	8.95
Bus Review 10 (Bus Enthusiast)	6.95
Austin - The Counties Years (Bus Enthusiast)	6.95
London Buses in Exile 2nd edition (Bus Enthusiast)	4.95
60 Years of A1 Service (Bus Enthusiast)	5.95

Maps and Track Diagrams (Quail Map Company)

British Rail Track Diagrams 5 - Southern	6.95
China Railway Station List 1988	4.00
Berlin Track Map	2.20
Portugal Railway Map	2.00
Czech Republic & Slovakia Railway Map	1.70
Greece Railway Map	1.70
Poland Railway Map	2.00
New York Railway Map	1.70
Estonia Railway Map	1.20
Latvia & Lithuania Railway Map	2.00

European Railway Atlases (Ian Allan)

European Railway Atlas: France, Benelux	10.99
European Railway Atlas: Germany, Austria, Switzerland	9.95
European Railway Atlas: Spain, Portugal, Italy, Greece	10.99
European Railway Atlas: Scandinavia & Eastern Europe	10.99

PVC Book Covers

A6 Pocket Book Covers in Blue, Red, Green or Grey	0.80
Locomotives & CS Covers in Blue, Red, Green or Grey	1.00
A5 Book Covers in Blue, Red, Green or Grey	1.40

Postcards

Sheffield Supertram - crosses Sheffield Canal	0.20
Manchester Metrolink - in Aytoun Street	0.20

Calendars (Rail Photoprint)

Modern Traction Calendar 1996	4.25
Steam Traction Calendar 1996	4.25

Locomotives & Coaching Stock Back Numbers

1986	3.30	1991	6.60
1987	3.30	1992	7.00
1988	3.95	1993	7.25
1989	4.95	1994	7.50
1990	5.95	1995	8.50

Reduced Price Titles*

Exeter-Newton Abbot - A Railway History (was 25.00)	12.50
Midland Railway Portrait (was 12.95)	6.95
The Handbook of British Railways Steam Motive Power Depots	
Volume 2 - Central England, East Anglia & Wales (was 8.95)	3.95
Volume 4 - Northern England & Scotland (was 9.95)	3.95
North West Rails in Colour (was 8.50)	3.95
The Battle for the Settle & Carlisle (was 6.95)	2.95
The Fifty 50s in Colour (was 5.95)	2.95
Portrait of the Fifties (was 4.95)	2.95
Canadian Trackside Guide 1990 (was 9.95)	5.95
Edinburgh's Transport - The Early Years (was 9.95)	4.95

* Postage on reduced price titles must be based on original book price.

How To Order

Please send your sterling cheque, money order, Eurocheque or British Postal Order made payable to ''Platform 5 Publishing Ltd.'', to:

> **Platform 5 Mail Order Department (LCS),**
> 3 Wyvern House,
> Sark Road,
> SHEFFIELD,
> S2 4HG,
> ENGLAND.
>
> Tel: (+44) 0114 255 2625   Fax: (+44) 0114 255 2471

Postage & packing - please add: 10% UK; 20% Europe or 30% Rest of World. (if P&P works out as less than 30p then please add 30p as the minimum charge)

* Postage on reduced price titles must be based on original price.

When ordering Platform 5 European publications in conjunction with a **Today's Railways** subscription offer please add on post and packing **before** deducting the voucher. Vouchers may not be combined.

Payment by Credit card. We accept Visa/Access/Mastercard/Eurocard. Please state type of card, cardholder's name and address, card number and expiry date. Minimum credit card order accepted is £2.50.

Please note we cannot accept foreign currency cheques, except those in French francs. *Les chèques en francs francais devraient être libellés à l'ordre de 'Mr P Fox'.*

For Order Form See Over

Quantity	Title	Price	Total
		SUB-TOTAL	
Postage & Packing (see previous page for details)			
	TOTAL REMITTANCE		

Name: ....

Address: ....

....

.... Postcode: ....

Daytime Telephone No.: ....

Payment (Delete as appropriate)

I enclose my cheque/postal order for £ .... made payable
to '**PLATFORM 5 PUBLISHING LTD**'.

Please debit my Access/Visa/Mastercard/Eurocard

Card Number: .... Card Expiry Date: ....

Signature: .... Date: ....